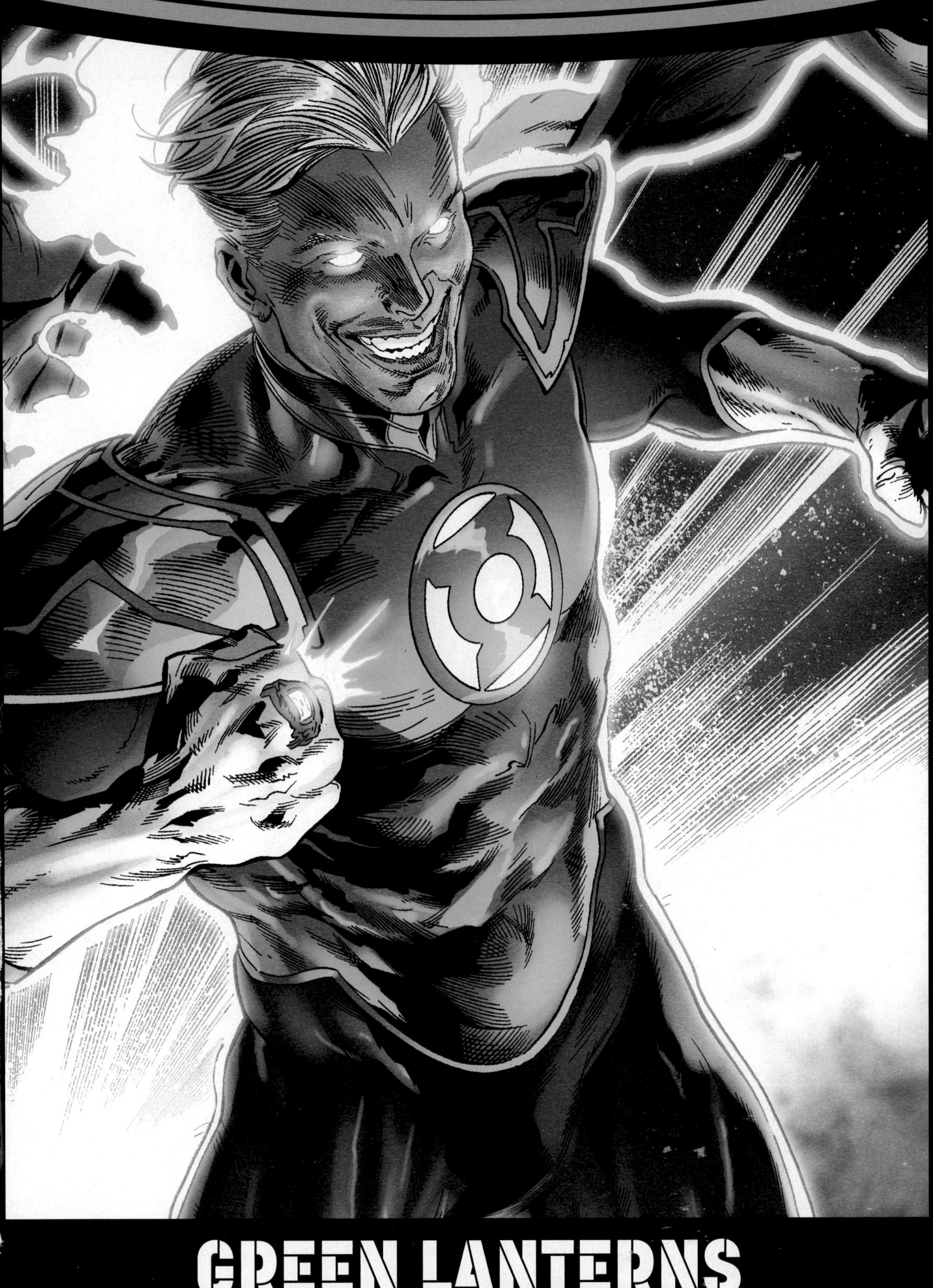

GREEN LANTERNS

VOL.2 THE PHANTOM LANTERN

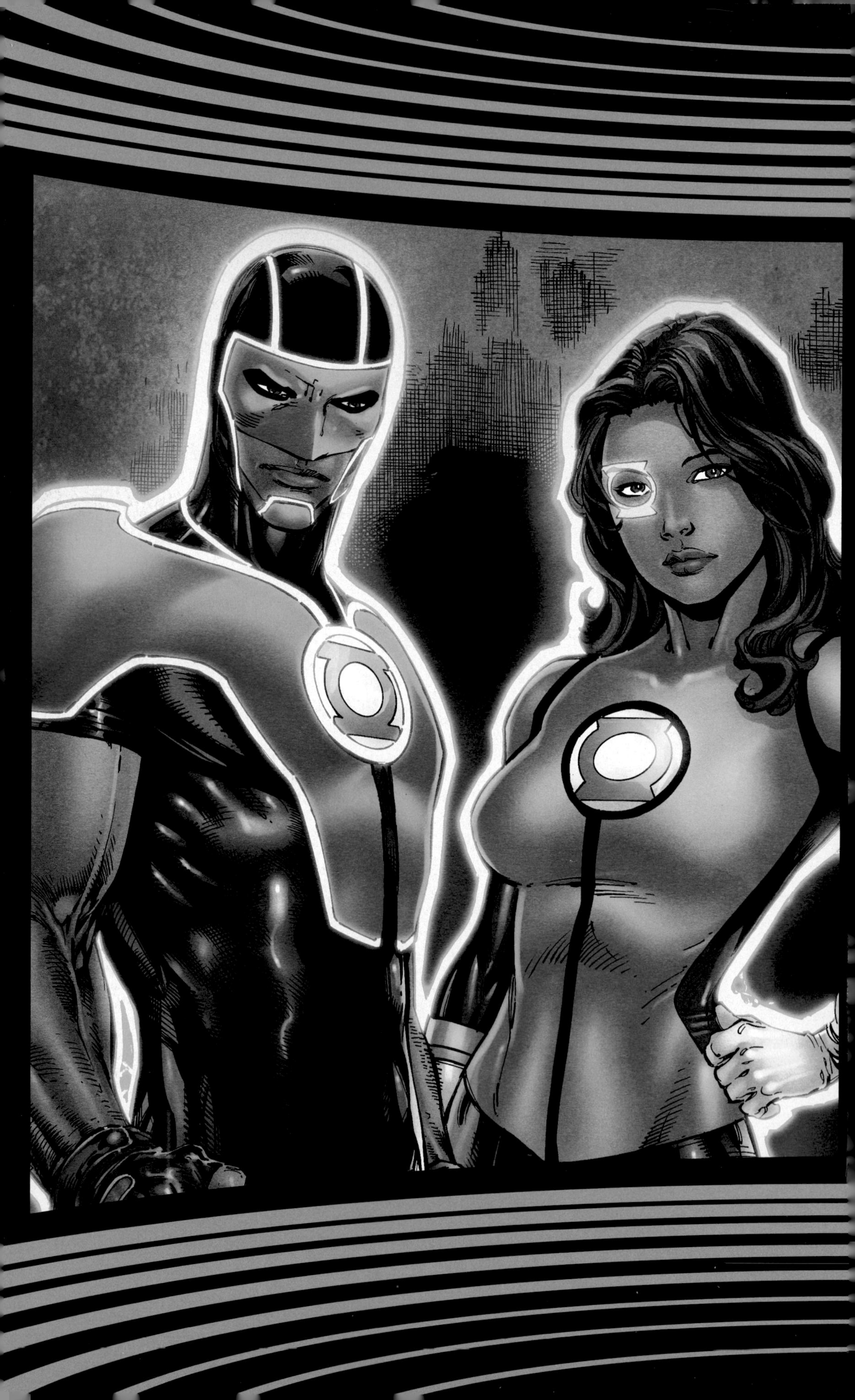

GREEN LANTERNS
VOL.2 THE PHANTOM LANTERN

SAM HUMPHRIES
writer

ED BENES * **RONAN CLIQUET** * **ROBSON ROCHA**
EDUARDO PANSICA * **JAY LEISTEN**
JULIO FERREIRA * **CAM SMITH**
artists

BLOND
colorist

DAVE SHARPE
letterer

ROBSON ROCHA, JOE PRADO and **ROD REIS**
collection cover artists

MIKE COTTON Editor – Original Series * **ANDREW MARINO** Associate Editor – Original Series
JEB WOODARD Group Editor – Collected Editions * **PAUL SANTOS** Editor – Collected Edition
STEVE COOK Design Director – Books * **MONIQUE GRUSPE** Publication Design

BOB HARRAS Senior VP – Editor-in-Chief, DC Comics

DIANE NELSON President * **DAN DiDIO** Publisher * **JIM LEE** Publisher * **GEOFF JOHNS** President & Chief Creative Officer
AMIT DESAI Executive VP – Business & Marketing Strategy, Direct to Consumer & Global Franchise Management * **SAM ADES** Senior VP – Direct to Consumer
BOBBIE CHASE VP – Talent Development * **MARK CHIARELLO** Senior VP – Art, Design & Collected Editions
JOHN CUNNINGHAM Senior VP – Sales & Trade Marketing * **ANNE DePIES** Senior VP – Business Strategy, Finance & Administration
DON FALLETTI VP – Manufacturing Operations * **LAWRENCE GANEM** VP – Editorial Administration & Talent Relations
ALISON GILL Senior VP – Manufacturing & Operations * **HANK KANALZ** Senior VP – Editorial Strategy & Administration
JAY KOGAN VP – Legal Affairs * **THOMAS LOFTUS** VP – Business Affairs
JACK MAHAN VP – Business Affairs * **NICK J. NAPOLITANO** VP – Manufacturing Administration
EDDIE SCANNELL VP – Consumer Marketing * **COURTNEY SIMMONS** Senior VP – Publicity & Communications
JIM (SKI) SOKOLOWSKI VP – Comic Book Specialty Sales & Trade Marketing * **NANCY SPEARS** VP – Mass, Book, Digital Sales & Trade Marketing

GREEN LANTERNS VOL. 2 THE PHANTOM LANTERN

Published by DC Comics. Compilation and all new material Copyright © 2017 DC Comics. All Rights Reserved.
Originally published in single magazine form in Green Lanterns 7-14. Copyright © 2016, 2017 DC Comics.
All Rights Reserved. All characters, their distinctive likenesses and related elements featured in this publication are trademarks of DC Comics.
The stories, characters and incidents featured in this publication are entirely fictional.
DC Comics does not read or accept unsolicited submissions of ideas, stories or artwork.

DC Comics, 2900 West Alameda Ave., Burbank, CA 91505.
Printed by LSC Communications, Salem, VA, USA. 3/24/17. First Printing.
ISBN: 978-1-4012-6849-7

Library of Congress Cataloging-in-Publication Data is available.

PEFC Certified

Printed on paper from
sustainably managed
forests, controlled
sources

PEFC/29-31-337   www.pefc.org

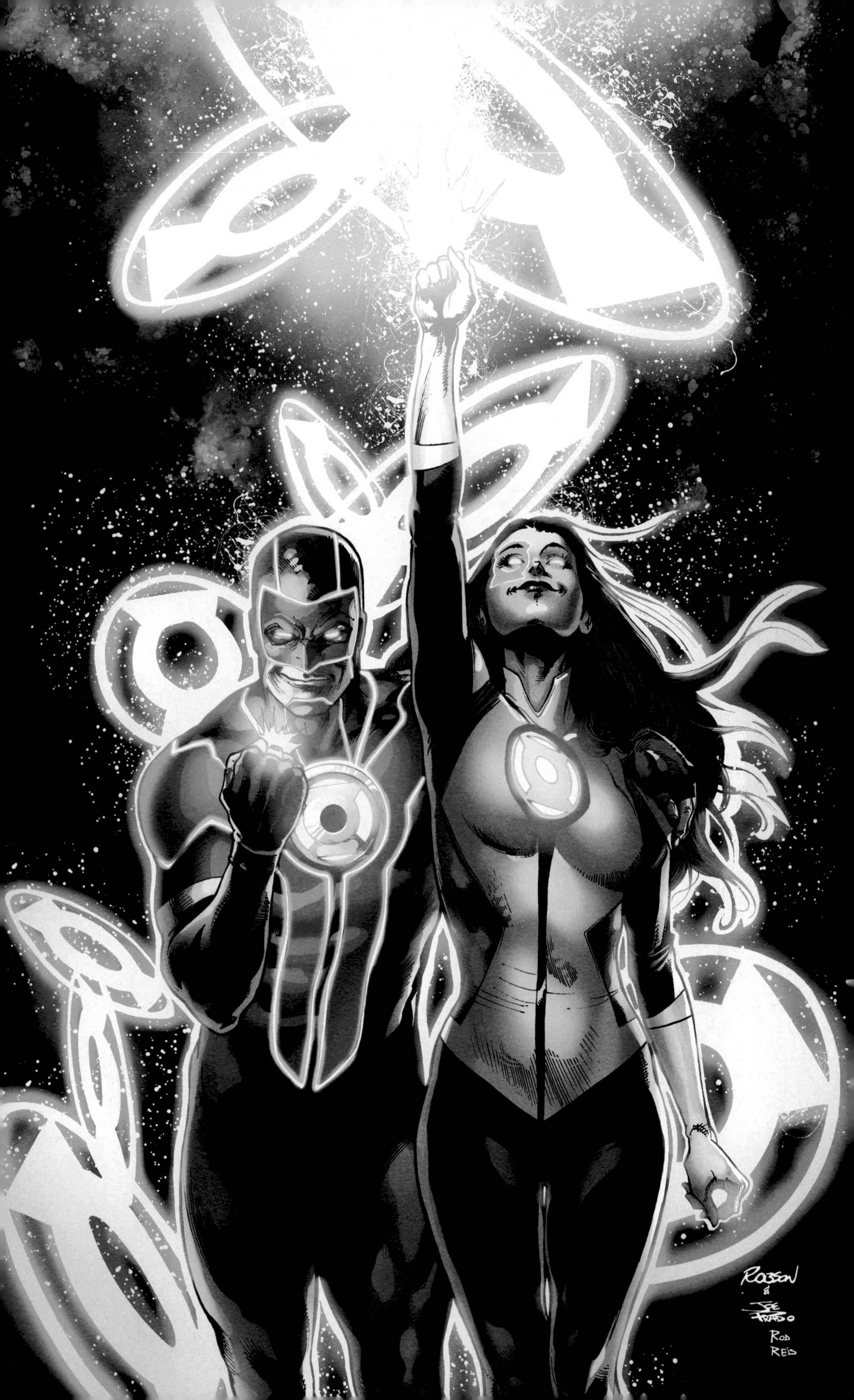

"FAMILY MATTERS PART ONE: KITCHEN NIGHTMARES"

SAM HUMPHRIES writer * RONAN CLIQUET artist

Cover by ROBSON ROCHA, JOE PRADO and ROD REIS

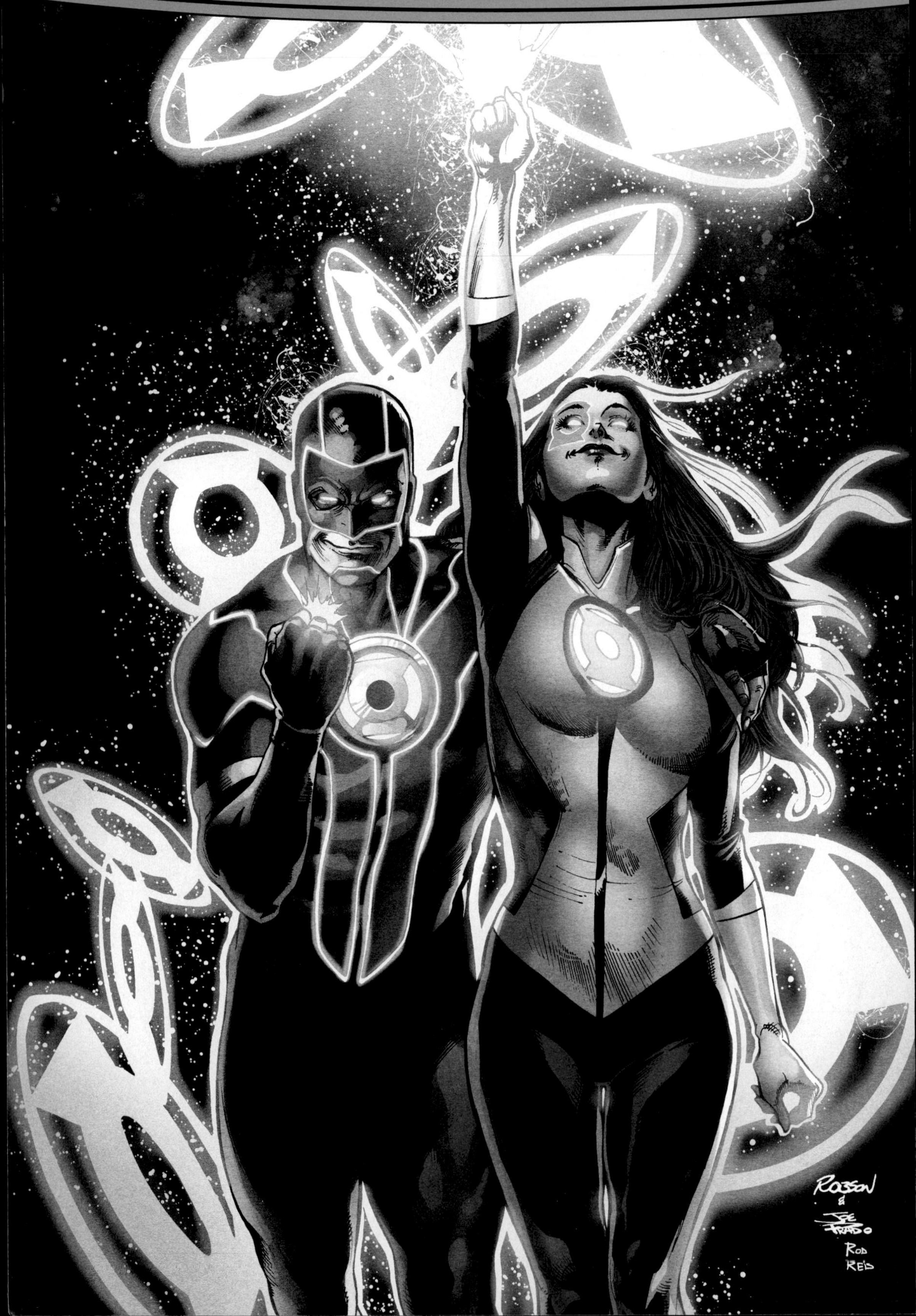
ROBSON
&
JOE PRADO
ROD
REIS

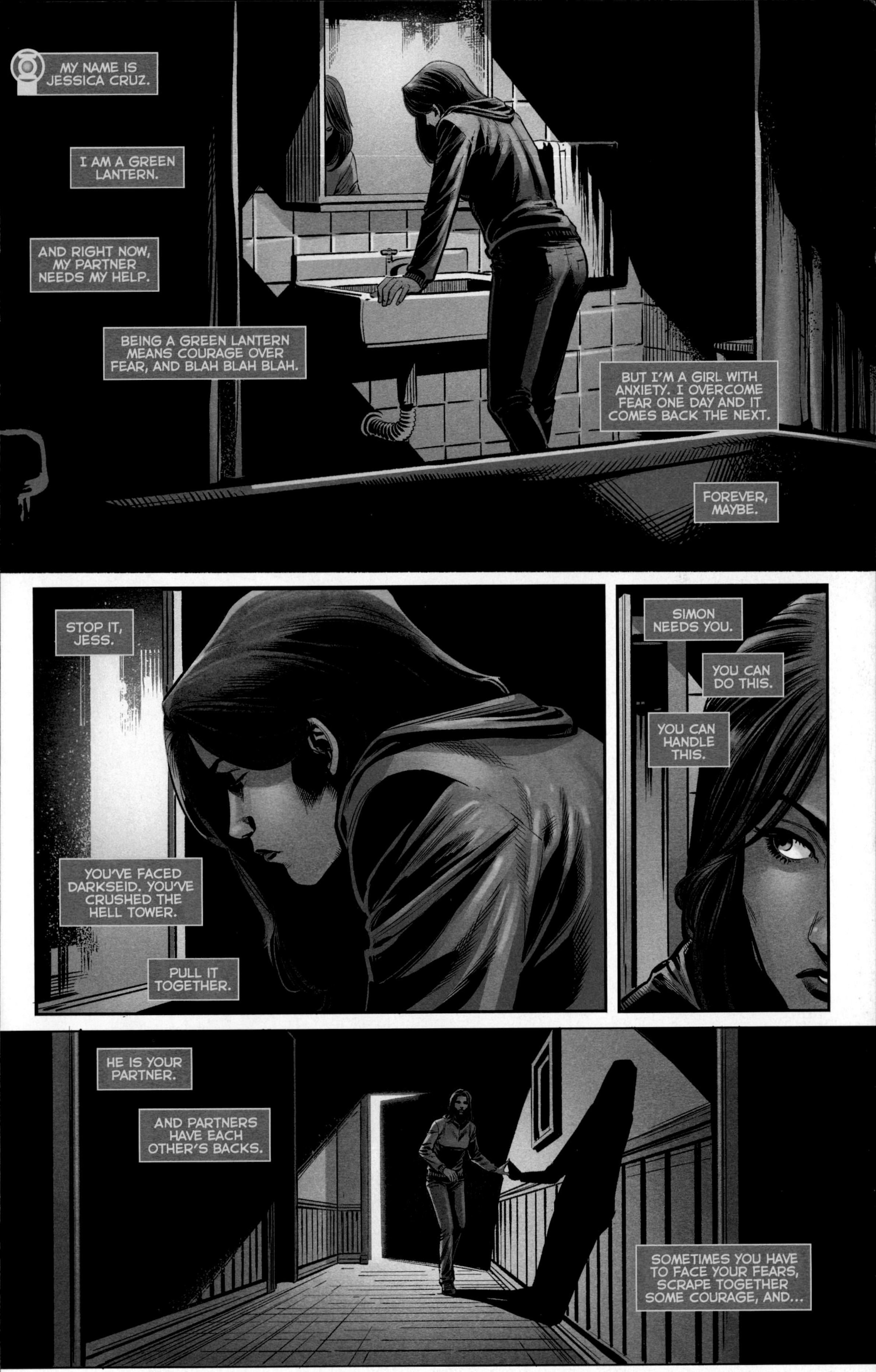

MY NAME IS JESSICA CRUZ.
I AM A GREEN LANTERN.
AND RIGHT NOW, MY PARTNER NEEDS MY HELP.
BEING A GREEN LANTERN MEANS COURAGE OVER FEAR, AND BLAH BLAH BLAH.
BUT I'M A GIRL WITH ANXIETY. I OVERCOME FEAR ONE DAY AND IT COMES BACK THE NEXT.
FOREVER, MAYBE.
STOP IT, JESS.
YOU'VE FACED DARKSEID. YOU'VE CRUSHED THE HELL TOWER.
PULL IT TOGETHER.
SIMON NEEDS YOU.
YOU CAN DO THIS.
YOU CAN HANDLE THIS.
HE IS YOUR PARTNER.
AND PARTNERS HAVE EACH OTHER'S BACKS.
SOMETIMES YOU HAVE TO FACE YOUR FEARS, SCRAPE TOGETHER SOME COURAGE, AND...

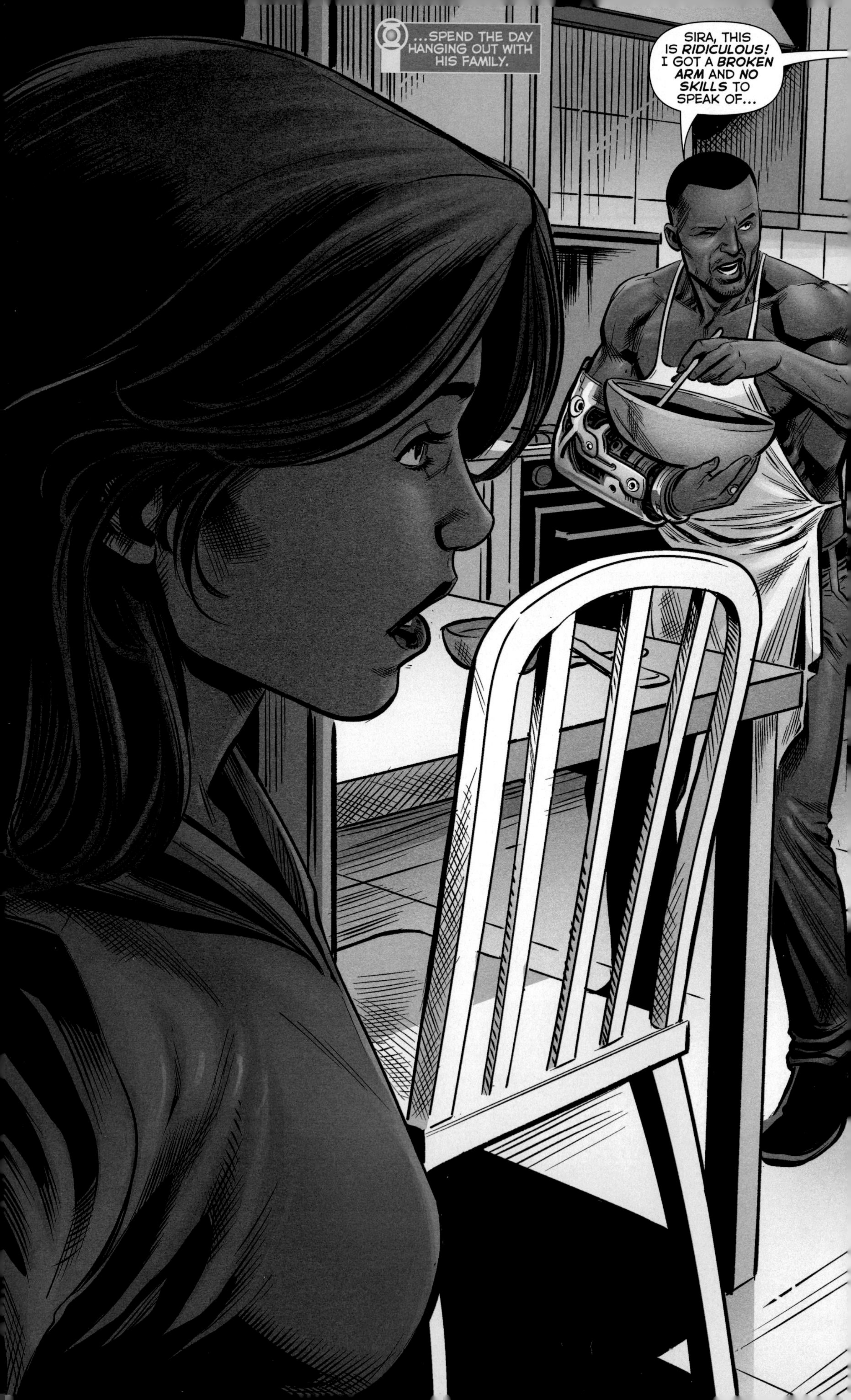
...SPEND THE DAY HANGING OUT WITH HIS FAMILY.
SIRA, THIS IS RIDICULOUS! I GOT A BROKEN ARM AND NO SKILLS TO SPEAK OF...

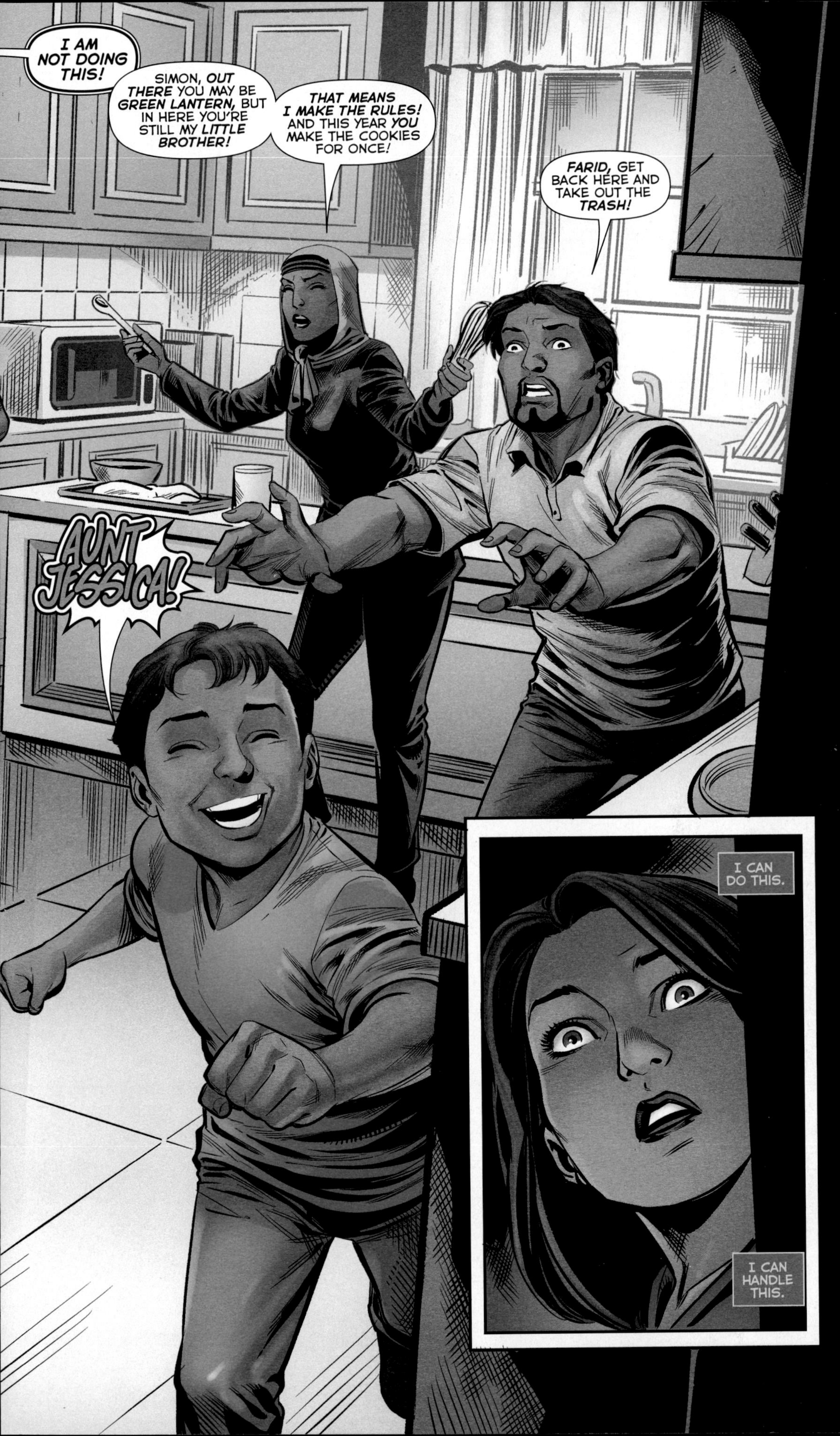
I AM NOT DOING THIS!
SIMON, OUT THERE YOU MAY BE GREEN LANTERN, BUT IN HERE YOU'RE STILL MY LITTLE BROTHER!
THAT MEANS I MAKE THE RULES! AND THIS YEAR YOU MAKE THE COOKIES FOR ONCE!
FARID, GET BACK HERE AND TAKE OUT THE TRASH!
AUNT JESSICA!
I CAN DO THIS.
I CAN HANDLE THIS.

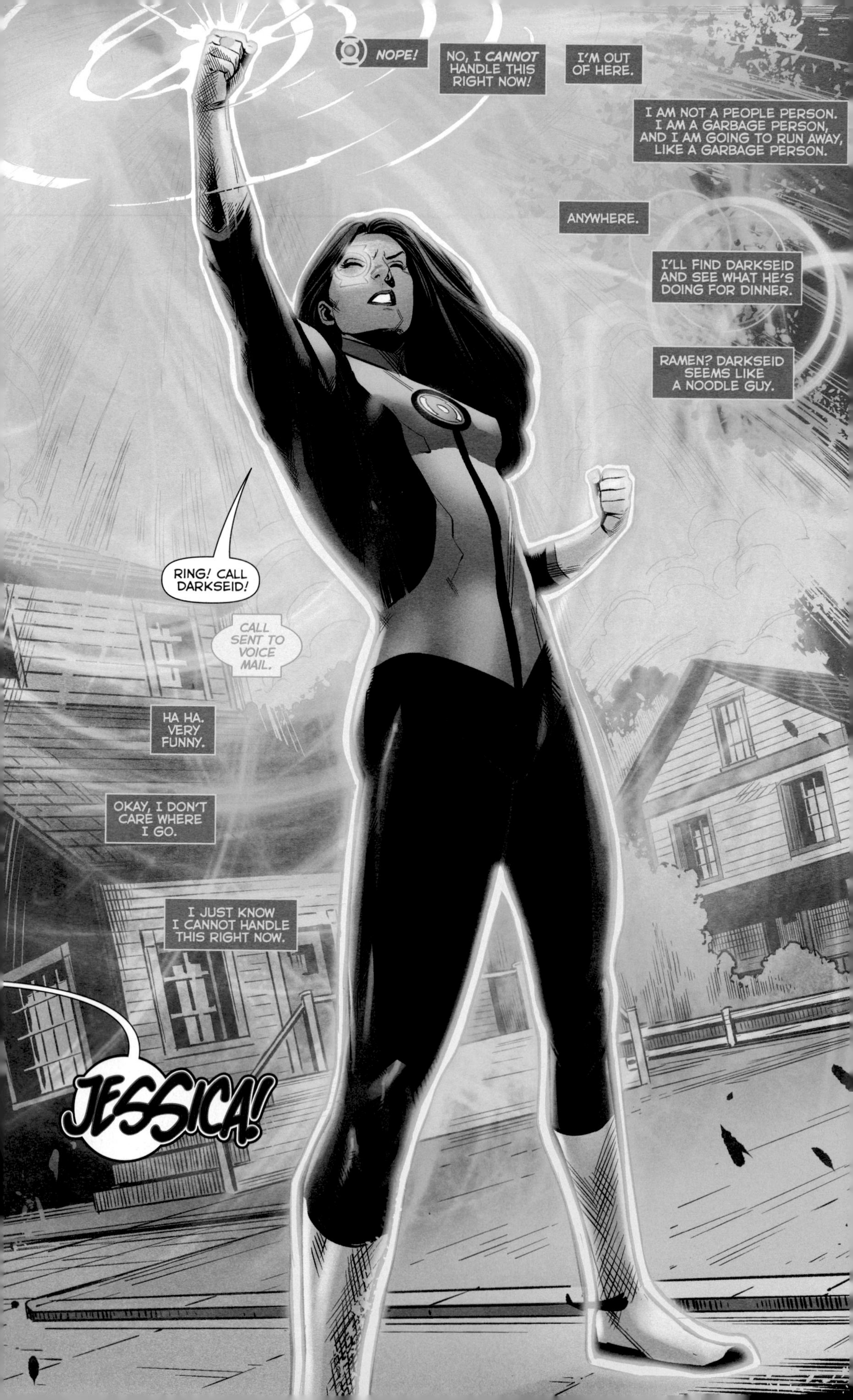
NOPE!
NO, I CANNOT HANDLE THIS RIGHT NOW!
I'M OUT OF HERE.
I AM NOT A PEOPLE PERSON. I AM A GARBAGE PERSON, AND I AM GOING TO RUN AWAY, LIKE A GARBAGE PERSON.
ANYWHERE.
I'LL FIND DARKSEID AND SEE WHAT HE'S DOING FOR DINNER.
RAMEN? DARKSEID SEEMS LIKE A NOODLE GUY.
RING! CALL DARKSEID!
CALL SENT TO VOICE MAIL.
HA HA. VERY FUNNY.
OKAY, I DON'T CARE WHERE I GO.
I JUST KNOW I CANNOT HANDLE THIS RIGHT NOW.
JESSICA!

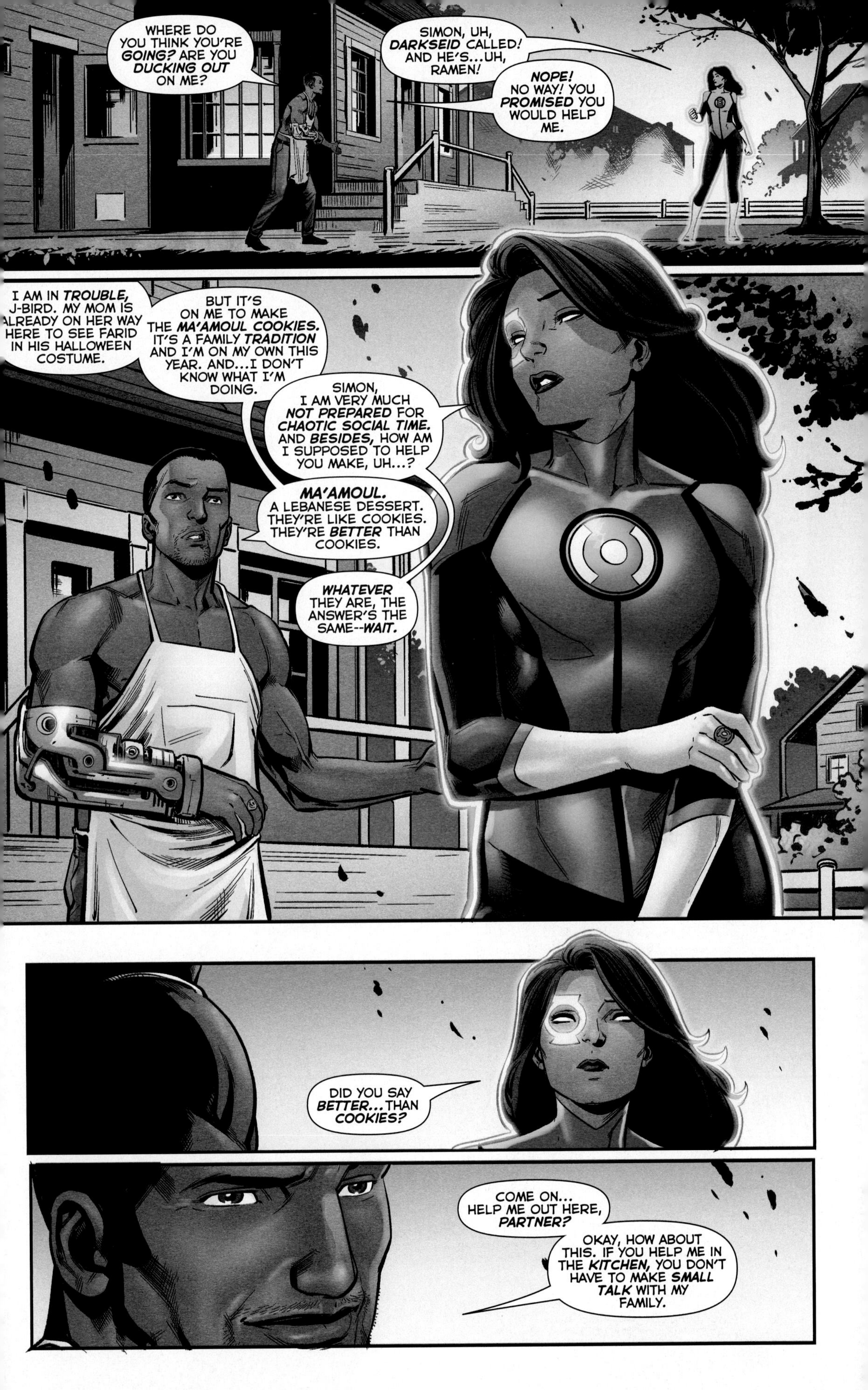
WHERE DO YOU THINK YOU'RE GOING? ARE YOU DUCKING OUT ON ME?
SIMON, UH, DARKSEID CALLED! AND HE'S...UH, RAMEN!
NOPE! NO WAY! YOU PROMISED YOU WOULD HELP ME.
I AM IN TROUBLE, J-BIRD. MY MOM IS ALREADY ON HER WAY HERE TO SEE FARID IN HIS HALLOWEEN COSTUME.
BUT IT'S ON ME TO MAKE THE MA'AMOUL COOKIES. IT'S A FAMILY TRADITION AND I'M ON MY OWN THIS YEAR. AND...I DON'T KNOW WHAT I'M DOING.
SIMON, I AM VERY MUCH NOT PREPARED FOR CHAOTIC SOCIAL TIME. AND BESIDES, HOW AM I SUPPOSED TO HELP YOU MAKE, UH...?
MA'AMOUL. A LEBANESE DESSERT. THEY'RE LIKE COOKIES. THEY'RE BETTER THAN COOKIES.
WHATEVER THEY ARE, THE ANSWER'S THE SAME--WAIT.
DID YOU SAY BETTER...THAN COOKIES?
COME ON... HELP ME OUT HERE, PARTNER?
OKAY, HOW ABOUT THIS. IF YOU HELP ME IN THE KITCHEN, YOU DON'T HAVE TO MAKE SMALL TALK WITH MY FAMILY.

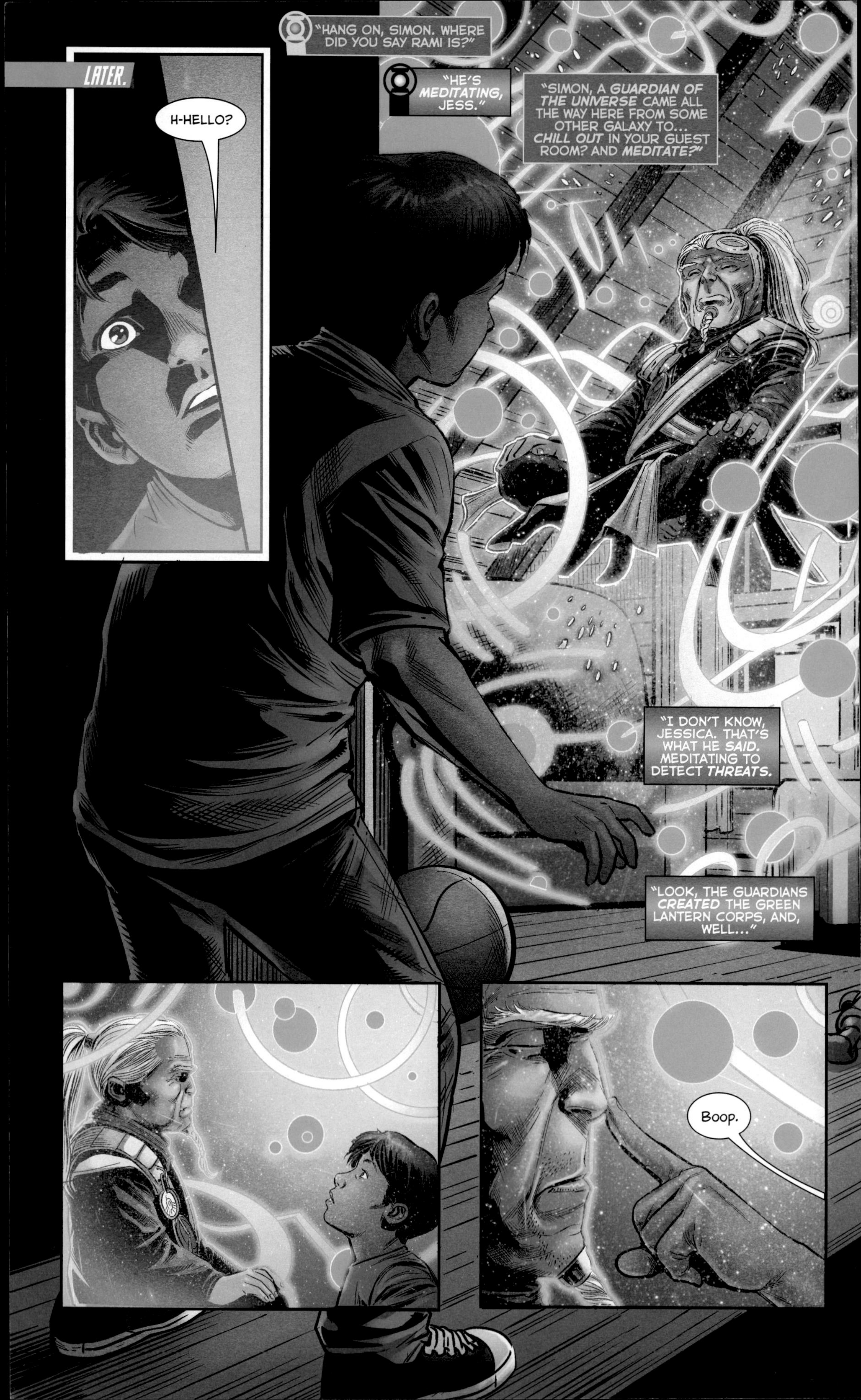
"HANG ON, SIMON. WHERE DID YOU SAY RAMI IS?"
LATER.
H-HELLO?
"HE'S MEDITATING, JESS."
"SIMON, A GUARDIAN OF THE UNIVERSE CAME ALL THE WAY HERE FROM SOME OTHER GALAXY TO... CHILL OUT IN YOUR GUEST ROOM? AND MEDITATE?"
"I DON'T KNOW, JESSICA. THAT'S WHAT HE SAID. MEDITATING TO DETECT THREATS.
"LOOK, THE GUARDIANS CREATED THE GREEN LANTERN CORPS, AND, WELL..."
Boop.

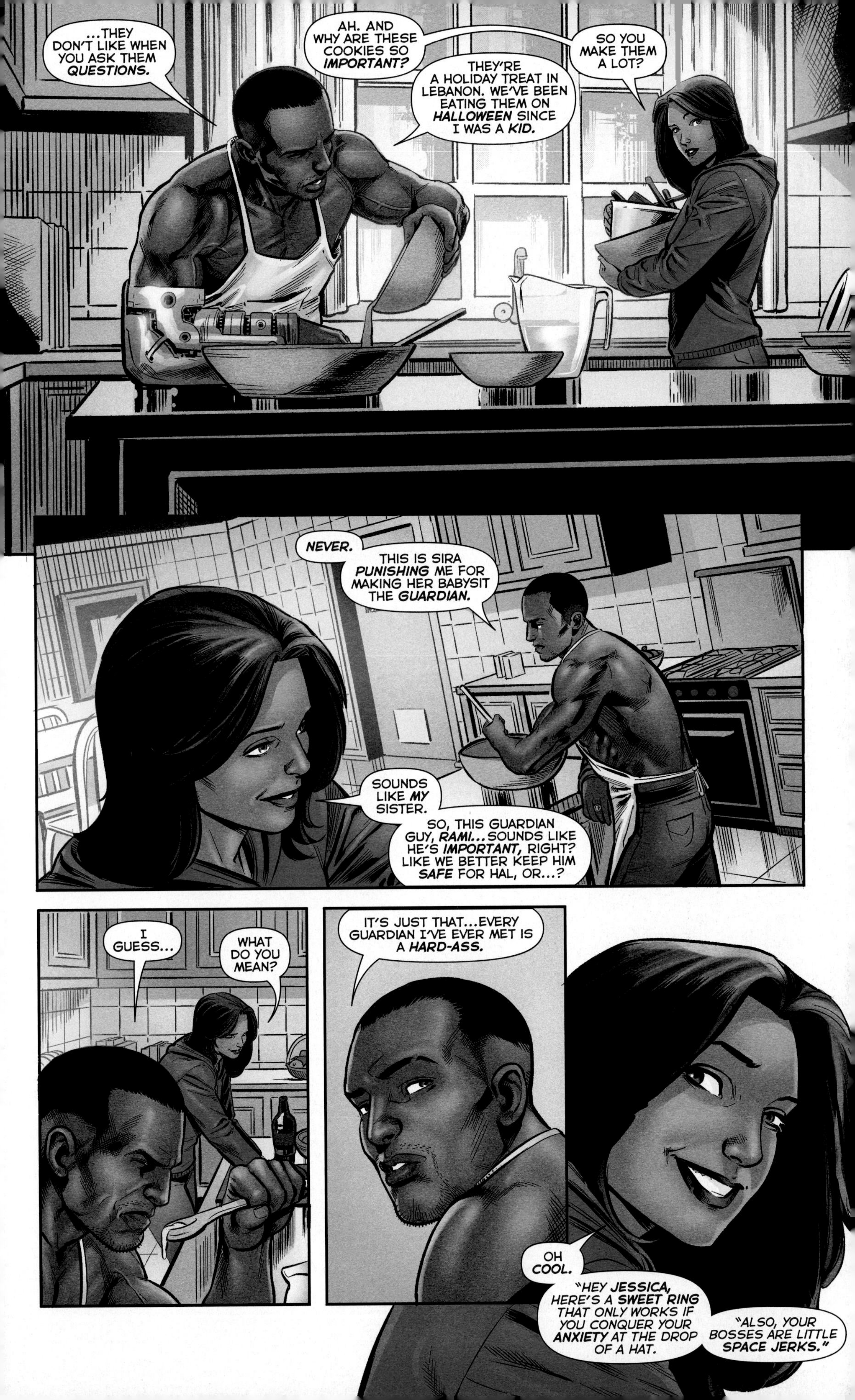

...THEY DON'T LIKE WHEN YOU ASK THEM QUESTIONS.
AH. AND WHY ARE THESE COOKIES SO IMPORTANT?
THEY'RE A HOLIDAY TREAT IN LEBANON. WE'VE BEEN EATING THEM ON HALLOWEEN SINCE I WAS A KID.
SO YOU MAKE THEM A LOT?
NEVER.
THIS IS SIRA PUNISHING ME FOR MAKING HER BABYSIT THE GUARDIAN.
SOUNDS LIKE MY SISTER.
SO, THIS GUARDIAN GUY, RAMI... SOUNDS LIKE HE'S IMPORTANT, RIGHT? LIKE WE BETTER KEEP HIM SAFE FOR HAL, OR...?
I GUESS...
WHAT DO YOU MEAN?
IT'S JUST THAT...EVERY GUARDIAN I'VE EVER MET IS A HARD-ASS.
OH COOL.
"HEY JESSICA, HERE'S A SWEET RING THAT ONLY WORKS IF YOU CONQUER YOUR ANXIETY AT THE DROP OF A HAT.
"ALSO, YOUR BOSSES ARE LITTLE SPACE JERKS."

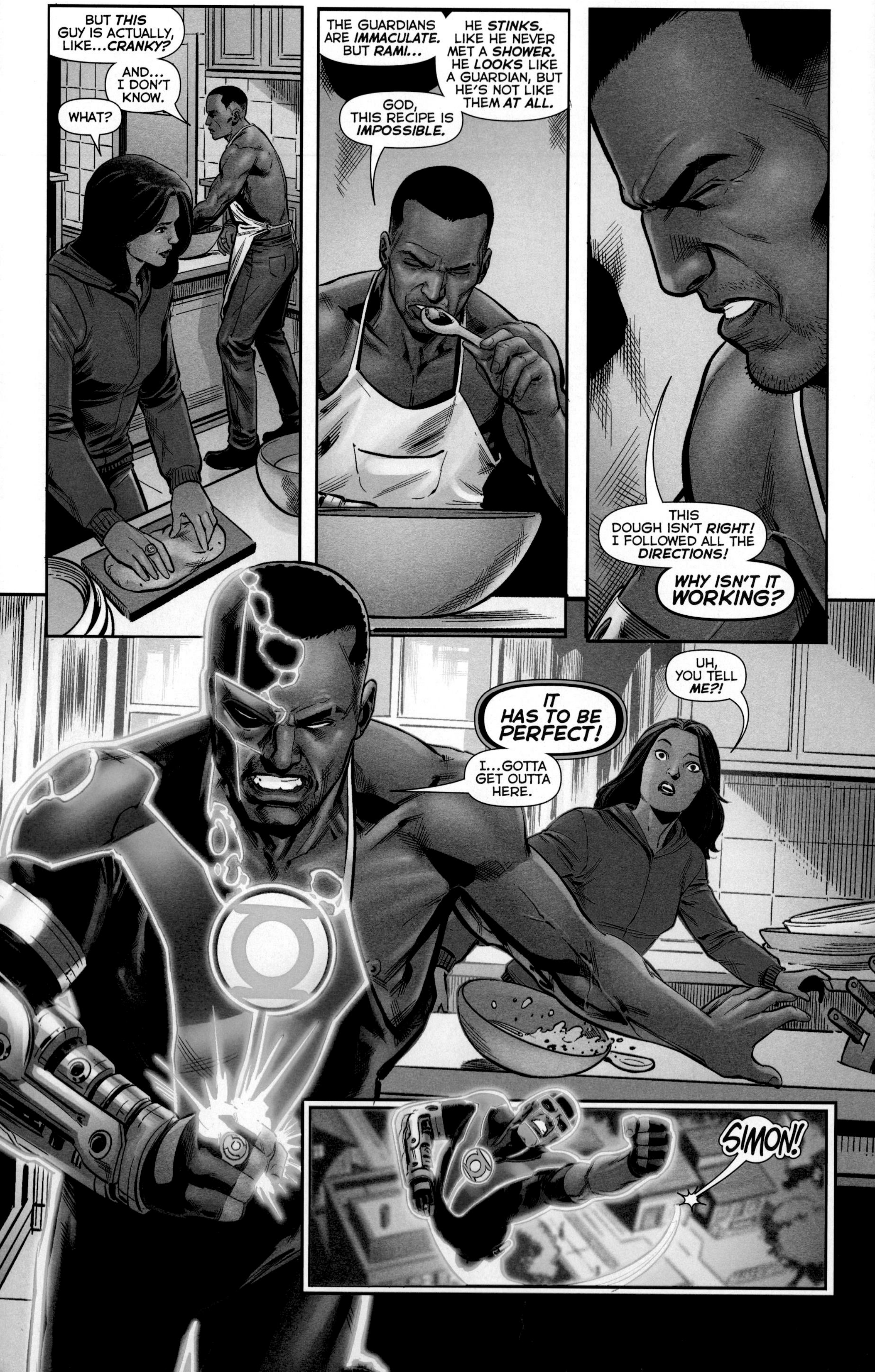
BUT THIS GUY IS ACTUALLY, LIKE...CRANKY?
AND... I DON'T KNOW.
WHAT?
THE GUARDIANS ARE IMMACULATE. BUT RAMI...
HE STINKS. LIKE HE NEVER MET A SHOWER. HE LOOKS LIKE A GUARDIAN, BUT HE'S NOT LIKE THEM AT ALL.
GOD, THIS RECIPE IS IMPOSSIBLE.
THIS DOUGH ISN'T RIGHT! I FOLLOWED ALL THE DIRECTIONS!
WHY ISN'T IT WORKING?
IT HAS TO BE PERFECT!
I...GOTTA GET OUTTA HERE.
UH, YOU TELL ME?!
SIMON!

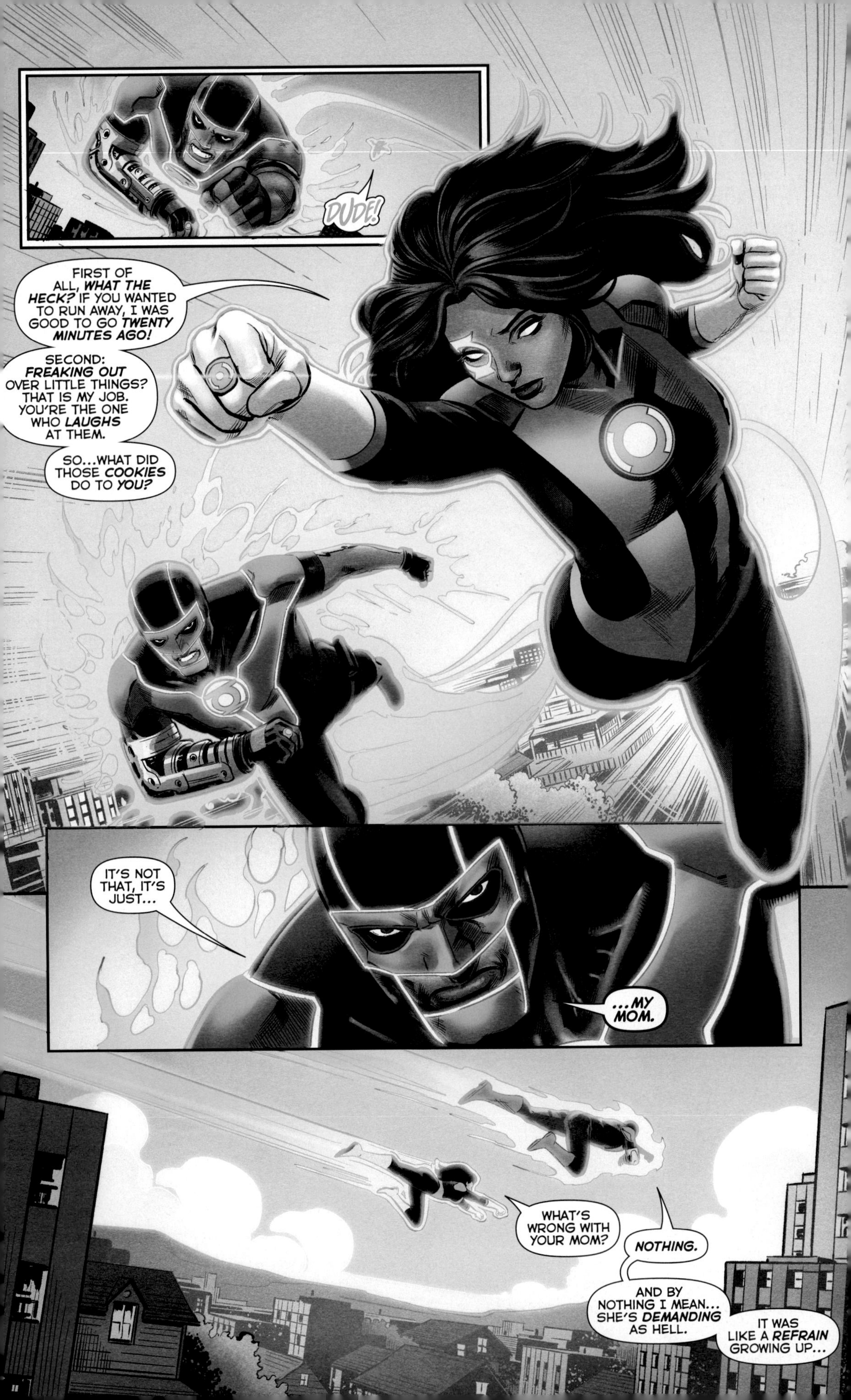
DUDE!
FIRST OF ALL, WHAT THE HECK? IF YOU WANTED TO RUN AWAY, I WAS GOOD TO GO TWENTY MINUTES AGO!
SECOND: FREAKING OUT OVER LITTLE THINGS? THAT IS MY JOB. YOU'RE THE ONE WHO LAUGHS AT THEM.
SO...WHAT DID THOSE COOKIES DO TO YOU?
IT'S NOT THAT, IT'S JUST...
...MY MOM.
WHAT'S WRONG WITH YOUR MOM?
NOTHING.
AND BY NOTHING I MEAN... SHE'S DEMANDING AS HELL.
IT WAS LIKE A REFRAIN GROWING UP...

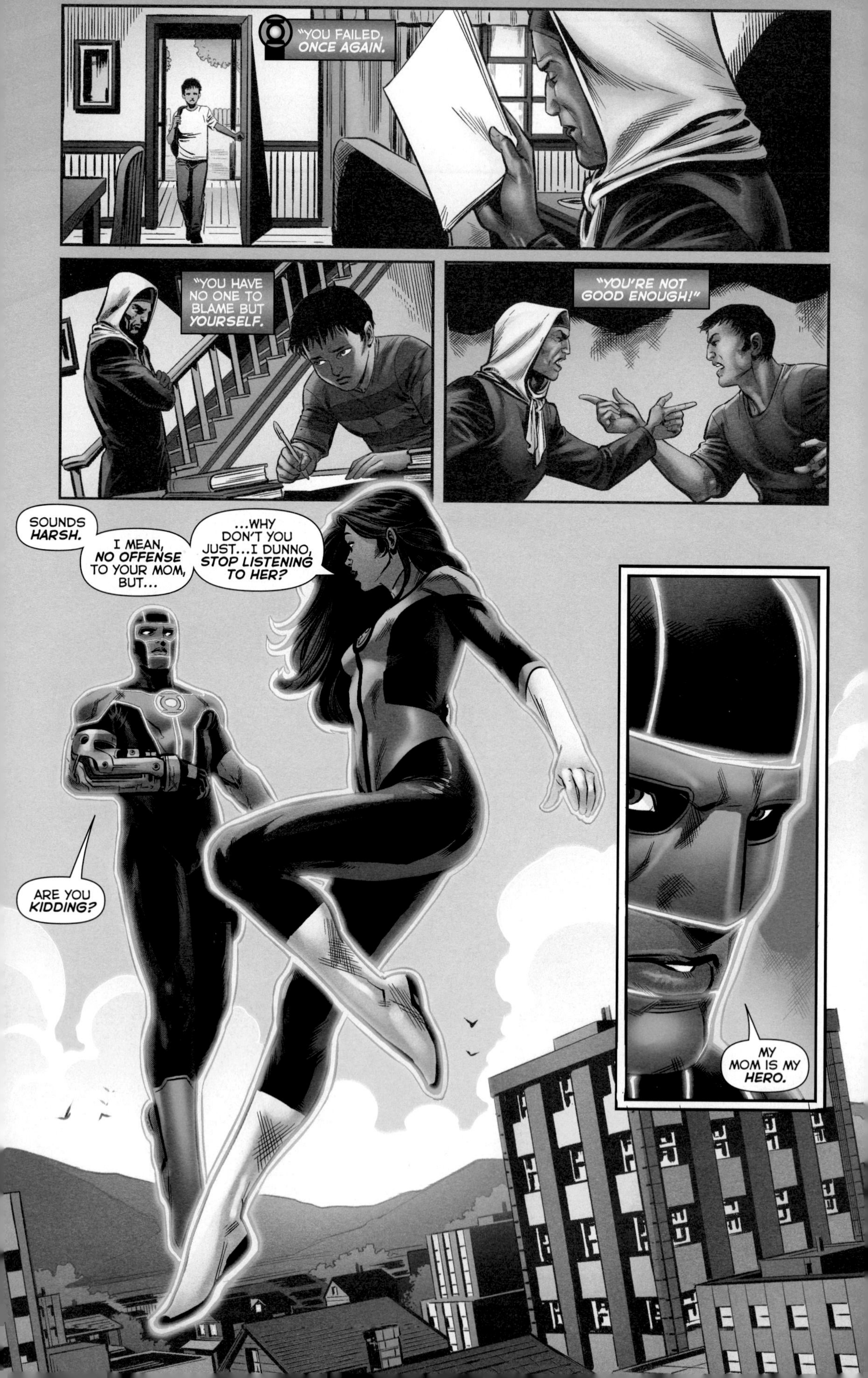
"YOU FAILED, ONCE AGAIN.
"YOU HAVE NO ONE TO BLAME BUT YOURSELF.
"YOU'RE NOT GOOD ENOUGH!"
SOUNDS HARSH.
I MEAN, NO OFFENSE TO YOUR MOM, BUT...
...WHY DON'T YOU JUST...I DUNNO, STOP LISTENING TO HER?
ARE YOU KIDDING?
MY MOM IS MY HERO.

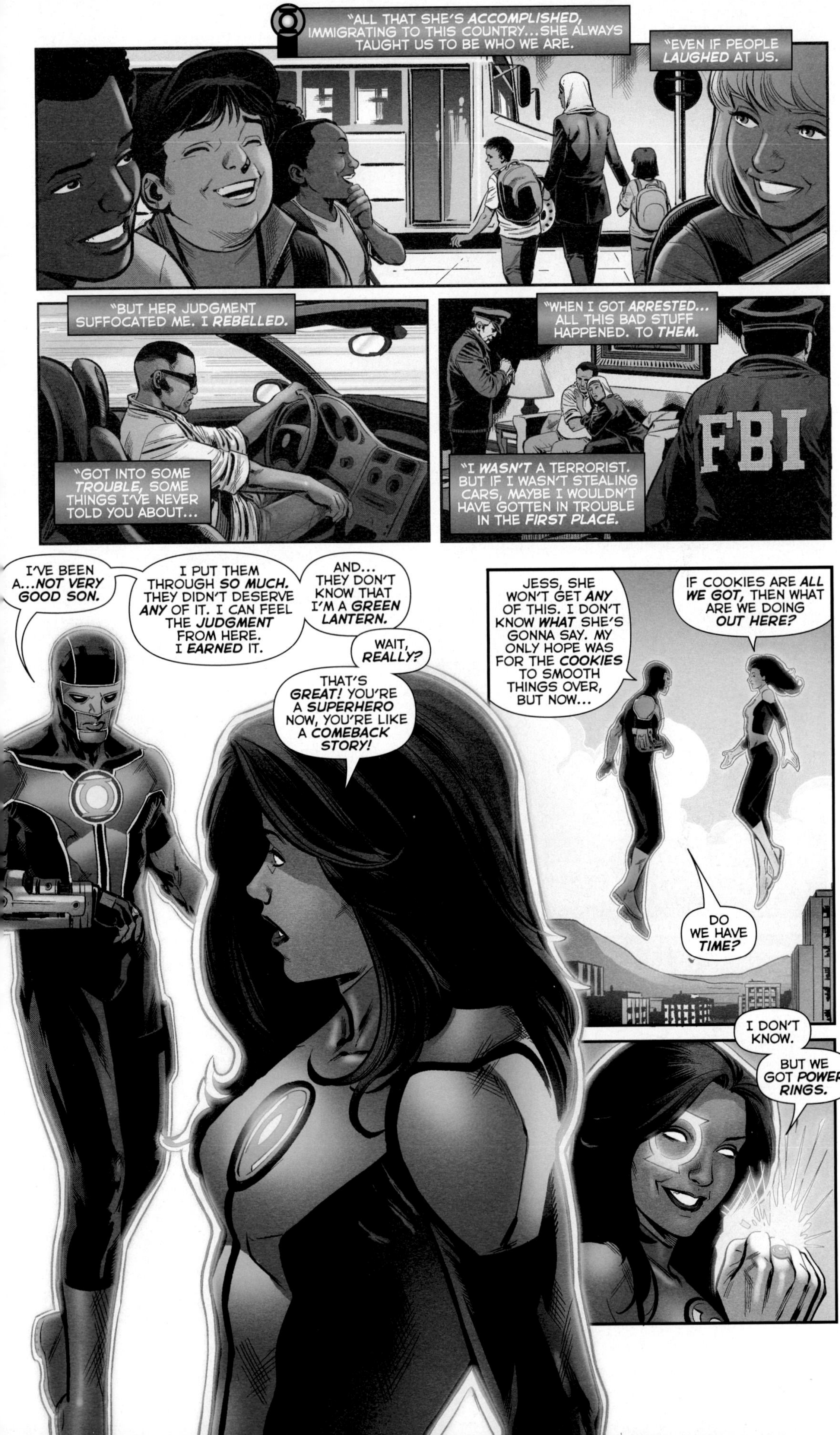
"ALL THAT SHE'S ACCOMPLISHED, IMMIGRATING TO THIS COUNTRY...SHE ALWAYS TAUGHT US TO BE WHO WE ARE.
"EVEN IF PEOPLE LAUGHED AT US.
"BUT HER JUDGMENT SUFFOCATED ME. I REBELLED.
"GOT INTO SOME TROUBLE, SOME THINGS I'VE NEVER TOLD YOU ABOUT...
"WHEN I GOT ARRESTED... ALL THIS BAD STUFF HAPPENED. TO THEM.
FBI
"I WASN'T A TERRORIST. BUT IF I WASN'T STEALING CARS, MAYBE I WOULDN'T HAVE GOTTEN IN TROUBLE IN THE FIRST PLACE.
I'VE BEEN A...NOT VERY GOOD SON.
I PUT THEM THROUGH SO MUCH. THEY DIDN'T DESERVE ANY OF IT. I CAN FEEL THE JUDGMENT FROM HERE. I EARNED IT.
AND... THEY DON'T KNOW THAT I'M A GREEN LANTERN.
WAIT, REALLY?
THAT'S GREAT! YOU'RE A SUPERHERO NOW, YOU'RE LIKE A COMEBACK STORY!
JESS, SHE WON'T GET ANY OF THIS. I DON'T KNOW WHAT SHE'S GONNA SAY. MY ONLY HOPE WAS FOR THE COOKIES TO SMOOTH THINGS OVER, BUT NOW...
IF COOKIES ARE ALL WE GOT, THEN WHAT ARE WE DOING OUT HERE?
DO WE HAVE TIME?
I DON'T KNOW.
BUT WE GOT POWER RINGS.

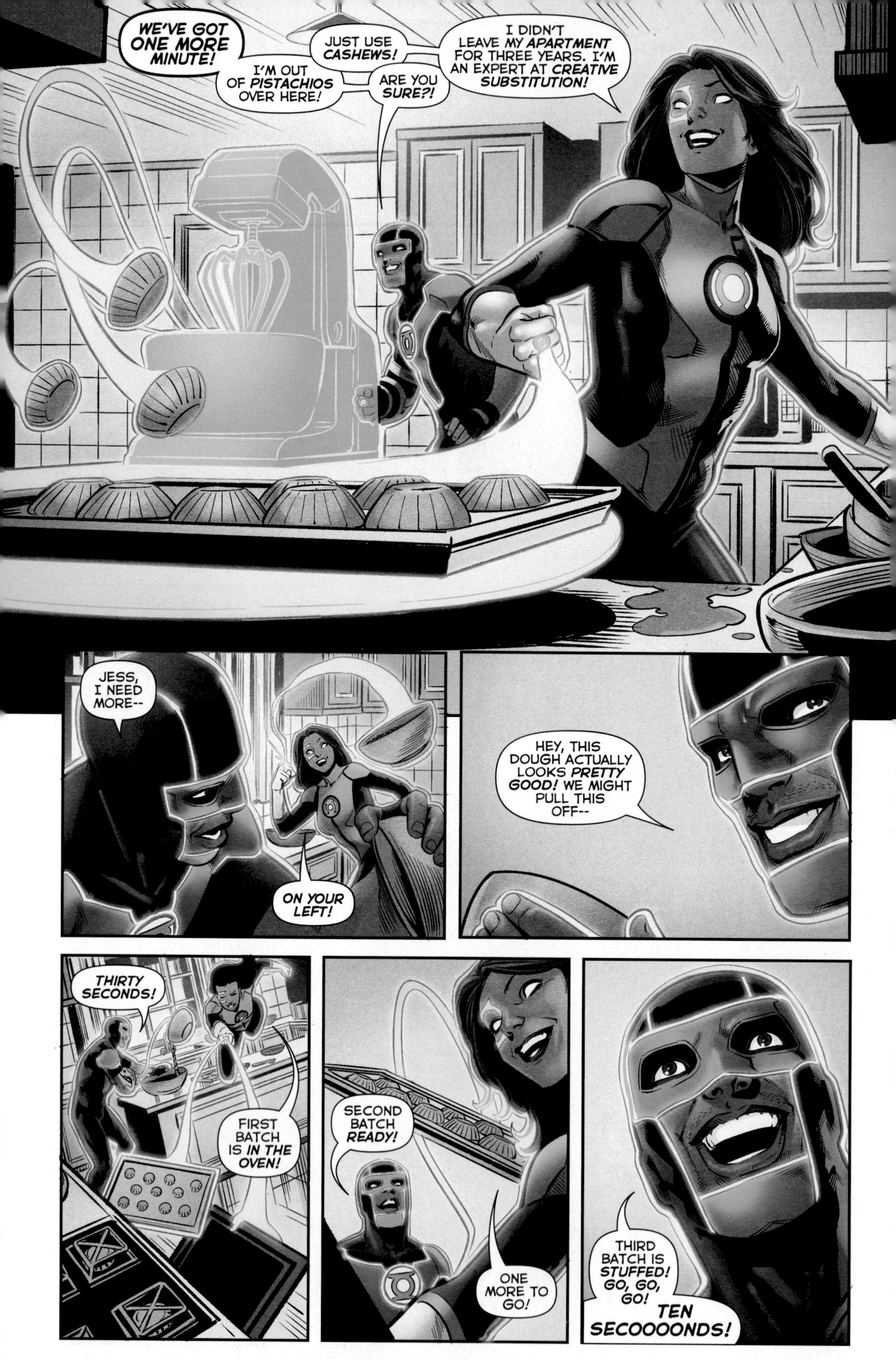
WE'VE GOT ONE MORE MINUTE!
I'M OUT OF PISTACHIOS OVER HERE!
JUST USE CASHEWS!
ARE YOU SURE?!
I DIDN'T LEAVE MY APARTMENT FOR THREE YEARS. I'M AN EXPERT AT CREATIVE SUBSTITUTION!
JESS, I NEED MORE--
ON YOUR LEFT!
HEY, THIS DOUGH ACTUALLY LOOKS PRETTY GOOD! WE MIGHT PULL THIS OFF--
THIRTY SECONDS!
FIRST BATCH IS IN THE OVEN!
SECOND BATCH READY!
ONE MORE TO GO!
THIRD BATCH IS STUFFED! GO, GO, GO!
TEN SECOOOONDS!

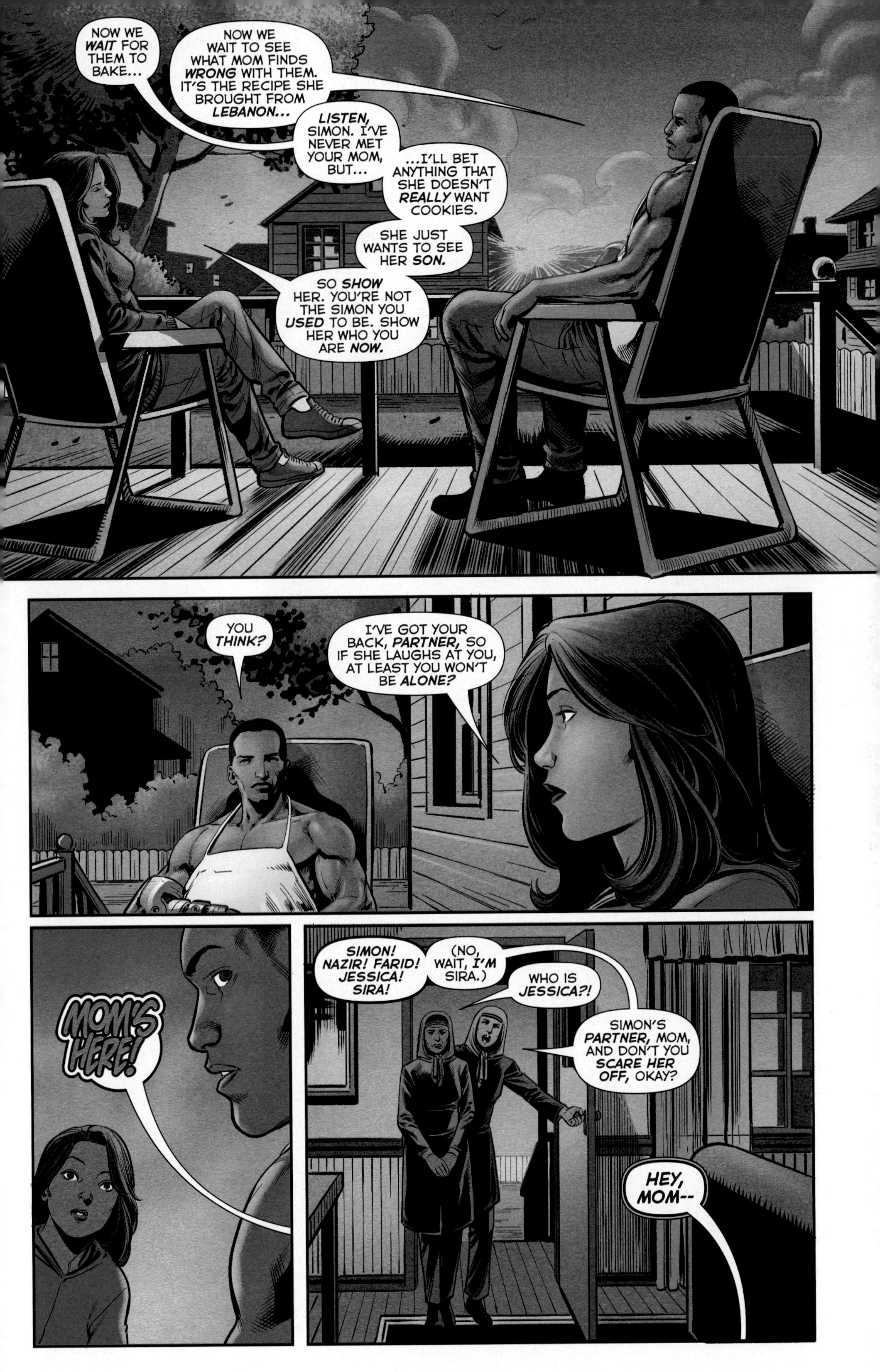
NOW WE WAIT FOR THEM TO BAKE...
NOW WE WAIT TO SEE WHAT MOM FINDS WRONG WITH THEM. IT'S THE RECIPE SHE BROUGHT FROM LEBANON...
LISTEN, SIMON. I'VE NEVER MET YOUR MOM, BUT...
...I'LL BET ANYTHING THAT SHE DOESN'T REALLY WANT COOKIES.
SHE JUST WANTS TO SEE HER SON.
SO SHOW HER. YOU'RE NOT THE SIMON YOU USED TO BE. SHOW HER WHO YOU ARE NOW.
YOU THINK?
I'VE GOT YOUR BACK, PARTNER, SO IF SHE LAUGHS AT YOU, AT LEAST YOU WON'T BE ALONE?
MOM'S HERE!
SIMON! NAZIR! FARID! JESSICA! SIRA!
(NO, WAIT, I'M SIRA.)
WHO IS JESSICA?!
SIMON'S PARTNER, MOM, AND DON'T YOU SCARE HER OFF, OKAY?
HEY, MOM--

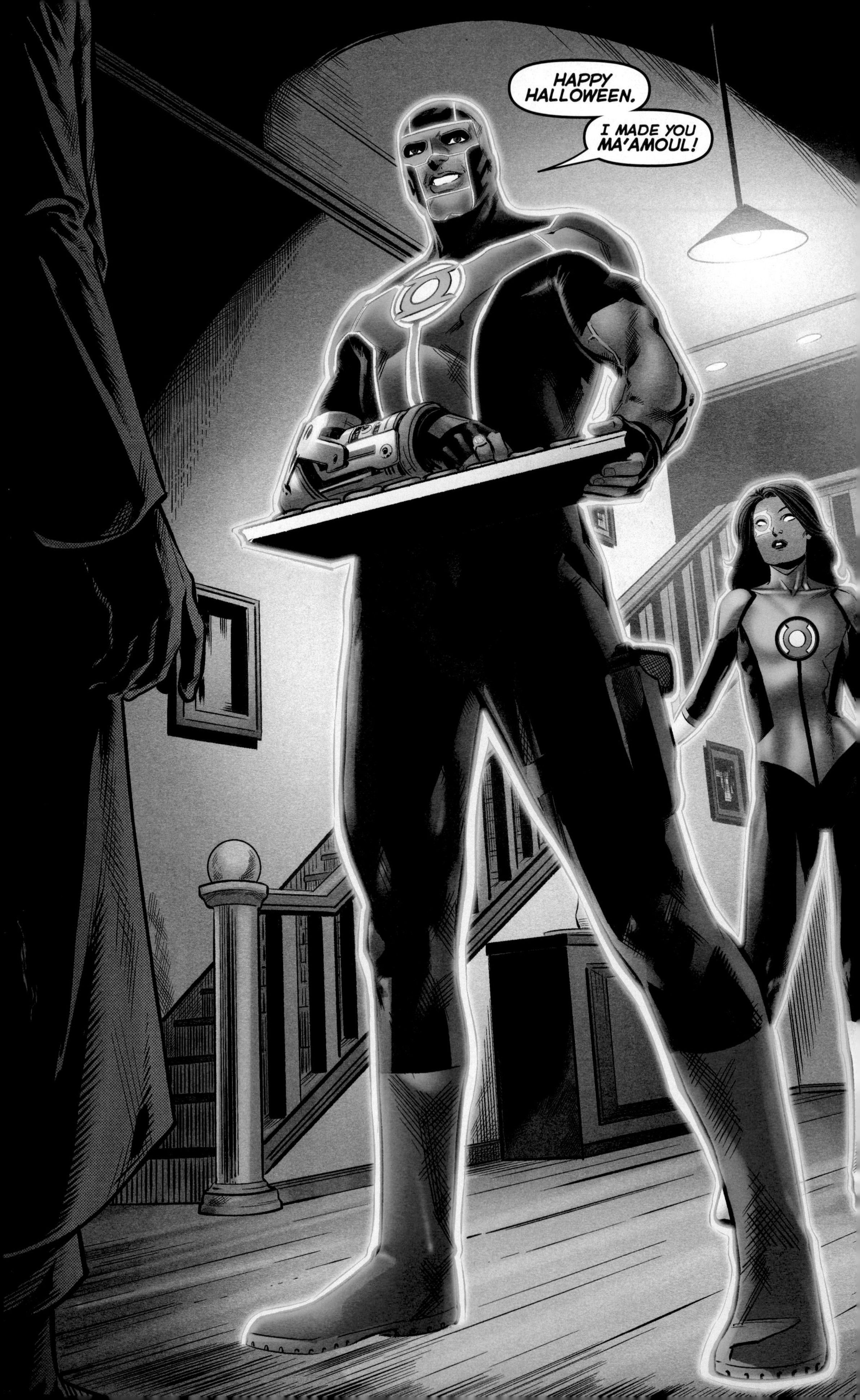
HAPPY HALLOWEEN.
I MADE YOU MA'AMOUL!

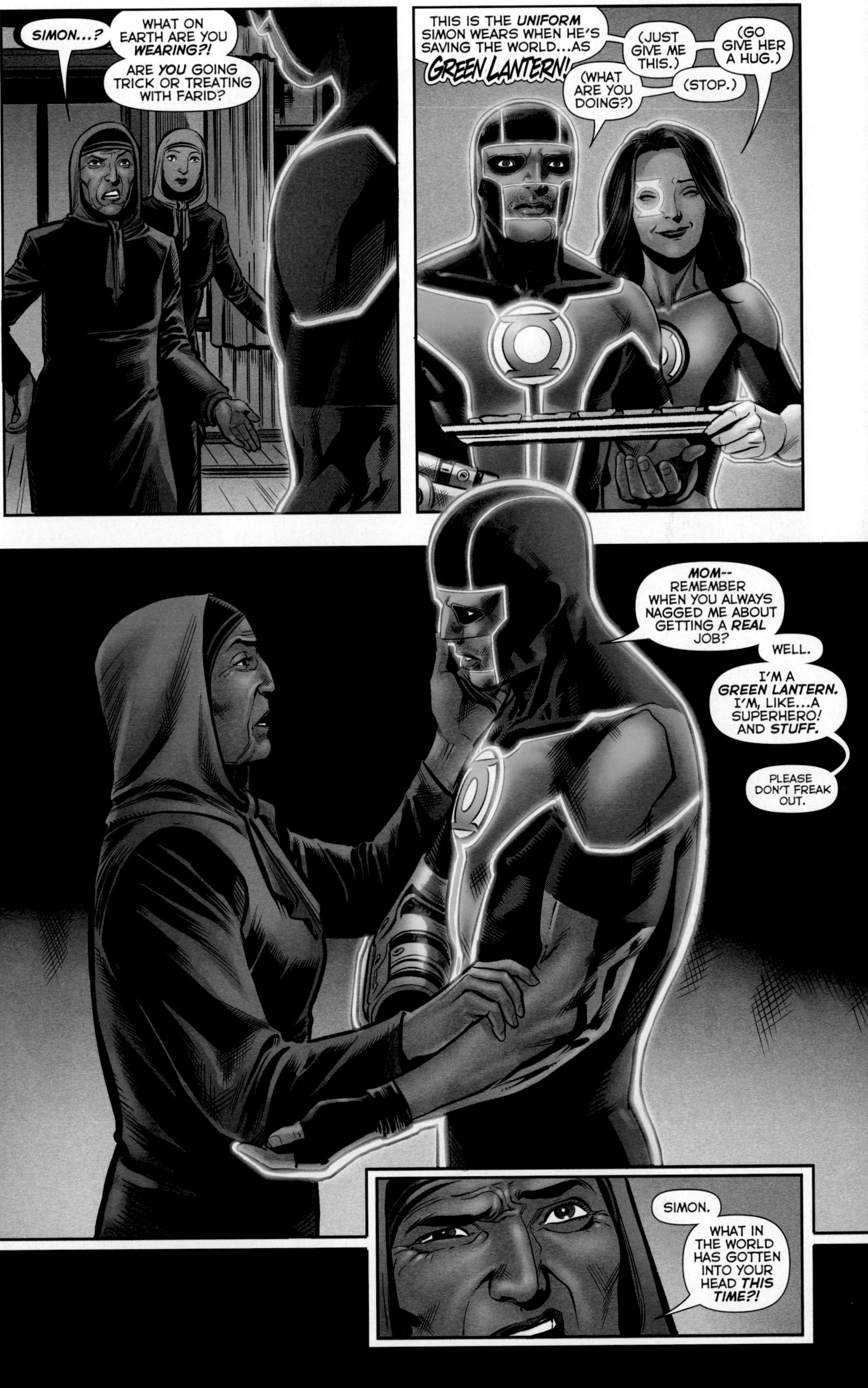
SIMON...?
WHAT ON EARTH ARE YOU WEARING?!
ARE YOU GOING TRICK OR TREATING WITH FARID?
THIS IS THE UNIFORM SIMON WEARS WHEN HE'S SAVING THE WORLD...AS GREEN LANTERN!
(JUST GIVE ME THIS.)
(GO GIVE HER A HUG.)
(WHAT ARE YOU DOING?)
(STOP.)
MOM-- REMEMBER WHEN YOU ALWAYS NAGGED ME ABOUT GETTING A REAL JOB?
WELL.
I'M A GREEN LANTERN. I'M, LIKE...A SUPERHERO! AND STUFF.
PLEASE DON'T FREAK OUT.
SIMON.
WHAT IN THE WORLD HAS GOTTEN INTO YOUR HEAD THIS TIME?!

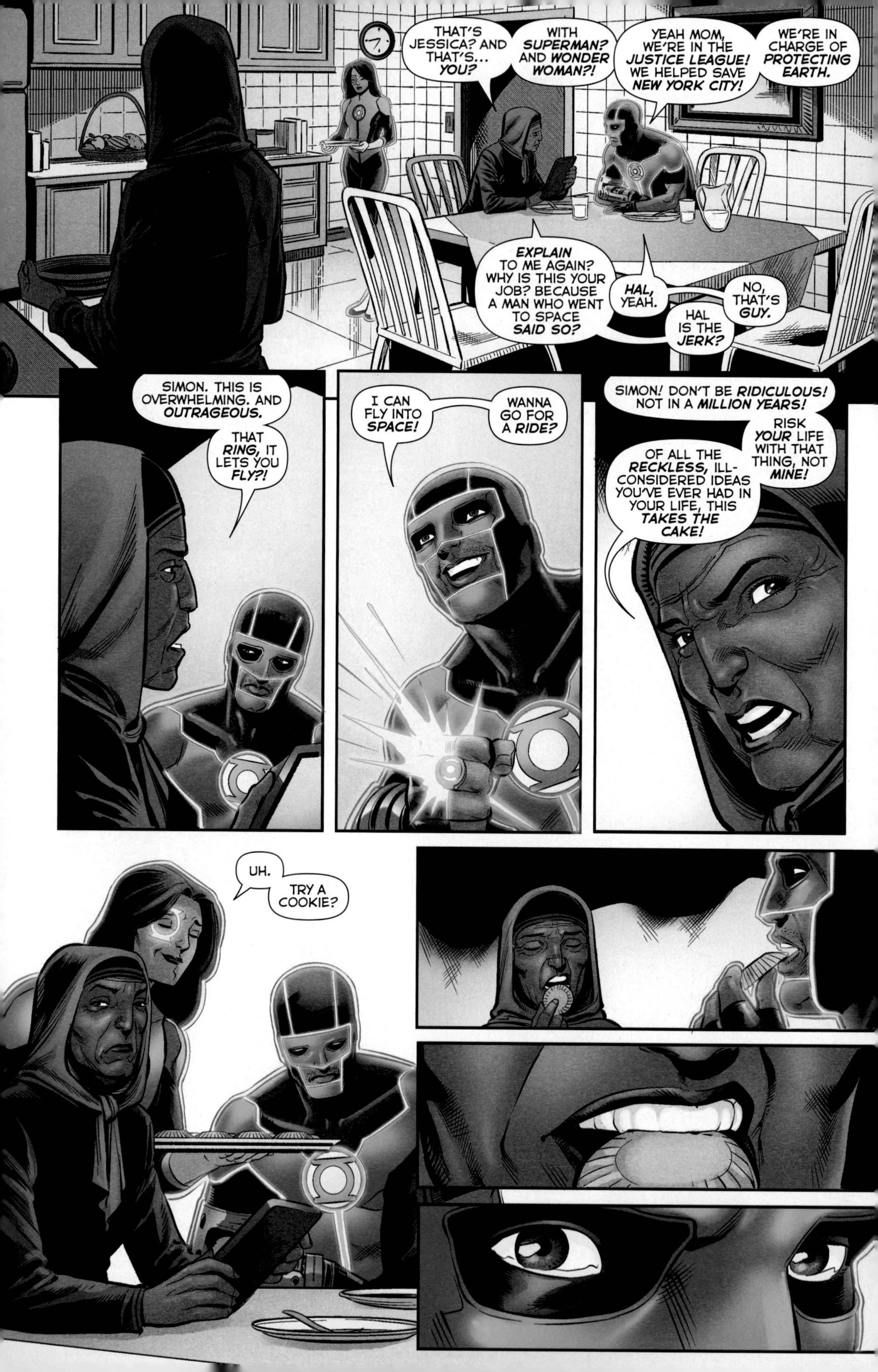
THAT'S JESSICA? AND THAT'S... YOU?
WITH SUPERMAN? AND WONDER WOMAN?!
YEAH MOM, WE'RE IN THE JUSTICE LEAGUE! WE HELPED SAVE NEW YORK CITY!
WE'RE IN CHARGE OF PROTECTING EARTH.
EXPLAIN TO ME AGAIN? WHY IS THIS YOUR JOB? BECAUSE A MAN WHO WENT TO SPACE SAID SO?
HAL, YEAH.
NO, THAT'S GUY.
HAL IS THE JERK?
SIMON. THIS IS OVERWHELMING. AND OUTRAGEOUS.
THAT RING, IT LETS YOU FLY?!
I CAN FLY INTO SPACE!
WANNA GO FOR A RIDE?
SIMON! DON'T BE RIDICULOUS! NOT IN A MILLION YEARS!
RISK YOUR LIFE WITH THAT THING, NOT MINE!
OF ALL THE RECKLESS, ILL-CONSIDERED IDEAS YOU'VE EVER HAD IN YOUR LIFE, THIS TAKES THE CAKE!
UH.
TRY A COOKIE?

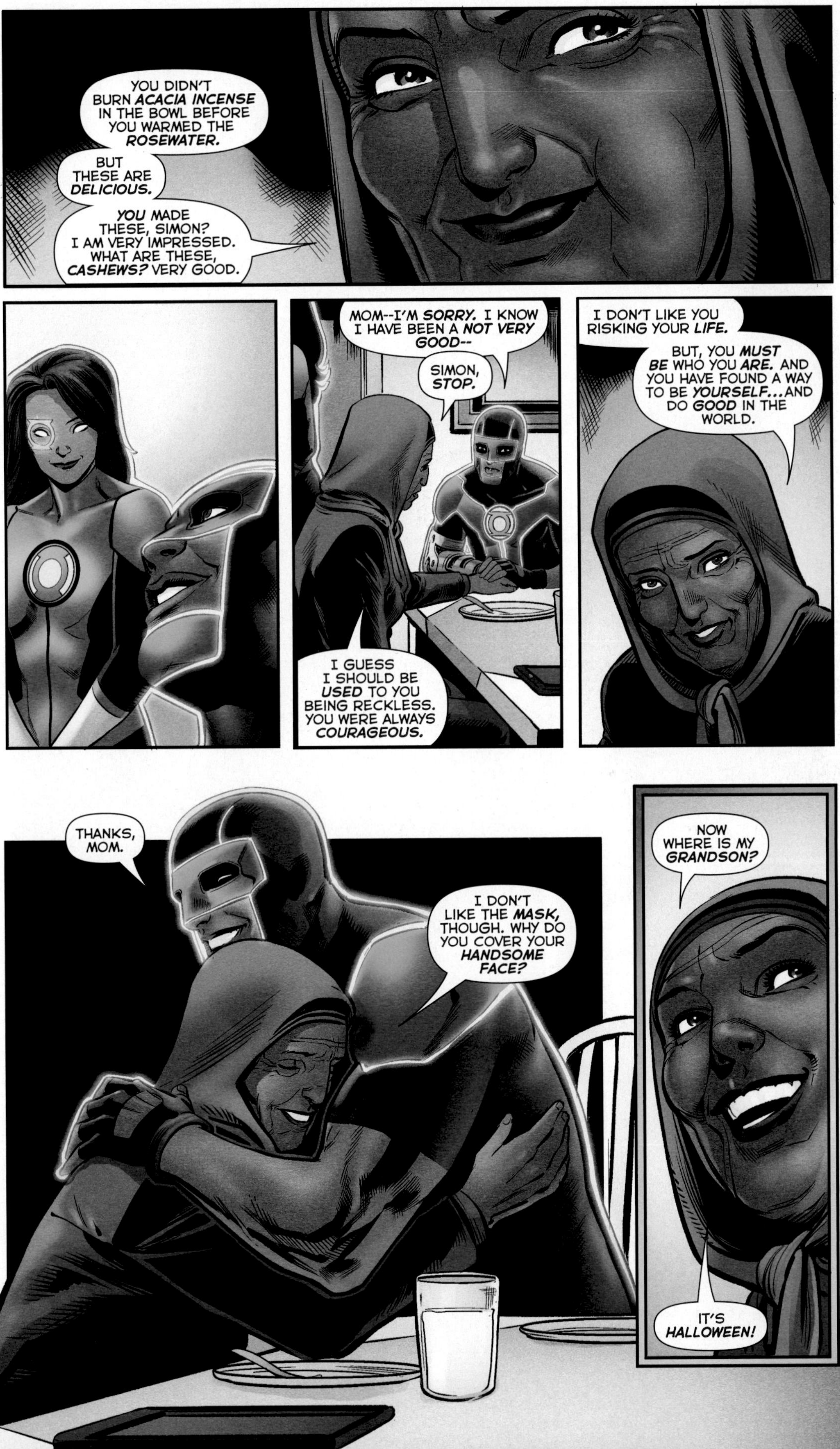
YOU DIDN'T BURN ACACIA INCENSE IN THE BOWL BEFORE YOU WARMED THE ROSEWATER.
BUT THESE ARE DELICIOUS.
YOU MADE THESE, SIMON? I AM VERY IMPRESSED. WHAT ARE THESE, CASHEWS? VERY GOOD.
MOM--I'M SORRY. I KNOW I HAVE BEEN A NOT VERY GOOD--
SIMON, STOP.
I GUESS I SHOULD BE USED TO YOU BEING RECKLESS. YOU WERE ALWAYS COURAGEOUS.
I DON'T LIKE YOU RISKING YOUR LIFE.
BUT, YOU MUST BE WHO YOU ARE. AND YOU HAVE FOUND A WAY TO BE YOURSELF...AND DO GOOD IN THE WORLD.
THANKS, MOM.
I DON'T LIKE THE MASK, THOUGH. WHY DO YOU COVER YOUR HANDSOME FACE?
NOW WHERE IS MY GRANDSON?
IT'S HALLOWEEN!

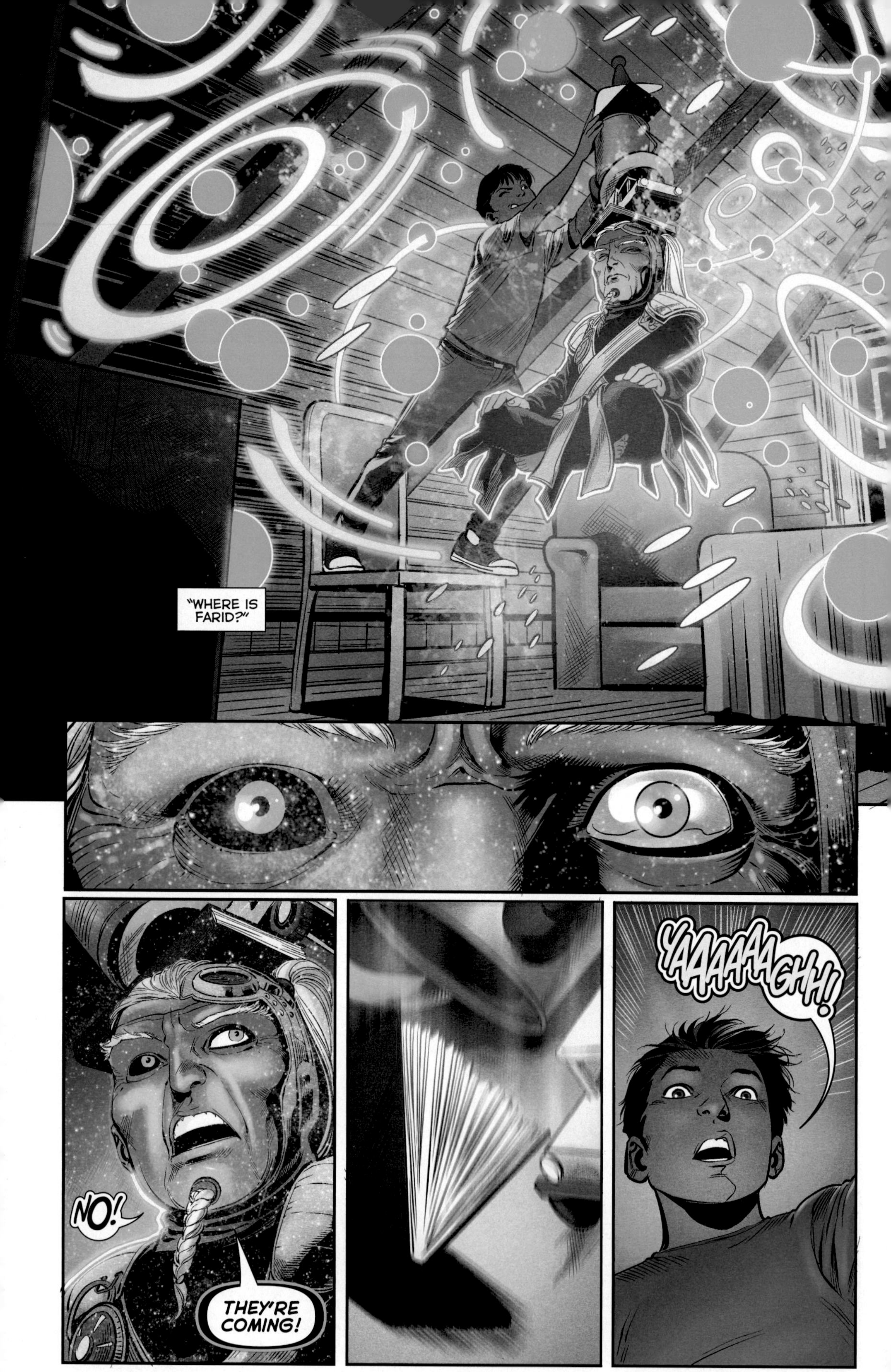
"WHERE IS FARID?"
NO!
THEY'RE COMING!
YAAAAAAGHH!

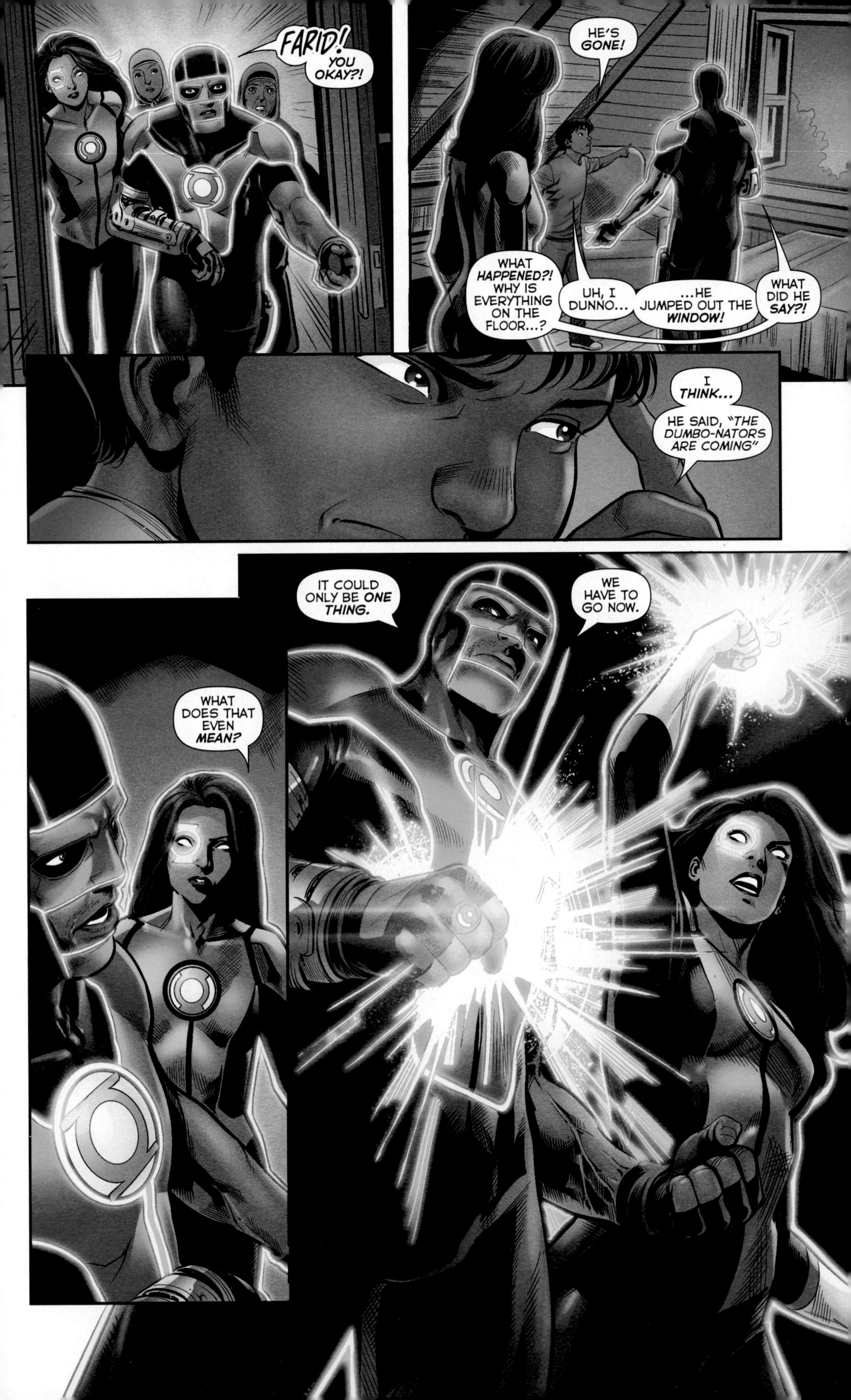
FARID! YOU OKAY?!
HE'S GONE!
WHAT HAPPENED?! WHY IS EVERYTHING ON THE FLOOR...?
UH, I DUNNO...
...HE JUMPED OUT THE WINDOW!
WHAT DID HE SAY?!
I THINK...
HE SAID, "THE DUMBO-NATORS ARE COMING"
WHAT DOES THAT EVEN MEAN?
IT COULD ONLY BE ONE THING.
WE HAVE TO GO NOW.

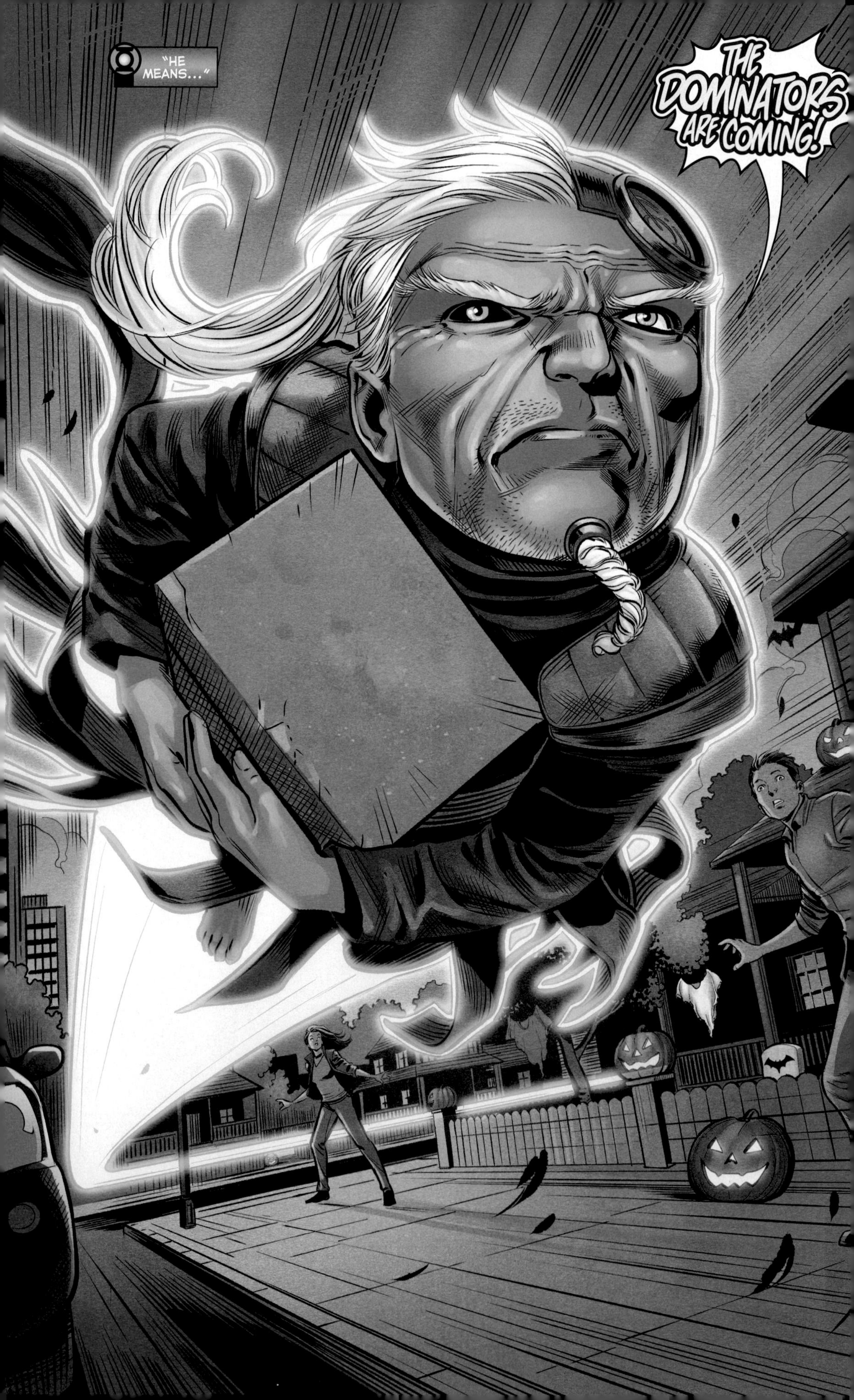
"HE MEANS..."
THE DOMINATORS ARE COMING!

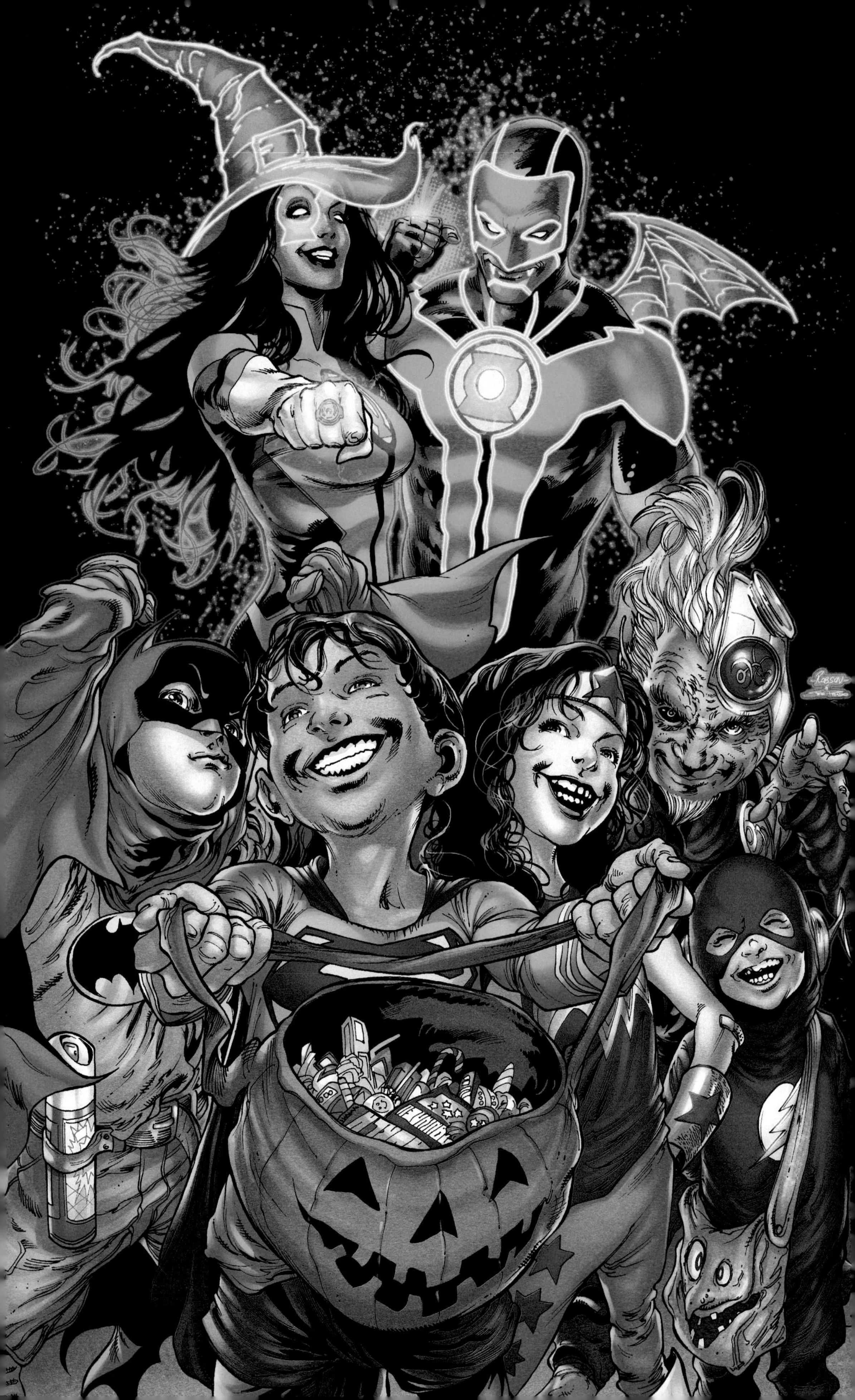

"FAMILY MATTERS PART TWO: ALL HALLOWS' EVE"

SAM HUMPHRIES writer * ED BENES artist

Cover by ROBSON ROCHA, JOE PRADO and ROD REIS

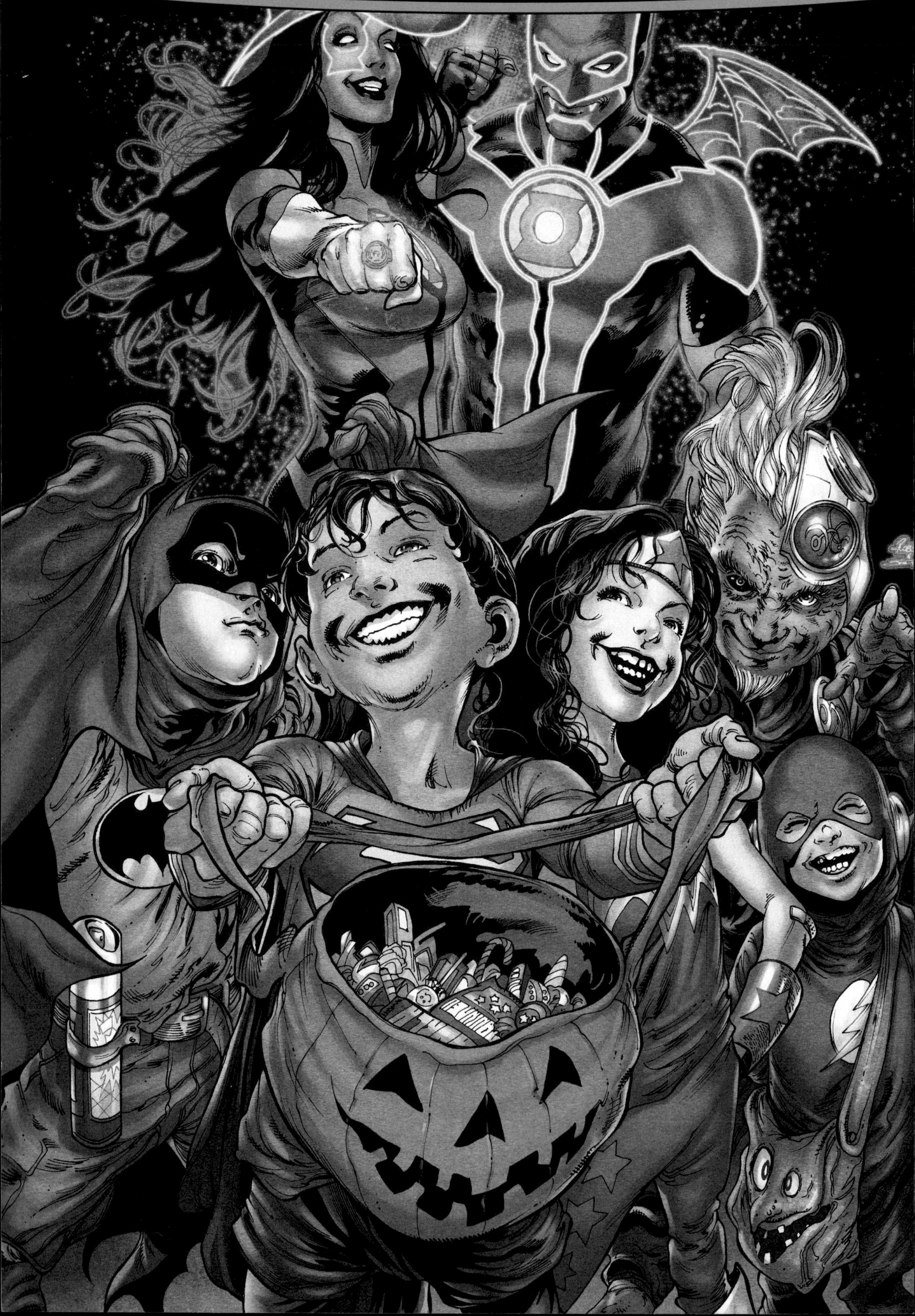

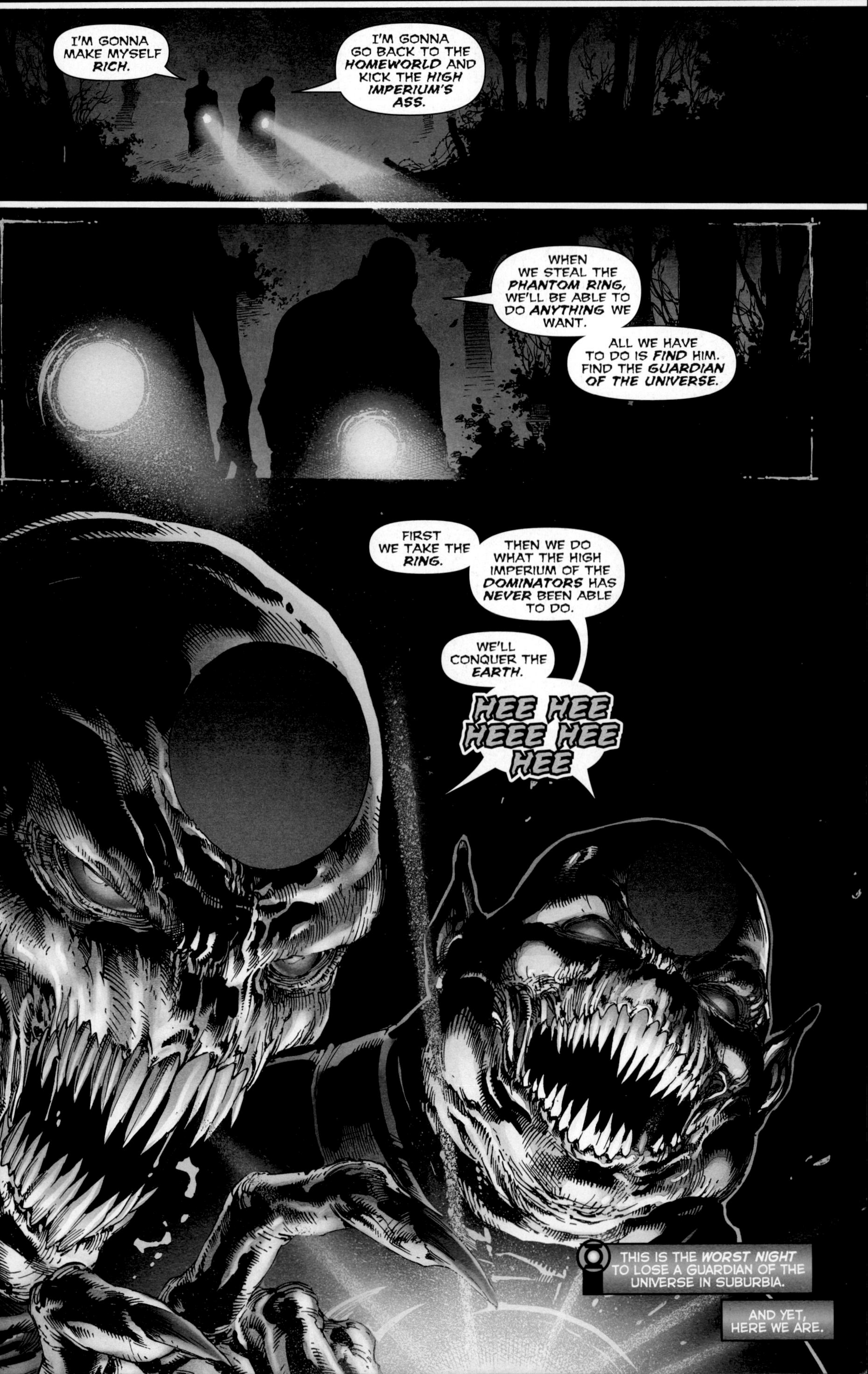
I'M GONNA MAKE MYSELF RICH.
I'M GONNA GO BACK TO THE HOMEWORLD AND KICK THE HIGH IMPERIUM'S ASS.
WHEN WE STEAL THE PHANTOM RING, WE'LL BE ABLE TO DO ANYTHING WE WANT.
ALL WE HAVE TO DO IS FIND HIM. FIND THE GUARDIAN OF THE UNIVERSE.
FIRST WE TAKE THE RING.
THEN WE DO WHAT THE HIGH IMPERIUM OF THE DOMINATORS HAS NEVER BEEN ABLE TO DO.
WE'LL CONQUER THE EARTH.
HEE HEE HEEE HEE HEE
THIS IS THE WORST NIGHT TO LOSE A GUARDIAN OF THE UNIVERSE IN SUBURBIA.
AND YET, HERE WE ARE.

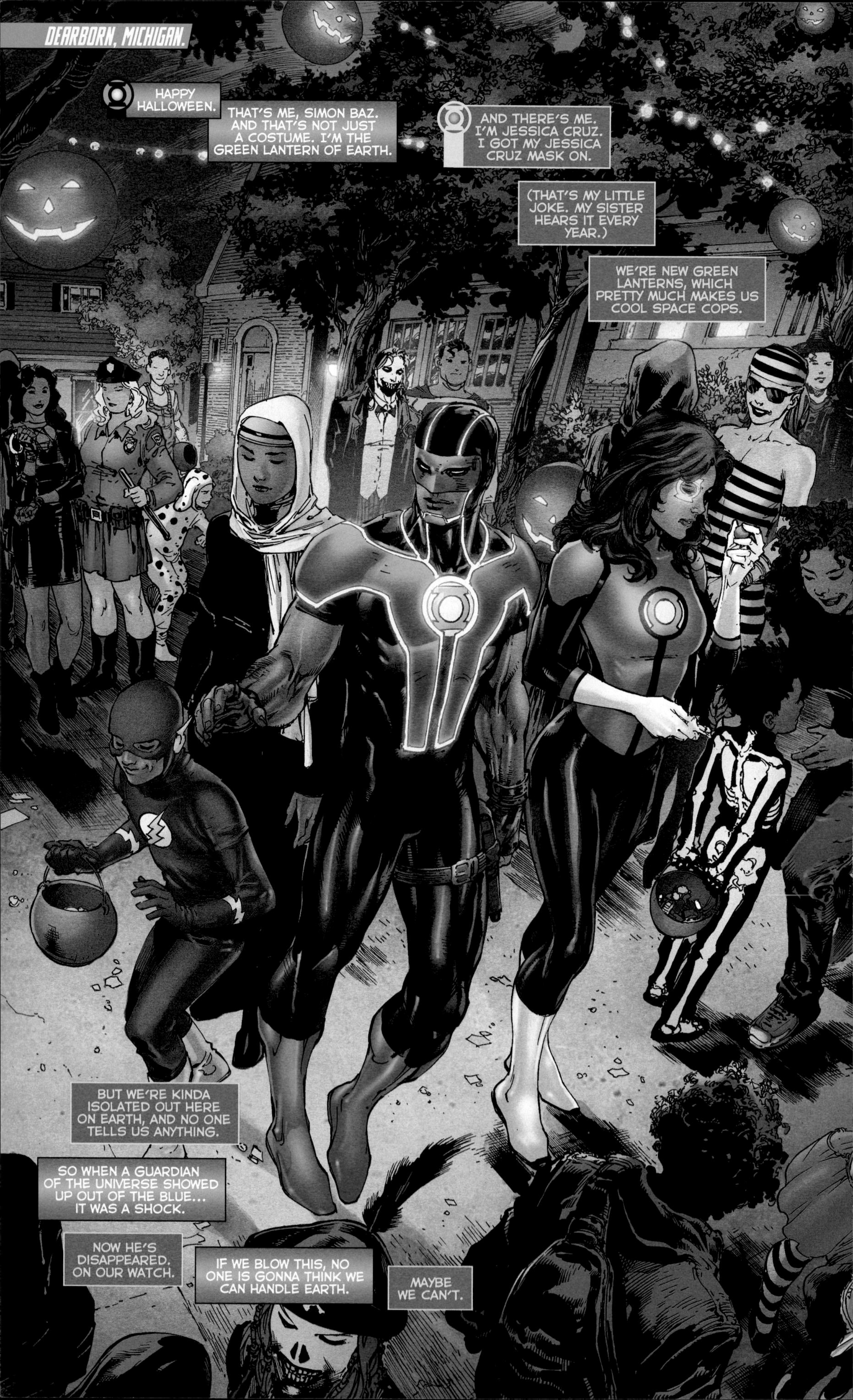
DEARBORN, MICHIGAN.
HAPPY HALLOWEEN.
THAT'S ME, SIMON BAZ. AND THAT'S NOT JUST A COSTUME. I'M THE GREEN LANTERN OF EARTH.
AND THERE'S ME. I'M JESSICA CRUZ. I GOT MY JESSICA CRUZ MASK ON.
(THAT'S MY LITTLE JOKE. MY SISTER HEARS IT EVERY YEAR.)
WE'RE NEW GREEN LANTERNS, WHICH PRETTY MUCH MAKES US COOL SPACE COPS.
BUT WE'RE KINDA ISOLATED OUT HERE ON EARTH, AND NO ONE TELLS US ANYTHING.
SO WHEN A GUARDIAN OF THE UNIVERSE SHOWED UP OUT OF THE BLUE... IT WAS A SHOCK.
NOW HE'S DISAPPEARED. ON OUR WATCH.
IF WE BLOW THIS, NO ONE IS GONNA THINK WE CAN HANDLE EARTH.
MAYBE WE CAN'T.

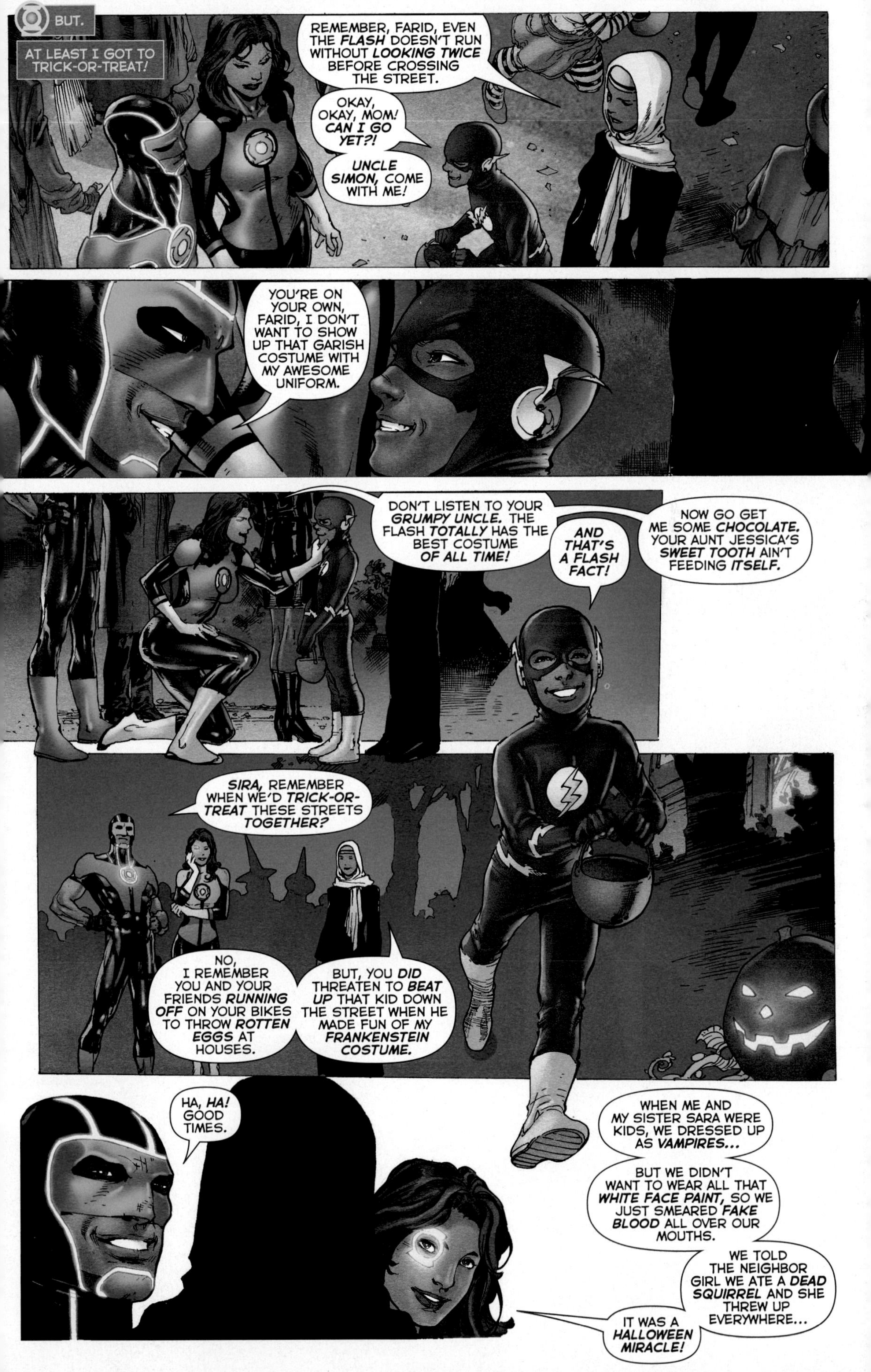
BUT.
AT LEAST I GOT TO TRICK-OR-TREAT!
REMEMBER, FARID, EVEN THE FLASH DOESN'T RUN WITHOUT LOOKING TWICE BEFORE CROSSING THE STREET.
OKAY, OKAY, MOM! CAN I GO YET?!
UNCLE SIMON, COME WITH ME!
YOU'RE ON YOUR OWN, FARID, I DON'T WANT TO SHOW UP THAT GARISH COSTUME WITH MY AWESOME UNIFORM.
DON'T LISTEN TO YOUR GRUMPY UNCLE. THE FLASH TOTALLY HAS THE BEST COSTUME OF ALL TIME!
AND THAT'S A FLASH FACT!
NOW GO GET ME SOME CHOCOLATE. YOUR AUNT JESSICA'S SWEET TOOTH AIN'T FEEDING ITSELF.
SIRA, REMEMBER WHEN WE'D TRICK-OR-TREAT THESE STREETS TOGETHER?
NO, I REMEMBER YOU AND YOUR FRIENDS RUNNING OFF ON YOUR BIKES TO THROW ROTTEN EGGS AT HOUSES.
BUT, YOU DID THREATEN TO BEAT UP THAT KID DOWN THE STREET WHEN HE MADE FUN OF MY FRANKENSTEIN COSTUME.
HA, HA! GOOD TIMES.
WHEN ME AND MY SISTER SARA WERE KIDS, WE DRESSED UP AS VAMPIRES...
BUT WE DIDN'T WANT TO WEAR ALL THAT WHITE FACE PAINT, SO WE JUST SMEARED FAKE BLOOD ALL OVER OUR MOUTHS.
WE TOLD THE NEIGHBOR GIRL WE ATE A DEAD SQUIRREL AND SHE THREW UP EVERYWHERE...
IT WAS A HALLOWEEN MIRACLE!

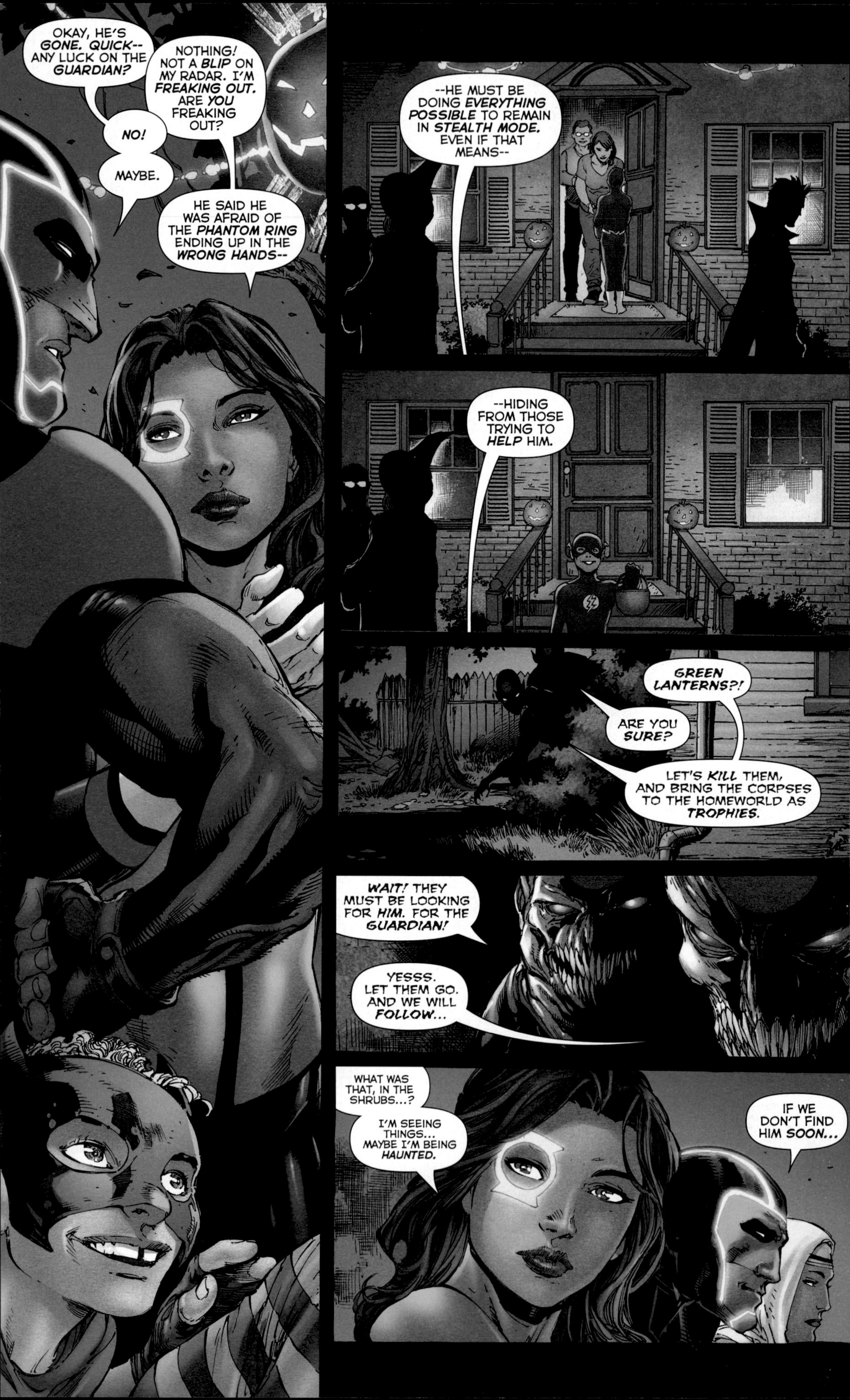
OKAY, HE'S GONE. QUICK-- ANY LUCK ON THE GUARDIAN?
NOTHING! NOT A BLIP ON MY RADAR. I'M FREAKING OUT. ARE YOU FREAKING OUT?
NO!
MAYBE.
HE SAID HE WAS AFRAID OF THE PHANTOM RING ENDING UP IN THE WRONG HANDS--
--HE MUST BE DOING EVERYTHING POSSIBLE TO REMAIN IN STEALTH MODE. EVEN IF THAT MEANS--
--HIDING FROM THOSE TRYING TO HELP HIM.
GREEN LANTERNS?!
ARE YOU SURE?
LET'S KILL THEM, AND BRING THE CORPSES TO THE HOMEWORLD AS TROPHIES.
WAIT! THEY MUST BE LOOKING FOR HIM. FOR THE GUARDIAN!
YESSS. LET THEM GO. AND WE WILL FOLLOW...
WHAT WAS THAT, IN THE SHRUBS...?
I'M SEEING THINGS... MAYBE I'M BEING HAUNTED.
IF WE DON'T FIND HIM SOON...

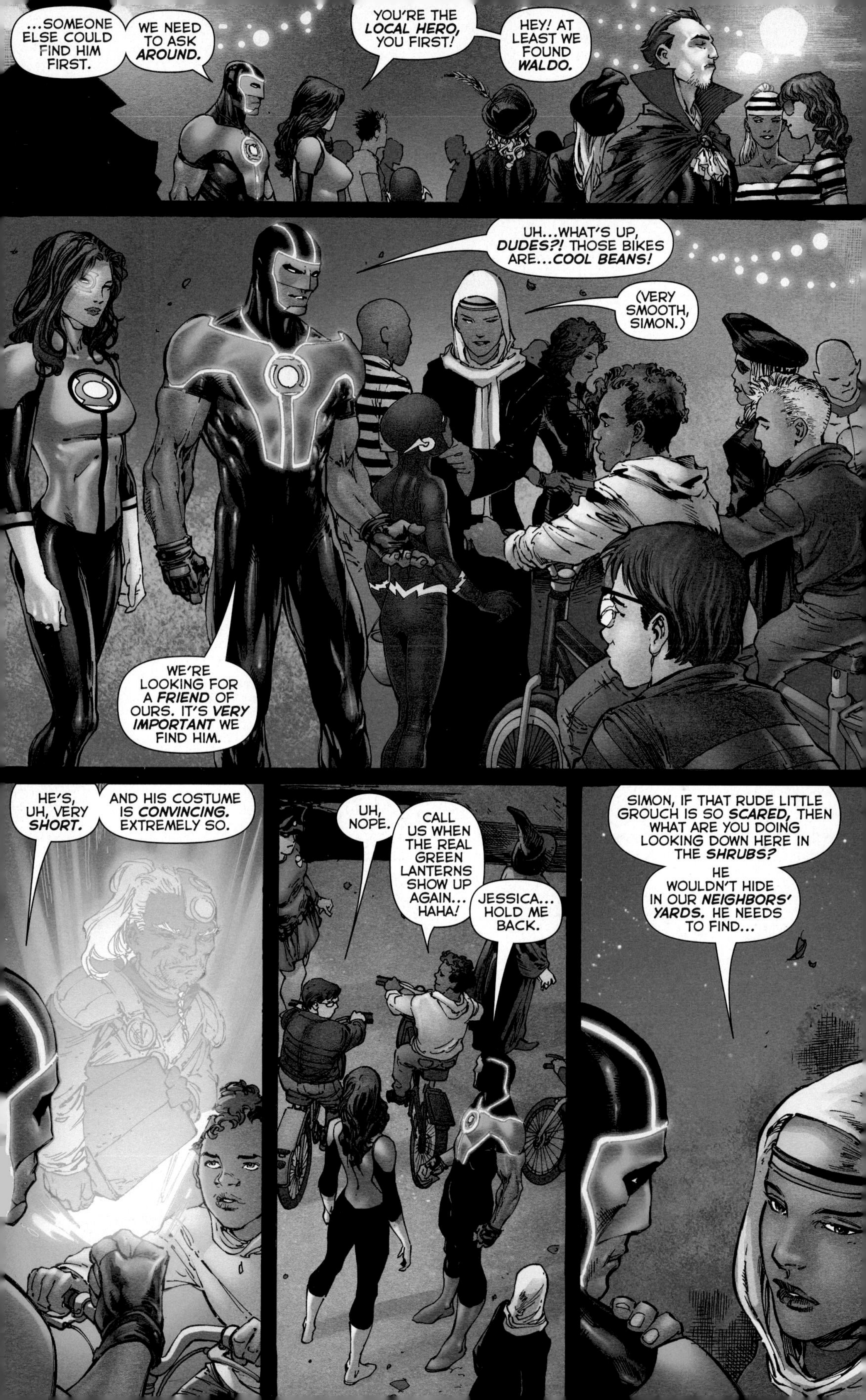
...SOMEONE ELSE COULD FIND HIM FIRST.
WE NEED TO ASK AROUND.
YOU'RE THE LOCAL HERO, YOU FIRST!
HEY! AT LEAST WE FOUND WALDO.
UH...WHAT'S UP, DUDES?! THOSE BIKES ARE...COOL BEANS!
(VERY SMOOTH, SIMON.)
WE'RE LOOKING FOR A FRIEND OF OURS. IT'S VERY IMPORTANT WE FIND HIM.
HE'S, UH, VERY SHORT.
AND HIS COSTUME IS CONVINCING. EXTREMELY SO.
UH, NOPE.
CALL US WHEN THE REAL GREEN LANTERNS SHOW UP AGAIN... HAHA!
JESSICA... HOLD ME BACK.
SIMON, IF THAT RUDE LITTLE GROUCH IS SO SCARED, THEN WHAT ARE YOU DOING LOOKING DOWN HERE IN THE SHRUBS?
HE WOULDN'T HIDE IN OUR NEIGHBORS' YARDS. HE NEEDS TO FIND...

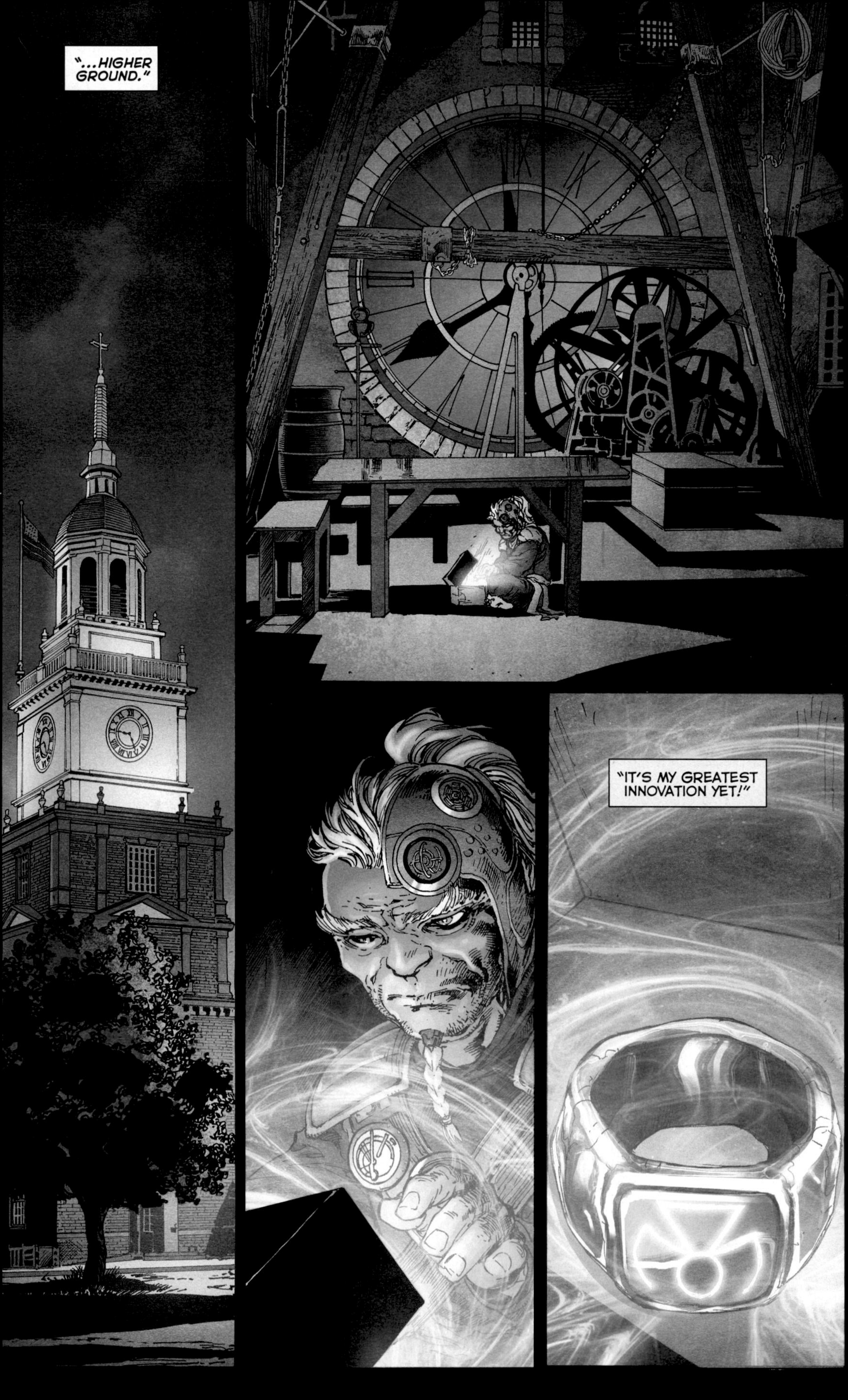
"...HIGHER GROUND."
"IT'S MY GREATEST INNOVATION YET!"

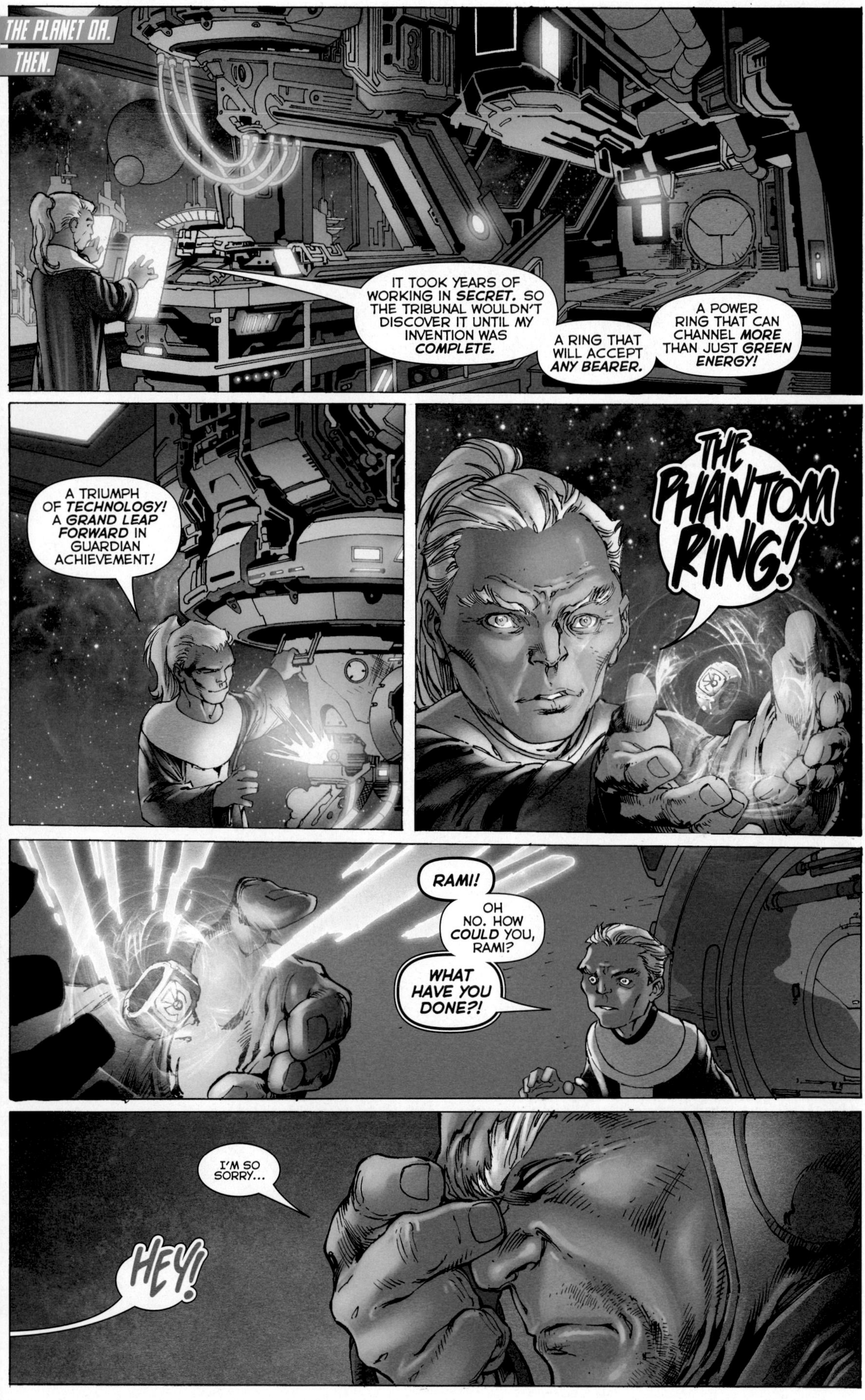
THE PLANET OA.
THEN.
IT TOOK YEARS OF WORKING IN SECRET. SO THE TRIBUNAL WOULDN'T DISCOVER IT UNTIL MY INVENTION WAS COMPLETE.
A RING THAT WILL ACCEPT ANY BEARER.
A POWER RING THAT CAN CHANNEL MORE THAN JUST GREEN ENERGY!
A TRIUMPH OF TECHNOLOGY! A GRAND LEAP FORWARD IN GUARDIAN ACHIEVEMENT!
THE PHANTOM RING!
RAMI!
OH NO. HOW COULD YOU, RAMI?
WHAT HAVE YOU DONE?!
I'M SO SORRY...
HEY!

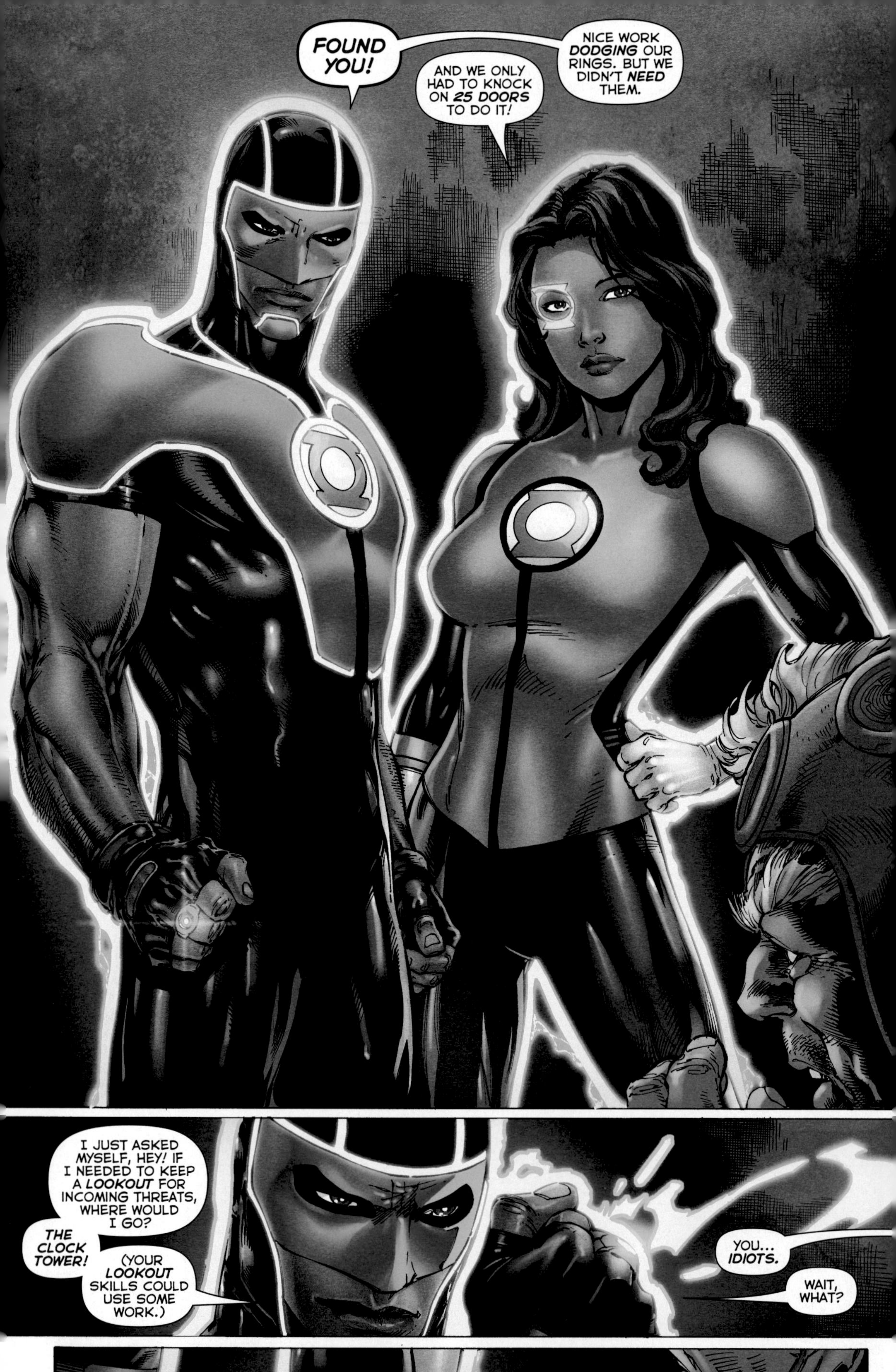
FOUND YOU!
AND WE ONLY HAD TO KNOCK ON 25 DOORS TO DO IT!
NICE WORK DODGING OUR RINGS. BUT WE DIDN'T NEED THEM.
I JUST ASKED MYSELF, HEY! IF I NEEDED TO KEEP A LOOKOUT FOR INCOMING THREATS, WHERE WOULD I GO?
THE CLOCK TOWER!
(YOUR LOOKOUT SKILLS COULD USE SOME WORK.)
YOU... IDIOTS.
WAIT, WHAT?

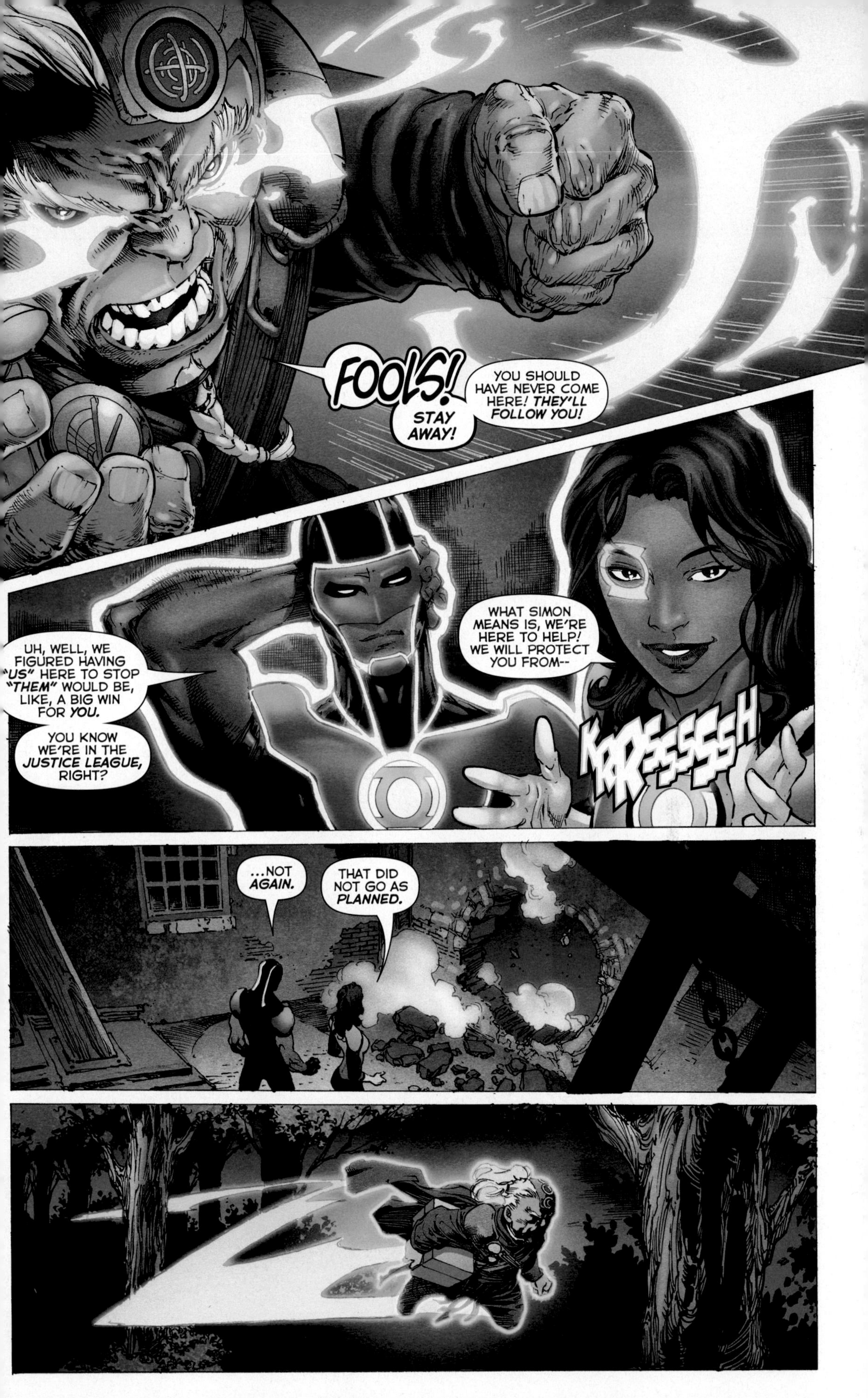
FOOLS!
STAY AWAY!
YOU SHOULD HAVE NEVER COME HERE! THEY'LL FOLLOW YOU!
UH, WELL, WE FIGURED HAVING "US" HERE TO STOP "THEM" WOULD BE, LIKE, A BIG WIN FOR YOU.
YOU KNOW WE'RE IN THE JUSTICE LEAGUE, RIGHT?
WHAT SIMON MEANS IS, WE'RE HERE TO HELP! WE WILL PROTECT YOU FROM--
KRRSSSSSH
...NOT AGAIN.
THAT DID NOT GO AS PLANNED.

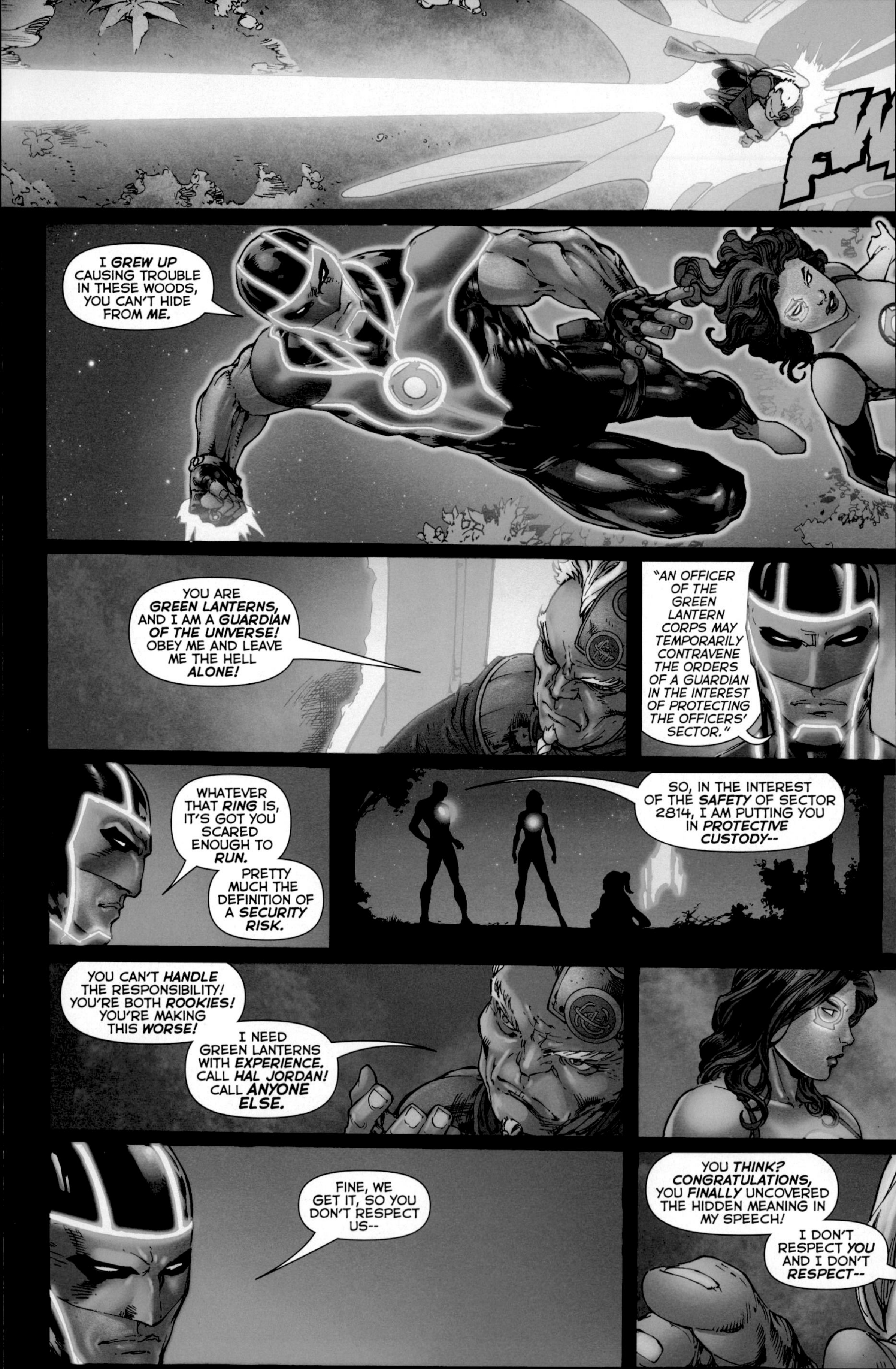

FW
I GREW UP CAUSING TROUBLE IN THESE WOODS, YOU CAN'T HIDE FROM ME.
YOU ARE GREEN LANTERNS, AND I AM A GUARDIAN OF THE UNIVERSE! OBEY ME AND LEAVE ME THE HELL ALONE!
"AN OFFICER OF THE GREEN LANTERN CORPS MAY TEMPORARILY CONTRAVENE THE ORDERS OF A GUARDIAN IN THE INTEREST OF PROTECTING THE OFFICERS' SECTOR."
WHATEVER THAT RING IS, IT'S GOT YOU SCARED ENOUGH TO RUN.
PRETTY MUCH THE DEFINITION OF A SECURITY RISK.
SO, IN THE INTEREST OF THE SAFETY OF SECTOR 2814, I AM PUTTING YOU IN PROTECTIVE CUSTODY--
YOU CAN'T HANDLE THE RESPONSIBILITY! YOU'RE BOTH ROOKIES! YOU'RE MAKING THIS WORSE!
I NEED GREEN LANTERNS WITH EXPERIENCE. CALL HAL JORDAN! CALL ANYONE ELSE.
FINE, WE GET IT, SO YOU DON'T RESPECT US--
YOU THINK? CONGRATULATIONS, YOU FINALLY UNCOVERED THE HIDDEN MEANING IN MY SPEECH!
I DON'T RESPECT YOU AND I DON'T RESPECT--

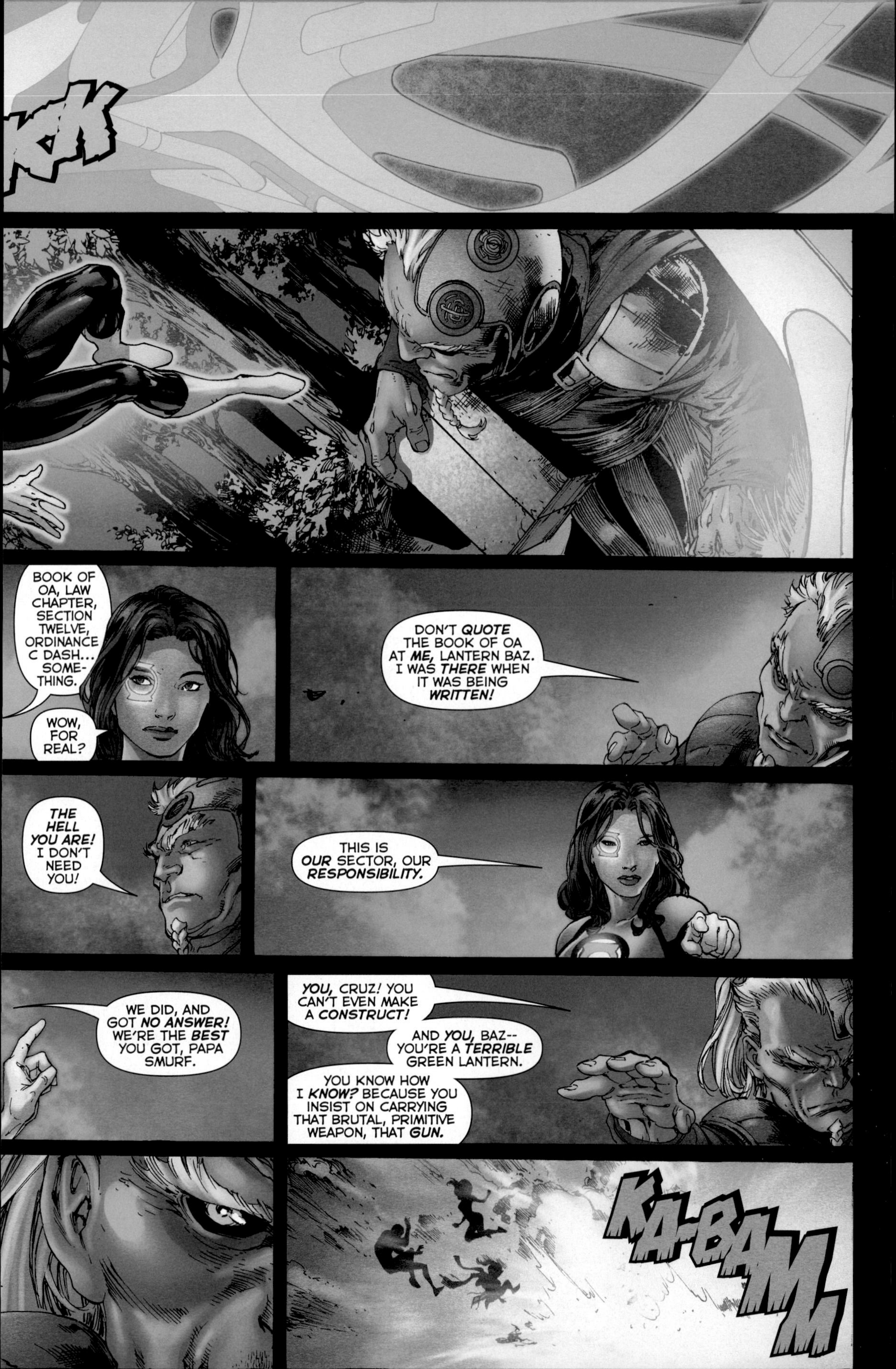
KK
BOOK OF OA, LAW CHAPTER, SECTION TWELVE, ORDINANCE C DASH... SOME-THING.
WOW, FOR REAL?
DON'T QUOTE THE BOOK OF OA AT ME, LANTERN BAZ. I WAS THERE WHEN IT WAS BEING WRITTEN!
THE HELL YOU ARE! I DON'T NEED YOU!
THIS IS OUR SECTOR, OUR RESPONSIBILITY.
WE DID, AND GOT NO ANSWER! WE'RE THE BEST YOU GOT, PAPA SMURF.
YOU, CRUZ! YOU CAN'T EVEN MAKE A CONSTRUCT!
AND YOU, BAZ-- YOU'RE A TERRIBLE GREEN LANTERN.
YOU KNOW HOW I KNOW? BECAUSE YOU INSIST ON CARRYING THAT BRUTAL, PRIMITIVE WEAPON, THAT GUN.
KA-BAMM

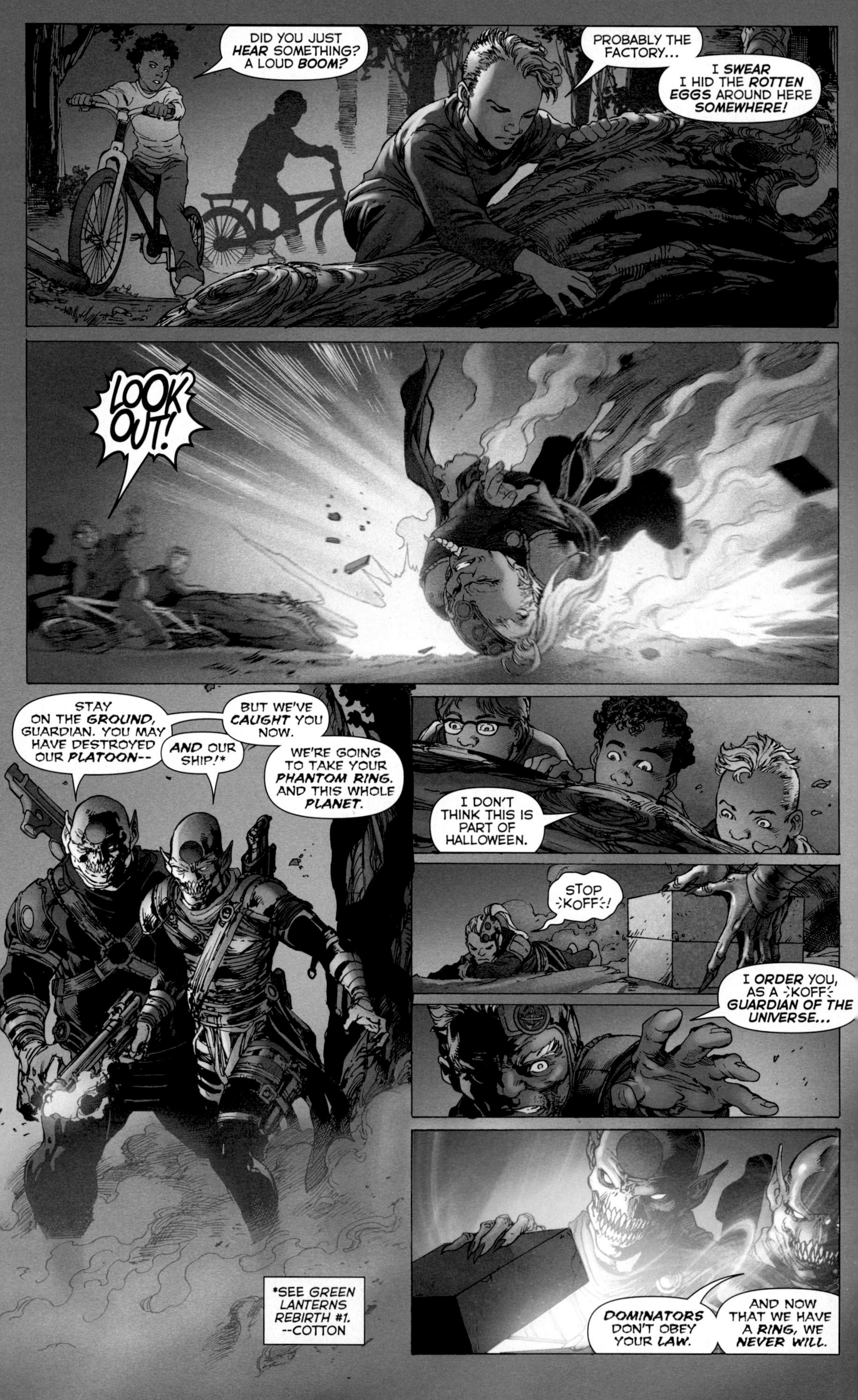

DID YOU JUST HEAR SOMETHING? A LOUD BOOM?
PROBABLY THE FACTORY...
I SWEAR I HID THE ROTTEN EGGS AROUND HERE SOMEWHERE!
LOOK OUT!
STAY ON THE GROUND, GUARDIAN. YOU MAY HAVE DESTROYED OUR PLATOON--
AND OUR SHIP!*
BUT WE'VE CAUGHT YOU NOW.
WE'RE GOING TO TAKE YOUR PHANTOM RING. AND THIS WHOLE PLANET.
*SEE GREEN LANTERNS REBIRTH #1. --COTTON
I DON'T THINK THIS IS PART OF HALLOWEEN.
STOP -KOFF-!
I ORDER YOU, AS A -KOFF- GUARDIAN OF THE UNIVERSE...
DOMINATORS DON'T OBEY YOUR LAW.
AND NOW THAT WE HAVE A RING, WE NEVER WILL.

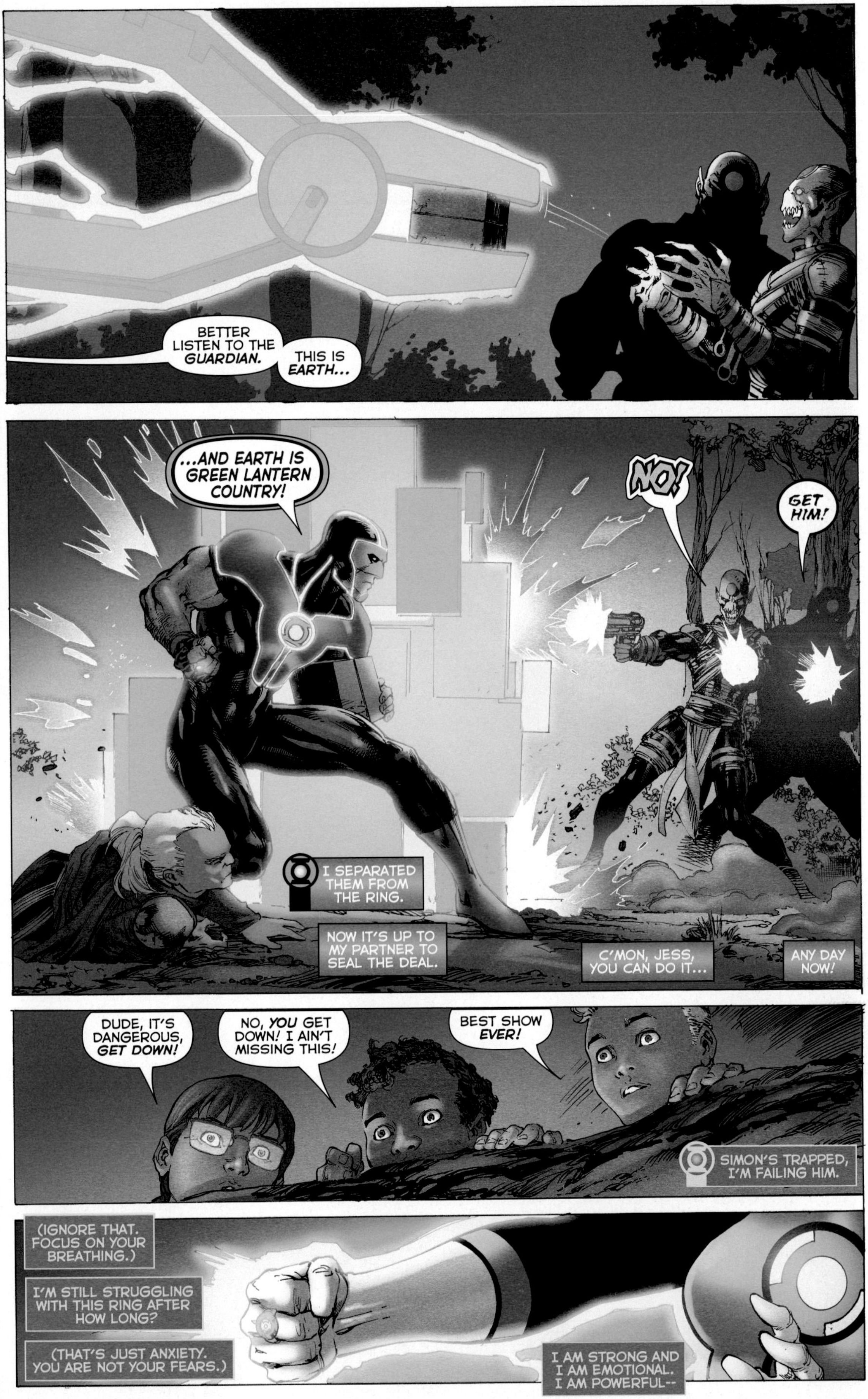

BETTER LISTEN TO THE GUARDIAN.
THIS IS EARTH...
...AND EARTH IS GREEN LANTERN COUNTRY!
NO!
GET HIM!
I SEPARATED THEM FROM THE RING.
NOW IT'S UP TO MY PARTNER TO SEAL THE DEAL.
C'MON, JESS, YOU CAN DO IT...
ANY DAY NOW!
DUDE, IT'S DANGEROUS, GET DOWN!
NO, YOU GET DOWN! I AIN'T MISSING THIS!
BEST SHOW EVER!
SIMON'S TRAPPED, I'M FAILING HIM.
(IGNORE THAT. FOCUS ON YOUR BREATHING.)
I'M STILL STRUGGLING WITH THIS RING AFTER HOW LONG?
(THAT'S JUST ANXIETY. YOU ARE NOT YOUR FEARS.)
I AM STRONG AND I AM EMOTIONAL. I AM POWERFUL--

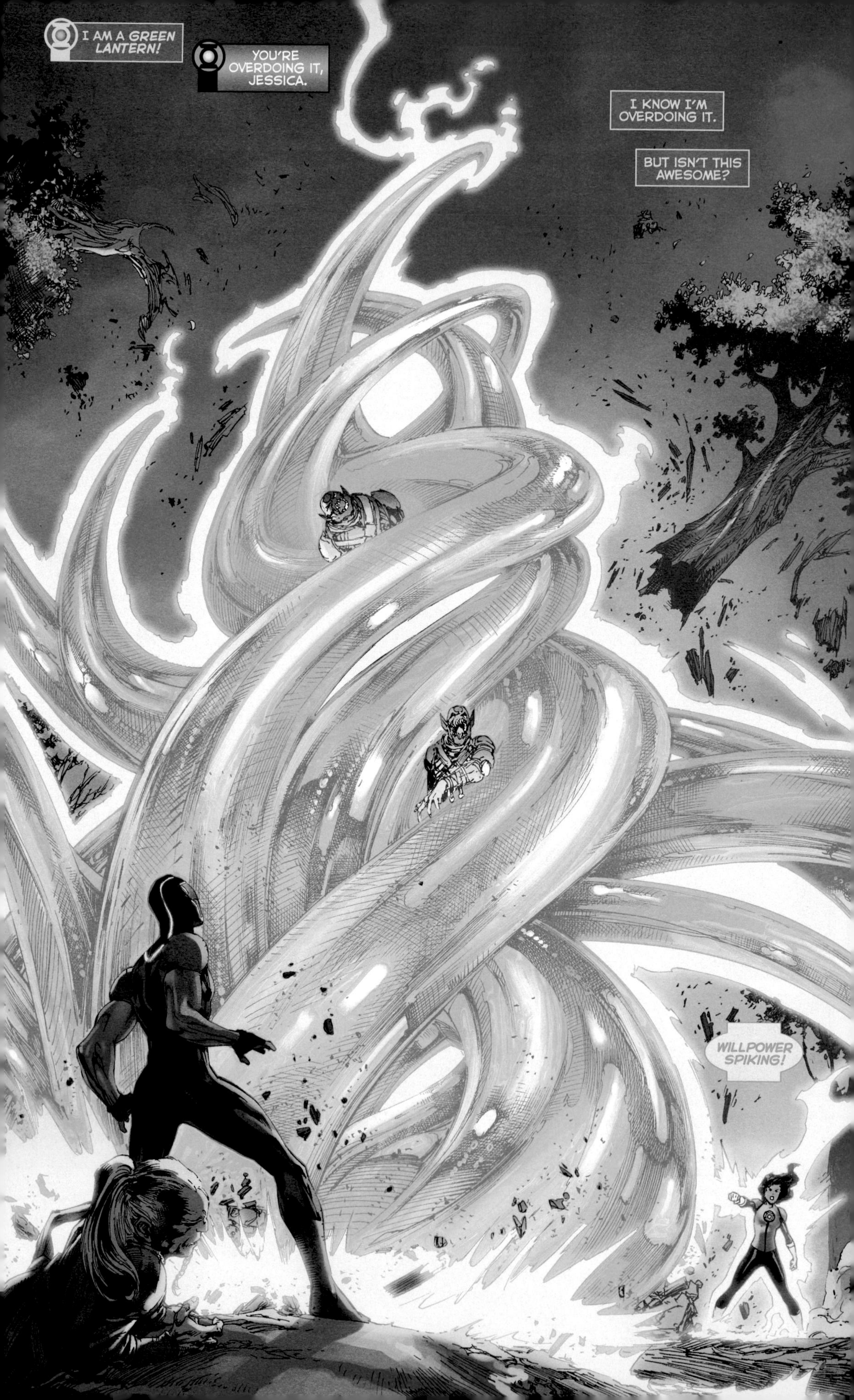
I AM A GREEN LANTERN!
YOU'RE OVERDOING IT, JESSICA.
I KNOW I'M OVERDOING IT.
BUT ISN'T THIS AWESOME?
WILLPOWER SPIKING!

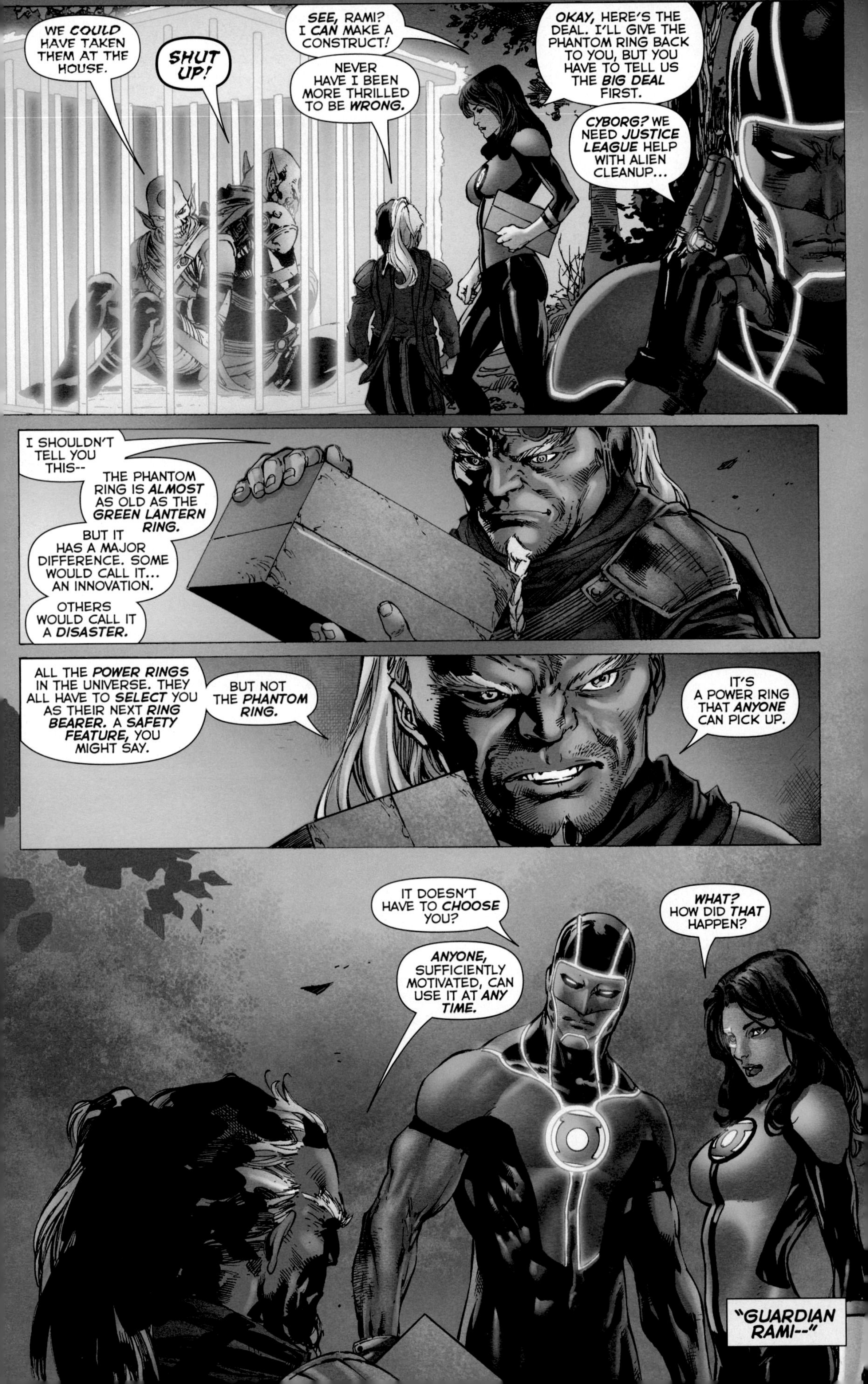

WE COULD HAVE TAKEN THEM AT THE HOUSE.
SHUT UP!
SEE, RAMI? I CAN MAKE A CONSTRUCT!
NEVER HAVE I BEEN MORE THRILLED TO BE WRONG.
OKAY, HERE'S THE DEAL. I'LL GIVE THE PHANTOM RING BACK TO YOU, BUT YOU HAVE TO TELL US THE BIG DEAL FIRST.
CYBORG? WE NEED JUSTICE LEAGUE HELP WITH ALIEN CLEANUP...
I SHOULDN'T TELL YOU THIS--
THE PHANTOM RING IS ALMOST AS OLD AS THE GREEN LANTERN RING.
BUT IT HAS A MAJOR DIFFERENCE. SOME WOULD CALL IT... AN INNOVATION.
OTHERS WOULD CALL IT A DISASTER.
ALL THE POWER RINGS IN THE UNIVERSE. THEY ALL HAVE TO SELECT YOU AS THEIR NEXT RING BEARER. A SAFETY FEATURE, YOU MIGHT SAY.
BUT NOT THE PHANTOM RING.
IT'S A POWER RING THAT ANYONE CAN PICK UP.
IT DOESN'T HAVE TO CHOOSE YOU?
ANYONE, SUFFICIENTLY MOTIVATED, CAN USE IT AT ANY TIME.
WHAT? HOW DID THAT HAPPEN?
"GUARDIAN RAMI--"

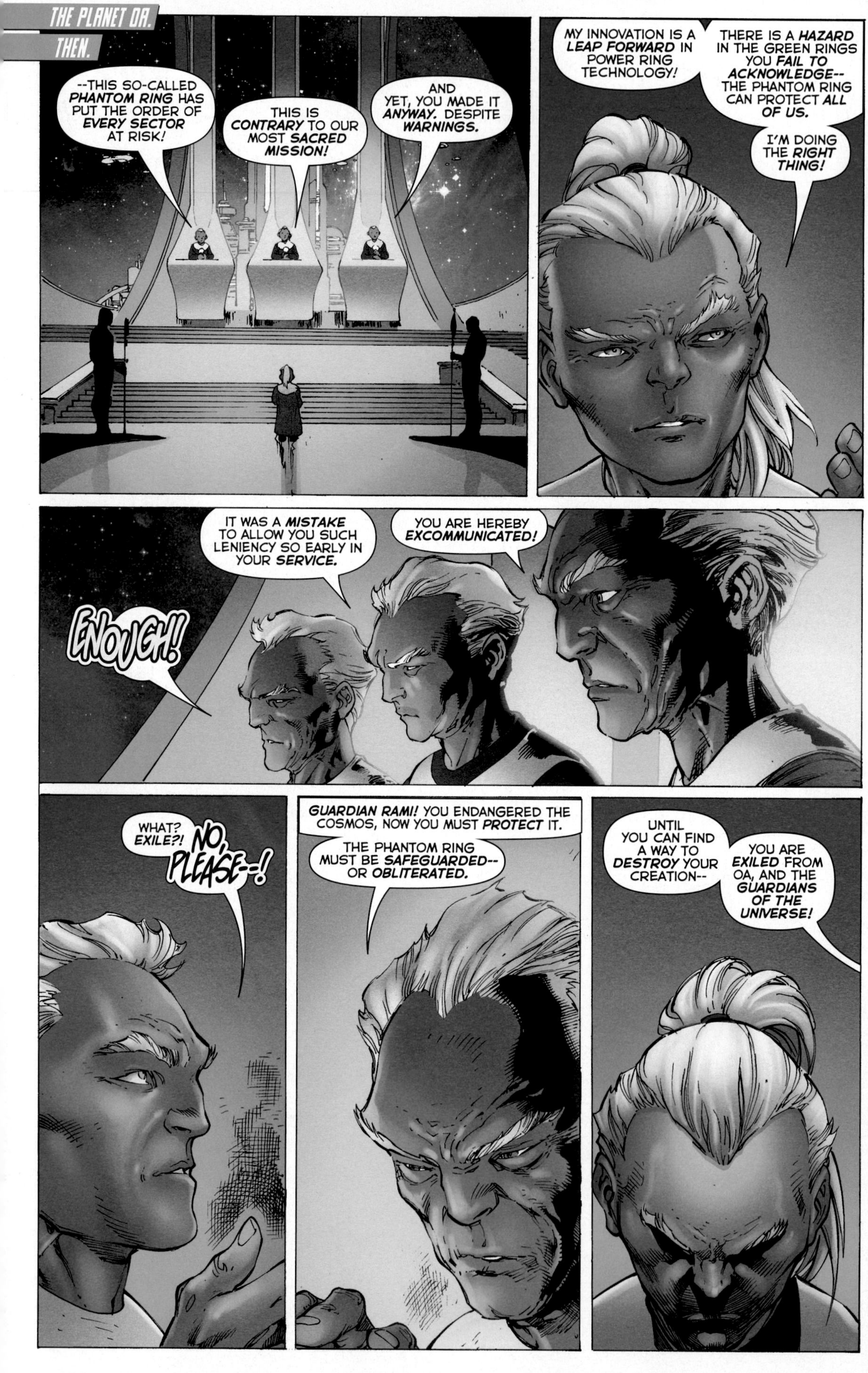
THE PLANET OA.
THEN.
--THIS SO-CALLED PHANTOM RING HAS PUT THE ORDER OF EVERY SECTOR AT RISK!
THIS IS CONTRARY TO OUR MOST SACRED MISSION!
AND YET, YOU MADE IT ANYWAY. DESPITE WARNINGS.
MY INNOVATION IS A LEAP FORWARD IN POWER RING TECHNOLOGY!
THERE IS A HAZARD IN THE GREEN RINGS YOU FAIL TO ACKNOWLEDGE-- THE PHANTOM RING CAN PROTECT ALL OF US.
I'M DOING THE RIGHT THING!
ENOUGH!
IT WAS A MISTAKE TO ALLOW YOU SUCH LENIENCY SO EARLY IN YOUR SERVICE.
YOU ARE HEREBY EXCOMMUNICATED!
WHAT? EXILE?!
NO, PLEASE--!
GUARDIAN RAMI! YOU ENDANGERED THE COSMOS, NOW YOU MUST PROTECT IT.
THE PHANTOM RING MUST BE SAFEGUARDED-- OR OBLITERATED.
UNTIL YOU CAN FIND A WAY TO DESTROY YOUR CREATION--
YOU ARE EXILED FROM OA, AND THE GUARDIANS OF THE UNIVERSE!

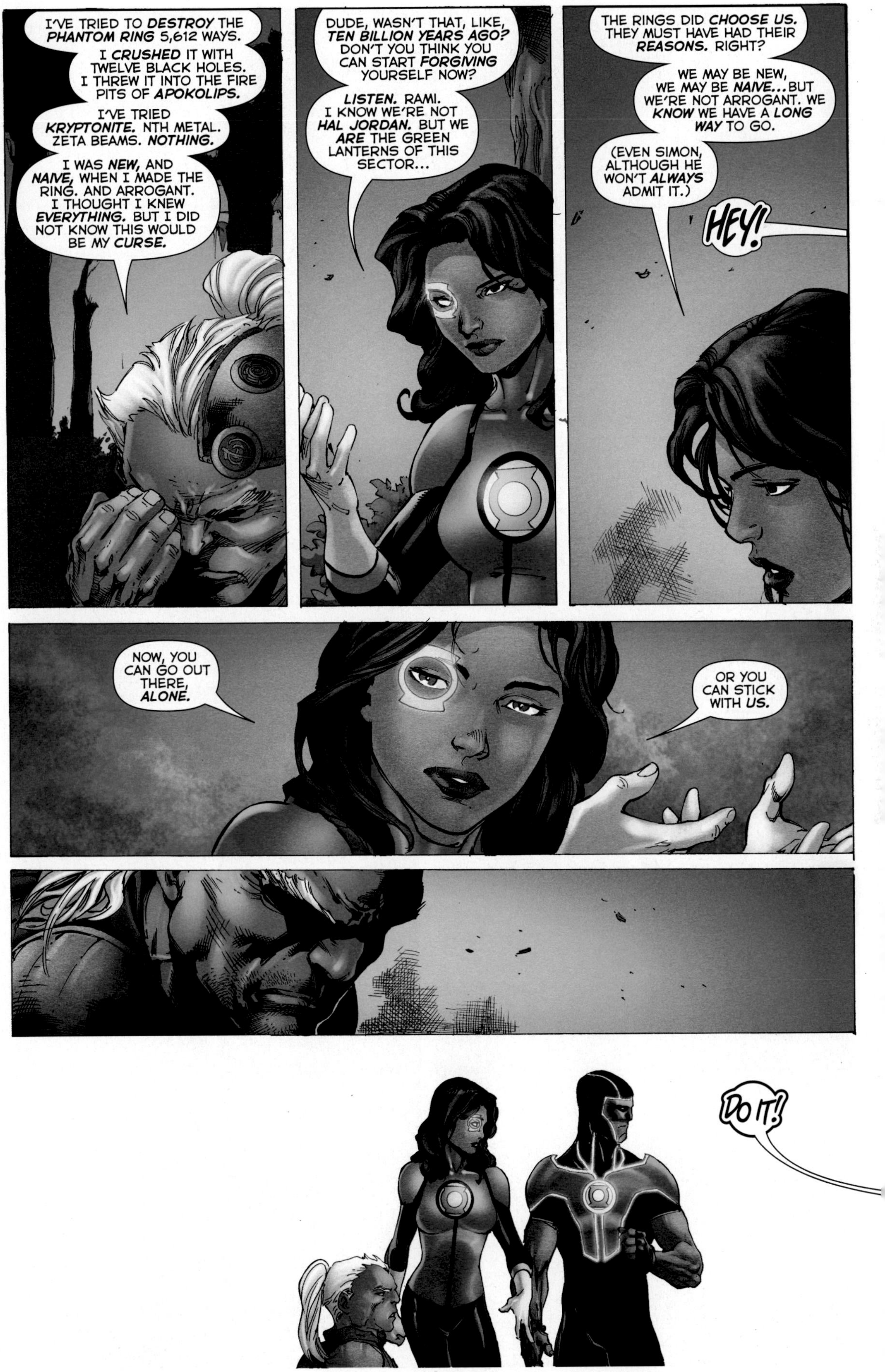

I'VE TRIED TO DESTROY THE PHANTOM RING 5,612 WAYS.
I CRUSHED IT WITH TWELVE BLACK HOLES. I THREW IT INTO THE FIRE PITS OF APOKOLIPS.
I'VE TRIED KRYPTONITE. NTH METAL. ZETA BEAMS. NOTHING.
I WAS NEW, AND NAIVE, WHEN I MADE THE RING. AND ARROGANT. I THOUGHT I KNEW EVERYTHING. BUT I DID NOT KNOW THIS WOULD BE MY CURSE.
DUDE, WASN'T THAT, LIKE, TEN BILLION YEARS AGO? DON'T YOU THINK YOU CAN START FORGIVING YOURSELF NOW?
LISTEN. RAMI. I KNOW WE'RE NOT HAL JORDAN. BUT WE ARE THE GREEN LANTERNS OF THIS SECTOR...
THE RINGS DID CHOOSE US. THEY MUST HAVE HAD THEIR REASONS. RIGHT?
WE MAY BE NEW, WE MAY BE NAIVE... BUT WE'RE NOT ARROGANT. WE KNOW WE HAVE A LONG WAY TO GO.
(EVEN SIMON, ALTHOUGH HE WON'T ALWAYS ADMIT IT.)
HEY!
NOW, YOU CAN GO OUT THERE, ALONE.
OR YOU CAN STICK WITH US.
DO IT!

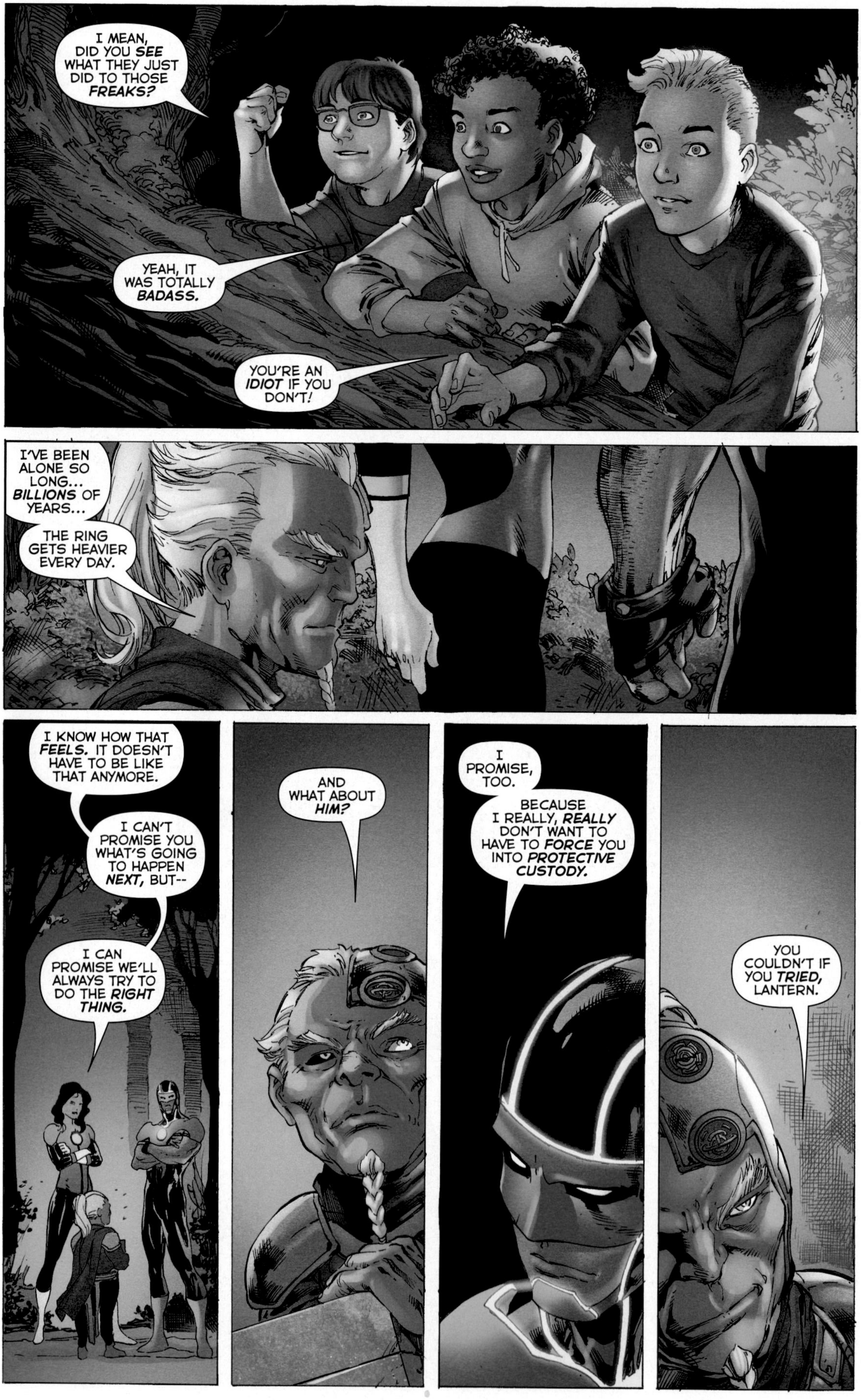
I MEAN, DID YOU SEE WHAT THEY JUST DID TO THOSE FREAKS?
YEAH, IT WAS TOTALLY BADASS.
YOU'RE AN IDIOT IF YOU DON'T!
I'VE BEEN ALONE SO LONG... BILLIONS OF YEARS...
THE RING GETS HEAVIER EVERY DAY.
I KNOW HOW THAT FEELS. IT DOESN'T HAVE TO BE LIKE THAT ANYMORE.
I CAN'T PROMISE YOU WHAT'S GOING TO HAPPEN NEXT, BUT--
I CAN PROMISE WE'LL ALWAYS TRY TO DO THE RIGHT THING.
AND WHAT ABOUT HIM?
I PROMISE, TOO.
BECAUSE I REALLY, REALLY DON'T WANT TO HAVE TO FORCE YOU INTO PROTECTIVE CUSTODY.
YOU COULDN'T IF YOU TRIED, LANTERN.

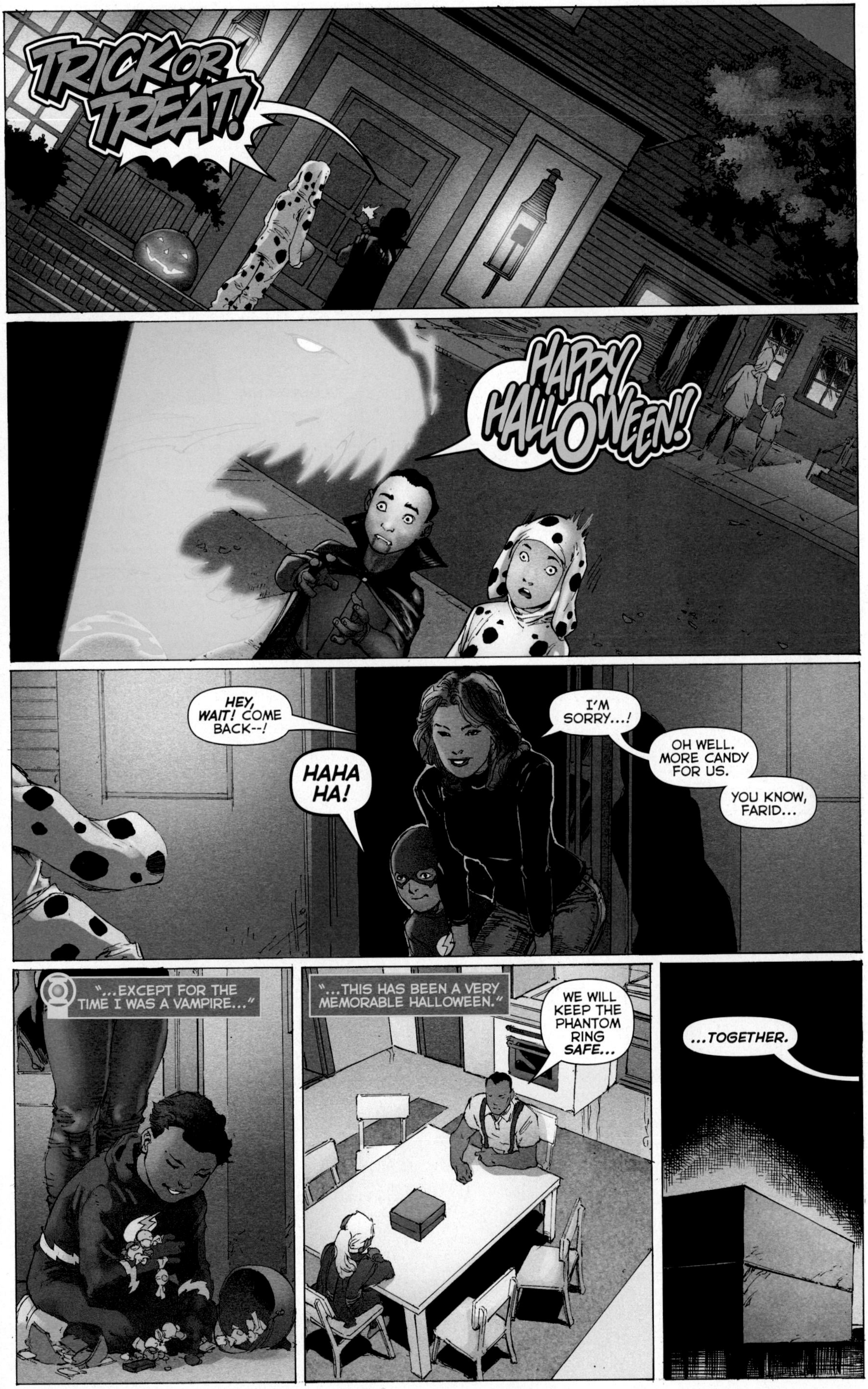
TRICK OR TREAT!
HAPPY HALLOWEEN!
HEY, WAIT! COME BACK--!
HAHA HA!
I'M SORRY...!
OH WELL. MORE CANDY FOR US.
YOU KNOW, FARID...
"...EXCEPT FOR THE TIME I WAS A VAMPIRE..."
"...THIS HAS BEEN A VERY MEMORABLE HALLOWEEN."
WE WILL KEEP THE PHANTOM RING SAFE...
...TOGETHER.

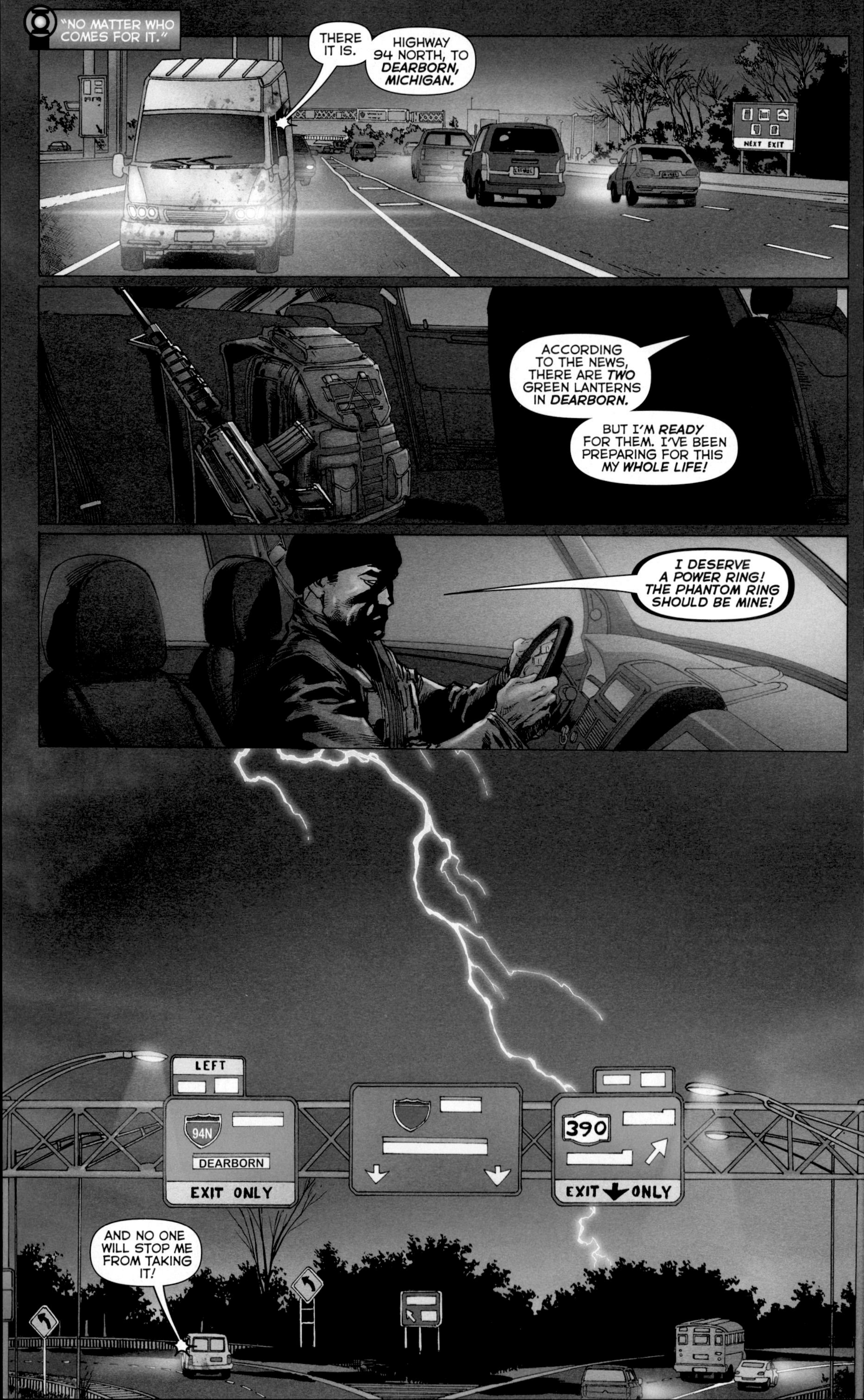
"NO MATTER WHO COMES FOR IT."
THERE IT IS.
HIGHWAY 94 NORTH, TO DEARBORN, MICHIGAN.
NEXT EXIT
ACCORDING TO THE NEWS, THERE ARE TWO GREEN LANTERNS IN DEARBORN.
BUT I'M READY FOR THEM. I'VE BEEN PREPARING FOR THIS MY WHOLE LIFE!
I DESERVE A POWER RING! THE PHANTOM RING SHOULD BE MINE!
LEFT
94N
DEARBORN
EXIT ONLY
390
EXIT ONLY
AND NO ONE WILL STOP ME FROM TAKING IT!

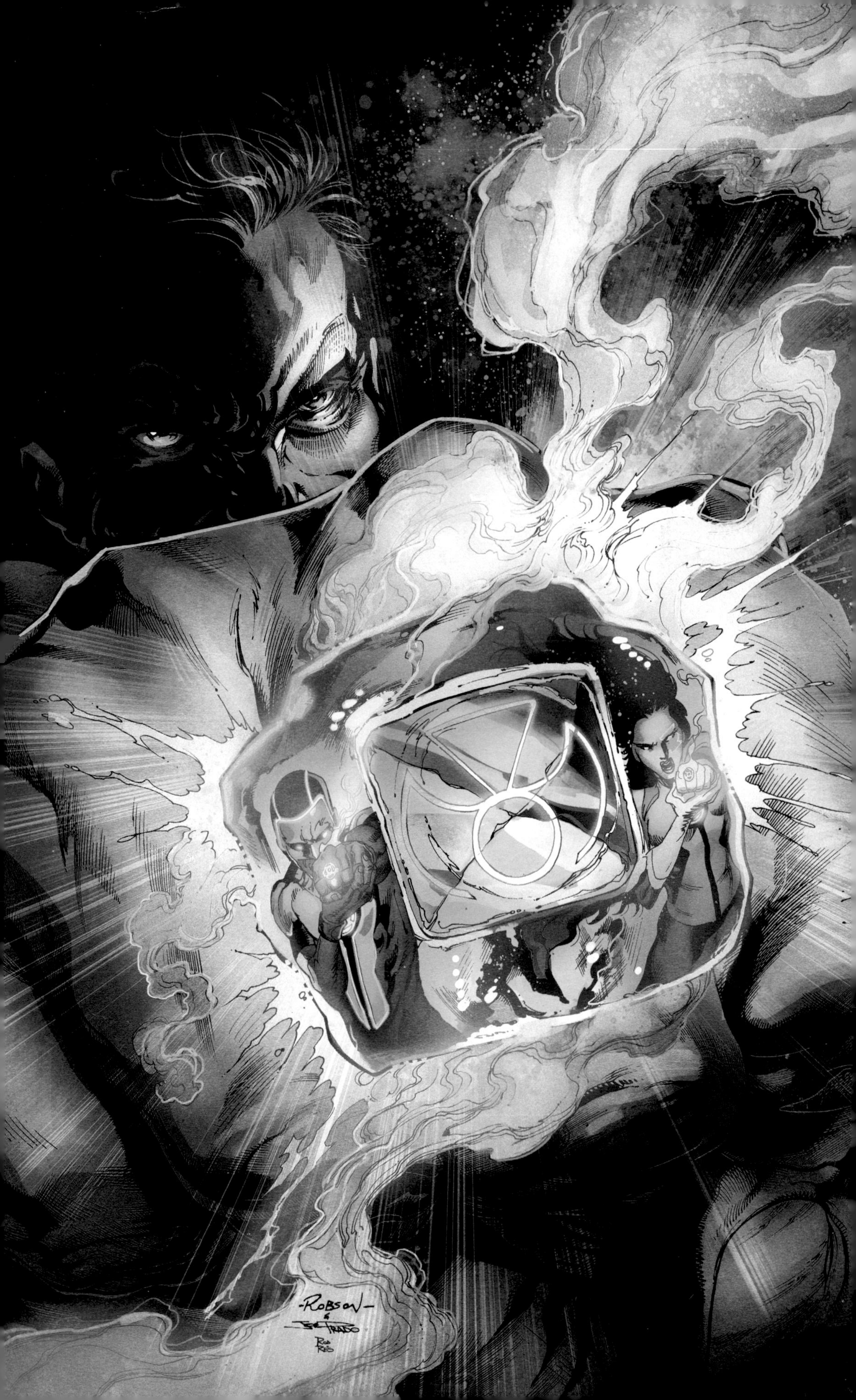
-ROBSON-

"THE PHANTOM LANTERN: PROLOGUE"

SAM HUMPHRIES writer * ROBSON ROCHA penciller * JAY LEISTEN inker

Cover by ROBSON ROCHA, JOE PRADO and ROD REIS

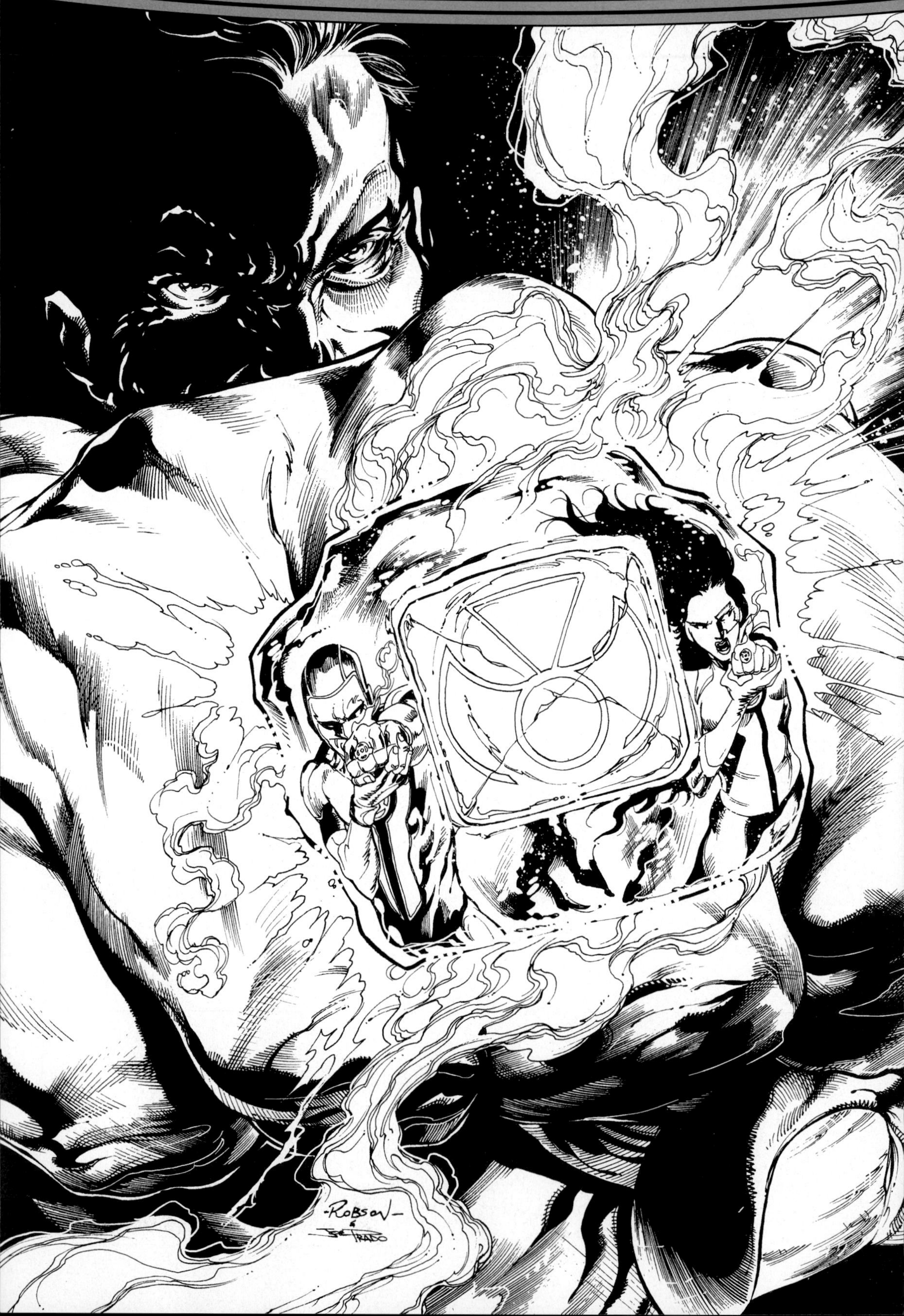
-ROBSON-

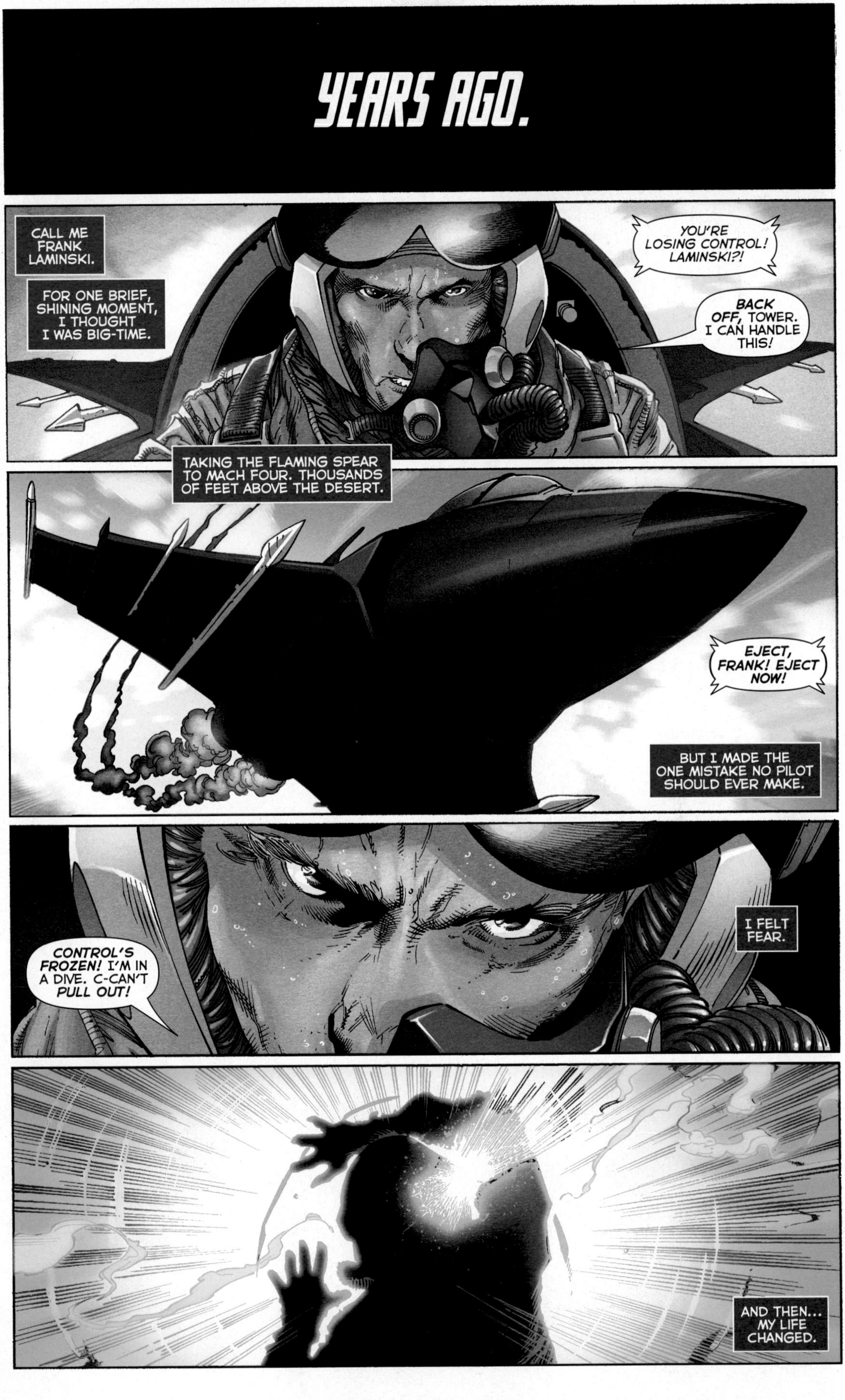
YEARS AGO.
CALL ME FRANK LAMINSKI.
FOR ONE BRIEF, SHINING MOMENT, I THOUGHT I WAS BIG-TIME.
YOU'RE LOSING CONTROL! LAMINSKI?!
BACK OFF, TOWER. I CAN HANDLE THIS!
TAKING THE FLAMING SPEAR TO MACH FOUR. THOUSANDS OF FEET ABOVE THE DESERT.
EJECT, FRANK! EJECT NOW!
BUT I MADE THE ONE MISTAKE NO PILOT SHOULD EVER MAKE.
I FELT FEAR.
CONTROL'S FROZEN! I'M IN A DIVE. C-CAN'T PULL OUT!
AND THEN... MY LIFE CHANGED.

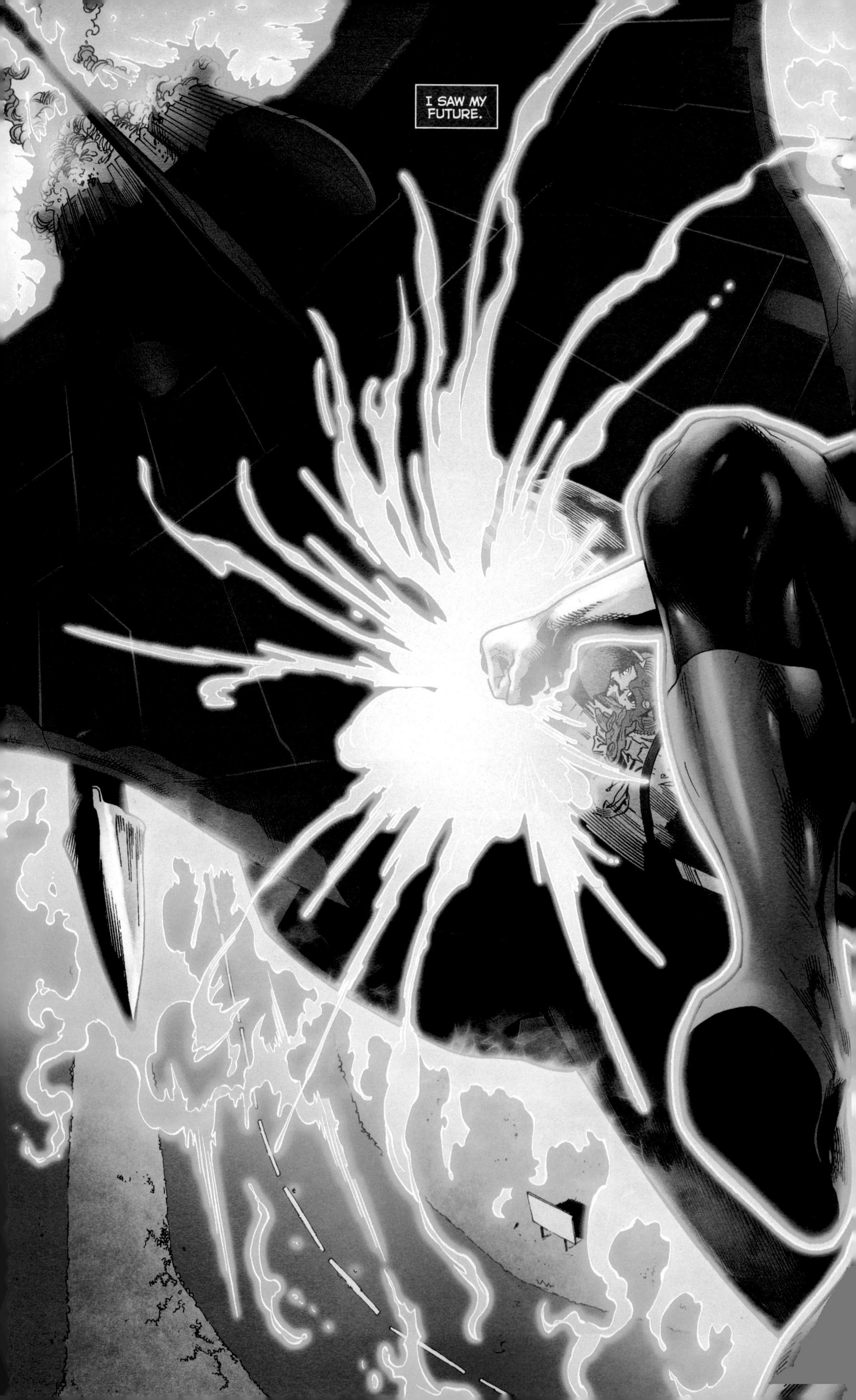
I SAW MY FUTURE.

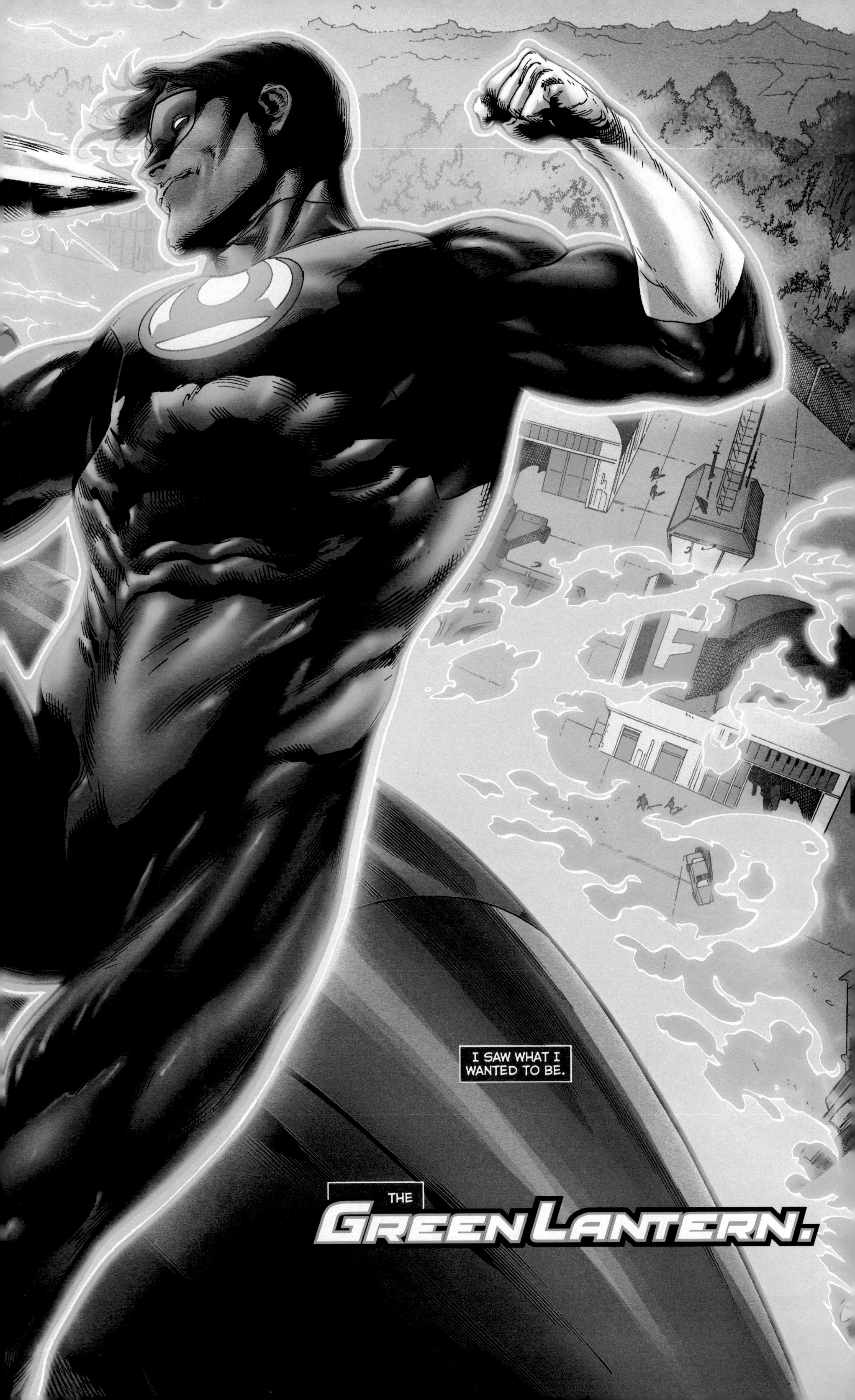
I SAW WHAT I WANTED TO BE.
THE
GREEN LANTERN.

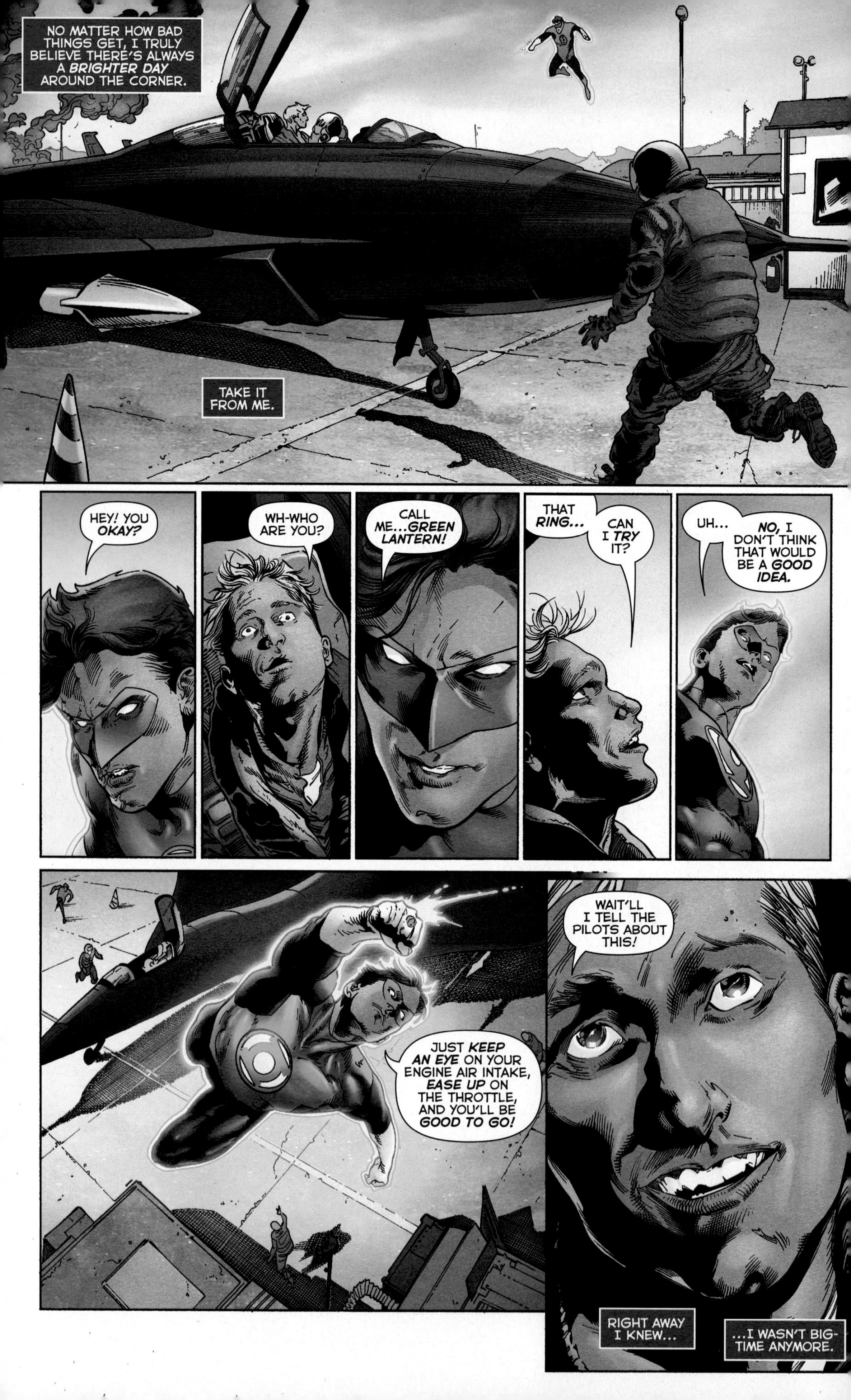
NO MATTER HOW BAD THINGS GET, I TRULY BELIEVE THERE'S ALWAYS A BRIGHTER DAY AROUND THE CORNER.
TAKE IT FROM ME.
HEY! YOU OKAY?
WH-WHO ARE YOU?
CALL ME...GREEN LANTERN!
THAT RING...
CAN I TRY IT?
UH...
NO, I DON'T THINK THAT WOULD BE A GOOD IDEA.
JUST KEEP AN EYE ON YOUR ENGINE AIR INTAKE, EASE UP ON THE THROTTLE, AND YOU'LL BE GOOD TO GO!
WAIT'LL I TELL THE PILOTS ABOUT THIS!
RIGHT AWAY I KNEW...
...I WASN'T BIG-TIME ANYMORE.

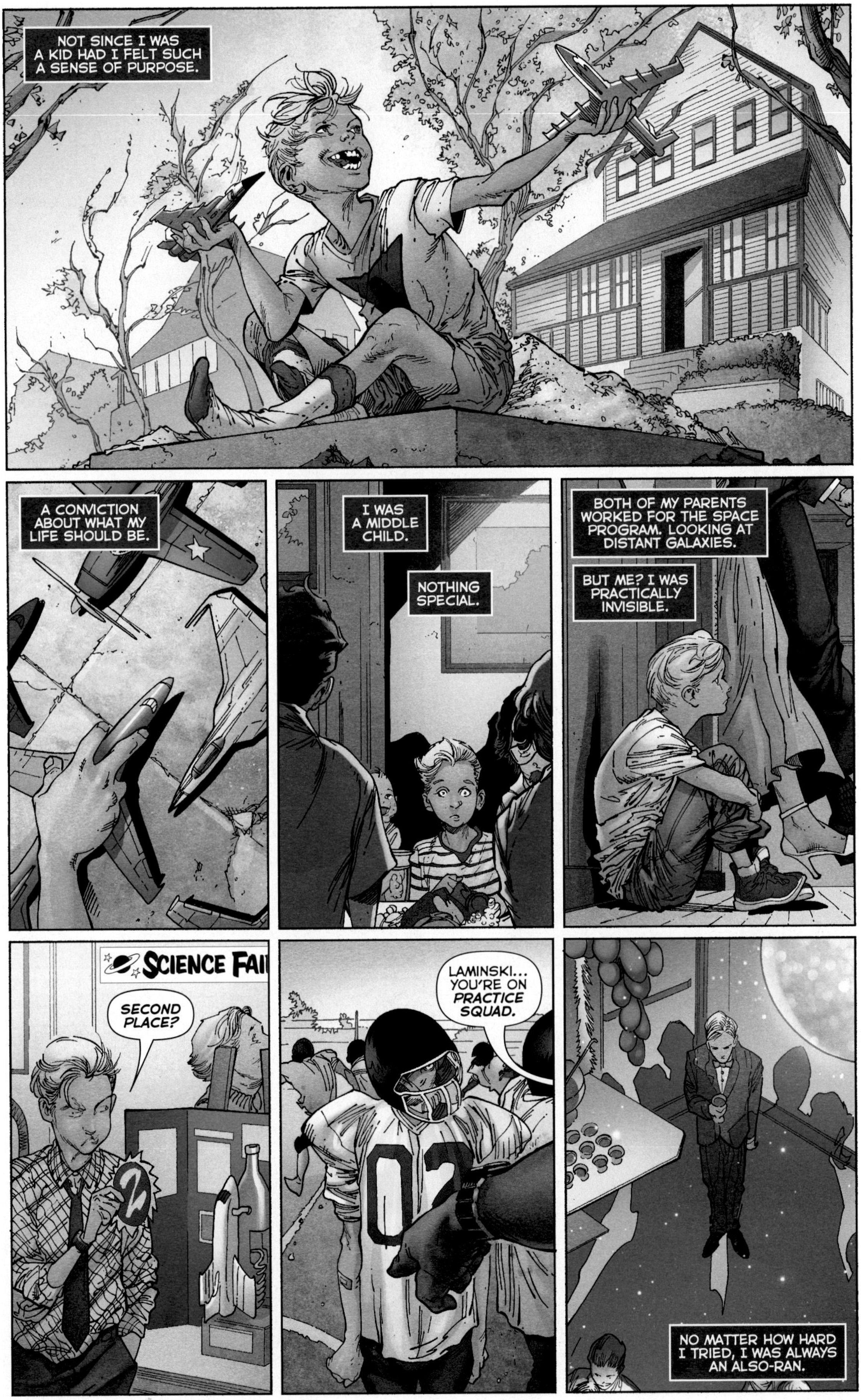
NOT SINCE I WAS A KID HAD I FELT SUCH A SENSE OF PURPOSE.
A CONVICTION ABOUT WHAT MY LIFE SHOULD BE.
I WAS A MIDDLE CHILD.
NOTHING SPECIAL.
BOTH OF MY PARENTS WORKED FOR THE SPACE PROGRAM. LOOKING AT DISTANT GALAXIES.
BUT ME? I WAS PRACTICALLY INVISIBLE.
SCIENCE FAI
SECOND PLACE?
LAMINSKI... YOU'RE ON *PRACTICE* SQUAD.
NO MATTER HOW HARD I TRIED, I WAS ALWAYS AN ALSO-RAN.

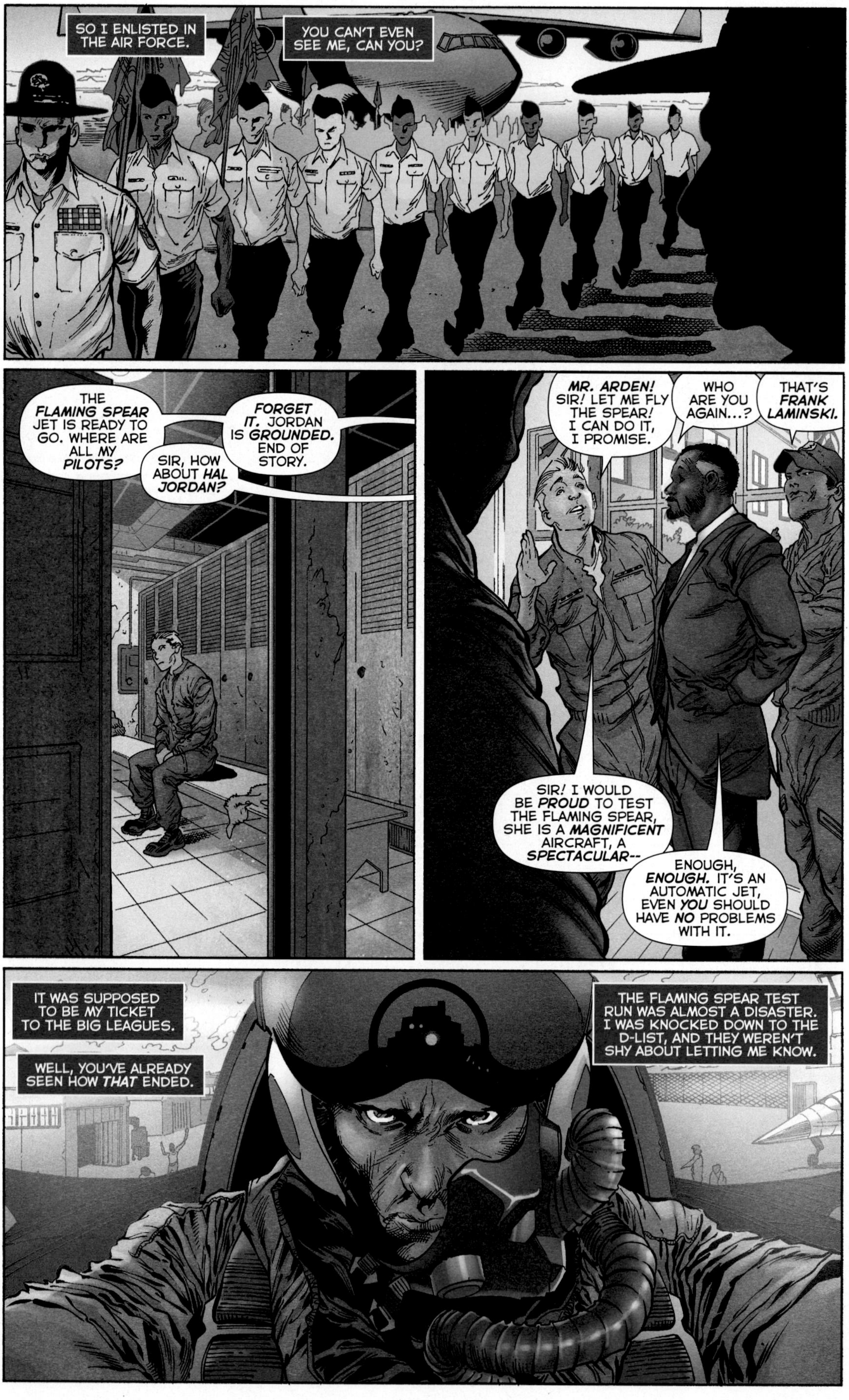
SO I ENLISTED IN THE AIR FORCE.
YOU CAN'T EVEN SEE ME, CAN YOU?
THE *FLAMING SPEAR* JET IS READY TO GO. WHERE ARE ALL MY *PILOTS?*
SIR, HOW ABOUT *HAL JORDAN?*
FORGET IT. JORDAN IS *GROUNDED.* END OF STORY.
MR. ARDEN! SIR*!* LET ME FLY THE SPEAR*!* I CAN DO IT, I PROMISE.
WHO ARE YOU AGAIN...?
THAT'S *FRANK LAMINSKI.*
SIR*!* I WOULD BE *PROUD* TO TEST THE FLAMING SPEAR, SHE IS A *MAGNIFICENT* AIRCRAFT, A *SPECTACULAR--*
ENOUGH, *ENOUGH.* IT'S AN AUTOMATIC JET, EVEN *YOU* SHOULD HAVE *NO* PROBLEMS WITH IT.
IT WAS SUPPOSED TO BE MY TICKET TO THE BIG LEAGUES.
WELL, YOU'VE ALREADY SEEN HOW *THAT* ENDED.
THE FLAMING SPEAR TEST RUN WAS ALMOST A DISASTER. I WAS KNOCKED DOWN TO THE D-LIST, AND THEY WEREN'T SHY ABOUT LETTING ME KNOW.

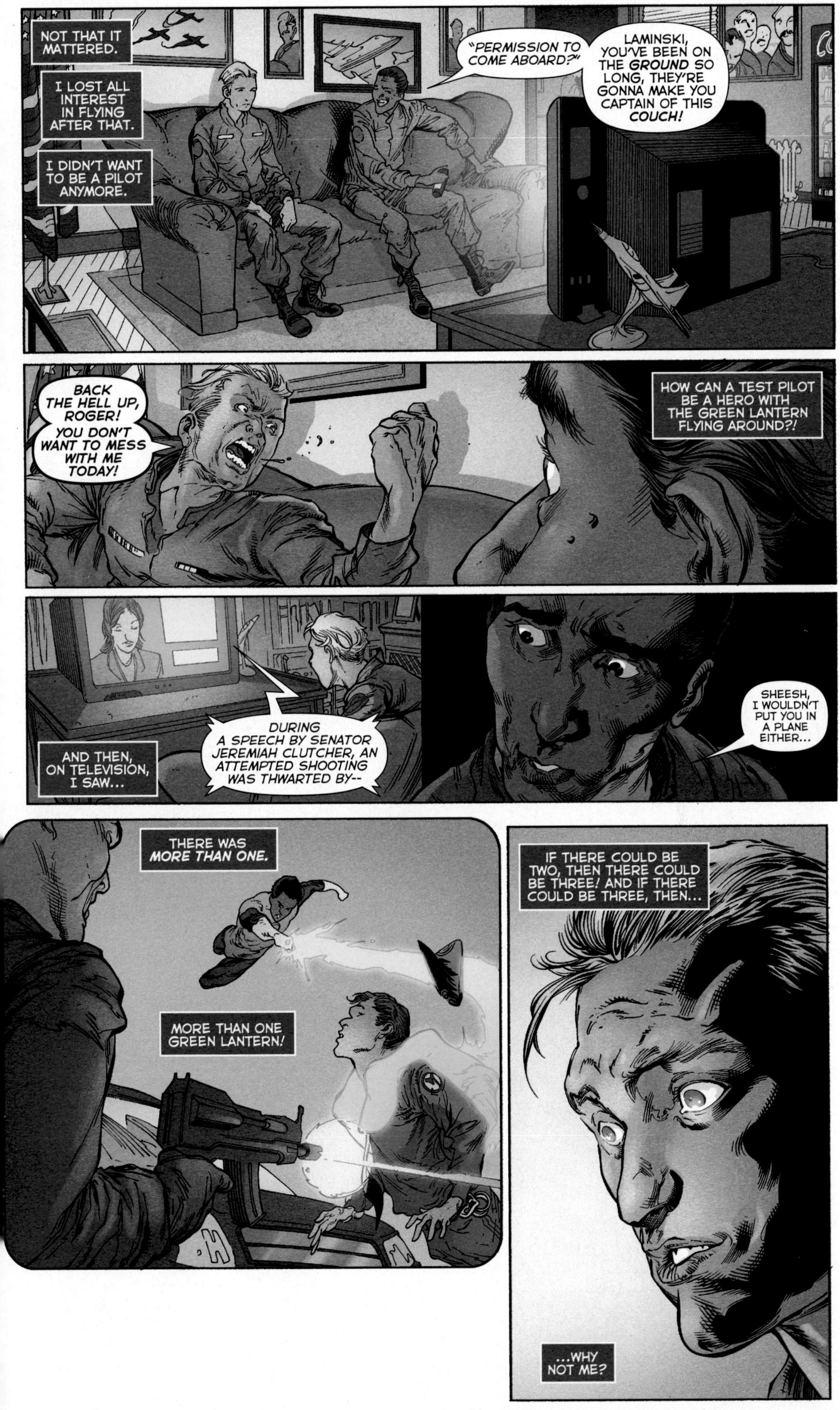
NOT THAT IT MATTERED.
I LOST ALL INTEREST IN FLYING AFTER THAT.
I DIDN'T WANT TO BE A PILOT ANYMORE.
"PERMISSION TO COME ABOARD?"
LAMINSKI, YOU'VE BEEN ON THE GROUND SO LONG, THEY'RE GONNA MAKE YOU CAPTAIN OF THIS COUCH!
BACK THE HELL UP, ROGER! YOU DON'T WANT TO MESS WITH ME TODAY!
HOW CAN A TEST PILOT BE A HERO WITH THE GREEN LANTERN FLYING AROUND?!
AND THEN, ON TELEVISION, I SAW...
DURING A SPEECH BY SENATOR JEREMIAH CLUTCHER, AN ATTEMPTED SHOOTING WAS THWARTED BY--
SHEESH, I WOULDN'T PUT YOU IN A PLANE EITHER...
THERE WAS MORE THAN ONE.
MORE THAN ONE GREEN LANTERN!
IF THERE COULD BE TWO, THEN THERE COULD BE THREE! AND IF THERE COULD BE THREE, THEN...
...WHY NOT ME?

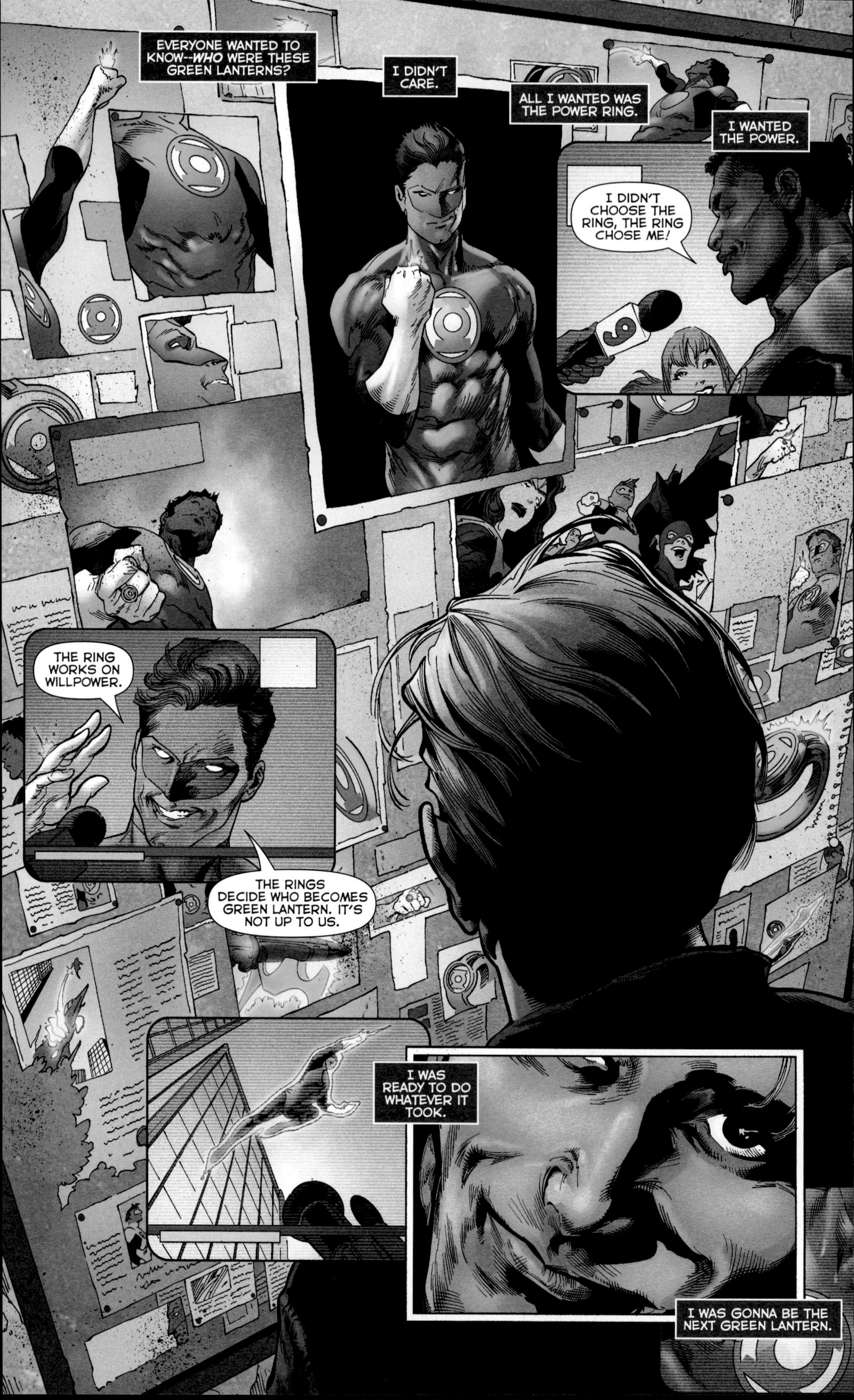
EVERYONE WANTED TO KNOW--*WHO* WERE THESE GREEN LANTERNS?
I DIDN'T CARE.
ALL I WANTED WAS THE POWER RING.
I WANTED THE POWER.
I DIDN'T CHOOSE THE RING, THE RING CHOSE ME!
9
THE RING WORKS ON WILLPOWER.
THE RINGS DECIDE WHO BECOMES GREEN LANTERN. IT'S NOT UP TO US.
I WAS READY TO DO WHATEVER IT TOOK.
I WAS GONNA BE THE NEXT GREEN LANTERN.

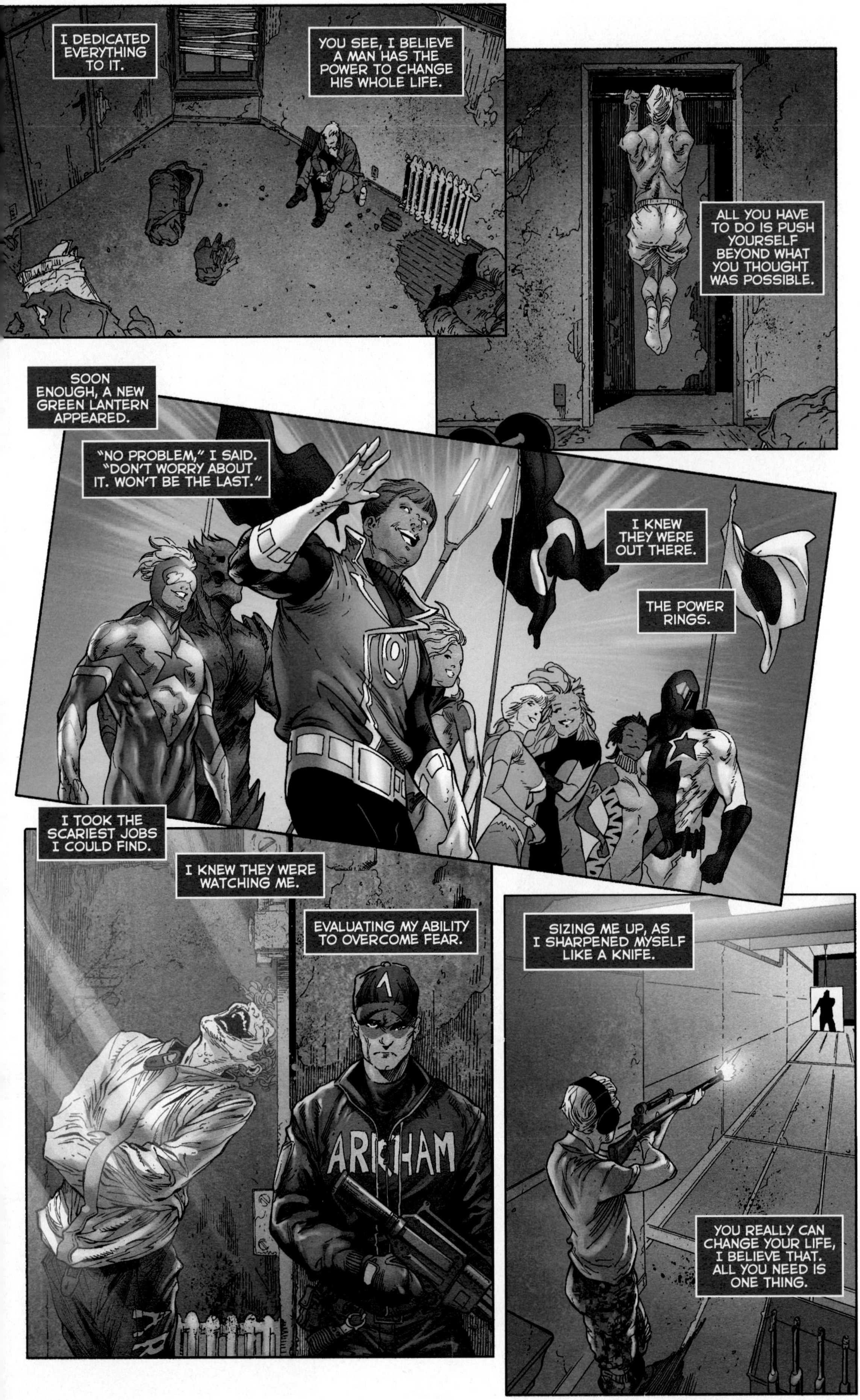

I DEDICATED EVERYTHING TO IT.
YOU SEE, I BELIEVE A MAN HAS THE POWER TO CHANGE HIS WHOLE LIFE.
ALL YOU HAVE TO DO IS PUSH YOURSELF BEYOND WHAT YOU THOUGHT WAS POSSIBLE.
SOON ENOUGH, A NEW GREEN LANTERN APPEARED.
"NO PROBLEM," I SAID. "DON'T WORRY ABOUT IT. WON'T BE THE LAST."
I KNEW THEY WERE OUT THERE.
THE POWER RINGS.
I TOOK THE SCARIEST JOBS I COULD FIND.
I KNEW THEY WERE WATCHING ME.
EVALUATING MY ABILITY TO OVERCOME FEAR.
ARKHAM
SIZING ME UP, AS I SHARPENED MYSELF LIKE A KNIFE.
YOU REALLY CAN CHANGE YOUR LIFE, I BELIEVE THAT. ALL YOU NEED IS ONE THING.

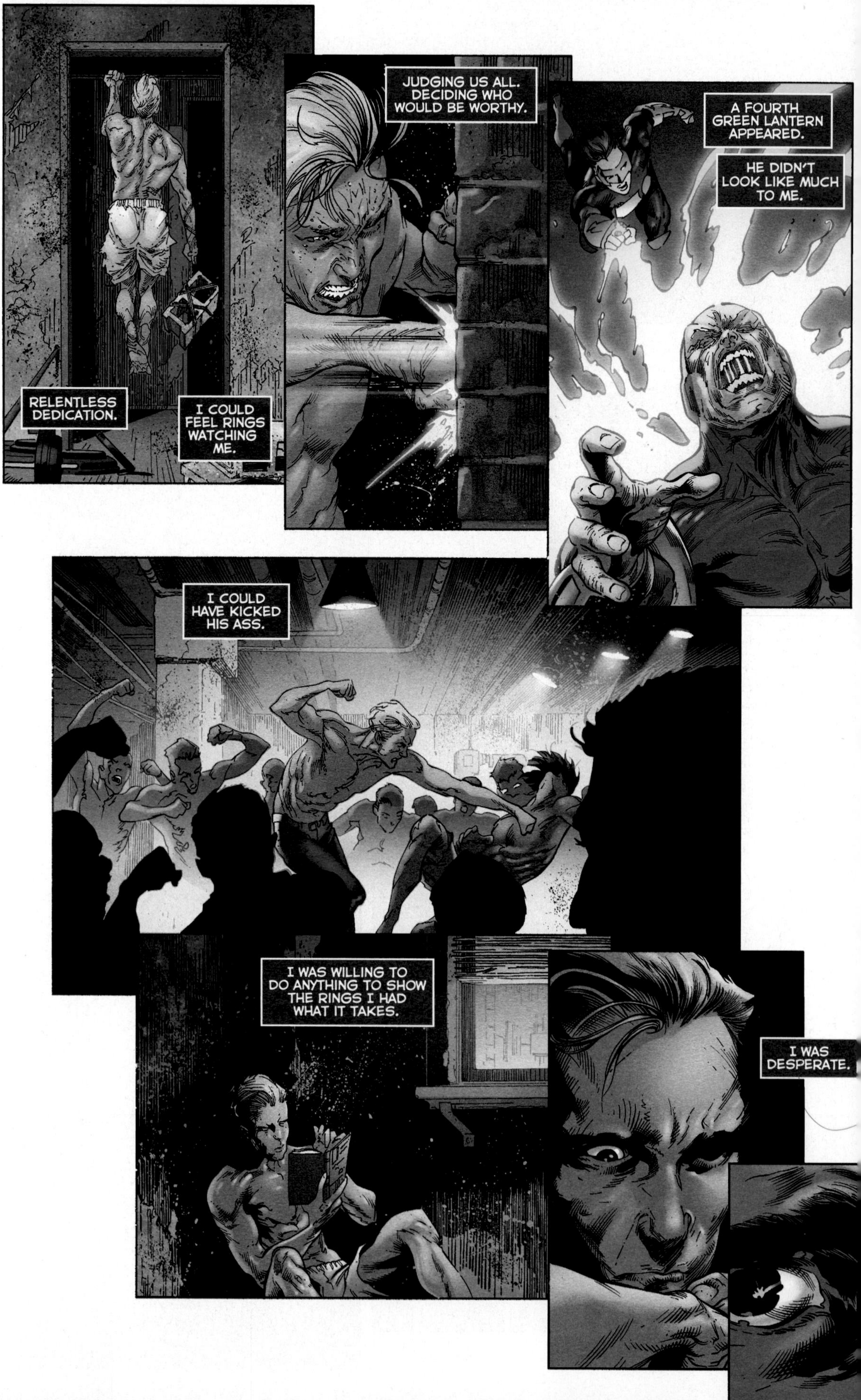
RELENTLESS DEDICATION.
I COULD FEEL RINGS WATCHING ME.
JUDGING US ALL. DECIDING WHO WOULD BE WORTHY.
A FOURTH GREEN LANTERN APPEARED.
HE DIDN'T LOOK LIKE MUCH TO ME.
I COULD HAVE KICKED HIS ASS.
I WAS WILLING TO DO ANYTHING TO SHOW THE RINGS I HAD WHAT IT TAKES.
I WAS DESPERATE.

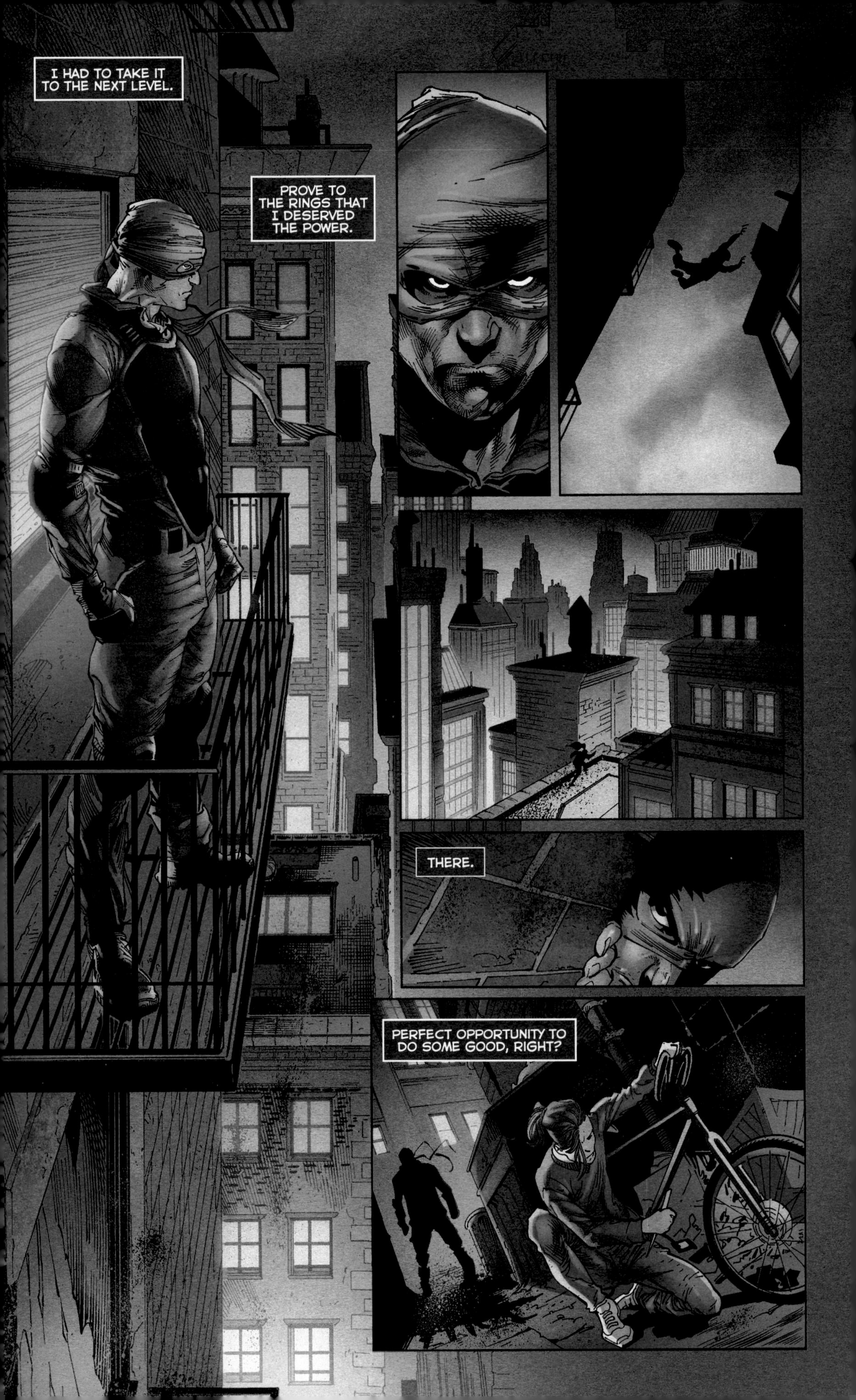
I HAD TO TAKE IT TO THE NEXT LEVEL.
PROVE TO THE RINGS THAT I DESERVED THE POWER.
THERE.
PERFECT OPPORTUNITY TO DO SOME GOOD, RIGHT?

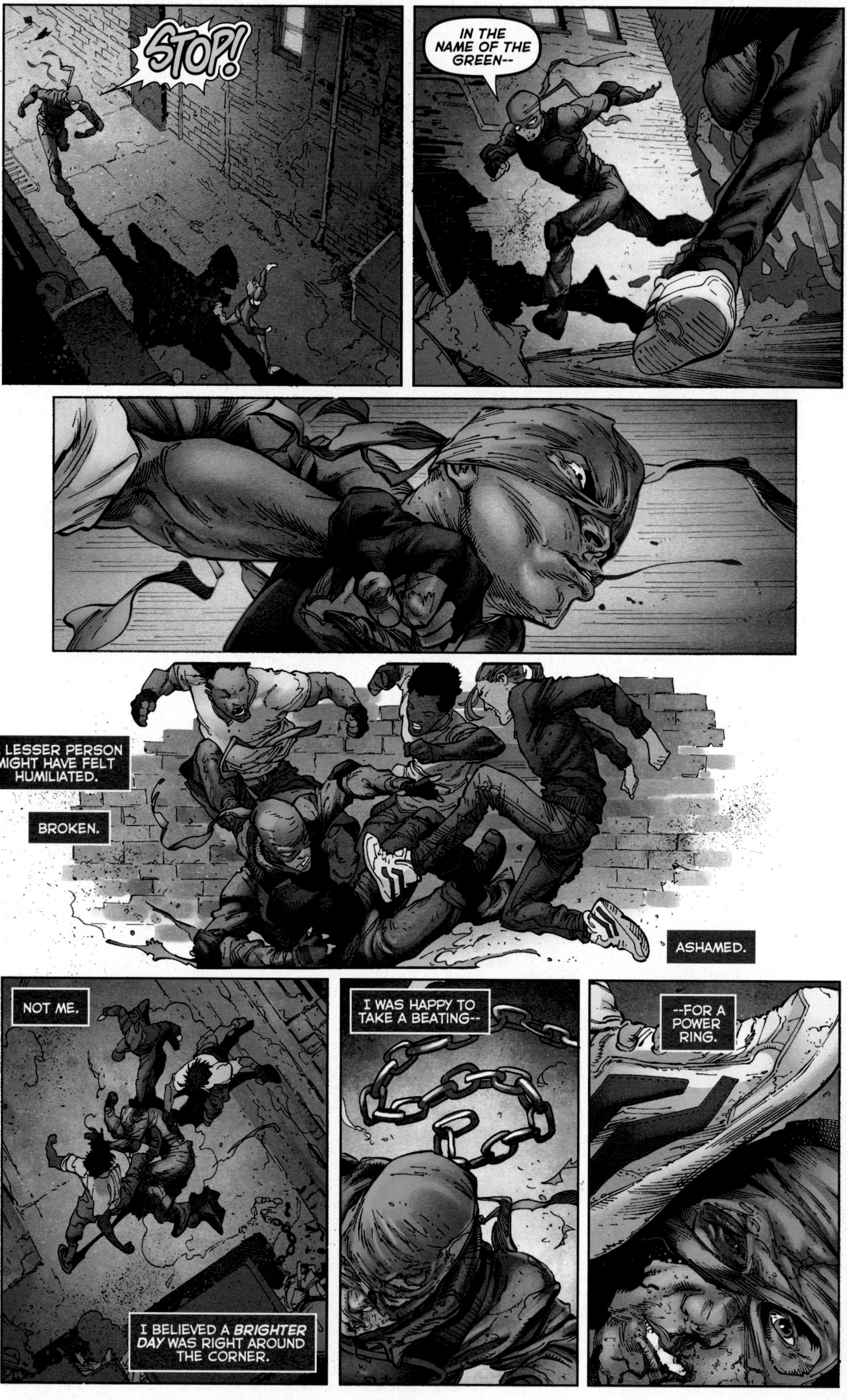
STOP!
IN THE NAME OF THE GREEN--
A LESSER PERSON MIGHT HAVE FELT HUMILIATED.
BROKEN.
ASHAMED.
NOT ME.
I BELIEVED A BRIGHTER DAY WAS RIGHT AROUND THE CORNER.
I WAS HAPPY TO TAKE A BEATING--
--FOR A POWER RING.

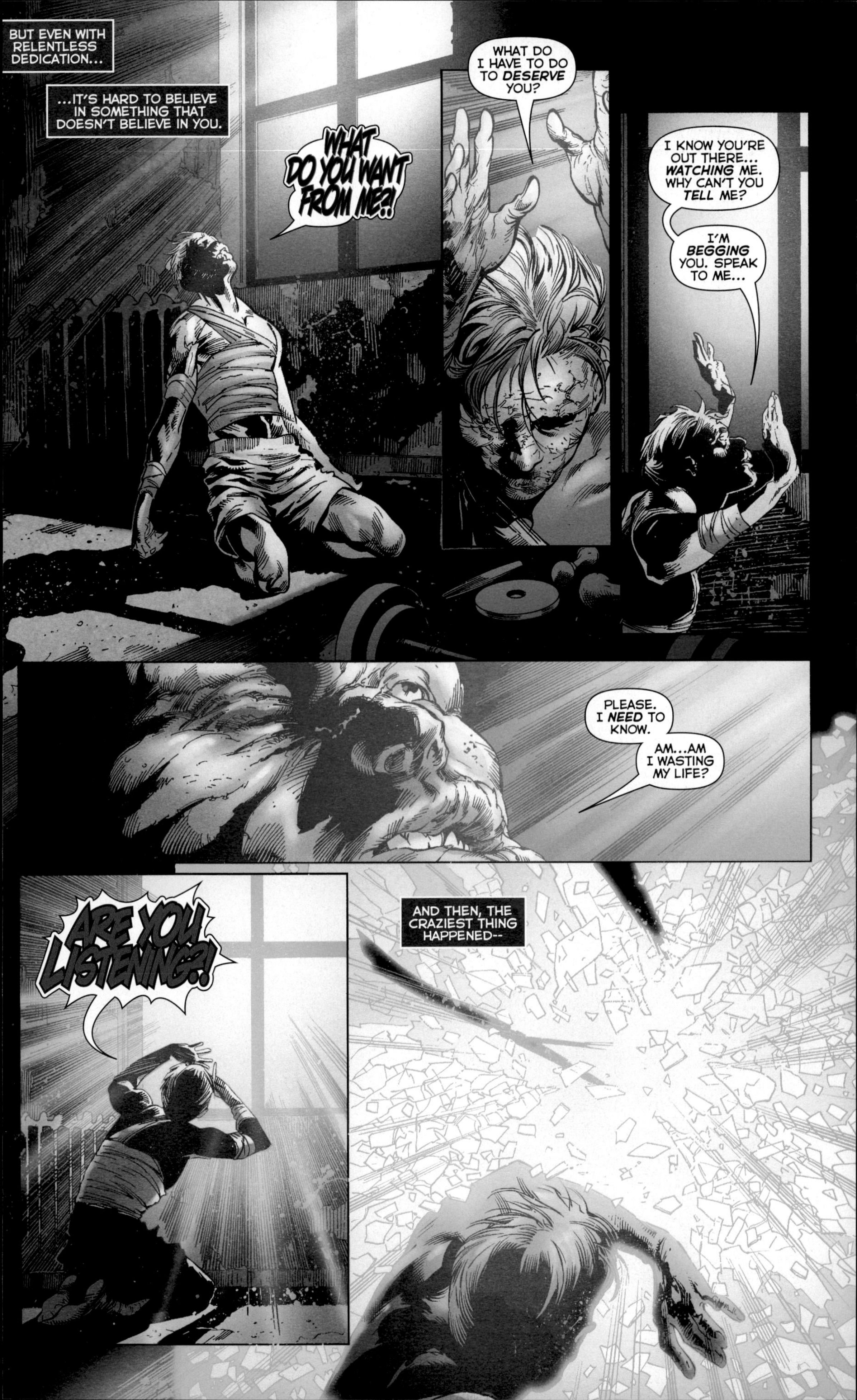
BUT EVEN WITH RELENTLESS DEDICATION...
...IT'S HARD TO BELIEVE IN SOMETHING THAT DOESN'T BELIEVE IN YOU.
WHAT DO YOU WANT FROM ME?!
WHAT DO I HAVE TO DO TO DESERVE YOU?
I KNOW YOU'RE OUT THERE... WATCHING ME. WHY CAN'T YOU TELL ME?
I'M BEGGING YOU. SPEAK TO ME...
PLEASE. I NEED TO KNOW.
AM...AM I WASTING MY LIFE?
ARE YOU LISTENING?!
AND THEN, THE CRAZIEST THING HAPPENED--

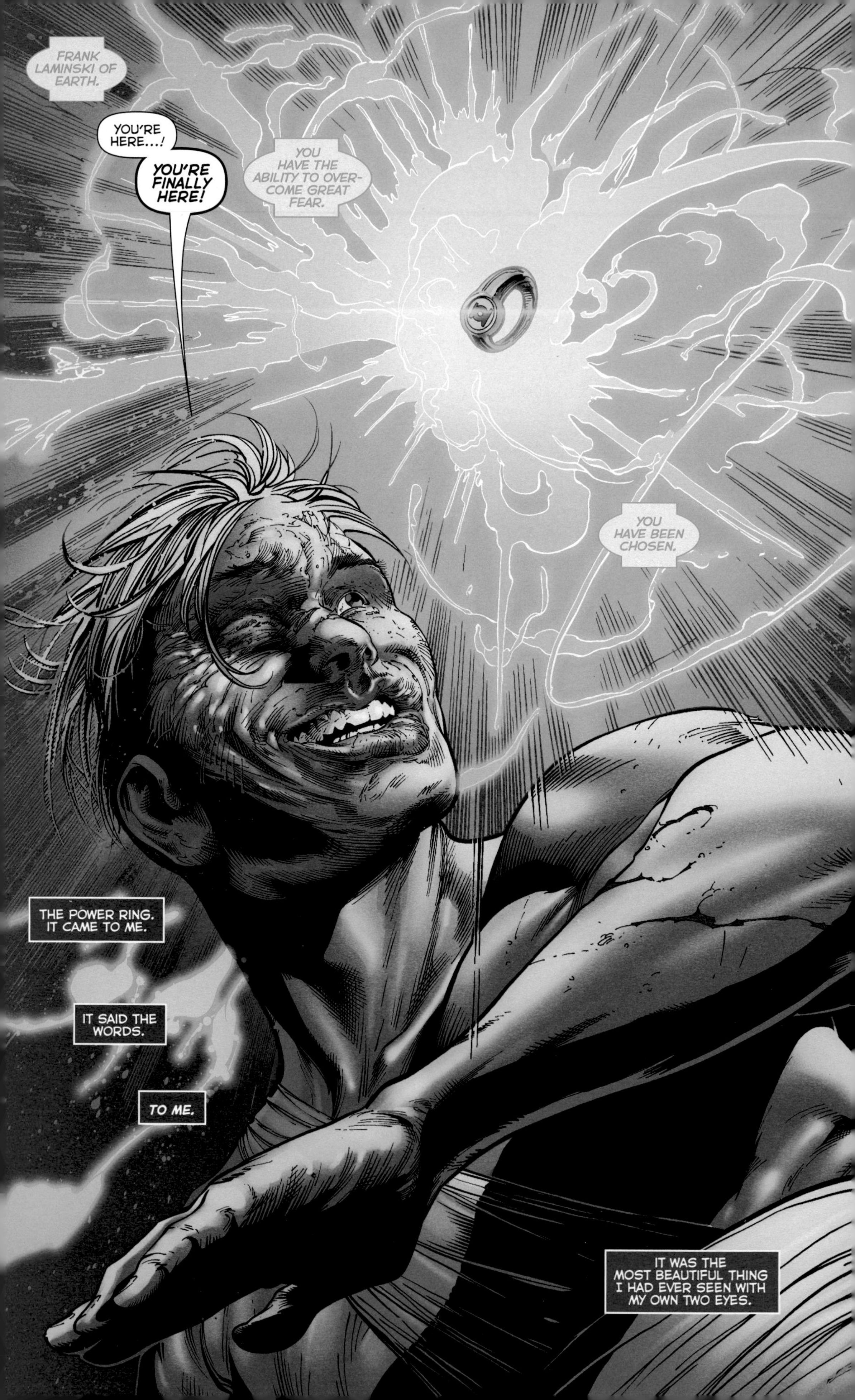
FRANK LAMINSKI OF EARTH.
YOU'RE HERE...!
YOU'RE FINALLY HERE!
YOU HAVE THE ABILITY TO OVER-COME GREAT FEAR.
YOU HAVE BEEN CHOSEN.
THE POWER RING. IT CAME TO ME.
IT SAID THE WORDS.
TO ME.
IT WAS THE MOST BEAUTIFUL THING I HAD EVER SEEN WITH MY OWN TWO EYES.

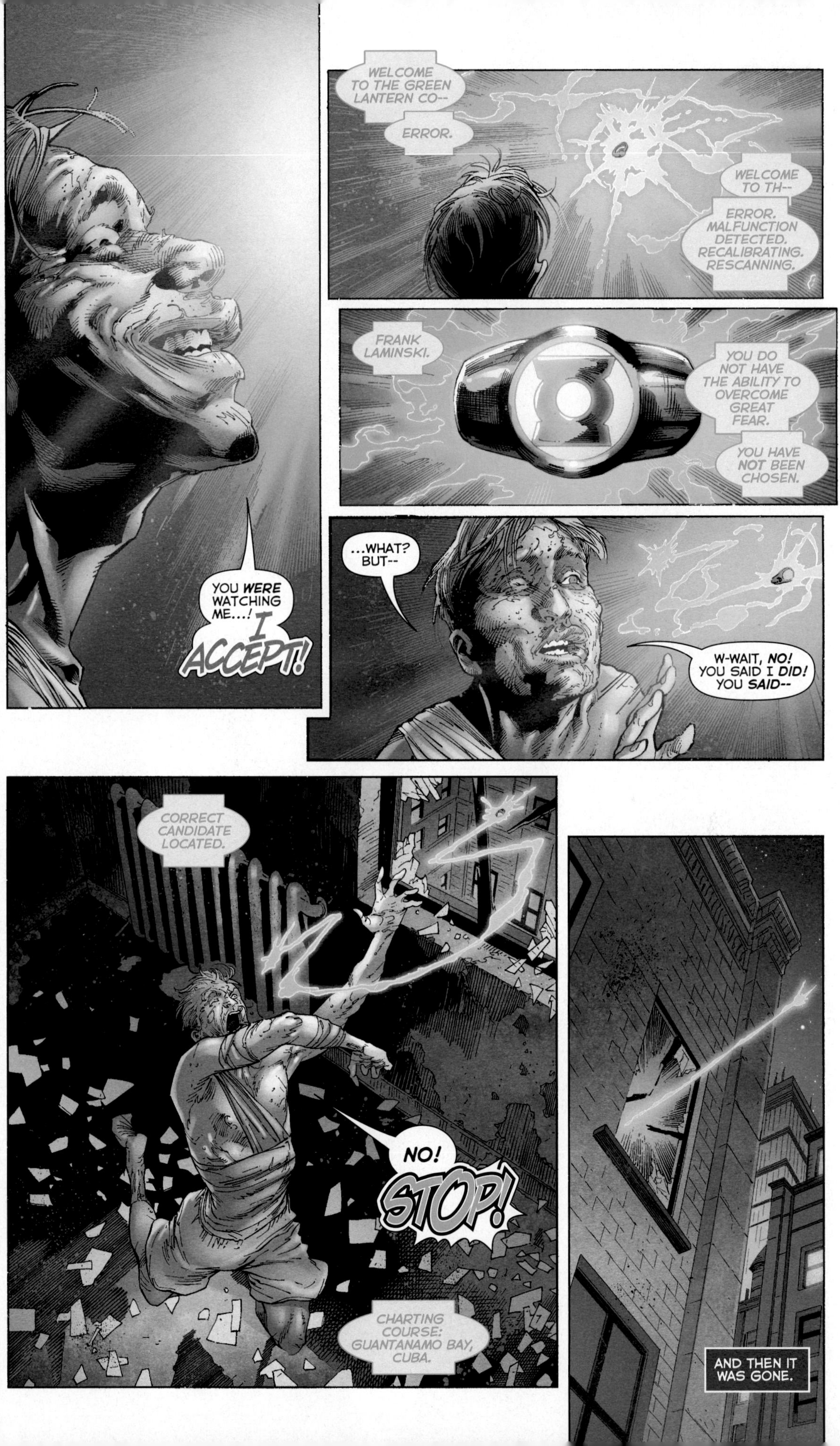

YOU WERE WATCHING ME...! I ACCEPT!
WELCOME TO THE GREEN LANTERN CO--
ERROR.
WELCOME TO TH--
ERROR. MALFUNCTION DETECTED. RECALIBRATING. RESCANNING.
FRANK LAMINSKI.
YOU DO NOT HAVE THE ABILITY TO OVERCOME GREAT FEAR.
YOU HAVE NOT BEEN CHOSEN.
...WHAT? BUT--
W-WAIT, NO! YOU SAID I DID! YOU SAID--
CORRECT CANDIDATE LOCATED.
NO! STOP!
CHARTING COURSE: GUANTANAMO BAY, CUBA.
AND THEN IT WAS GONE.

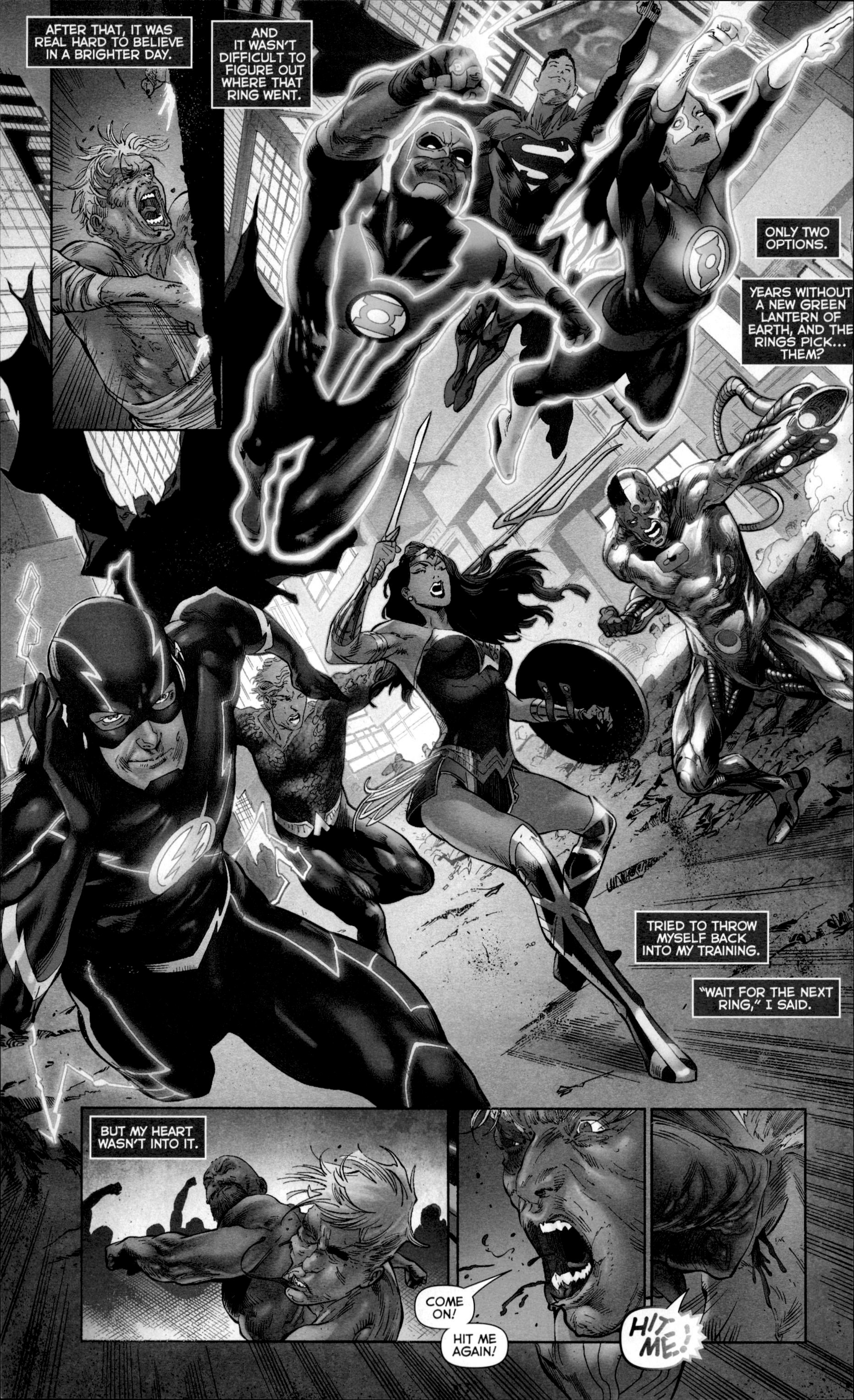
AFTER THAT, IT WAS REAL HARD TO BELIEVE IN A BRIGHTER DAY.
AND IT WASN'T DIFFICULT TO FIGURE OUT WHERE THAT RING WENT.
ONLY TWO OPTIONS.
YEARS WITHOUT A NEW GREEN LANTERN OF EARTH, AND THE RINGS PICK... THEM?
TRIED TO THROW MYSELF BACK INTO MY TRAINING.
"WAIT FOR THE NEXT RING," I SAID.
BUT MY HEART WASN'T INTO IT.
COME ON!
HIT ME AGAIN!
HIT ME!

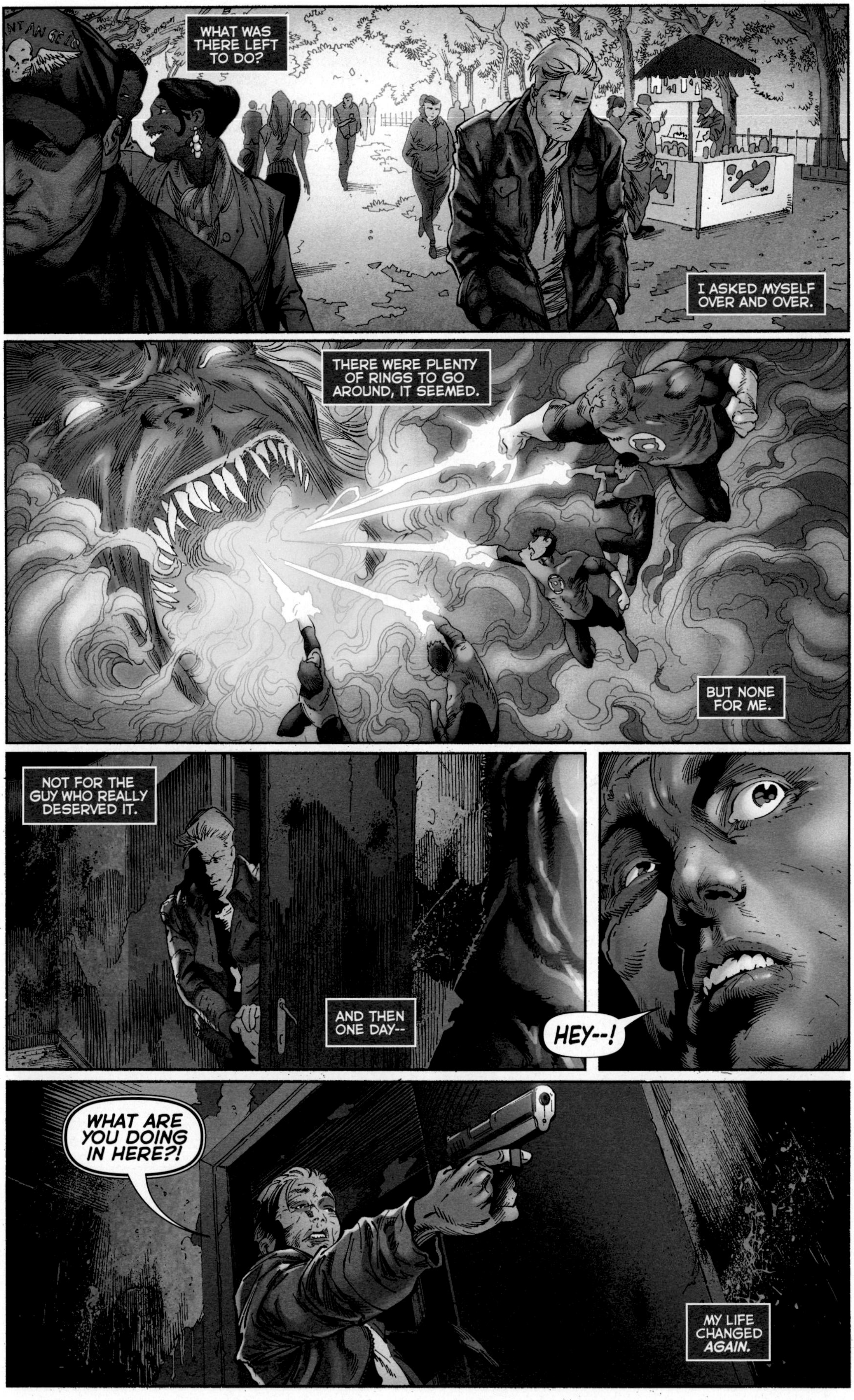
WHAT WAS THERE LEFT TO DO?
I ASKED MYSELF OVER AND OVER.
THERE WERE PLENTY OF RINGS TO GO AROUND, IT SEEMED.
BUT NONE FOR ME.
NOT FOR THE GUY WHO REALLY DESERVED IT.
AND THEN ONE DAY--
HEY--!
WHAT ARE YOU DOING IN HERE?!
MY LIFE CHANGED AGAIN.

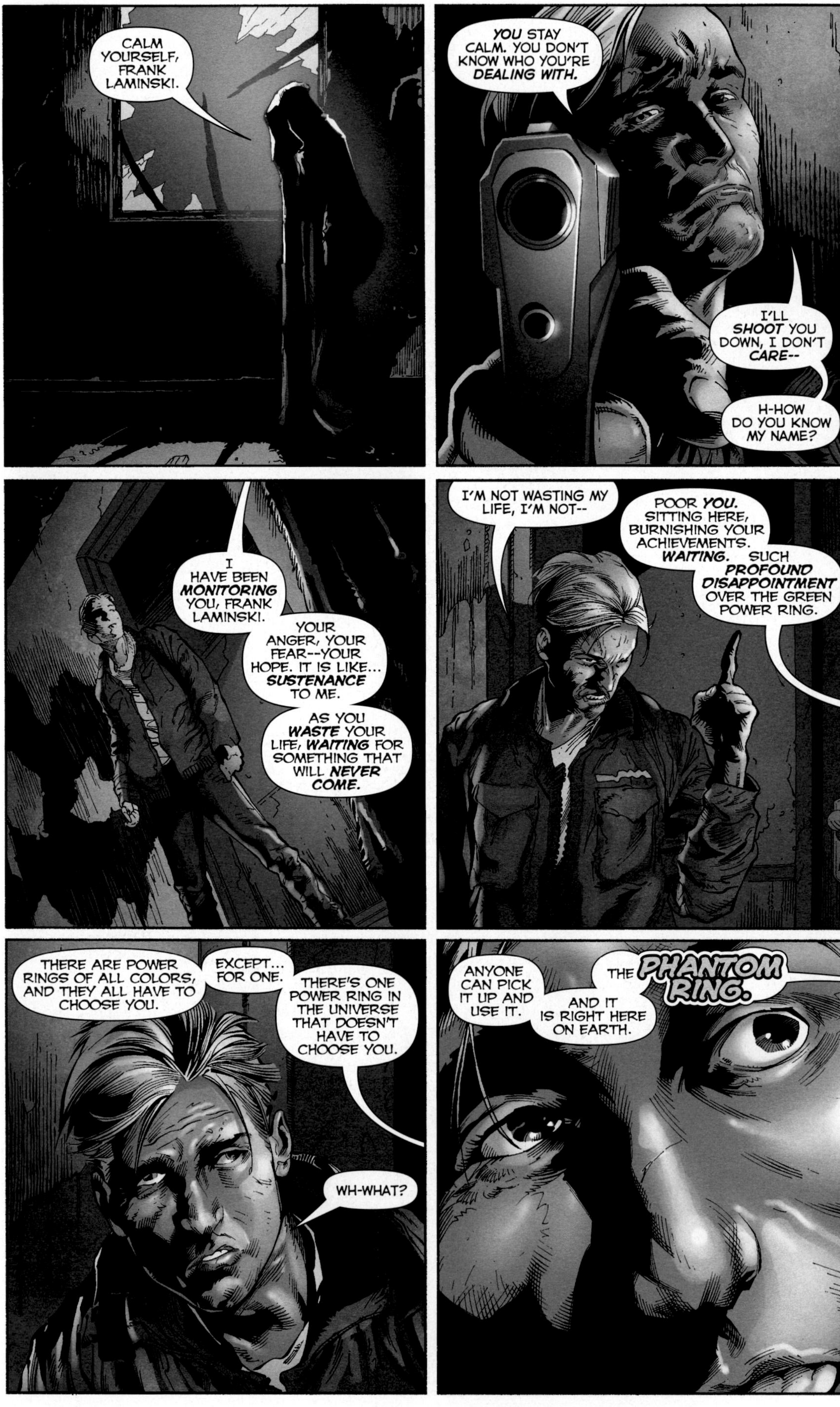
CALM YOURSELF, FRANK LAMINSKI.
YOU STAY CALM. YOU DON'T KNOW WHO YOU'RE *DEALING WITH.*
I'LL *SHOOT* YOU DOWN, I DON'T *CARE--*
H-HOW DO YOU KNOW MY NAME?
I HAVE BEEN *MONITORING* YOU, FRANK LAMINSKI.
YOUR ANGER, YOUR FEAR--YOUR HOPE. IT IS LIKE... *SUSTENANCE* TO ME.
AS YOU *WASTE* YOUR LIFE, *WAITING* FOR SOMETHING THAT WILL *NEVER COME.*
I'M NOT WASTING MY LIFE, I'M NOT--
POOR *YOU.* SITTING HERE, BURNISHING YOUR ACHIEVEMENTS. *WAITING.* SUCH *PROFOUND DISAPPOINTMENT* OVER THE GREEN POWER RING.
THERE ARE POWER RINGS OF ALL COLORS, AND THEY ALL HAVE TO CHOOSE YOU.
EXCEPT... FOR ONE.
THERE'S ONE POWER RING IN THE UNIVERSE THAT DOESN'T HAVE TO CHOOSE YOU.
WH-WHAT?
ANYONE CAN PICK IT UP AND USE IT.
THE PHANTOM RING.
AND IT IS RIGHT HERE ON EARTH.

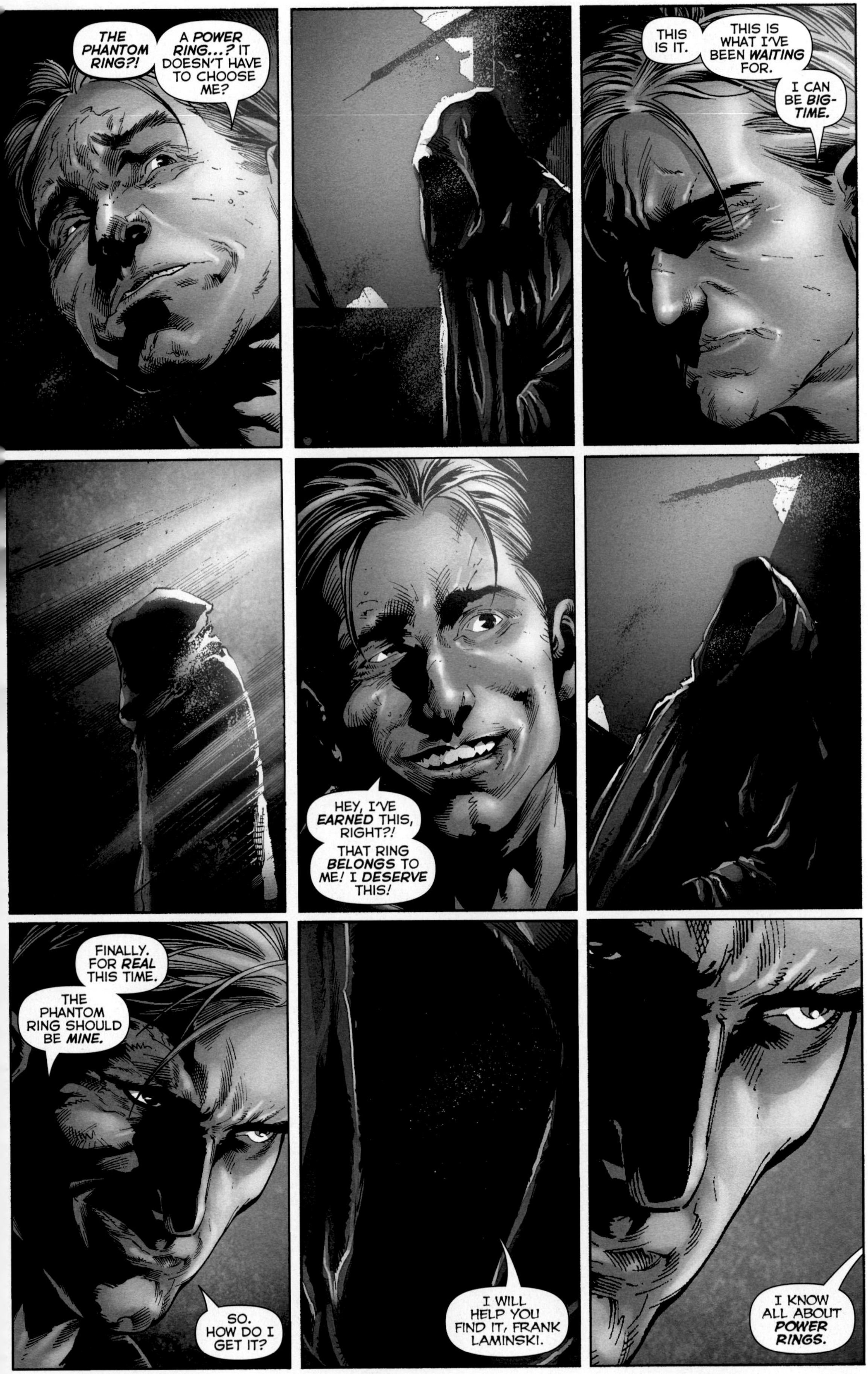
THE PHANTOM RING?!
A POWER RING...? IT DOESN'T HAVE TO CHOOSE ME?
THIS IS IT.
THIS IS WHAT I'VE BEEN WAITING FOR.
I CAN BE BIG-TIME.
HEY, I'VE EARNED THIS, RIGHT?!
THAT RING BELONGS TO ME! I DESERVE THIS!
FINALLY. FOR REAL THIS TIME.
THE PHANTOM RING SHOULD BE MINE.
SO. HOW DO I GET IT?
I WILL HELP YOU FIND IT, FRANK LAMINSKI.
I KNOW ALL ABOUT POWER RINGS.

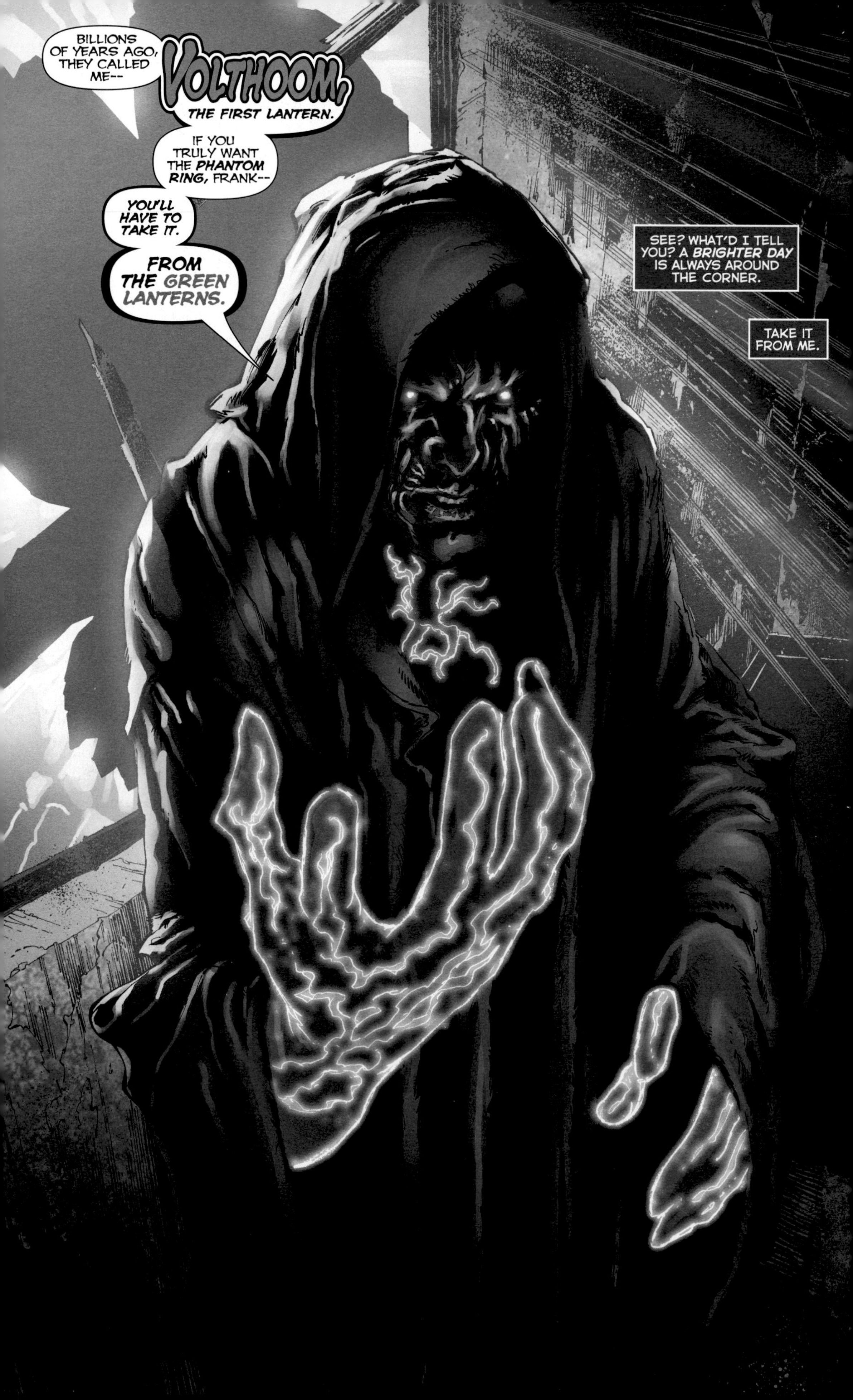
BILLIONS OF YEARS AGO, THEY CALLED ME--
VOLTHOOM, THE FIRST LANTERN.
IF YOU TRULY WANT THE PHANTOM RING, FRANK--
YOU'LL HAVE TO TAKE IT.
FROM THE GREEN LANTERNS.
SEE? WHAT'D I TELL YOU? A BRIGHTER DAY IS ALWAYS AROUND THE CORNER.
TAKE IT FROM ME.

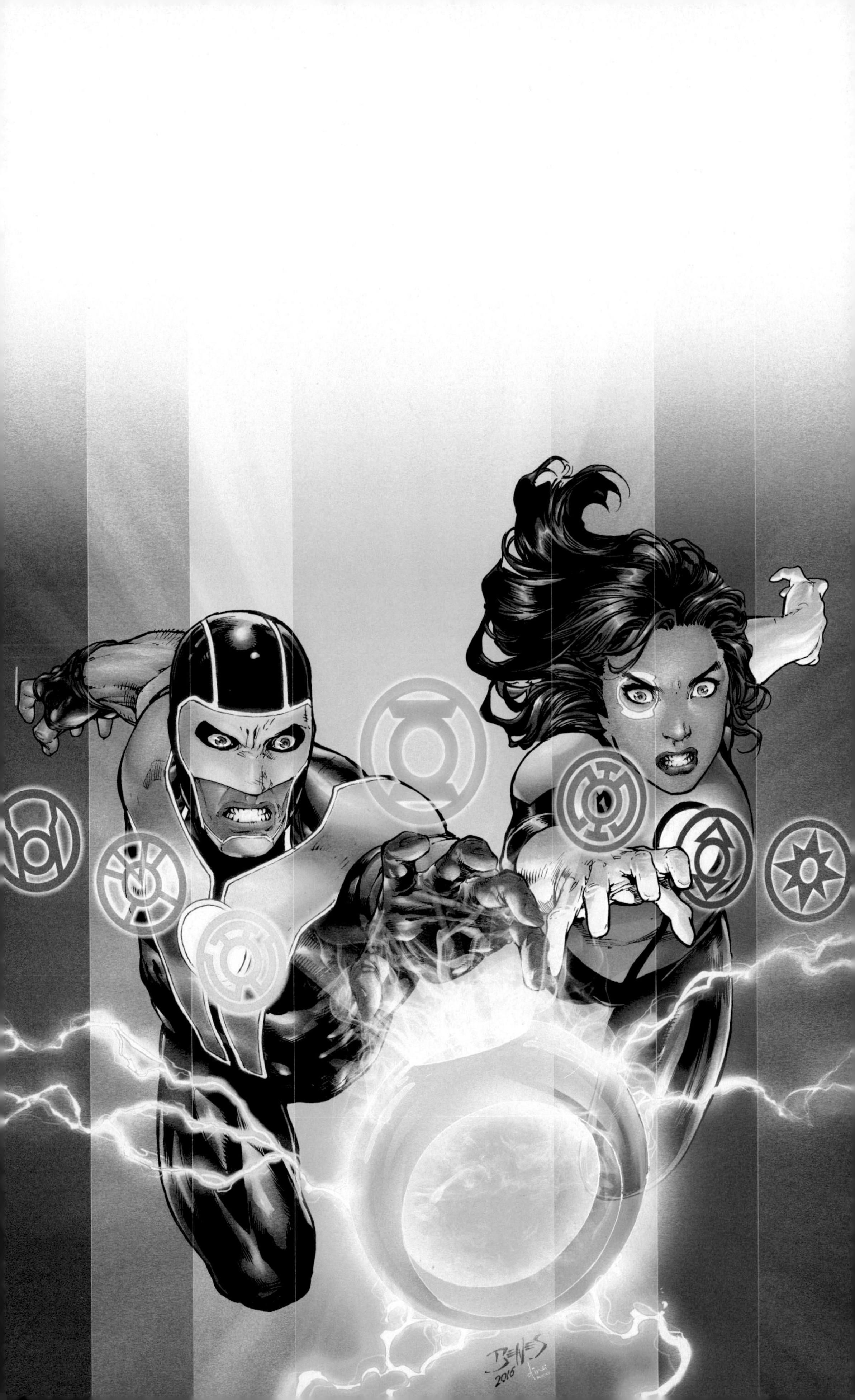

"THE PHANTOM LANTERN: PART ONE"

SAM HUMPHRIES writer * EDUARDO PANSICA penciller * JULIO FERREIRA inker

Cover by ED BENES and DINEI RIBEIRO

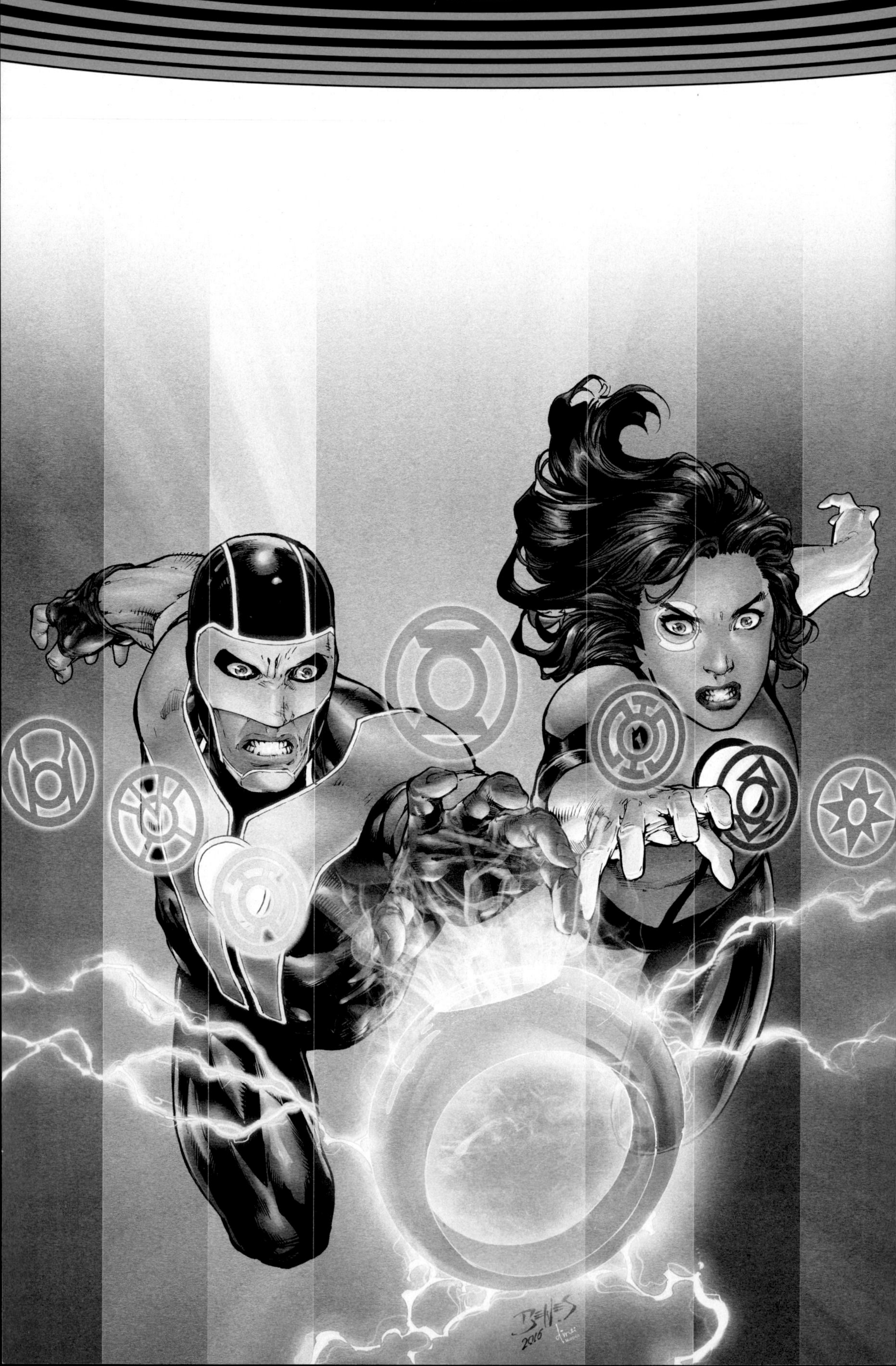

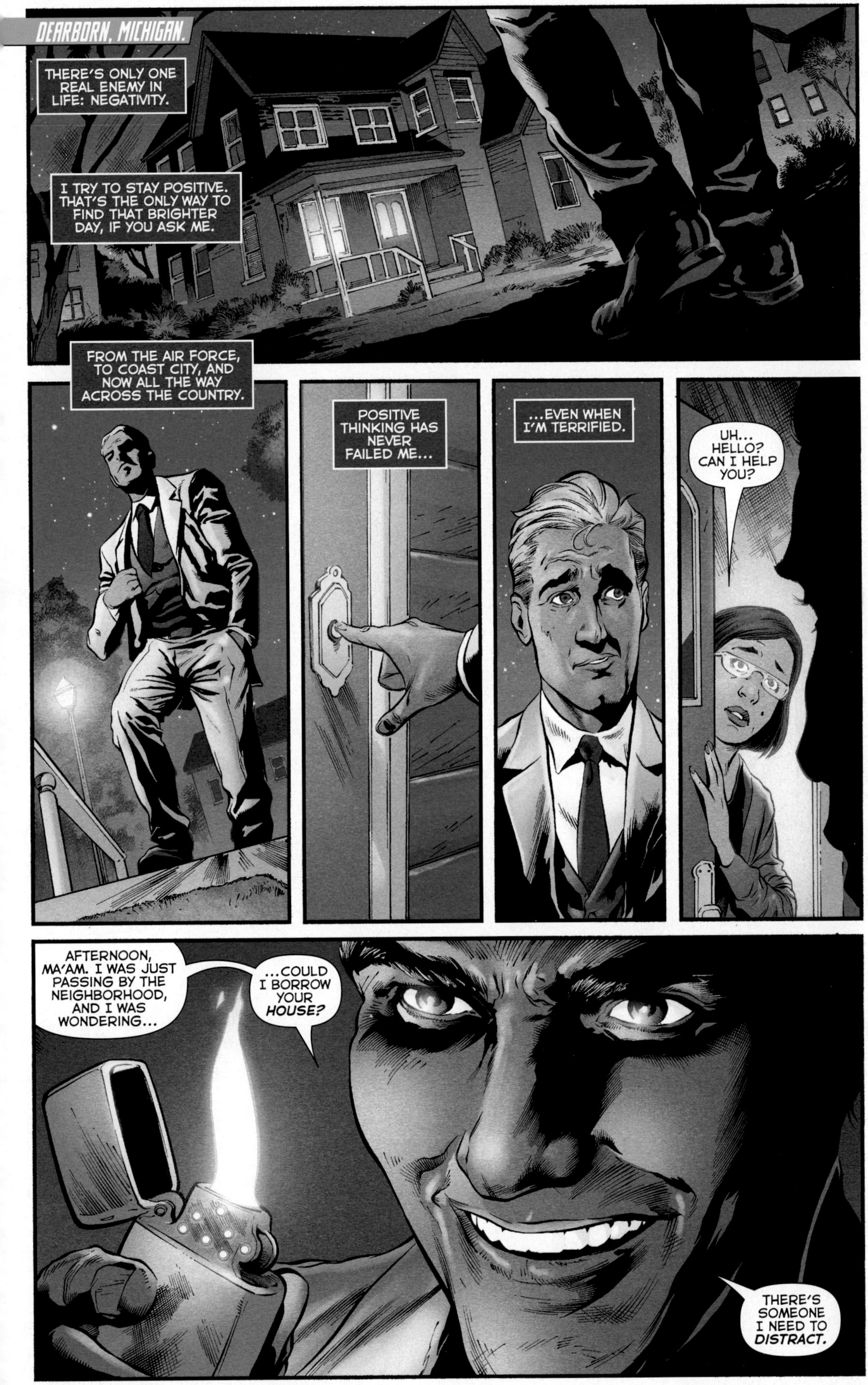
DEARBORN, MICHIGAN.
THERE'S ONLY ONE REAL ENEMY IN LIFE: NEGATIVITY.
I TRY TO STAY POSITIVE. THAT'S THE ONLY WAY TO FIND THAT BRIGHTER DAY, IF YOU ASK ME.
FROM THE AIR FORCE, TO COAST CITY, AND NOW ALL THE WAY ACROSS THE COUNTRY.
POSITIVE THINKING HAS NEVER FAILED ME...
...EVEN WHEN I'M TERRIFIED.
UH... HELLO? CAN I HELP YOU?
AFTERNOON, MA'AM. I WAS JUST PASSING BY THE NEIGHBORHOOD, AND I WAS WONDERING...
...COULD I BORROW YOUR *HOUSE?*
THERE'S SOMEONE I NEED TO *DISTRACT.*

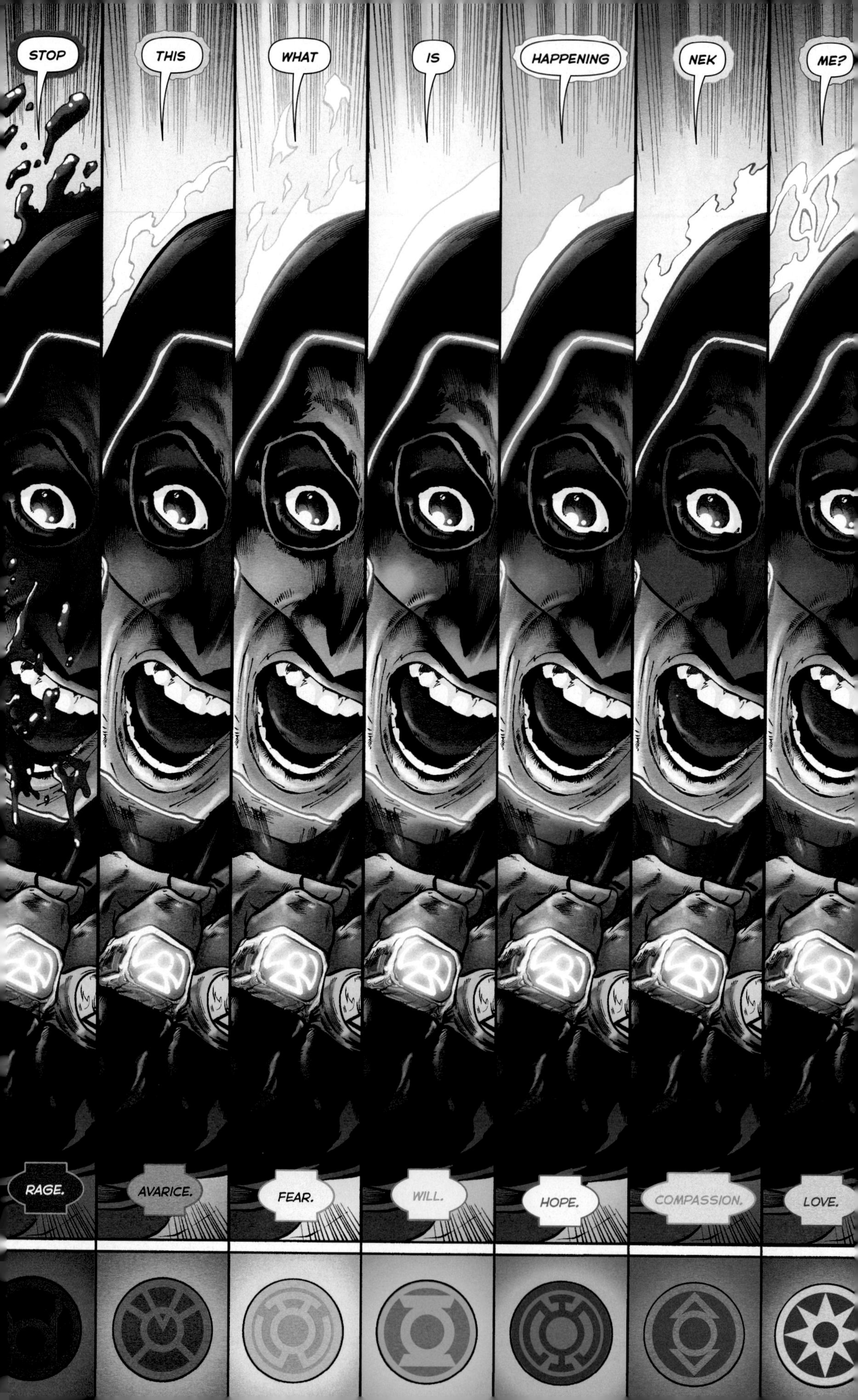
STOP
THIS
WHAT
IS
HAPPENING
NEK
ME?
RAGE.
AVARICE.
FEAR.
WILL.
HOPE.
COMPASSION.
LOVE.

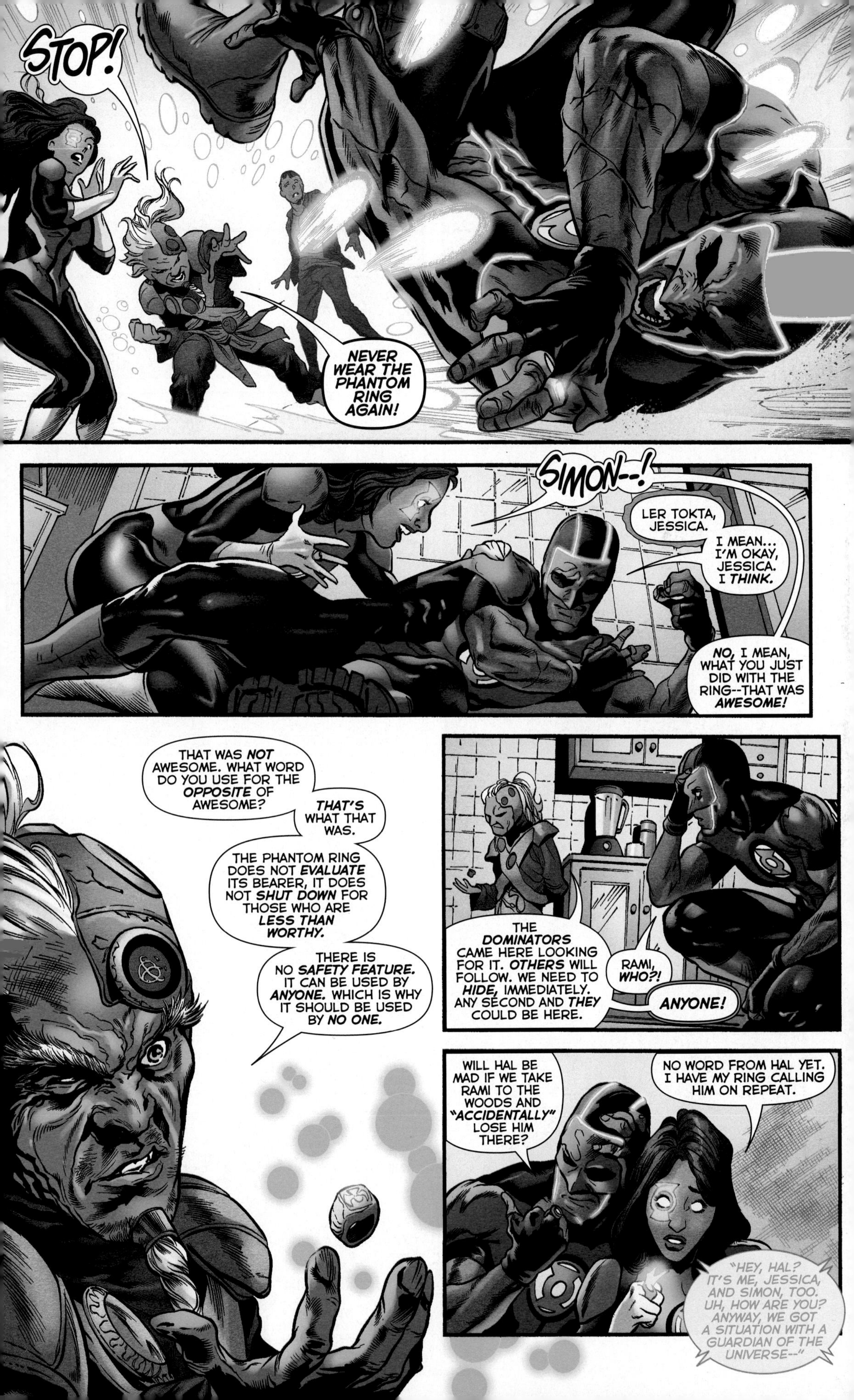
STOP!
NEVER WEAR THE PHANTOM RING AGAIN!
SIMON--!
LER TOKTA, JESSICA.
I MEAN... I'M OKAY, JESSICA. I THINK.
NO, I MEAN, WHAT YOU JUST DID WITH THE RING--THAT WAS AWESOME!
THAT WAS NOT AWESOME. WHAT WORD DO YOU USE FOR THE OPPOSITE OF AWESOME?
THAT'S WHAT THAT WAS.
THE PHANTOM RING DOES NOT EVALUATE ITS BEARER, IT DOES NOT SHUT DOWN FOR THOSE WHO ARE LESS THAN WORTHY.
THERE IS NO SAFETY FEATURE. IT CAN BE USED BY ANYONE. WHICH IS WHY IT SHOULD BE USED BY NO ONE.
THE DOMINATORS CAME HERE LOOKING FOR IT. OTHERS WILL FOLLOW. WE NEED TO HIDE, IMMEDIATELY. ANY SECOND AND THEY COULD BE HERE.
RAMI, WHO?!
ANYONE!
WILL HAL BE MAD IF WE TAKE RAMI TO THE WOODS AND "ACCIDENTALLY" LOSE HIM THERE?
NO WORD FROM HAL YET. I HAVE MY RING CALLING HIM ON REPEAT.
"HEY, HAL? IT'S ME, JESSICA, AND SIMON, TOO. UH, HOW ARE YOU? ANYWAY, WE GOT A SITUATION WITH A GUARDIAN OF THE UNIVERSE--"

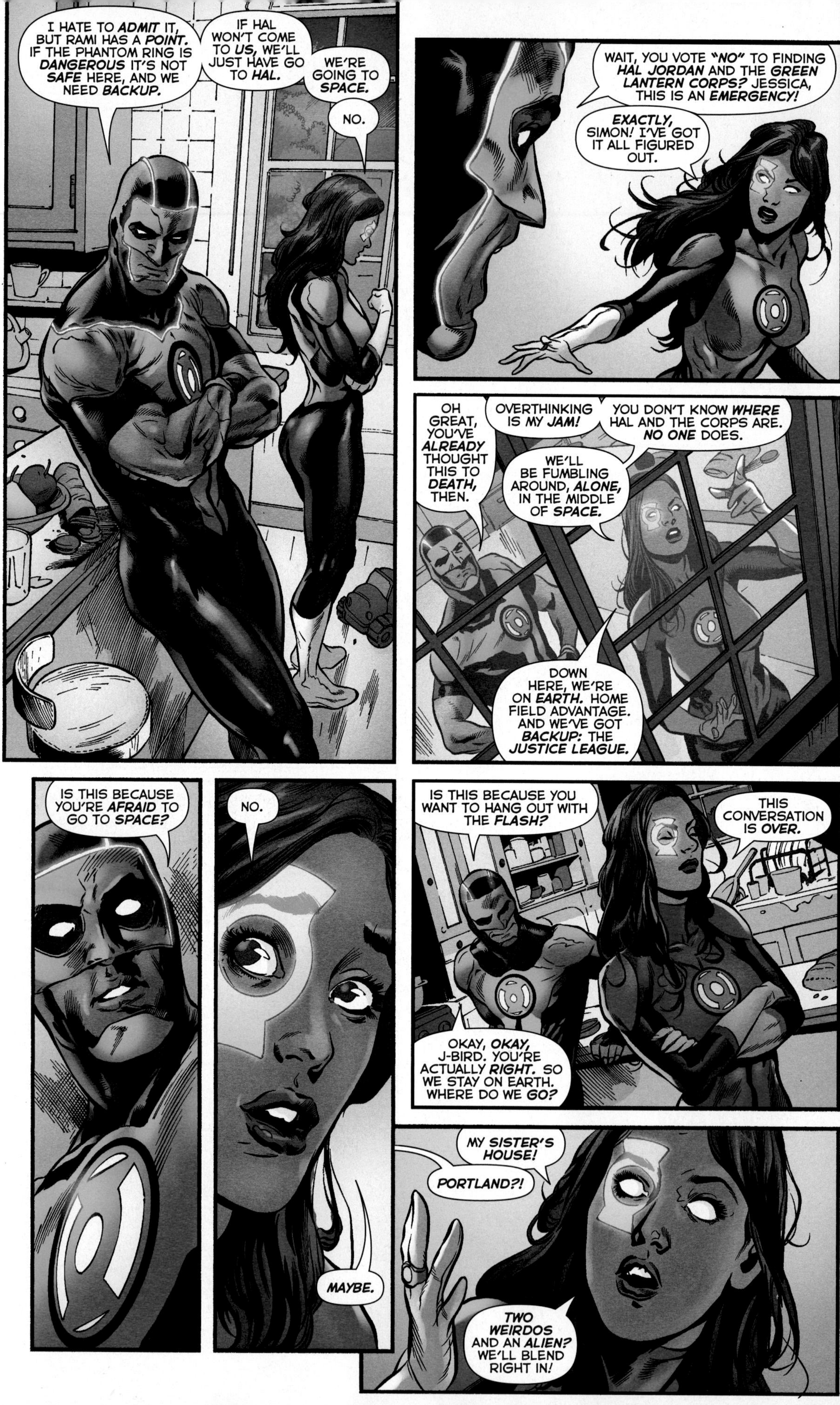
I HATE TO ADMIT IT, BUT RAMI HAS A POINT. IF THE PHANTOM RING IS DANGEROUS IT'S NOT SAFE HERE, AND WE NEED BACKUP.
IF HAL WON'T COME TO US, WE'LL JUST HAVE GO TO HAL.
WE'RE GOING TO SPACE.
NO.
WAIT, YOU VOTE "NO" TO FINDING HAL JORDAN AND THE GREEN LANTERN CORPS? JESSICA, THIS IS AN EMERGENCY!
EXACTLY, SIMON! I'VE GOT IT ALL FIGURED OUT.
OH GREAT, YOU'VE ALREADY THOUGHT THIS TO DEATH, THEN.
OVERTHINKING IS MY JAM!
YOU DON'T KNOW WHERE HAL AND THE CORPS ARE. NO ONE DOES.
WE'LL BE FUMBLING AROUND, ALONE, IN THE MIDDLE OF SPACE.
DOWN HERE, WE'RE ON EARTH. HOME FIELD ADVANTAGE. AND WE'VE GOT BACKUP: THE JUSTICE LEAGUE.
IS THIS BECAUSE YOU'RE AFRAID TO GO TO SPACE?
NO.
MAYBE.
IS THIS BECAUSE YOU WANT TO HANG OUT WITH THE FLASH?
THIS CONVERSATION IS OVER.
OKAY, OKAY, J-BIRD. YOU'RE ACTUALLY RIGHT. SO WE STAY ON EARTH. WHERE DO WE GO?
MY SISTER'S HOUSE!
PORTLAND?!
TWO WEIRDOS AND AN ALIEN? WE'LL BLEND RIGHT IN!

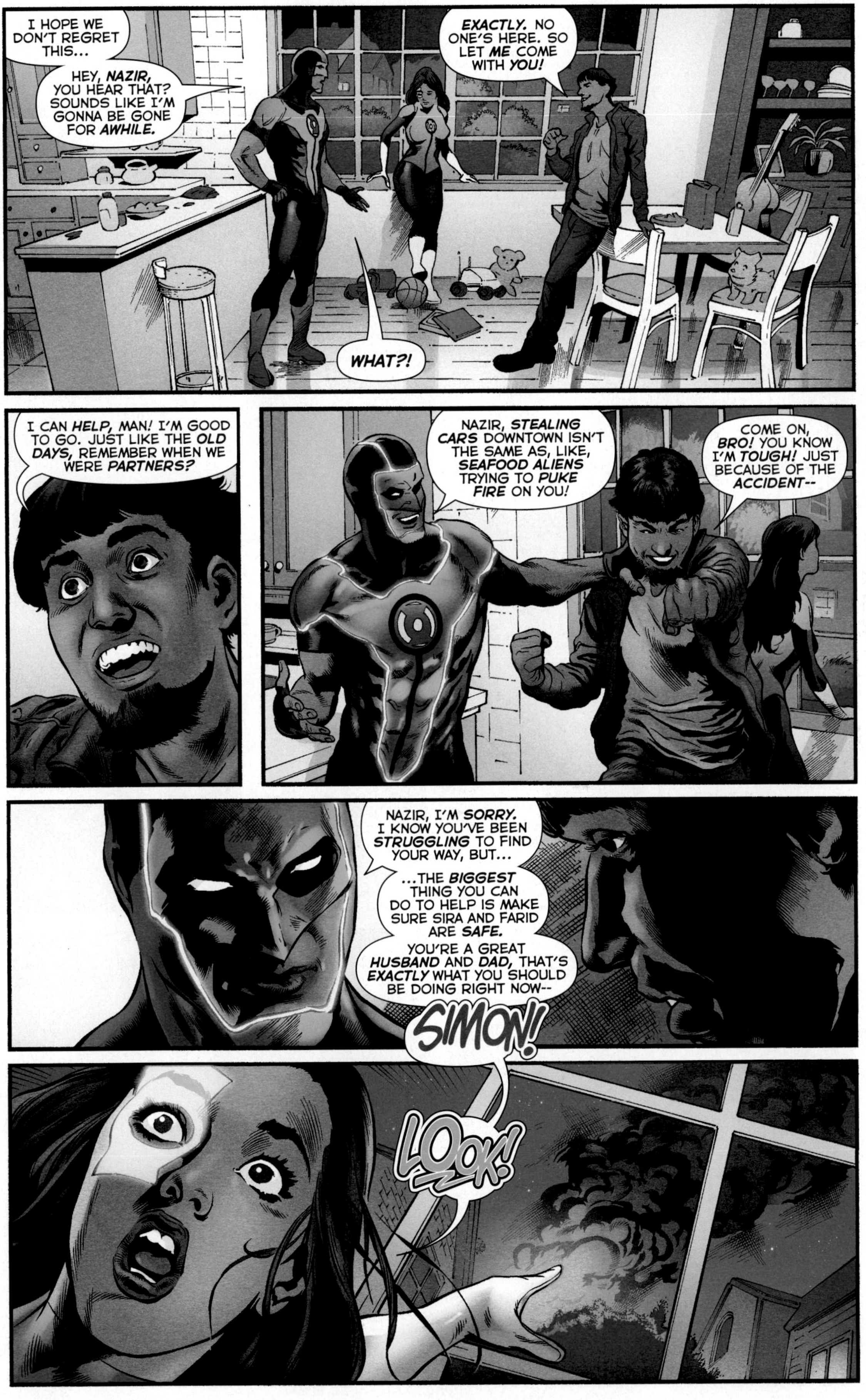
I HOPE WE DON'T REGRET THIS...
HEY, NAZIR, YOU HEAR THAT? SOUNDS LIKE I'M GONNA BE GONE FOR AWHILE.
EXACTLY. NO ONE'S HERE. SO LET ME COME WITH YOU!
WHAT?!
I CAN HELP, MAN! I'M GOOD TO GO. JUST LIKE THE OLD DAYS, REMEMBER WHEN WE WERE PARTNERS?
NAZIR, STEALING CARS DOWNTOWN ISN'T THE SAME AS, LIKE, SEAFOOD ALIENS TRYING TO PUKE FIRE ON YOU!
COME ON, BRO! YOU KNOW I'M TOUGH! JUST BECAUSE OF THE ACCIDENT--
NAZIR, I'M SORRY. I KNOW YOU'VE BEEN STRUGGLING TO FIND YOUR WAY, BUT...
...THE BIGGEST THING YOU CAN DO TO HELP IS MAKE SURE SIRA AND FARID ARE SAFE.
YOU'RE A GREAT HUSBAND AND DAD, THAT'S EXACTLY WHAT YOU SHOULD BE DOING RIGHT NOW--
SIMON!
LOOK!

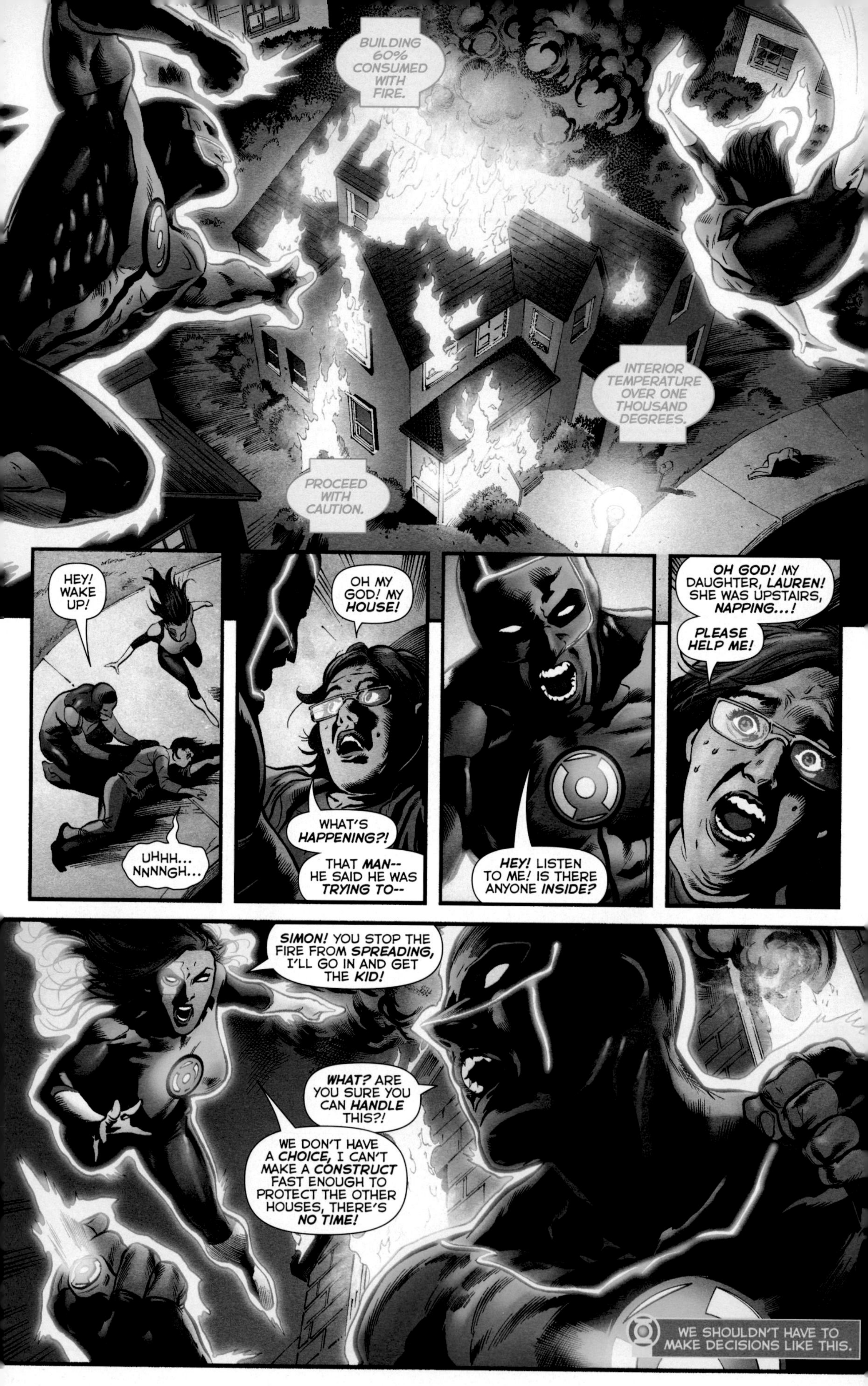
BUILDING 60% CONSUMED WITH FIRE.
INTERIOR TEMPERATURE OVER ONE THOUSAND DEGREES.
PROCEED WITH CAUTION.
HEY! WAKE UP!
UHHH... NNNNGH...
OH MY GOD! MY HOUSE!
WHAT'S HAPPENING?!
THAT MAN-- HE SAID HE WAS TRYING TO--
HEY! LISTEN TO ME! IS THERE ANYONE INSIDE?
OH GOD! MY DAUGHTER, LAUREN! SHE WAS UPSTAIRS, NAPPING...!
PLEASE HELP ME!
SIMON! YOU STOP THE FIRE FROM SPREADING, I'LL GO IN AND GET THE KID!
WHAT? ARE YOU SURE YOU CAN HANDLE THIS?!
WE DON'T HAVE A CHOICE, I CAN'T MAKE A CONSTRUCT FAST ENOUGH TO PROTECT THE OTHER HOUSES, THERE'S NO TIME!
WE SHOULDN'T HAVE TO MAKE DECISIONS LIKE THIS.

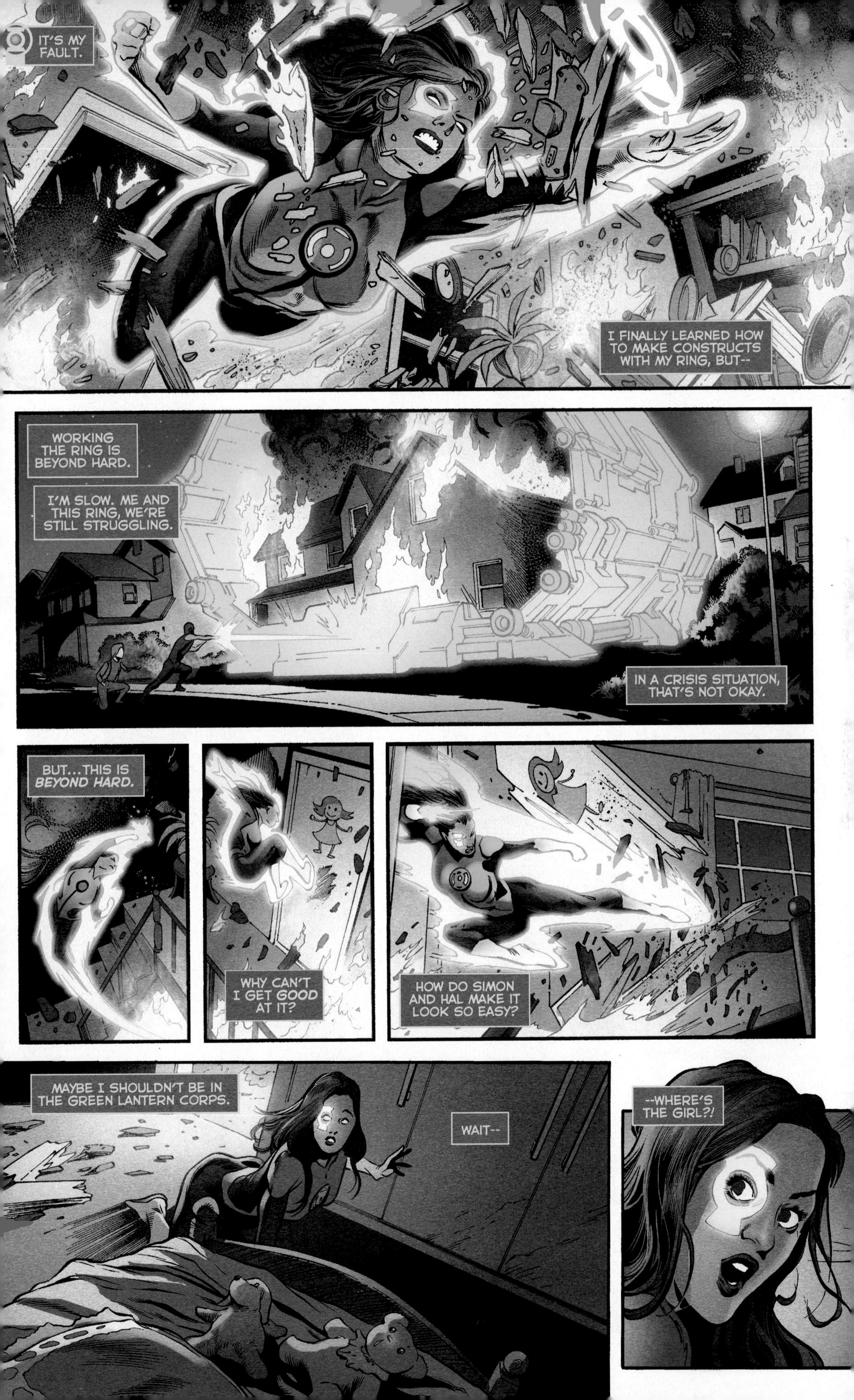
IT'S MY FAULT.
I FINALLY LEARNED HOW TO MAKE CONSTRUCTS WITH MY RING, BUT--
WORKING THE RING IS BEYOND HARD.
I'M SLOW. ME AND THIS RING, WE'RE STILL STRUGGLING.
IN A CRISIS SITUATION, THAT'S NOT OKAY.
BUT...THIS IS *BEYOND HARD.*
WHY CAN'T I GET *GOOD* AT IT?
HOW DO SIMON AND HAL MAKE IT LOOK SO EASY?
MAYBE I SHOULDN'T BE IN THE GREEN LANTERN CORPS.
WAIT--
--WHERE'S THE GIRL?!

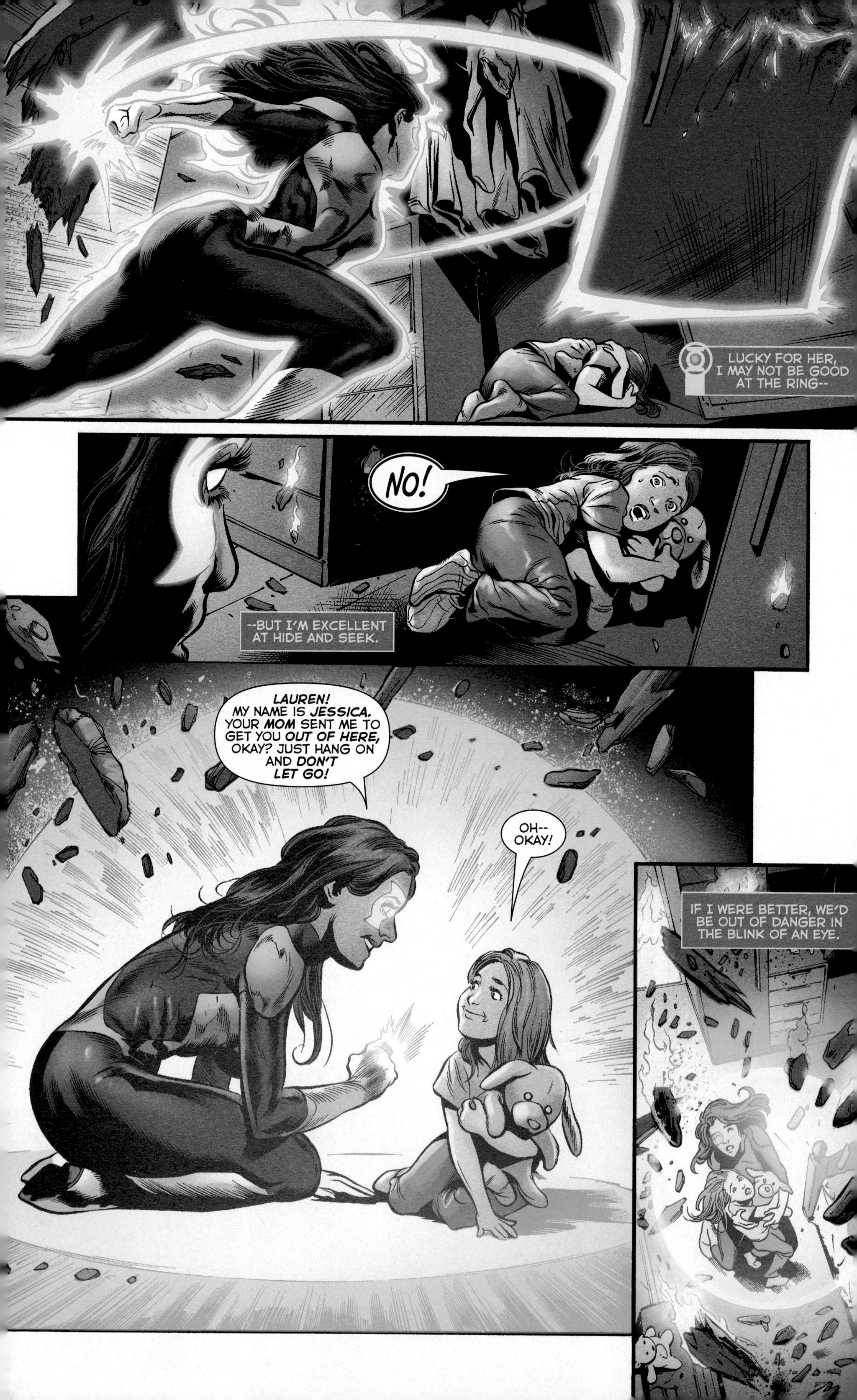
LUCKY FOR HER, I MAY NOT BE GOOD AT THE RING--
NO!
--BUT I'M EXCELLENT AT HIDE AND SEEK.
LAUREN! MY NAME IS JESSICA. YOUR MOM SENT ME TO GET YOU OUT OF HERE, OKAY? JUST HANG ON AND DON'T LET GO!
OH-- OKAY!
IF I WERE BETTER, WE'D BE OUT OF DANGER IN THE BLINK OF AN EYE.

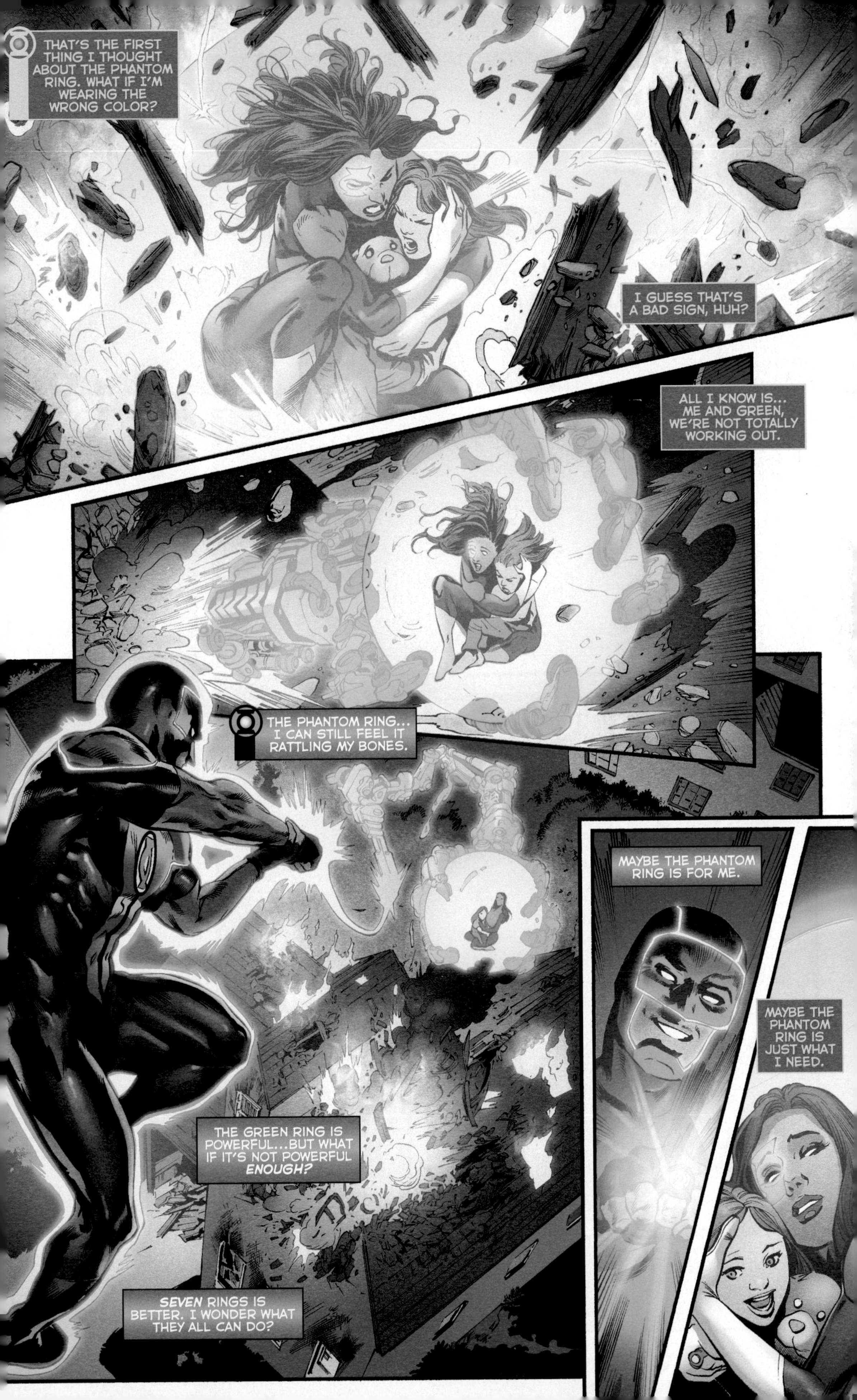
THAT'S THE FIRST THING I THOUGHT ABOUT THE PHANTOM RING. WHAT IF I'M WEARING THE WRONG COLOR?
I GUESS THAT'S A BAD SIGN, HUH?
ALL I KNOW IS... ME AND GREEN, WE'RE NOT TOTALLY WORKING OUT.
THE PHANTOM RING... I CAN STILL FEEL IT RATTLING MY BONES.
MAYBE THE PHANTOM RING IS FOR ME.
MAYBE THE PHANTOM RING IS JUST WHAT I NEED.
THE GREEN RING IS POWERFUL...BUT WHAT IF IT'S NOT POWERFUL *ENOUGH?*
SEVEN RINGS IS BETTER. I WONDER WHAT THEY ALL CAN DO?

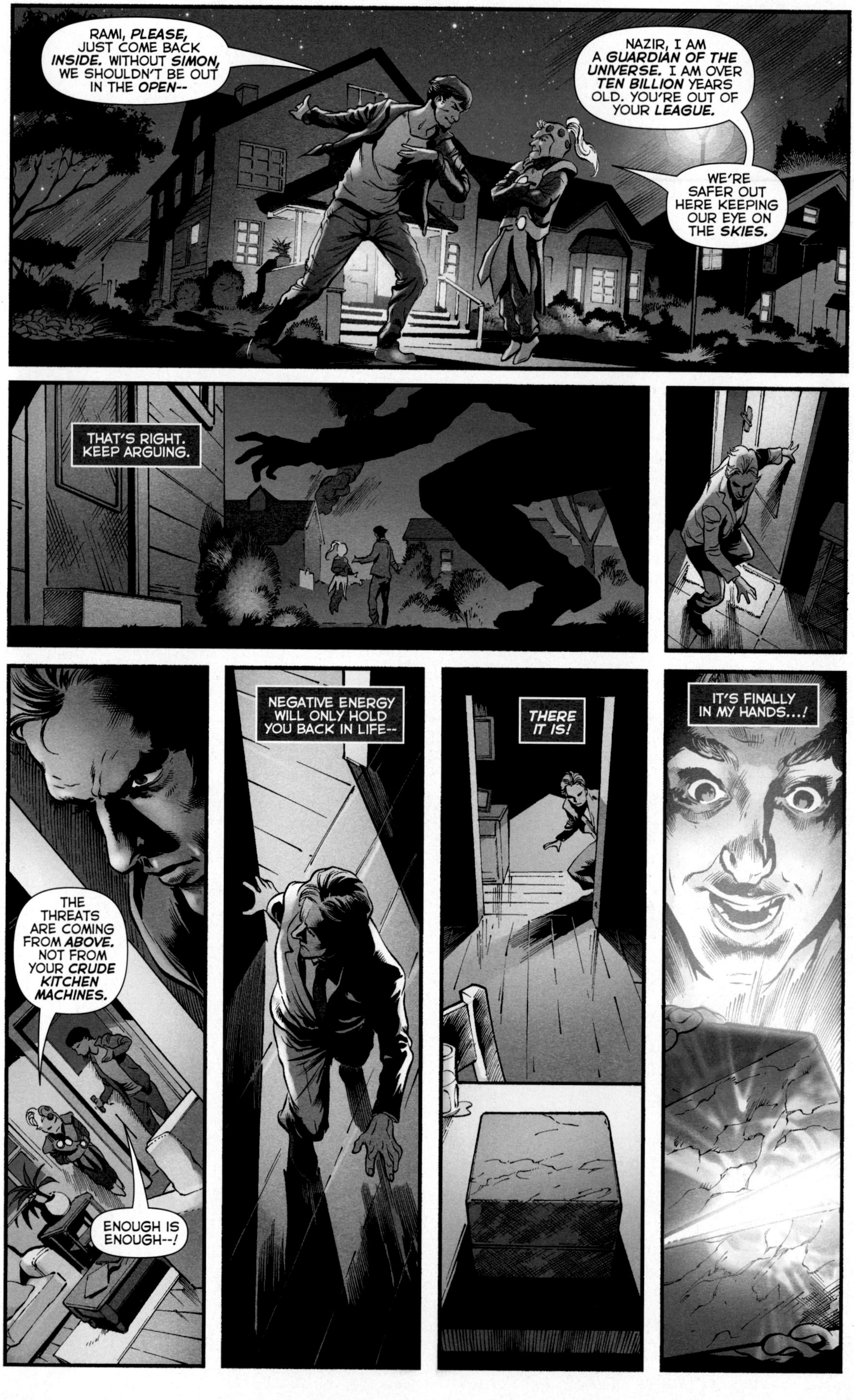
RAMI, PLEASE, JUST COME BACK INSIDE. WITHOUT SIMON, WE SHOULDN'T BE OUT IN THE OPEN--
NAZIR, I AM A GUARDIAN OF THE UNIVERSE. I AM OVER TEN BILLION YEARS OLD. YOU'RE OUT OF YOUR LEAGUE.
WE'RE SAFER OUT HERE KEEPING OUR EYE ON THE SKIES.
THAT'S RIGHT. KEEP ARGUING.
THE THREATS ARE COMING FROM ABOVE. NOT FROM YOUR CRUDE KITCHEN MACHINES.
ENOUGH IS ENOUGH--!
NEGATIVE ENERGY WILL ONLY HOLD YOU BACK IN LIFE--
THERE IT IS!
IT'S FINALLY IN MY HANDS...!

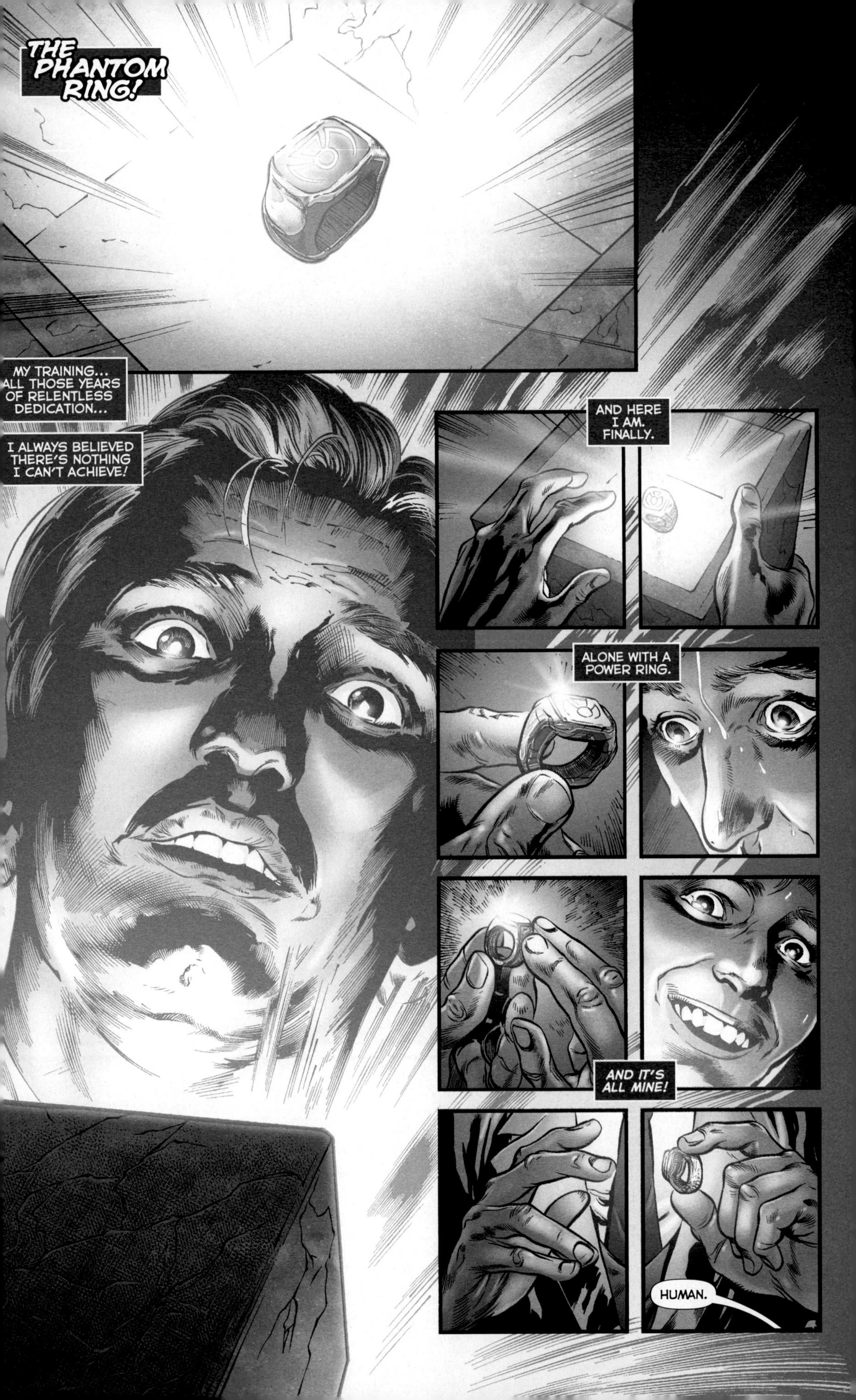
THE PHANTOM RING!
MY TRAINING... ALL THOSE YEARS OF RELENTLESS DEDICATION...
I ALWAYS BELIEVED THERE'S NOTHING I CAN'T ACHIEVE!
AND HERE I AM. FINALLY.
ALONE WITH A POWER RING.
AND IT'S ALL MINE!
HUMAN.

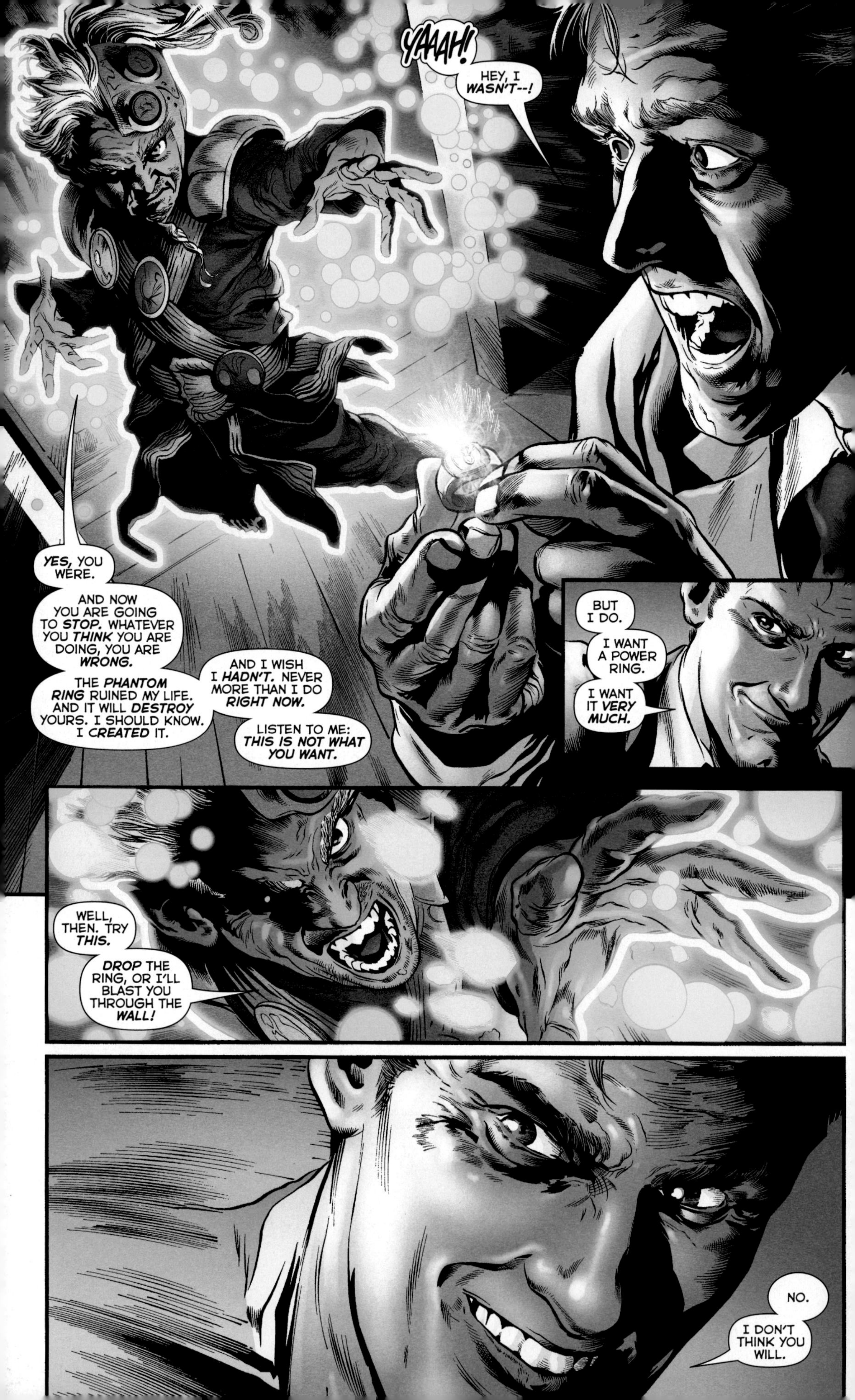

YAAAH!
HEY, I WASN'T--!
YES, YOU WERE.
AND NOW YOU ARE GOING TO STOP. WHATEVER YOU THINK YOU ARE DOING, YOU ARE WRONG.
THE PHANTOM RING RUINED MY LIFE. AND IT WILL DESTROY YOURS. I SHOULD KNOW. I CREATED IT.
AND I WISH I HADN'T. NEVER MORE THAN I DO RIGHT NOW.
LISTEN TO ME: THIS IS NOT WHAT YOU WANT.
BUT I DO.
I WANT A POWER RING.
I WANT IT VERY MUCH.
WELL, THEN. TRY THIS.
DROP THE RING, OR I'LL BLAST YOU THROUGH THE WALL!
NO.
I DON'T THINK YOU WILL.

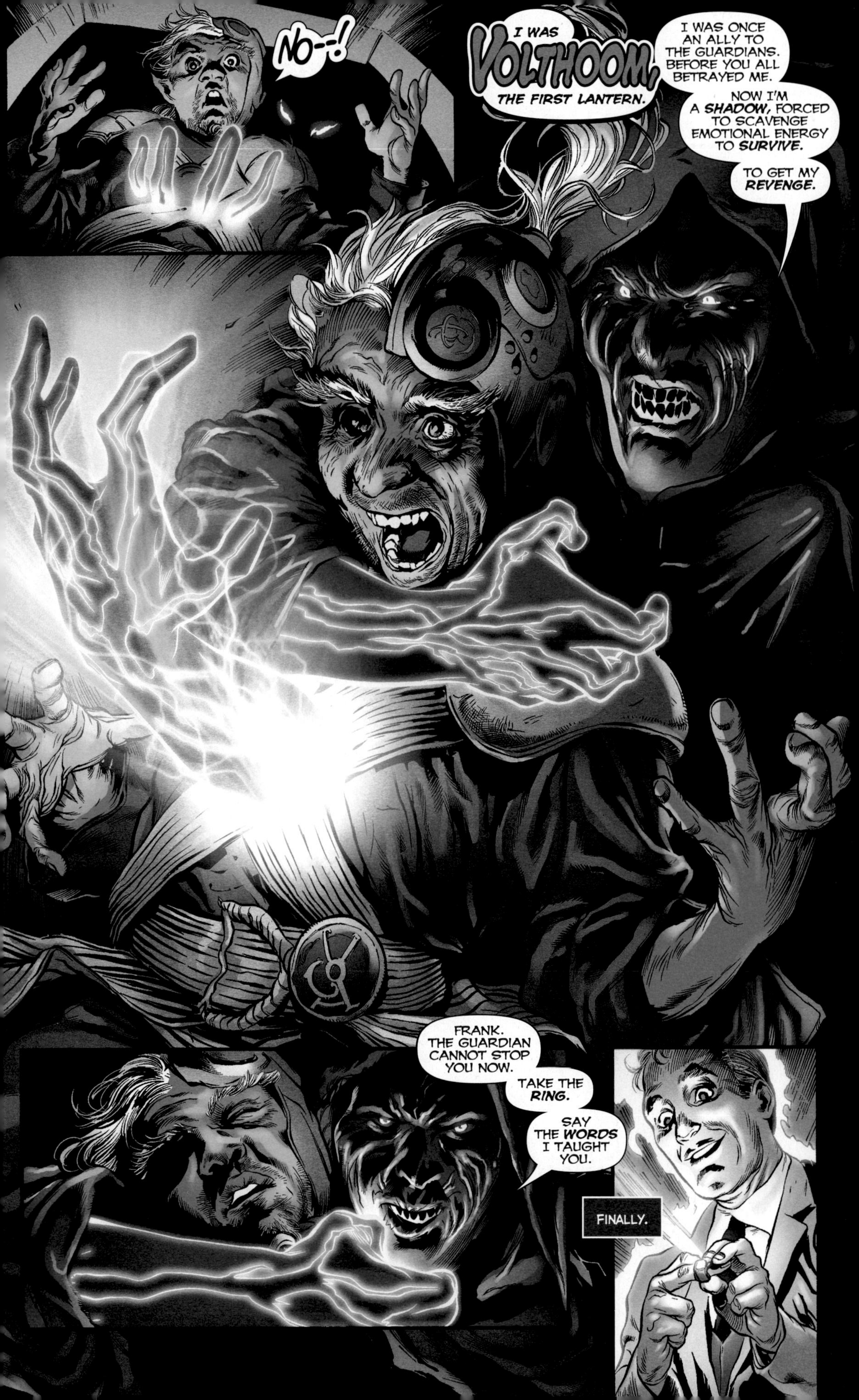
NO--!
I WAS VOLTHOOM, THE FIRST LANTERN.
I WAS ONCE AN ALLY TO THE GUARDIANS. BEFORE YOU ALL BETRAYED ME.
NOW I'M A SHADOW, FORCED TO SCAVENGE EMOTIONAL ENERGY TO SURVIVE.
TO GET MY REVENGE.
FRANK. THE GUARDIAN CANNOT STOP YOU NOW.
TAKE THE RING.
SAY THE WORDS I TAUGHT YOU.
FINALLY.

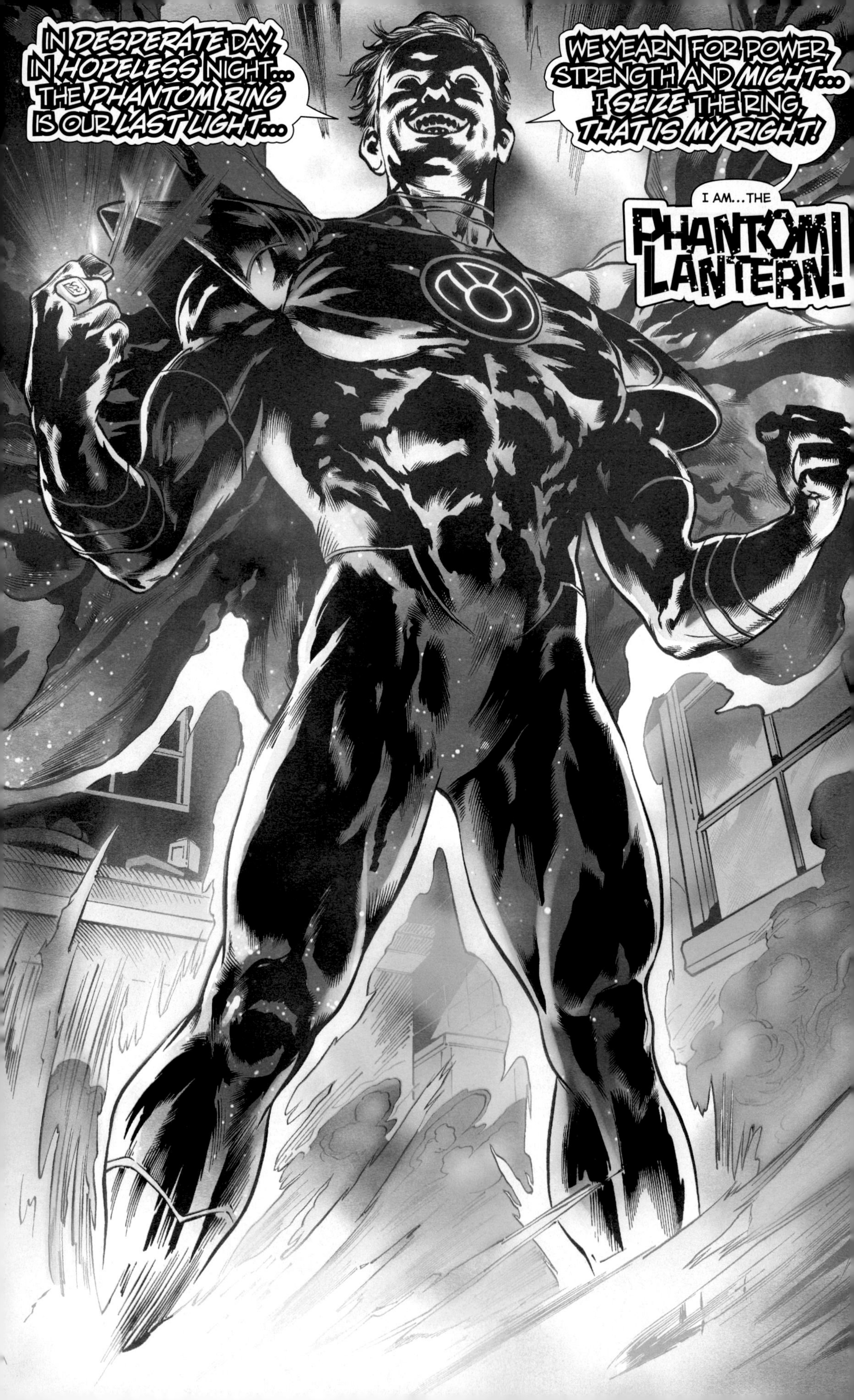
IN DESPERATE DAY, IN HOPELESS NIGHT... THE PHANTOM RING IS OUR LAST LIGHT...
WE YEARN FOR POWER, STRENGTH AND MIGHT... I SEIZE THE RING, THAT IS MY RIGHT!
I AM...THE
PHANTOM LANTERN!

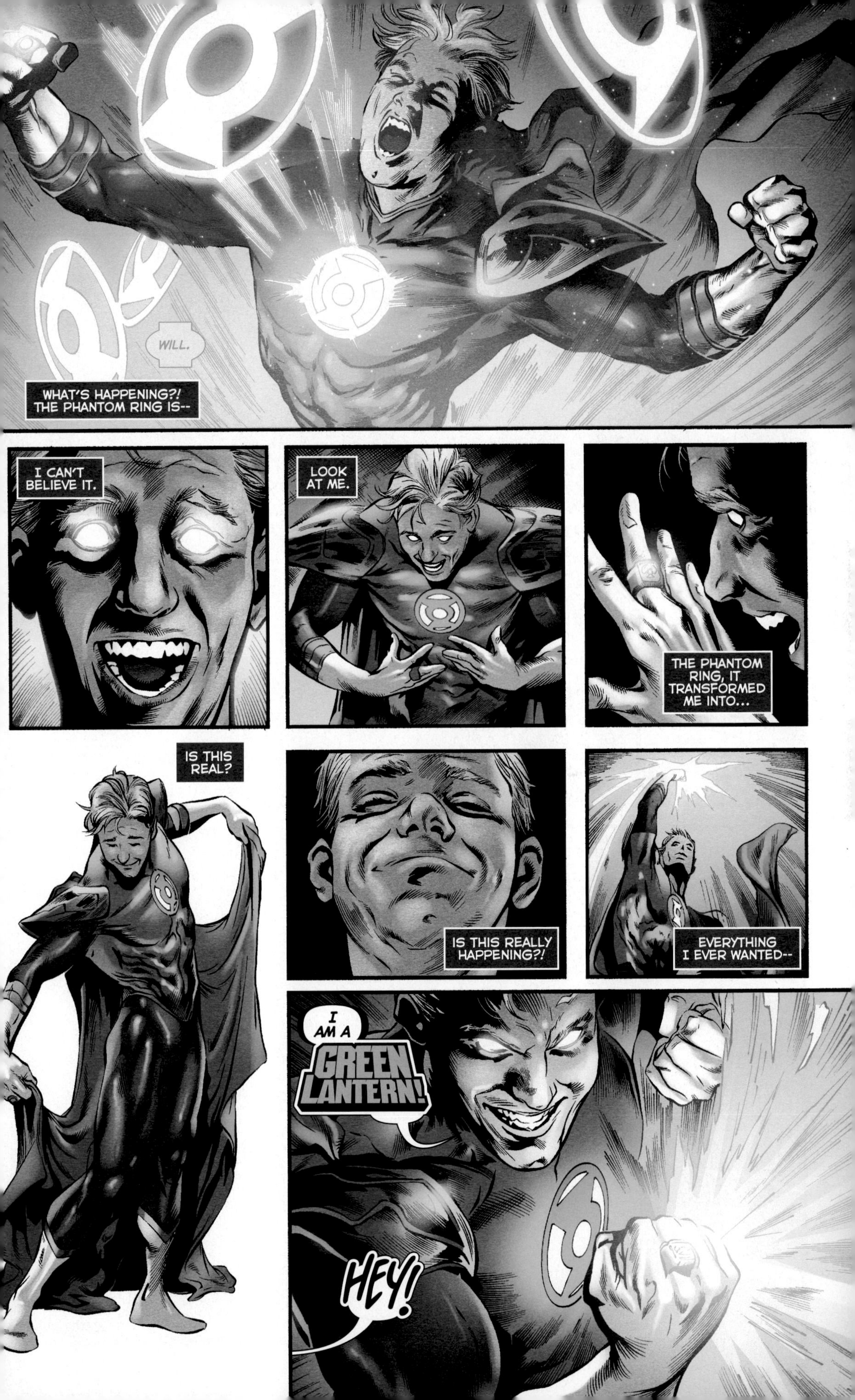
WILL.
WHAT'S HAPPENING?! THE PHANTOM RING IS--
I CAN'T BELIEVE IT.
LOOK AT ME.
THE PHANTOM RING, IT TRANSFORMED ME INTO...
IS THIS REAL?
IS THIS REALLY HAPPENING?!
EVERYTHING I EVER WANTED--
I AM A GREEN LANTERN!
HEY!

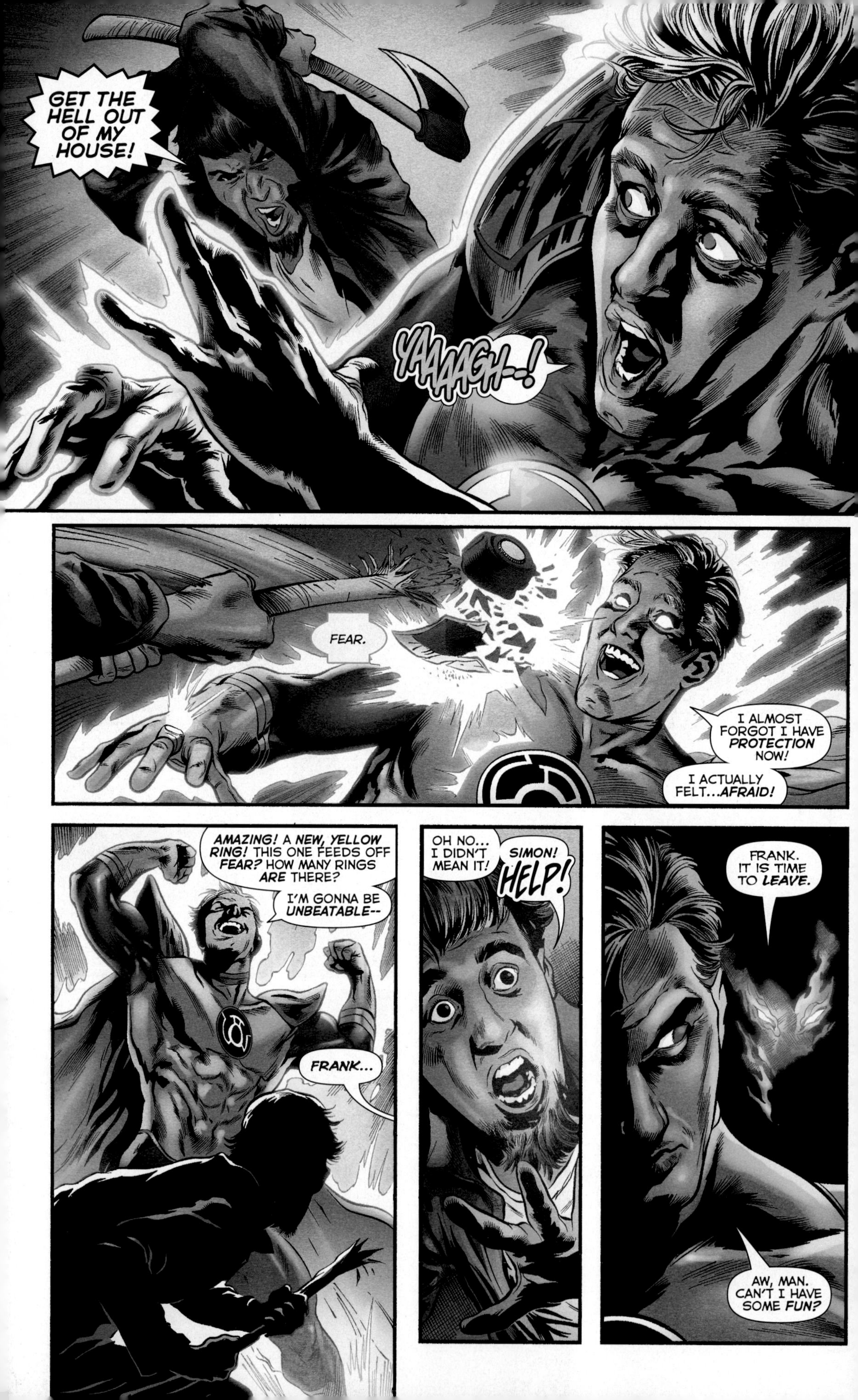
GET THE HELL OUT OF MY HOUSE!
YAAAAGH--!
FEAR.
I ALMOST FORGOT I HAVE *PROTECTION* NOW!
I ACTUALLY FELT...*AFRAID!*
AMAZING! A *NEW, YELLOW RING!* THIS ONE FEEDS OFF *FEAR?* HOW MANY RINGS *ARE* THERE?
I'M GONNA BE *UNBEATABLE*--
FRANK...
OH NO... I DIDN'T MEAN IT!
SIMON!
HELP!
FRANK. IT IS TIME TO *LEAVE.*
AW, MAN. CAN'T I HAVE SOME *FUN?*

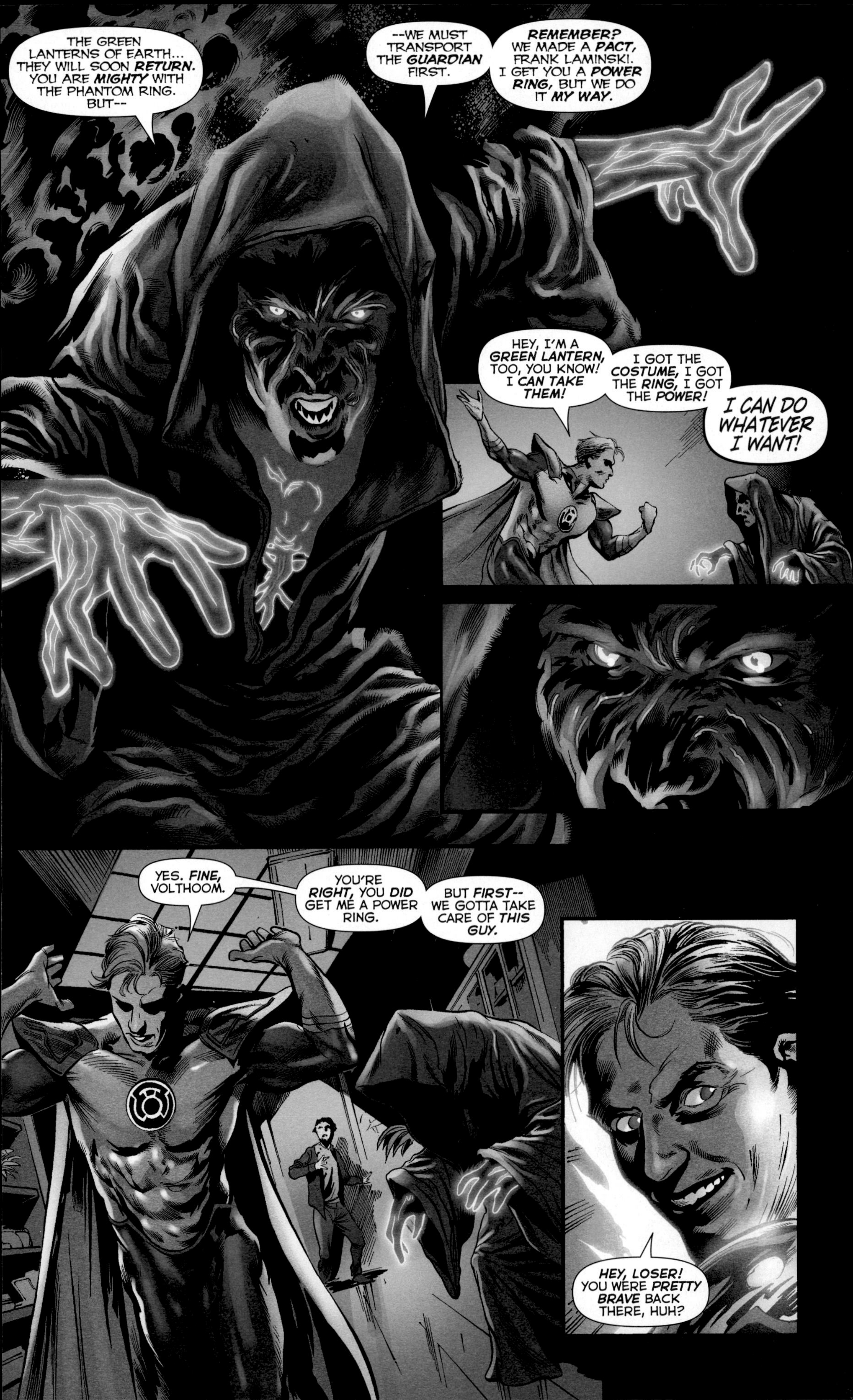
THE GREEN LANTERNS OF EARTH... THEY WILL SOON RETURN. YOU ARE MIGHTY WITH THE PHANTOM RING. BUT--
--WE MUST TRANSPORT THE GUARDIAN FIRST.
REMEMBER? WE MADE A PACT, FRANK LAMINSKI. I GET YOU A POWER RING, BUT WE DO IT MY WAY.
HEY, I'M A GREEN LANTERN, TOO, YOU KNOW! I CAN TAKE THEM!
I GOT THE COSTUME, I GOT THE RING, I GOT THE POWER!
I CAN DO WHATEVER I WANT!
YES. FINE, VOLTHOOM.
YOU'RE RIGHT, YOU DID GET ME A POWER RING.
BUT FIRST-- WE GOTTA TAKE CARE OF THIS GUY.
HEY, LOSER! YOU WERE PRETTY BRAVE BACK THERE, HUH?

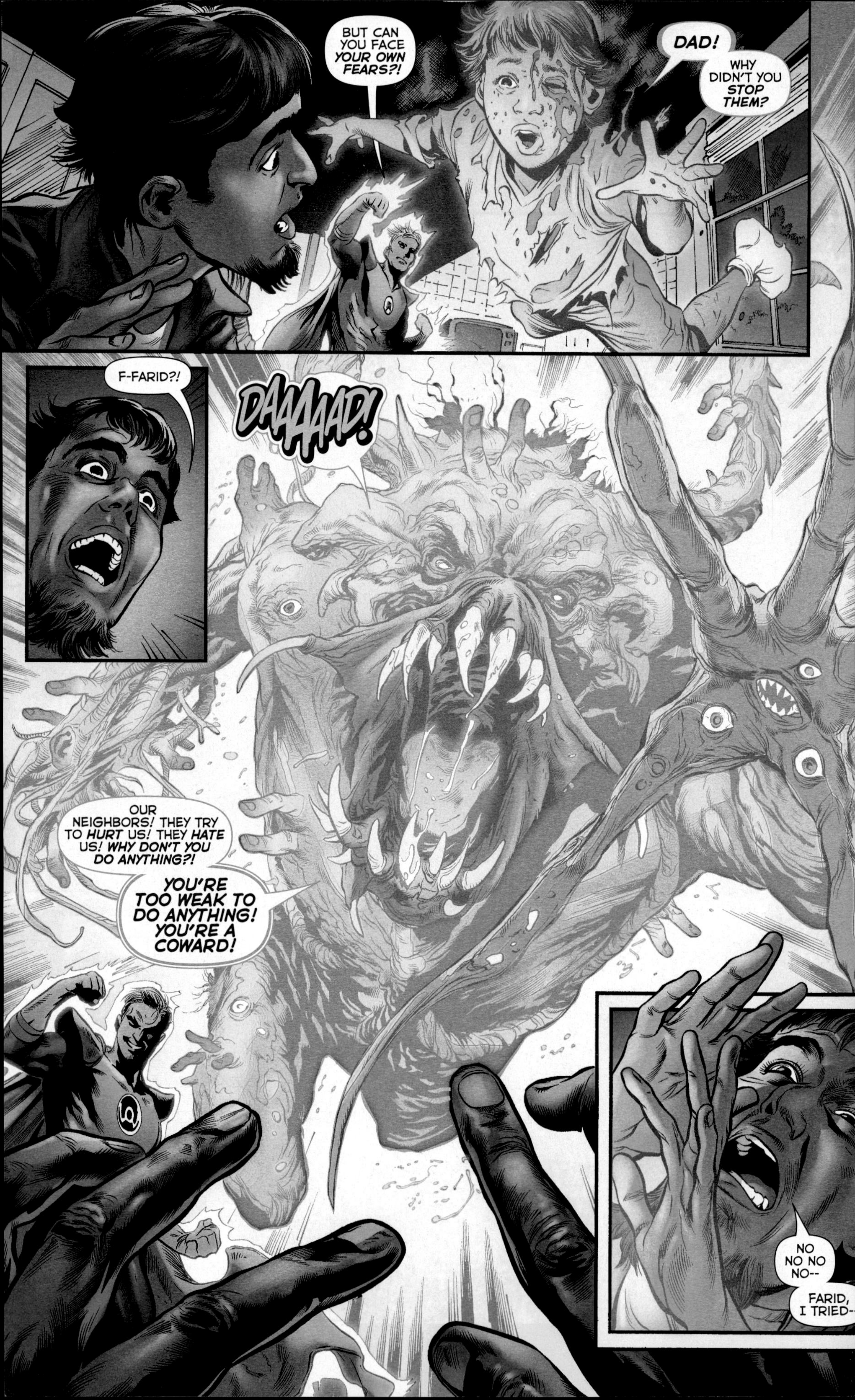
BUT CAN YOU FACE YOUR OWN FEARS?!
DAD!
WHY DIDN'T YOU STOP THEM?
F-FARID?!
DAAAAAD!
OUR NEIGHBORS! THEY TRY TO HURT US! THEY HATE US! WHY DON'T YOU DO ANYTHING?!
YOU'RE TOO WEAK TO DO ANYTHING! YOU'RE A COWARD!
NO NO NO NO--
FARID, I TRIED--

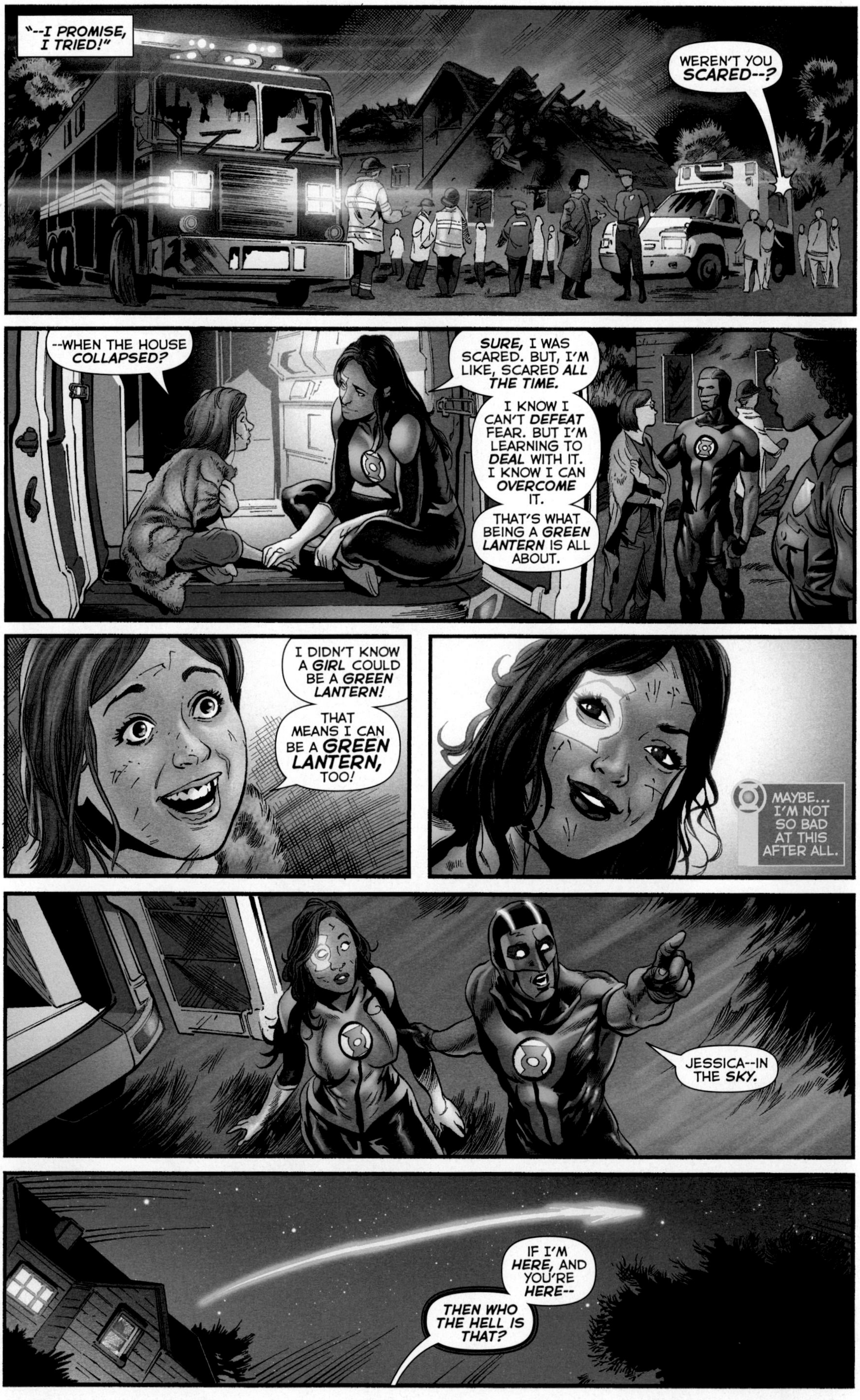
"--I PROMISE, I TRIED!"
WEREN'T YOU SCARED--?
--WHEN THE HOUSE COLLAPSED?
SURE, I WAS SCARED. BUT, I'M LIKE, SCARED ALL THE TIME.
I KNOW I CAN'T DEFEAT FEAR. BUT I'M LEARNING TO DEAL WITH IT. I KNOW I CAN OVERCOME IT.
THAT'S WHAT BEING A GREEN LANTERN IS ALL ABOUT.
I DIDN'T KNOW A GIRL COULD BE A GREEN LANTERN!
THAT MEANS I CAN BE A GREEN LANTERN, TOO!
MAYBE... I'M NOT SO BAD AT THIS AFTER ALL.
JESSICA--IN THE SKY.
IF I'M HERE, AND YOU'RE HERE--
THEN WHO THE HELL IS THAT?

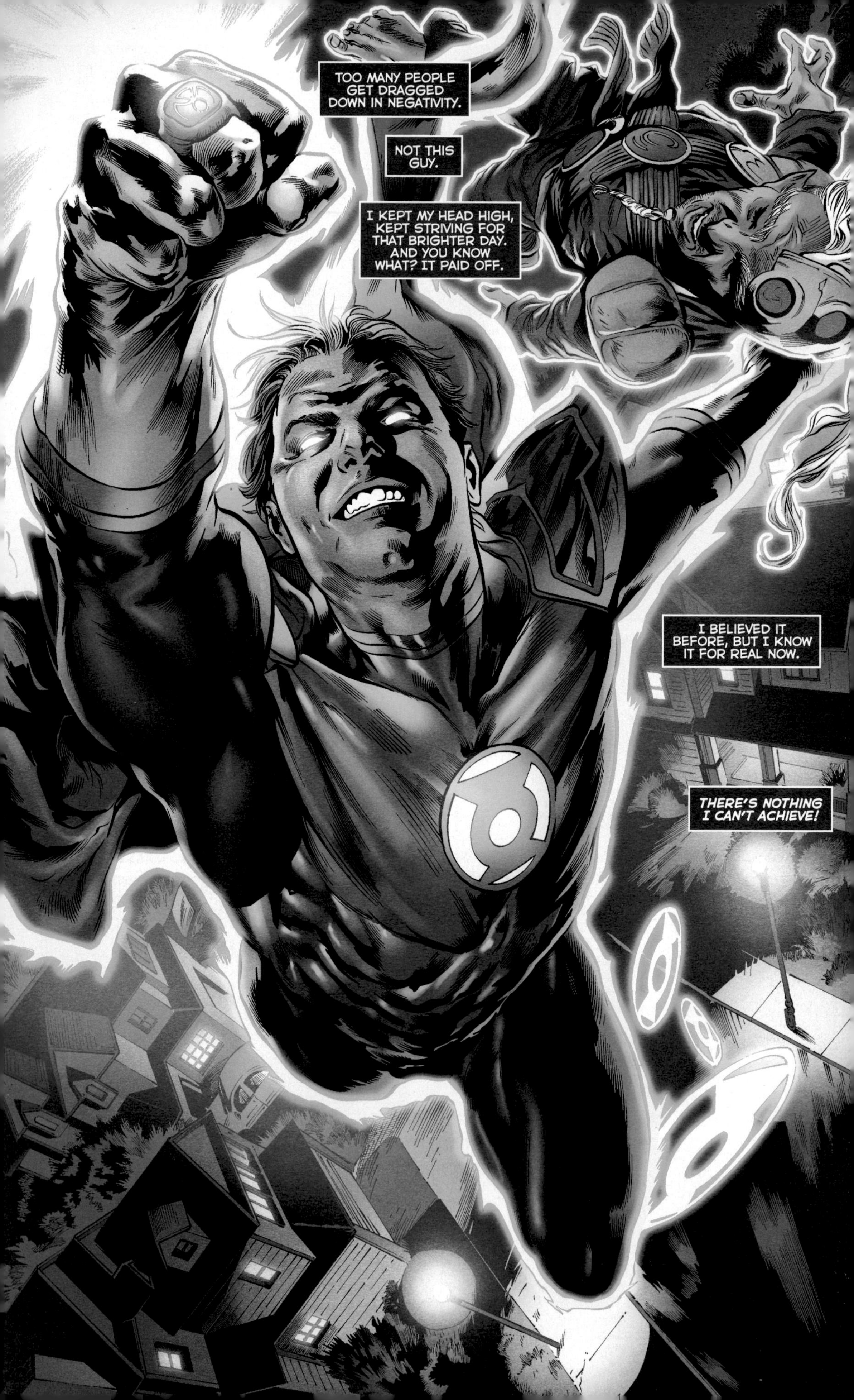
TOO MANY PEOPLE GET DRAGGED DOWN IN NEGATIVITY.
NOT THIS GUY.
I KEPT MY HEAD HIGH, KEPT STRIVING FOR THAT BRIGHTER DAY. AND YOU KNOW WHAT? IT PAID OFF.
I BELIEVED IT BEFORE, BUT I KNOW IT FOR REAL NOW.
THERE'S NOTHING I CAN'T ACHIEVE!

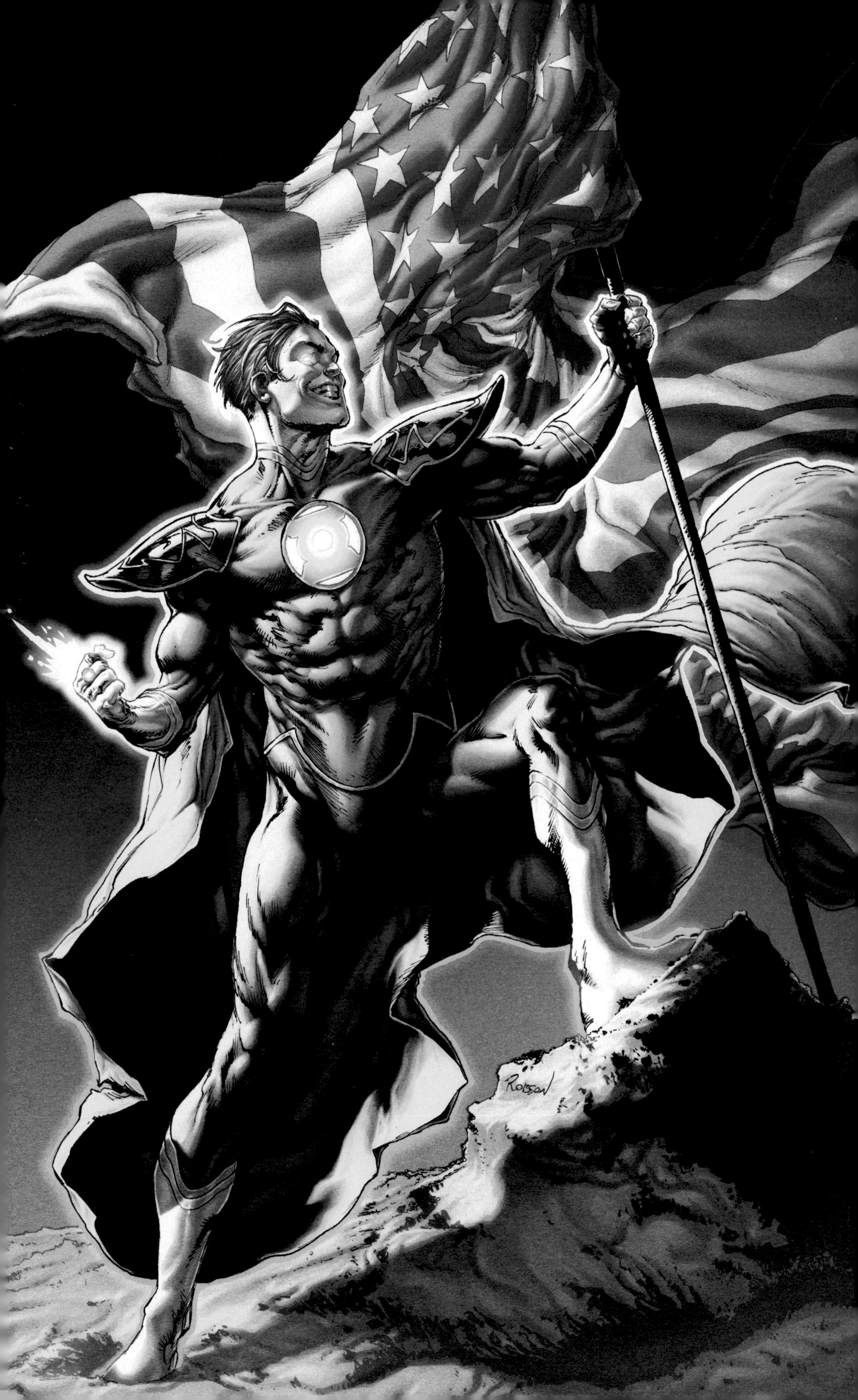
ROBSON

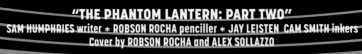

"THE PHANTOM LANTERN: PART TWO"

SAM HUMPHRIES writer * ROBSON ROCHA penciller * JAY LEISTEN CAM SMITH inkers

Cover by ROBSON ROCHA and ALEX SOLLAZZO

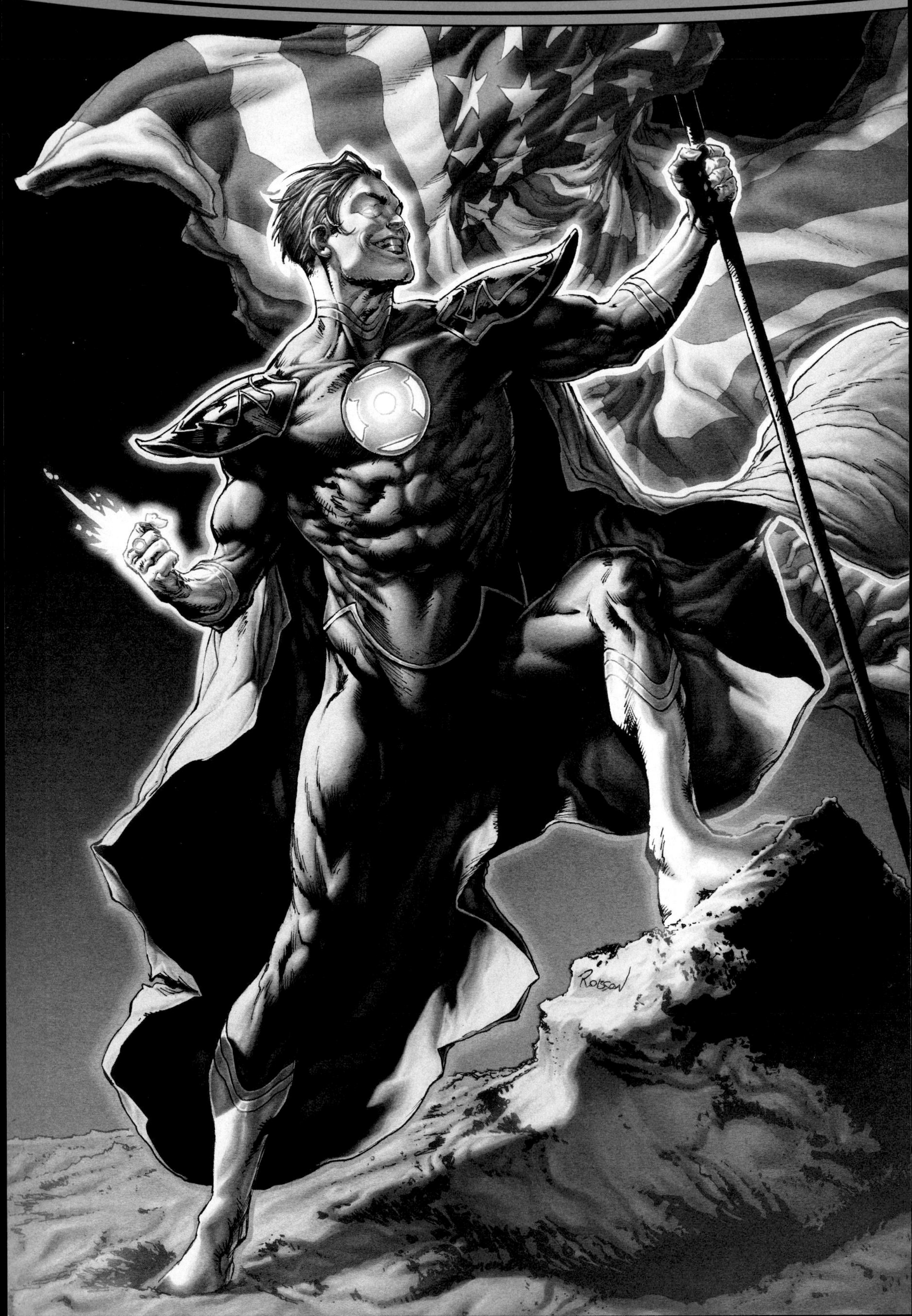
ROBSON

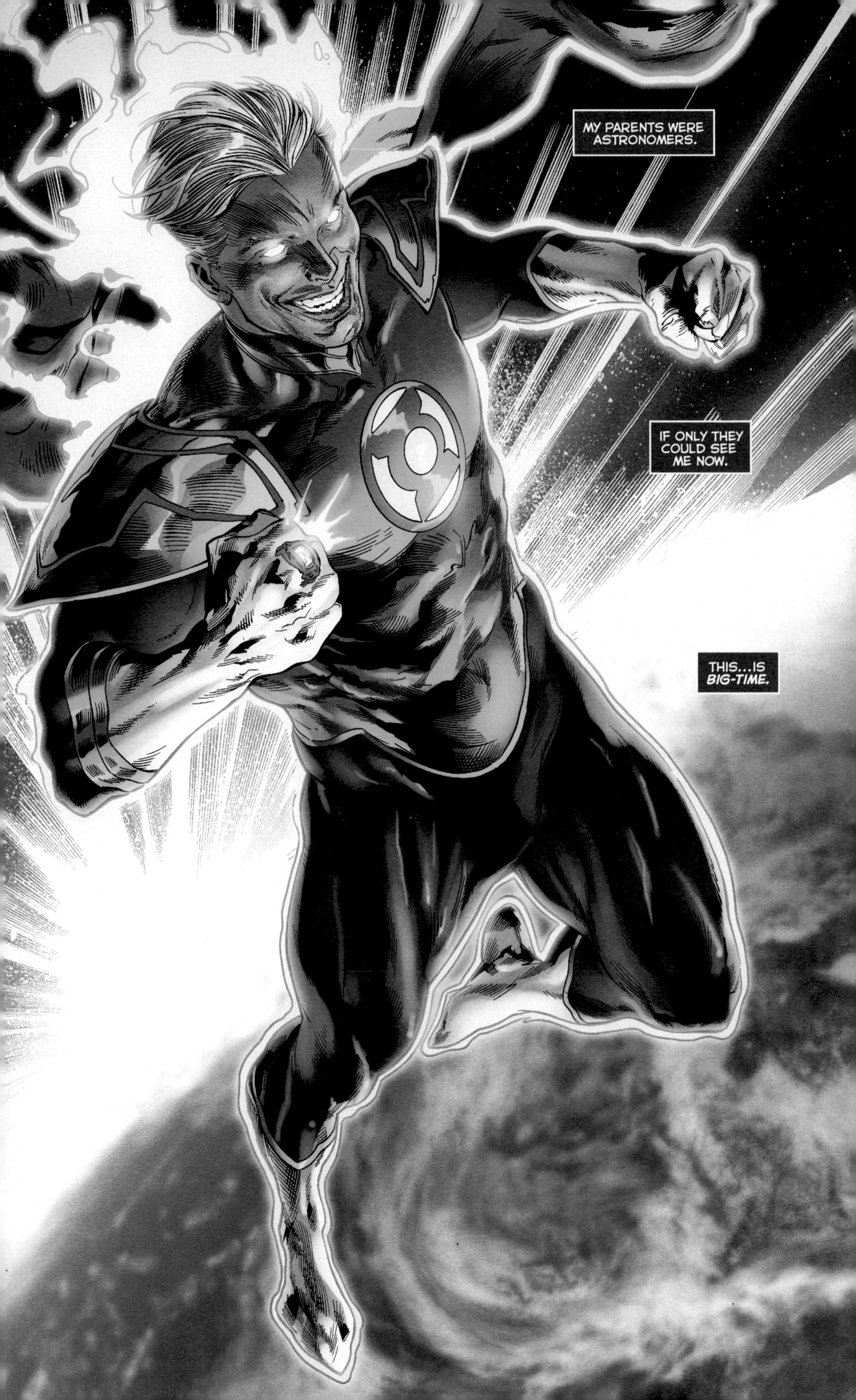
MY PARENTS WERE ASTRONOMERS.
IF ONLY THEY COULD SEE ME NOW.
THIS...IS *BIG-TIME.*

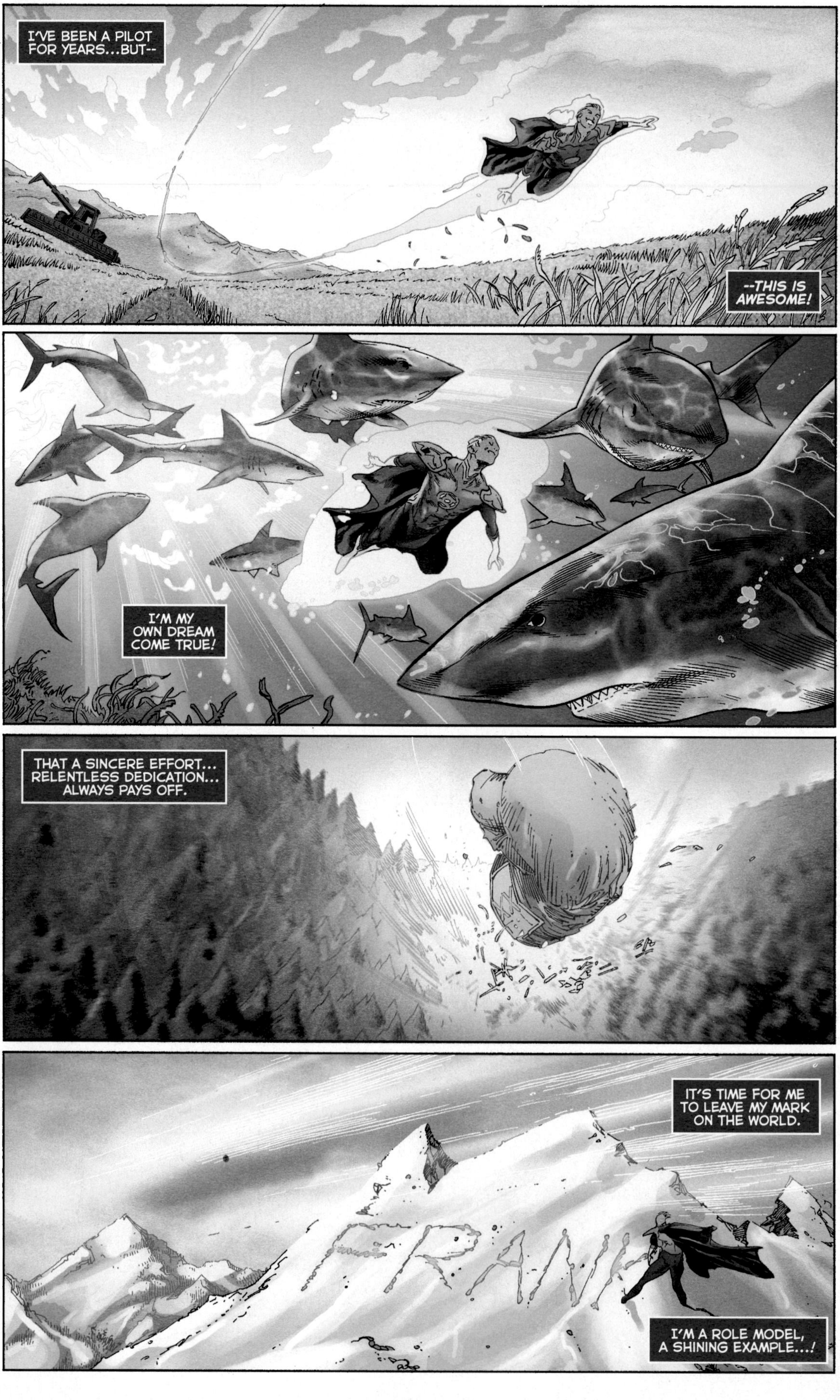
I'VE BEEN A PILOT FOR YEARS...BUT--
--THIS IS AWESOME!
I'M MY OWN DREAM COME TRUE!
THAT A SINCERE EFFORT... RELENTLESS DEDICATION... ALWAYS PAYS OFF.
IT'S TIME FOR ME TO LEAVE MY MARK ON THE WORLD.
I'M A ROLE MODEL, A SHINING EXAMPLE...!

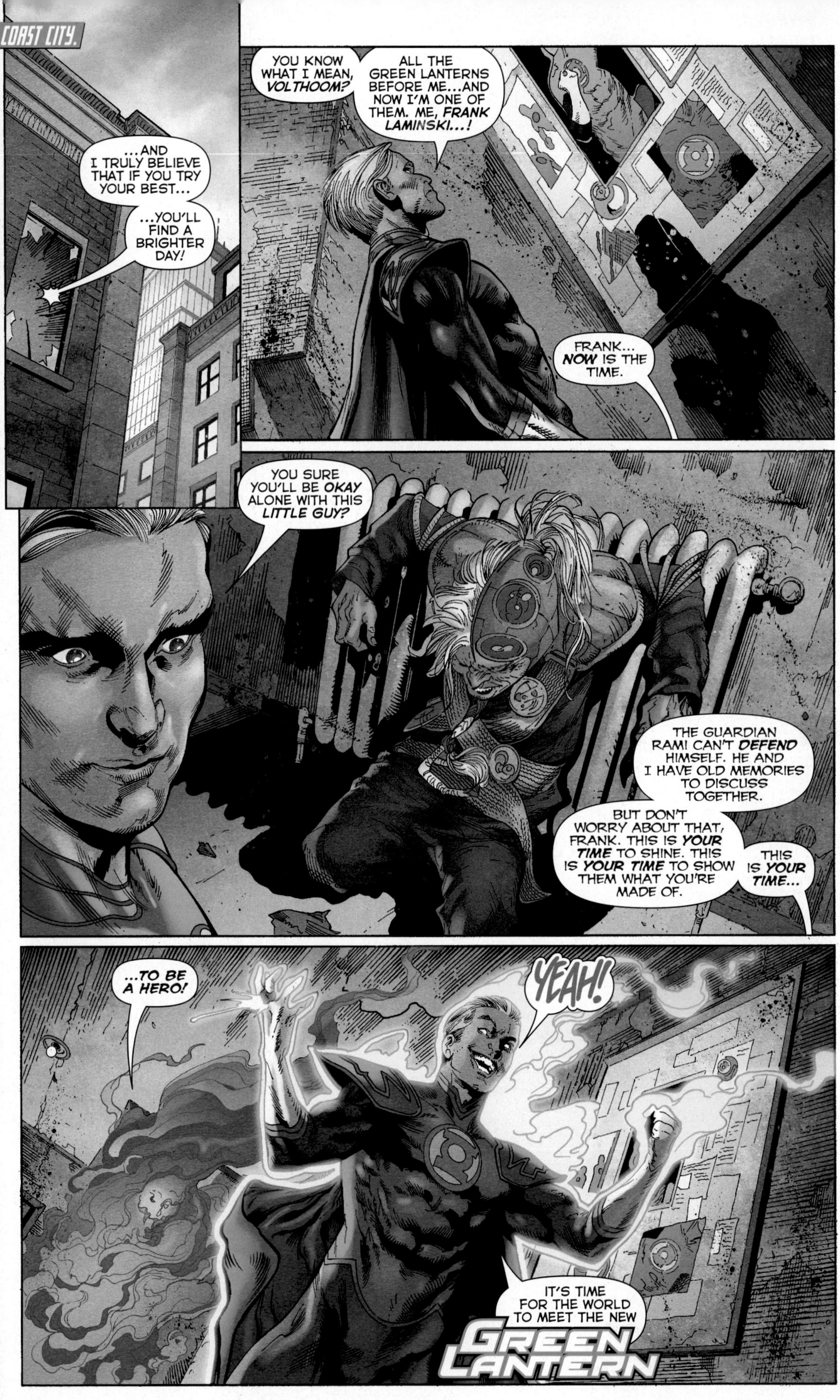
COAST CITY.
...AND I TRULY BELIEVE THAT IF YOU TRY YOUR BEST...
...YOU'LL FIND A BRIGHTER DAY!
YOU KNOW WHAT I MEAN, VOLTHOOM?
ALL THE GREEN LANTERNS BEFORE ME...AND NOW I'M ONE OF THEM. ME, FRANK LAMINSKI...!
FRANK... NOW IS THE TIME.
YOU SURE YOU'LL BE OKAY ALONE WITH THIS LITTLE GUY?
THE GUARDIAN RAMI CAN'T DEFEND HIMSELF. HE AND I HAVE OLD MEMORIES TO DISCUSS TOGETHER.
BUT DON'T WORRY ABOUT THAT, FRANK. THIS IS YOUR TIME TO SHINE. THIS IS YOUR TIME TO SHOW THEM WHAT YOU'RE MADE OF.
THIS IS YOUR TIME...
...TO BE A HERO!
YEAH!
IT'S TIME FOR THE WORLD TO MEET THE NEW
GREEN LANTERN

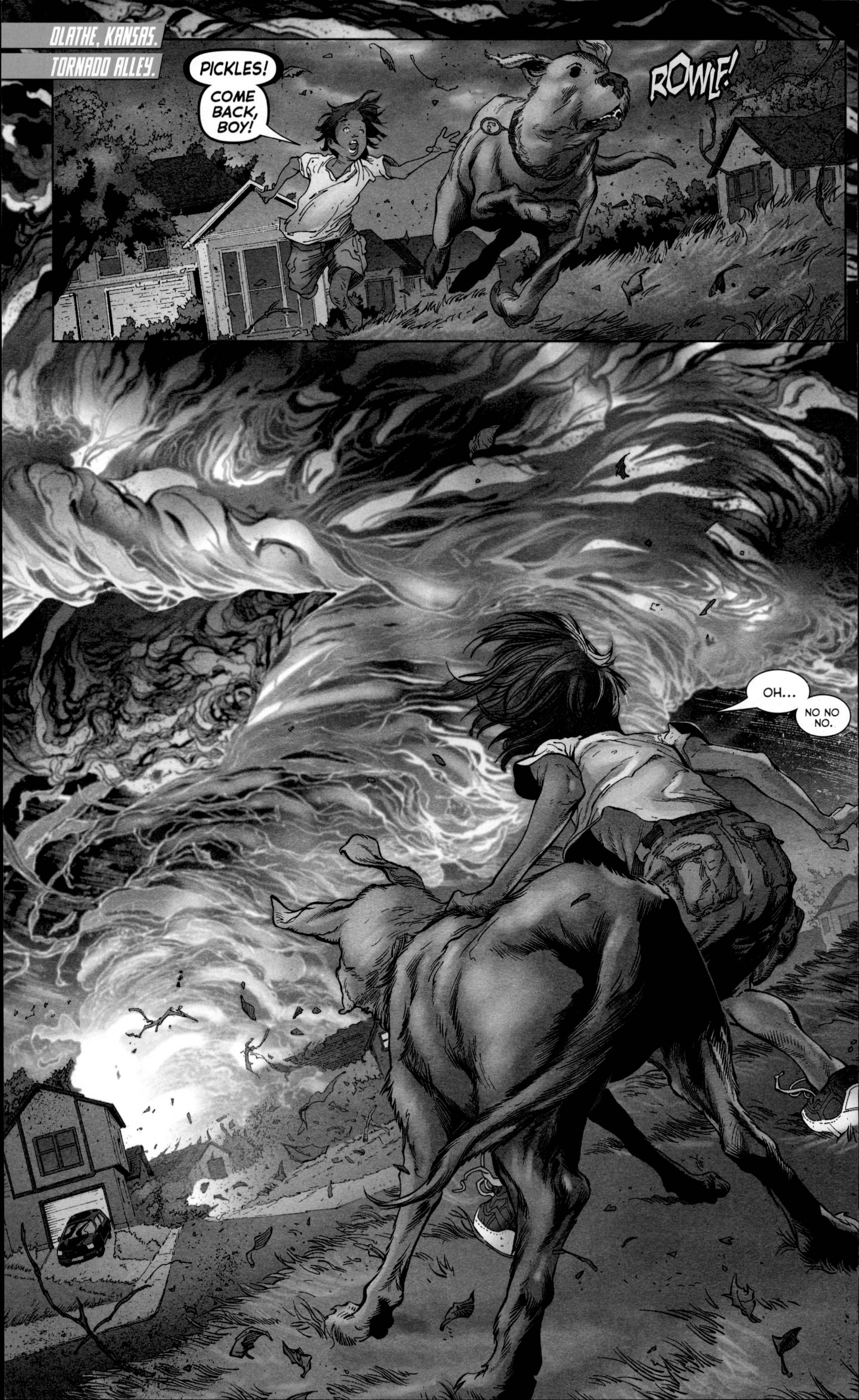
OLATHE, KANSAS.
TORNADO ALLEY.
PICKLES! COME BACK, BOY!
ROWLF!
OH...
NO NO NO.

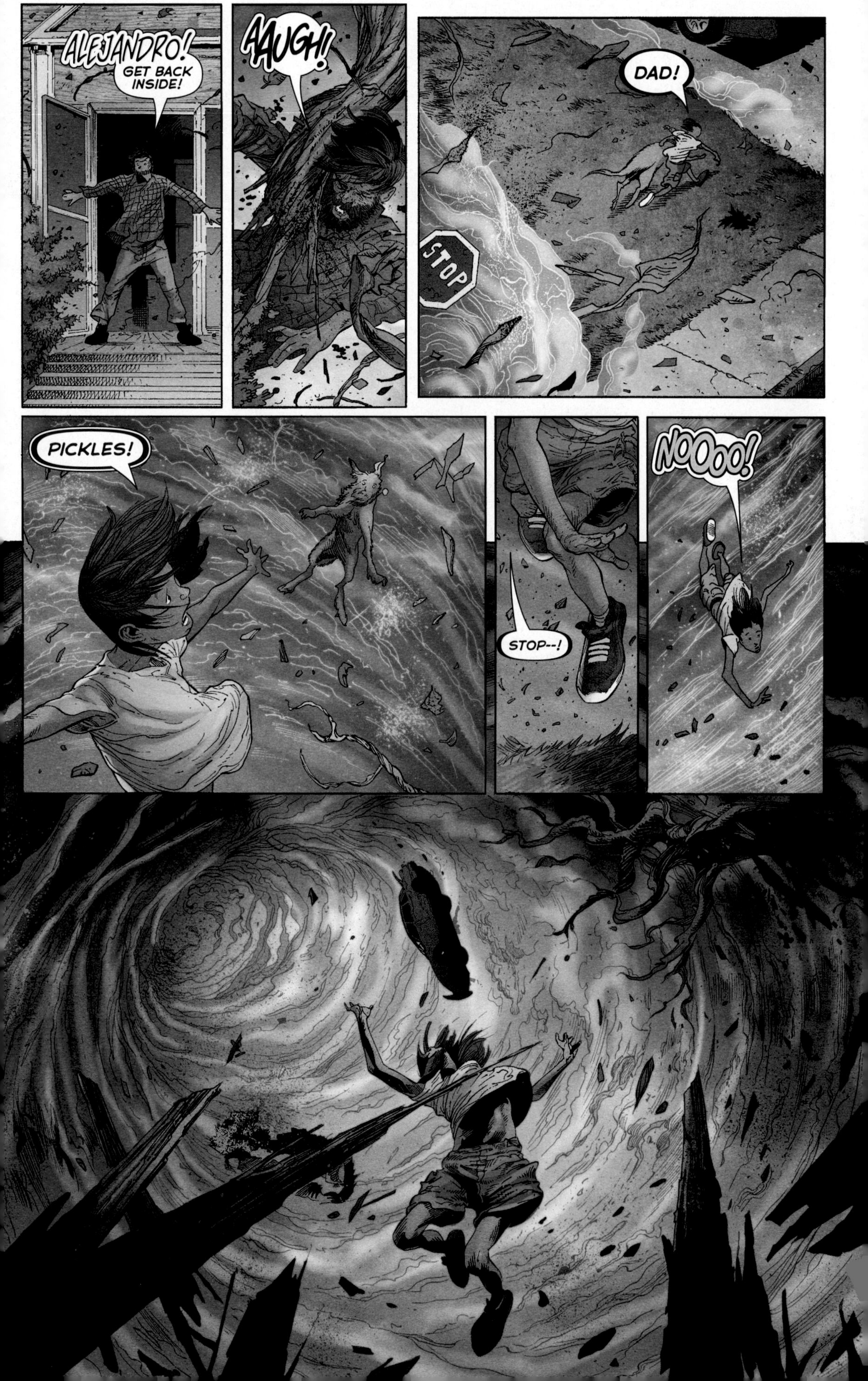
ALEJANDRO!
GET BACK INSIDE!
AAUGH!
DAD!
STOP
PICKLES!
STOP--!
NOOOO!

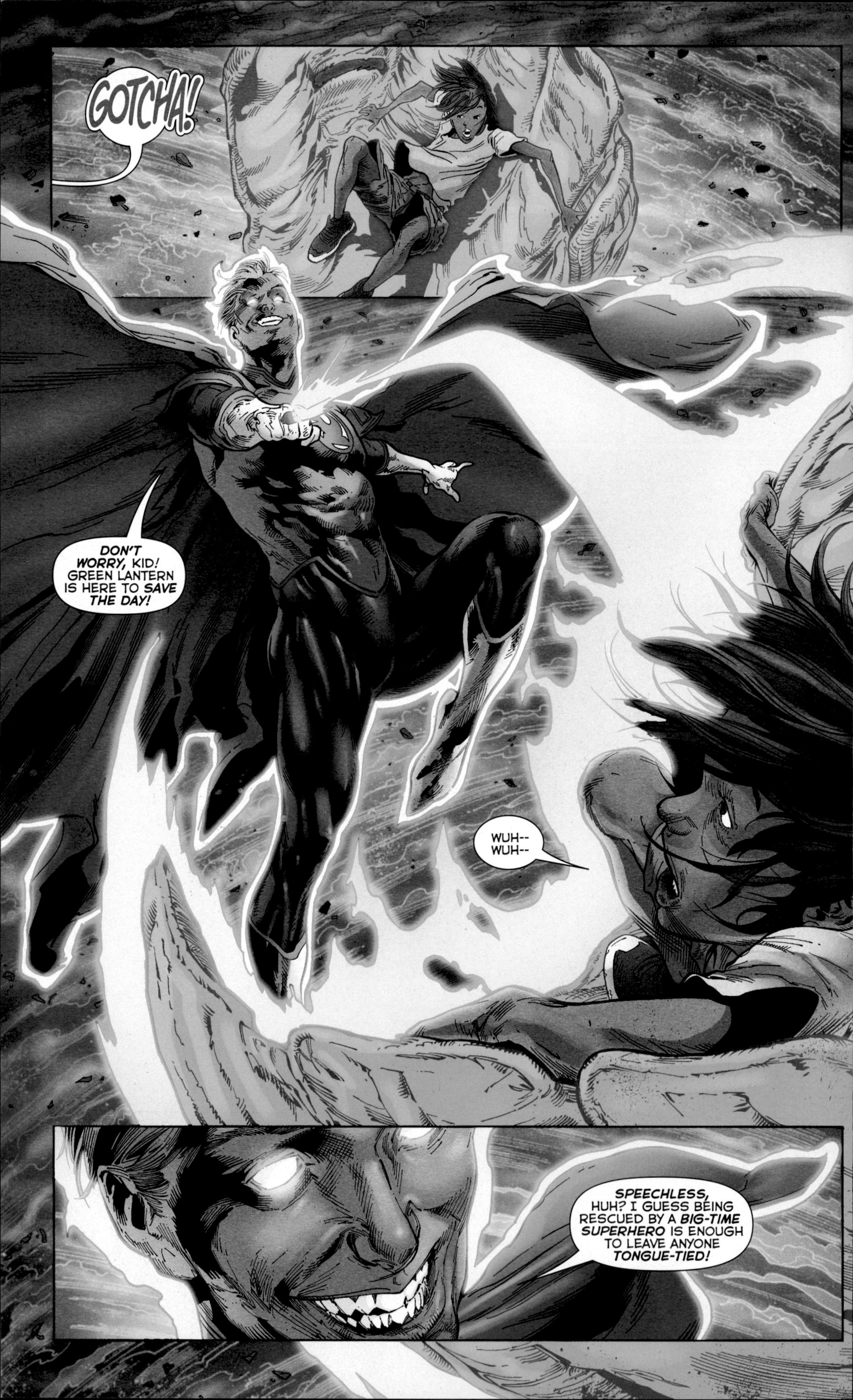
GOTCHA!
DON'T WORRY, KID! GREEN LANTERN IS HERE TO SAVE THE DAY!
WUH-- WUH--
SPEECHLESS, HUH? I GUESS BEING RESCUED BY A BIG-TIME SUPERHERO IS ENOUGH TO LEAVE ANYONE TONGUE-TIED!

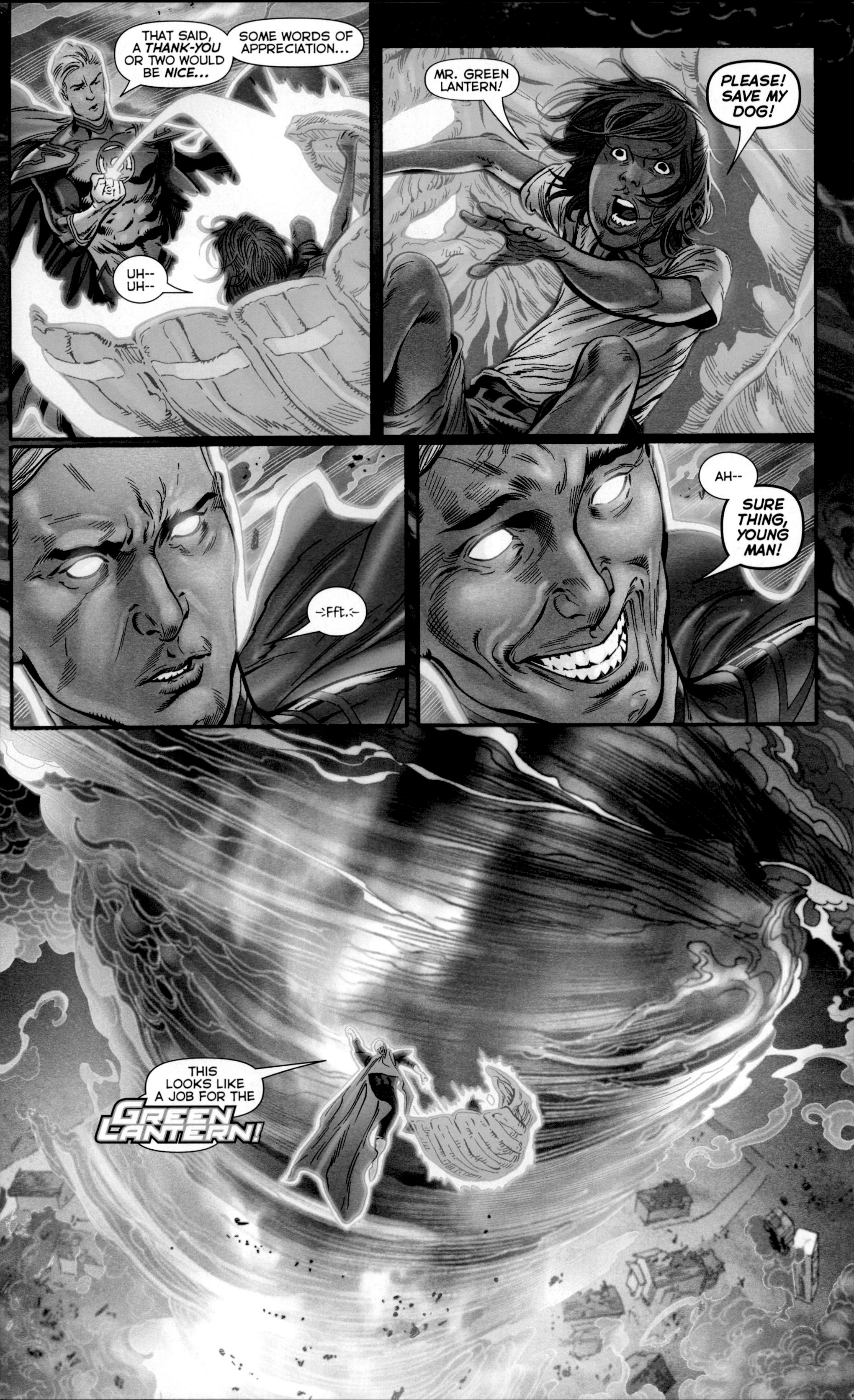
THAT SAID, A *THANK-YOU* OR TWO WOULD BE *NICE*...
SOME WORDS OF APPRECIATION...
UH-- UH--
MR. GREEN LANTERN!
PLEASE! SAVE MY DOG!
FFT.
AH--
SURE THING, YOUNG MAN!
THIS LOOKS LIKE A JOB FOR THE
GREEN LANTERN!

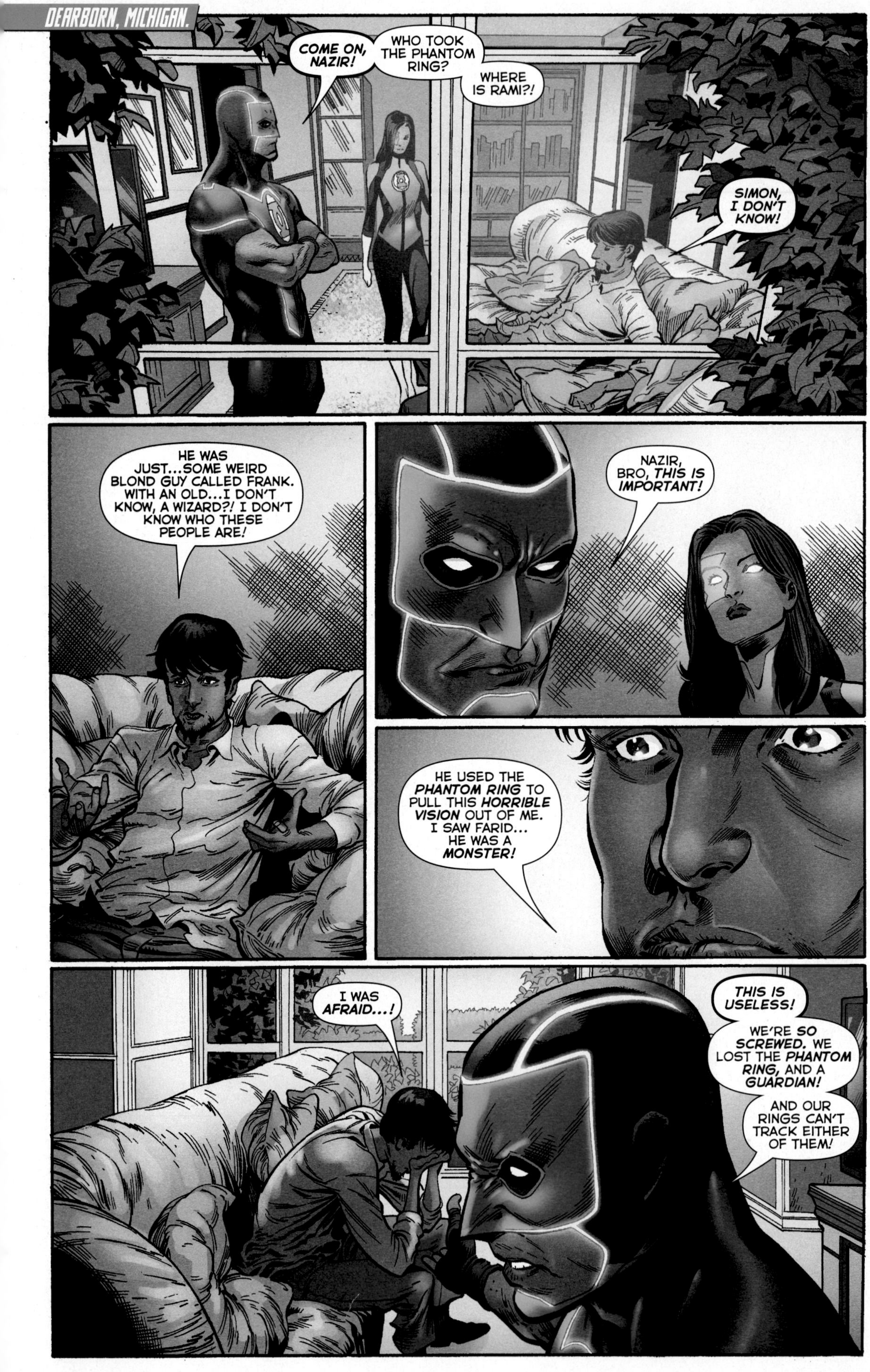
DEARBORN, MICHIGAN.
COME ON, NAZIR!
WHO TOOK THE PHANTOM RING?
WHERE IS RAMI?!
SIMON, I DON'T KNOW!
HE WAS JUST...SOME WEIRD BLOND GUY CALLED FRANK. WITH AN OLD...I DON'T KNOW, A WIZARD?! I DON'T KNOW WHO THESE PEOPLE ARE!
NAZIR, BRO, THIS IS IMPORTANT!
HE USED THE PHANTOM RING TO PULL THIS HORRIBLE VISION OUT OF ME. I SAW FARID... HE WAS A MONSTER!
I WAS AFRAID...!
THIS IS USELESS!
WE'RE SO SCREWED. WE LOST THE PHANTOM RING, AND A GUARDIAN!
AND OUR RINGS CAN'T TRACK EITHER OF THEM!

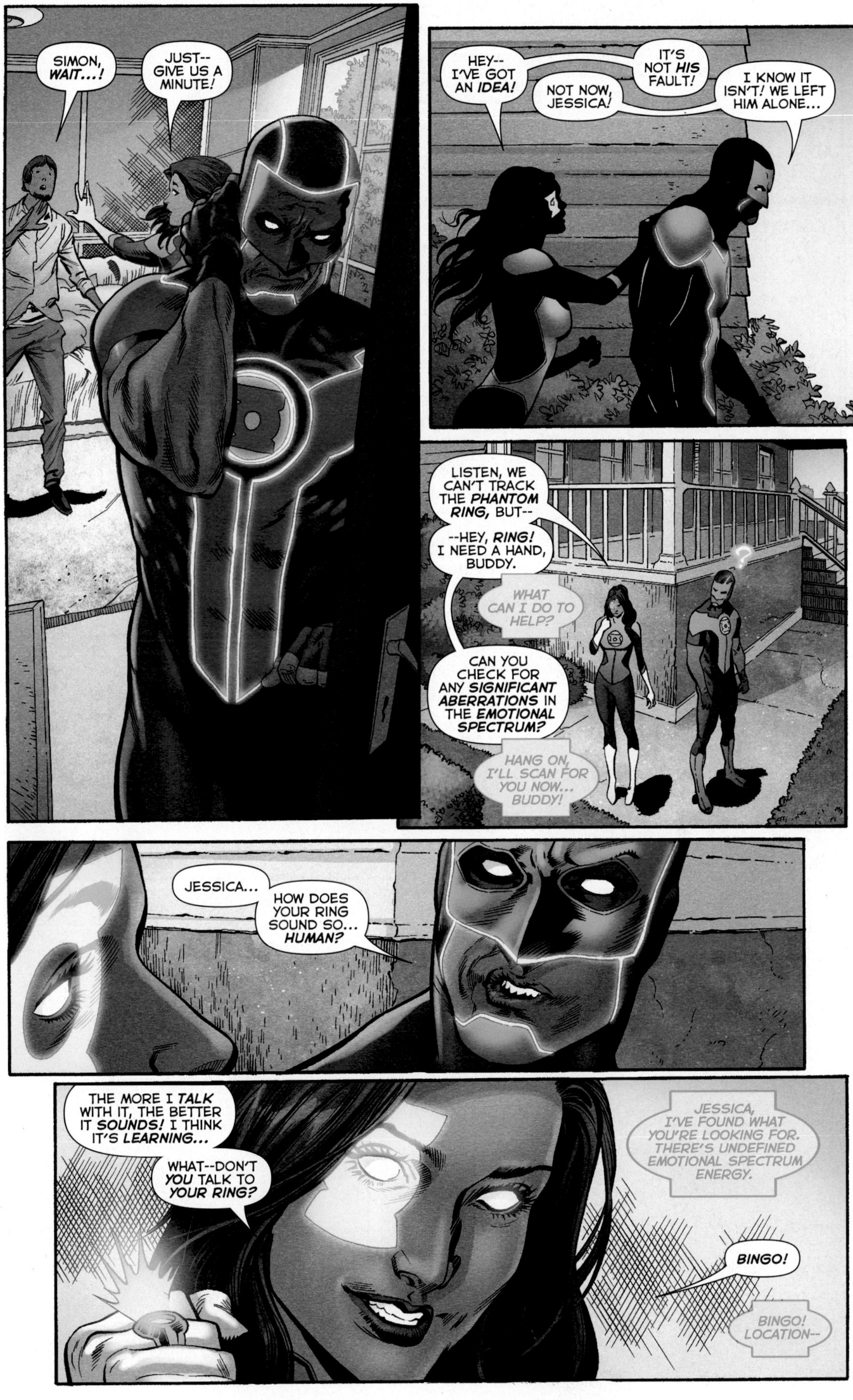
SIMON, WAIT...!
JUST-- GIVE US A MINUTE!
HEY-- I'VE GOT AN IDEA!
NOT NOW, JESSICA!
IT'S NOT HIS FAULT!
I KNOW IT ISN'T! WE LEFT HIM ALONE...
LISTEN, WE CAN'T TRACK THE PHANTOM RING, BUT--
--HEY, RING! I NEED A HAND, BUDDY.
WHAT CAN I DO TO HELP?
CAN YOU CHECK FOR ANY SIGNIFICANT ABERRATIONS IN THE EMOTIONAL SPECTRUM?
HANG ON, I'LL SCAN FOR YOU NOW... BUDDY!
JESSICA...
HOW DOES YOUR RING SOUND SO... HUMAN?
THE MORE I TALK WITH IT, THE BETTER IT SOUNDS! I THINK IT'S LEARNING...
WHAT--DON'T YOU TALK TO YOUR RING?
JESSICA, I'VE FOUND WHAT YOU'RE LOOKING FOR. THERE'S UNDEFINED EMOTIONAL SPECTRUM ENERGY.
BINGO!
BINGO! LOCATION--

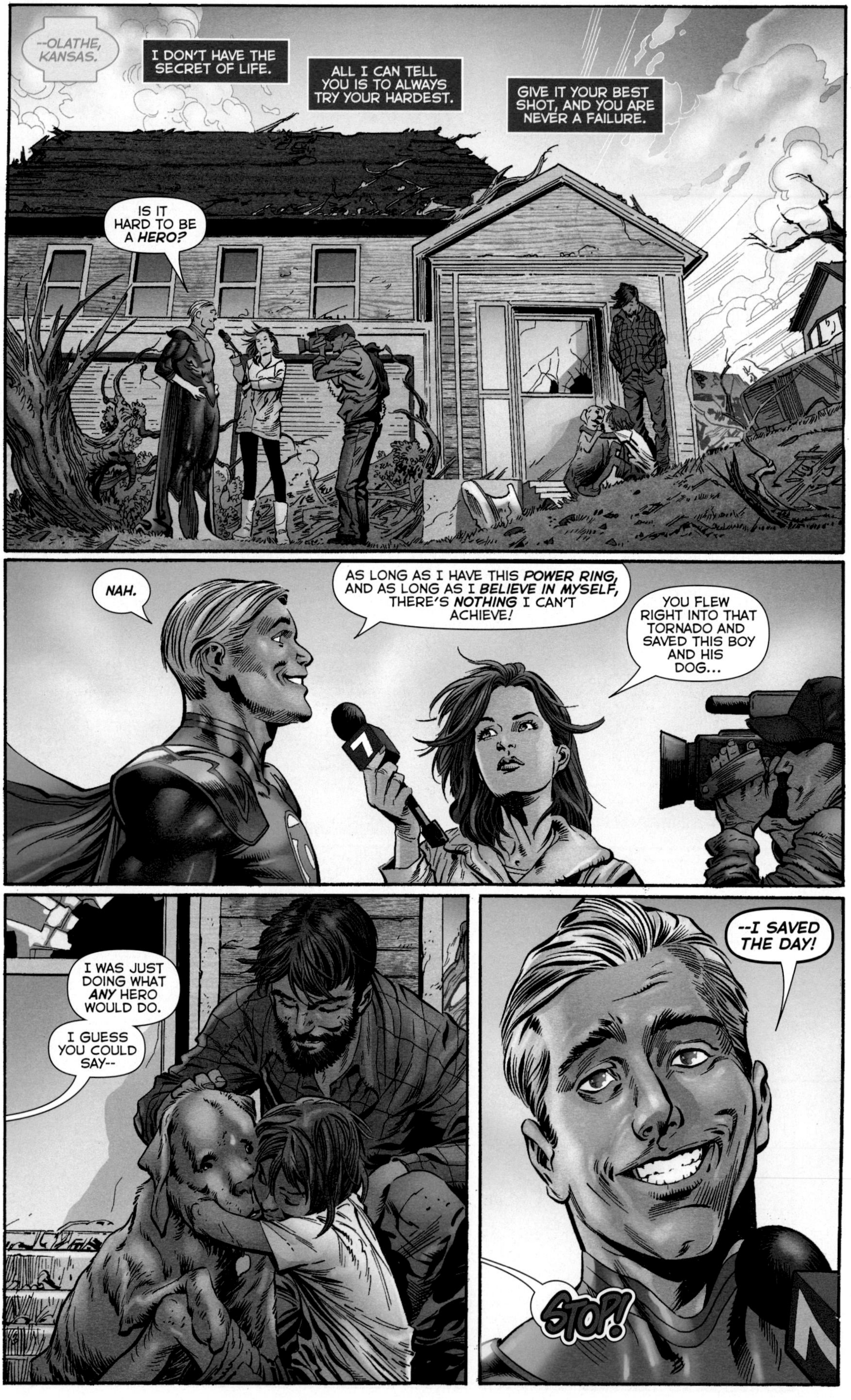
--OLATHE, KANSAS.
I DON'T HAVE THE SECRET OF LIFE.
ALL I CAN TELL YOU IS TO ALWAYS TRY YOUR HARDEST.
GIVE IT YOUR BEST SHOT, AND YOU ARE NEVER A FAILURE.
IS IT HARD TO BE A HERO?
NAH.
AS LONG AS I HAVE THIS POWER RING, AND AS LONG AS I BELIEVE IN MYSELF, THERE'S NOTHING I CAN'T ACHIEVE!
YOU FLEW RIGHT INTO THAT TORNADO AND SAVED THIS BOY AND HIS DOG...
I WAS JUST DOING WHAT ANY HERO WOULD DO.
I GUESS YOU COULD SAY--
--I SAVED THE DAY!
STOP!

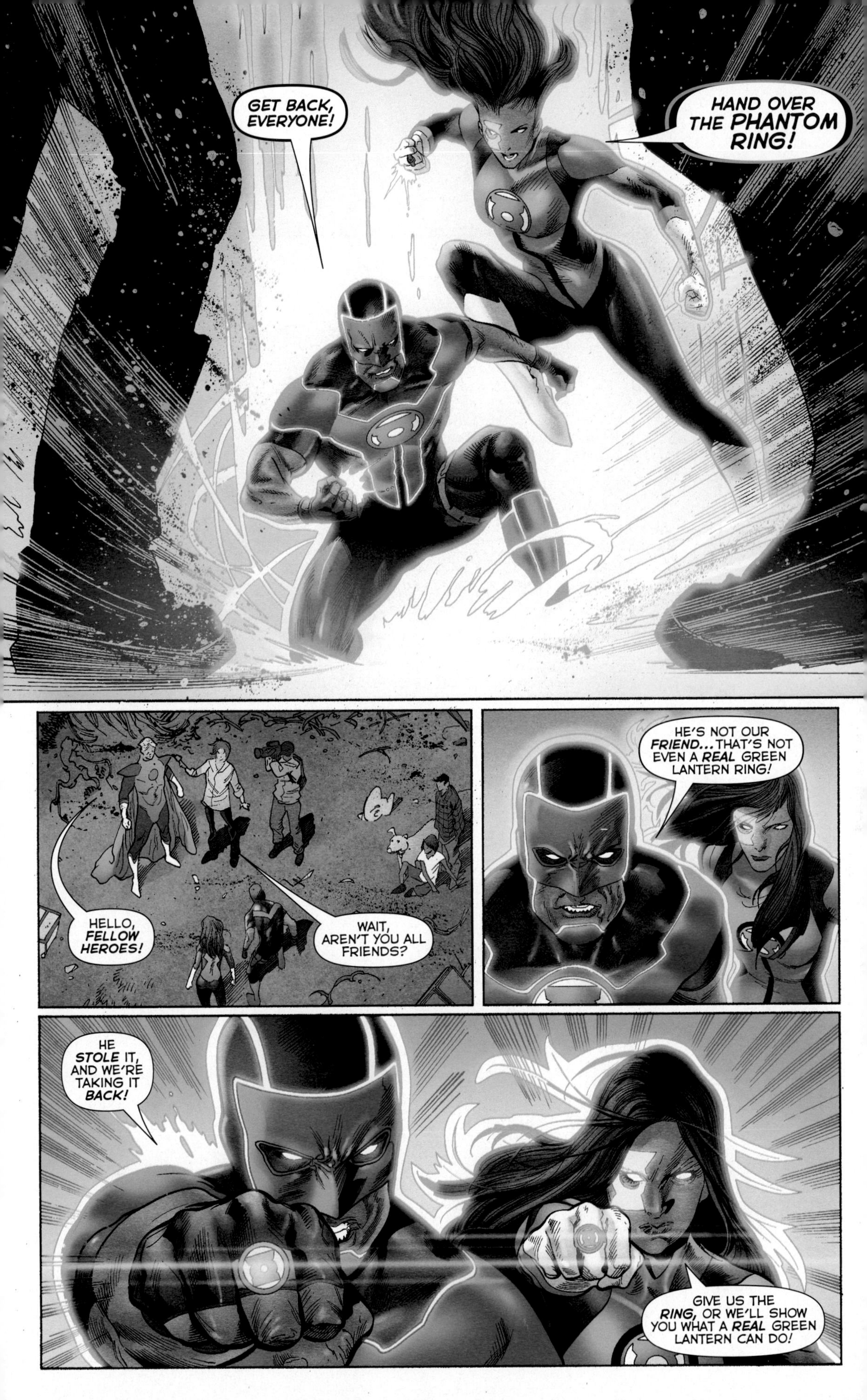
GET BACK, EVERYONE!
HAND OVER THE PHANTOM RING!
HELLO, FELLOW HEROES!
WAIT, AREN'T YOU ALL FRIENDS?
HE'S NOT OUR FRIEND... THAT'S NOT EVEN A REAL GREEN LANTERN RING!
HE STOLE IT, AND WE'RE TAKING IT BACK!
GIVE US THE RING, OR WE'LL SHOW YOU WHAT A REAL GREEN LANTERN CAN DO!

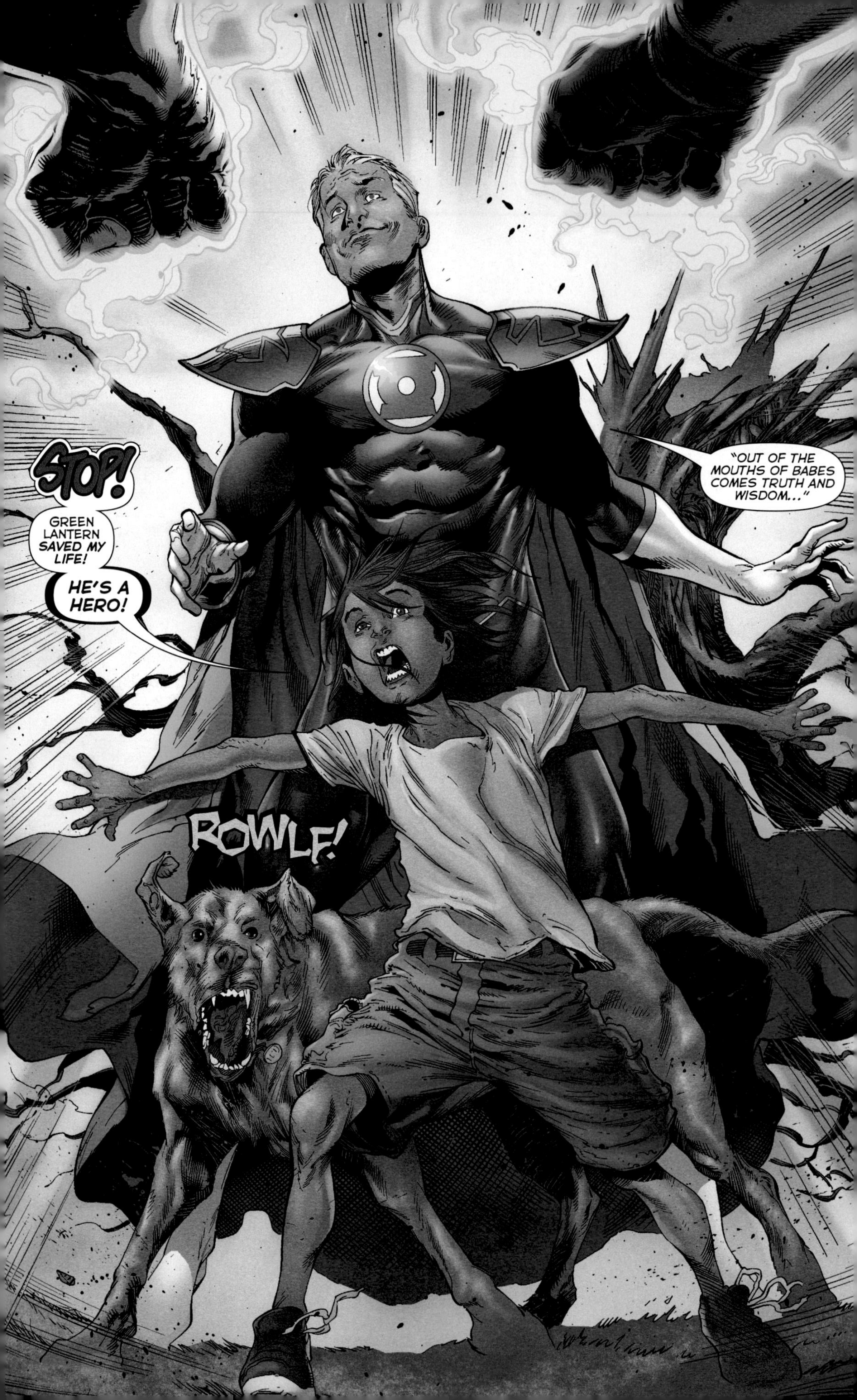
"OUT OF THE MOUTHS OF BABES COMES TRUTH AND WISDOM..."
STOP!
GREEN LANTERN SAVED MY LIFE!
HE'S A HERO!
ROWLF!

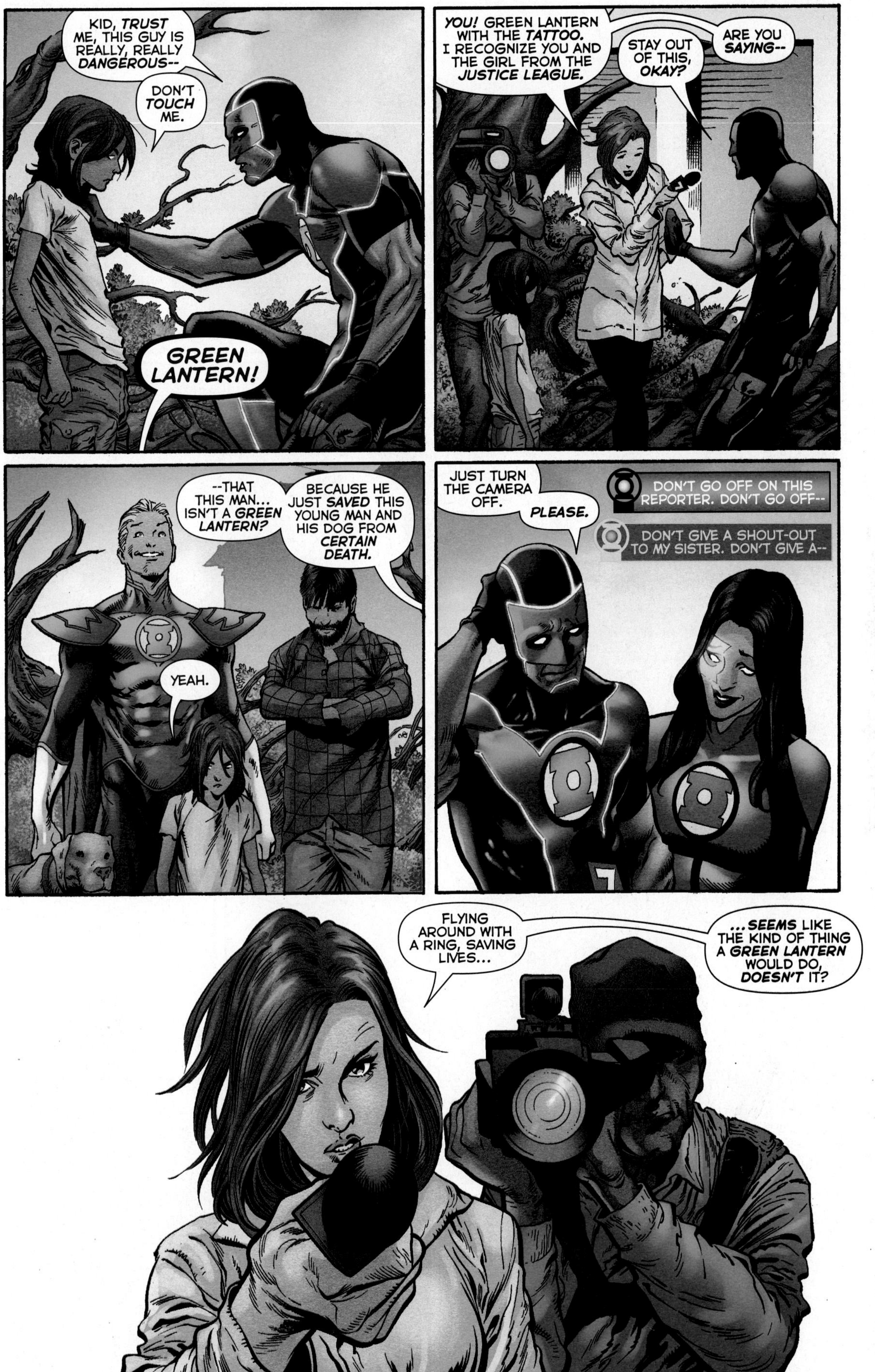

KID, TRUST ME, THIS GUY IS REALLY, REALLY DANGEROUS--
DON'T TOUCH ME.
GREEN LANTERN!
YOU! GREEN LANTERN WITH THE TATTOO. I RECOGNIZE YOU AND THE GIRL FROM THE JUSTICE LEAGUE.
STAY OUT OF THIS, OKAY?
ARE YOU SAYING--
--THAT THIS MAN... ISN'T A GREEN LANTERN?
BECAUSE HE JUST SAVED THIS YOUNG MAN AND HIS DOG FROM CERTAIN DEATH.
YEAH.
JUST TURN THE CAMERA OFF.
PLEASE.
DON'T GO OFF ON THIS REPORTER. DON'T GO OFF--
DON'T GIVE A SHOUT-OUT TO MY SISTER. DON'T GIVE A--
FLYING AROUND WITH A RING, SAVING LIVES...
...SEEMS LIKE THE KIND OF THING A GREEN LANTERN WOULD DO, DOESN'T IT?

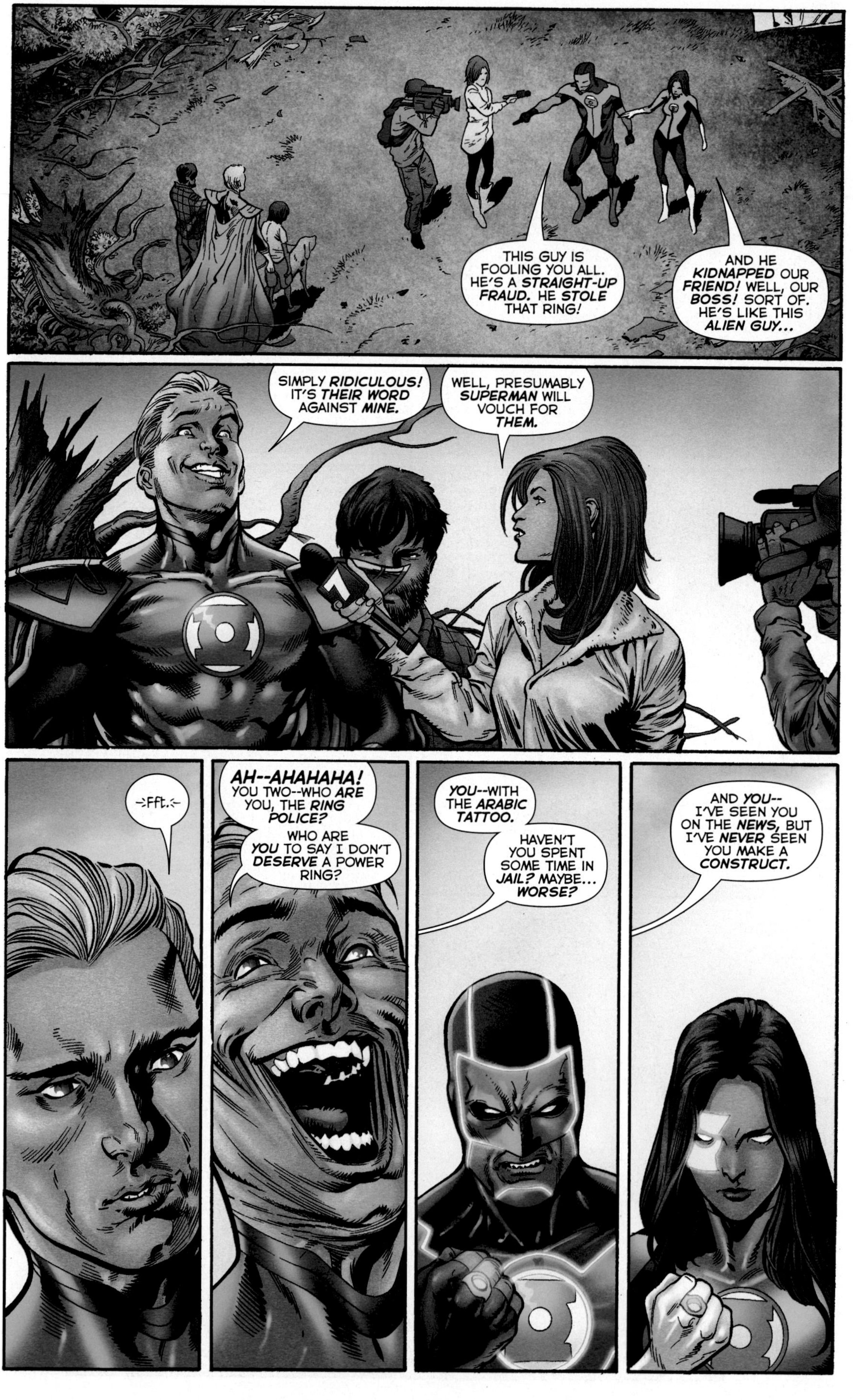
THIS GUY IS FOOLING YOU ALL. HE'S A STRAIGHT-UP FRAUD. HE STOLE THAT RING!
AND HE KIDNAPPED OUR FRIEND! WELL, OUR BOSS! SORT OF. HE'S LIKE THIS ALIEN GUY...
SIMPLY RIDICULOUS! IT'S THEIR WORD AGAINST MINE.
WELL, PRESUMABLY SUPERMAN WILL VOUCH FOR THEM.
-Fft.-
AH--AHAHAHA! YOU TWO--WHO ARE YOU, THE RING POLICE?
WHO ARE YOU TO SAY I DON'T DESERVE A POWER RING?
YOU--WITH THE ARABIC TATTOO.
HAVEN'T YOU SPENT SOME TIME IN JAIL? MAYBE... WORSE?
AND YOU-- I'VE SEEN YOU ON THE NEWS, BUT I'VE NEVER SEEN YOU MAKE A CONSTRUCT.

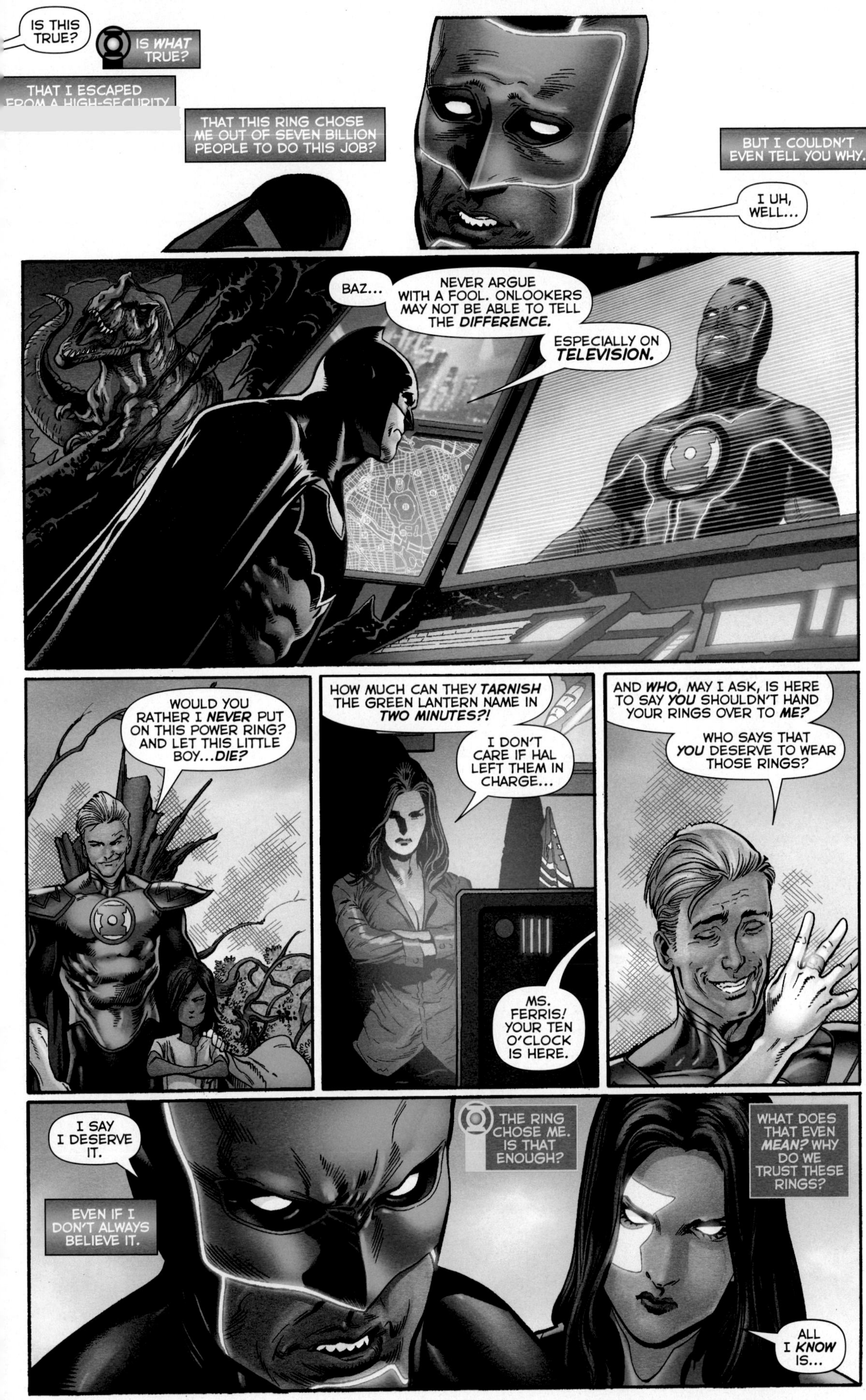
IS THIS TRUE?
IS WHAT TRUE?
THAT I ESCAPED
THAT THIS RING CHOSE ME OUT OF SEVEN BILLION PEOPLE TO DO THIS JOB?
BUT I COULDN'T EVEN TELL YOU WHY.
I UH, WELL...
BAZ...
NEVER ARGUE WITH A FOOL. ONLOOKERS MAY NOT BE ABLE TO TELL THE DIFFERENCE.
ESPECIALLY ON TELEVISION.
WOULD YOU RATHER I NEVER PUT ON THIS POWER RING? AND LET THIS LITTLE BOY...DIE?
HOW MUCH CAN THEY TARNISH THE GREEN LANTERN NAME IN TWO MINUTES?!
I DON'T CARE IF HAL LEFT THEM IN CHARGE...
MS. FERRIS! YOUR TEN O'CLOCK IS HERE.
AND WHO, MAY I ASK, IS HERE TO SAY YOU SHOULDN'T HAND YOUR RINGS OVER TO ME?
WHO SAYS THAT YOU DESERVE TO WEAR THOSE RINGS?
I SAY I DESERVE IT.
EVEN IF I DON'T ALWAYS BELIEVE IT.
THE RING CHOSE ME. IS THAT ENOUGH?
WHAT DOES THAT EVEN MEAN? WHY DO WE TRUST THESE RINGS?
ALL I KNOW IS...

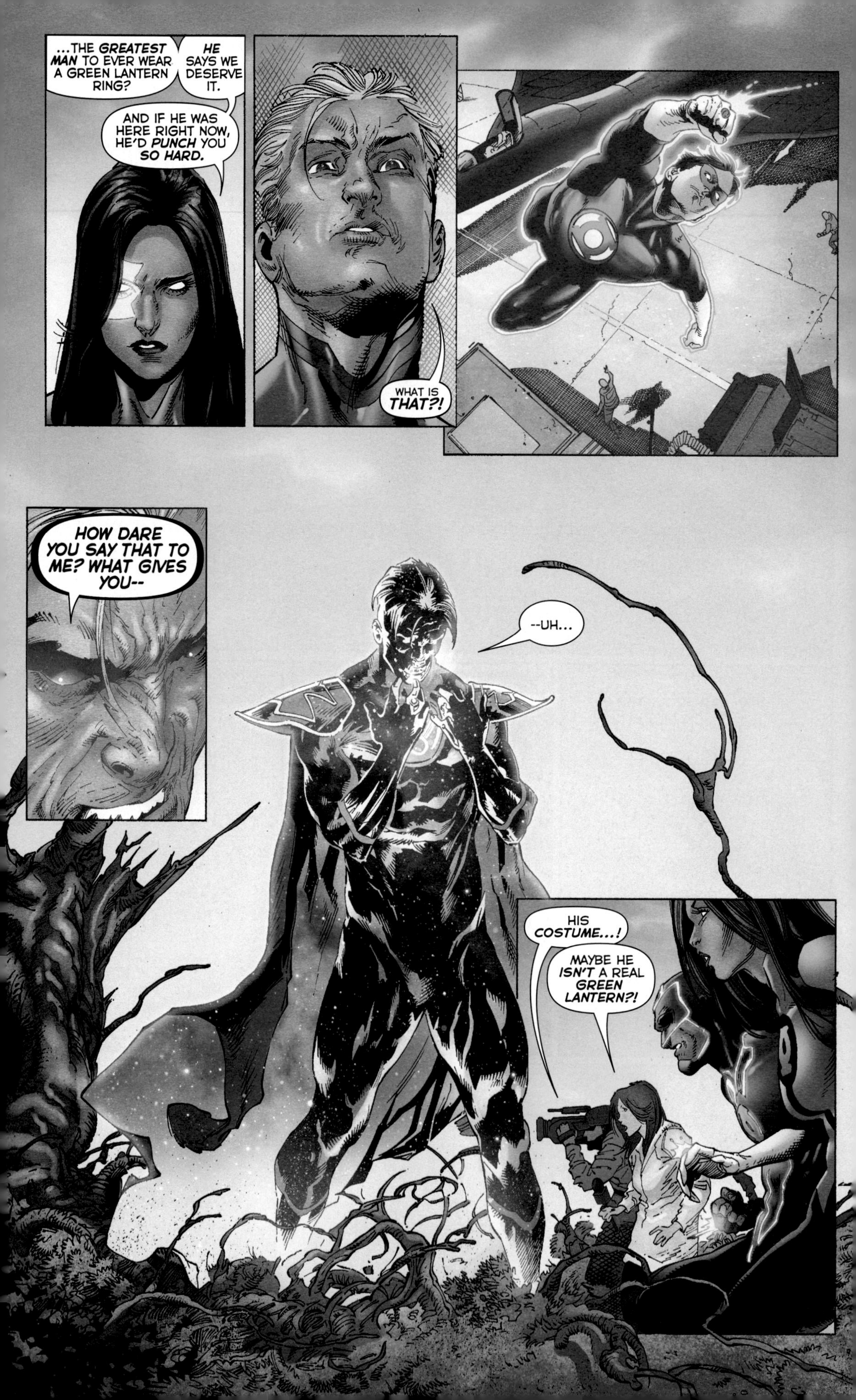

...THE GREATEST MAN TO EVER WEAR A GREEN LANTERN RING?
HE SAYS WE DESERVE IT.
AND IF HE WAS HERE RIGHT NOW, HE'D PUNCH YOU SO HARD.
WHAT IS THAT?!
HOW DARE YOU SAY THAT TO ME? WHAT GIVES YOU--
--UH...
HIS COSTUME...!
MAYBE HE ISN'T A REAL GREEN LANTERN?!

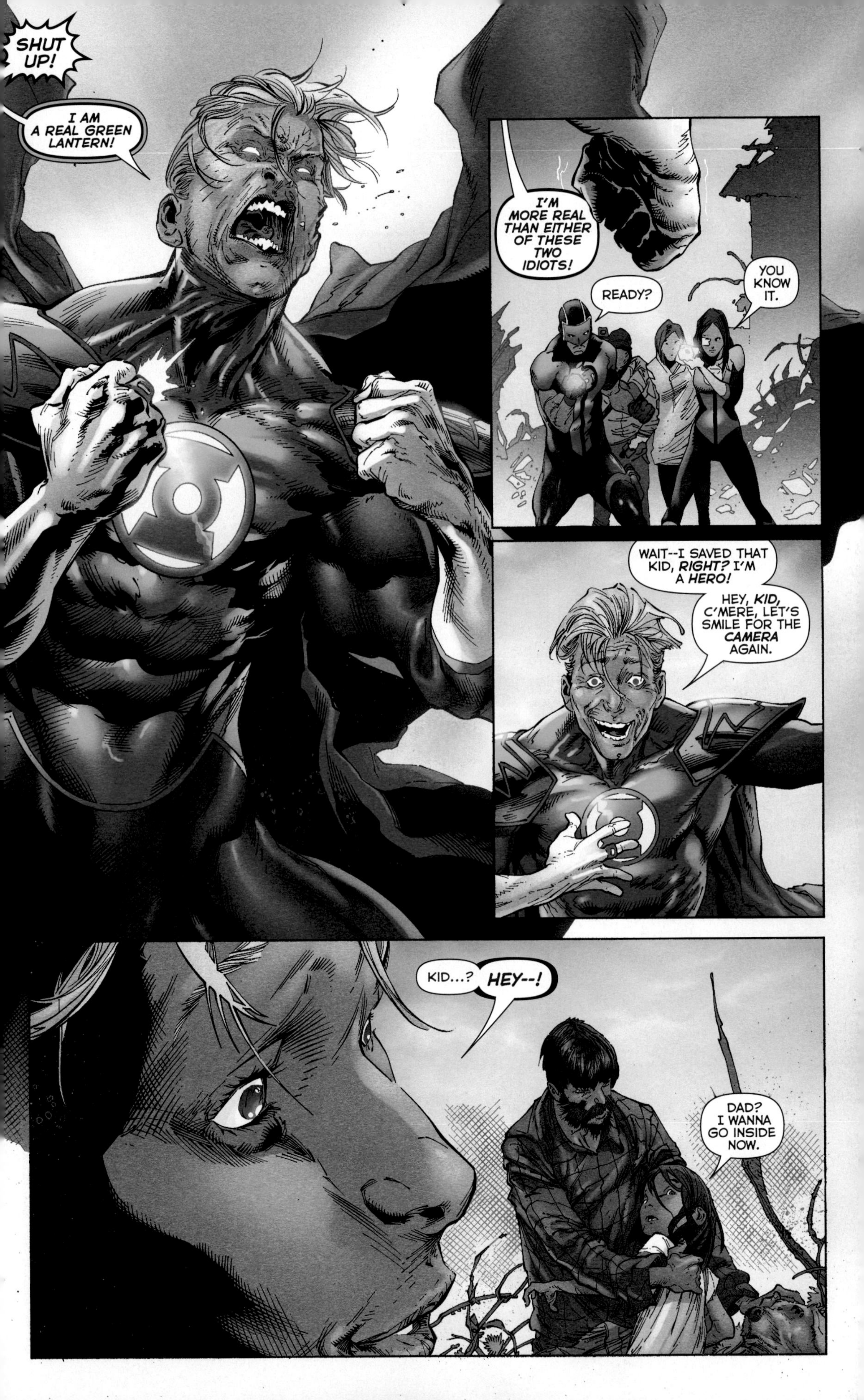
SHUT UP!
I AM A REAL GREEN LANTERN!
I'M MORE REAL THAN EITHER OF THESE TWO IDIOTS!
READY?
YOU KNOW IT.
WAIT--I SAVED THAT KID, RIGHT? I'M A HERO!
HEY, KID, C'MERE, LET'S SMILE FOR THE CAMERA AGAIN.
KID...? HEY--!
DAD? I WANNA GO INSIDE NOW.

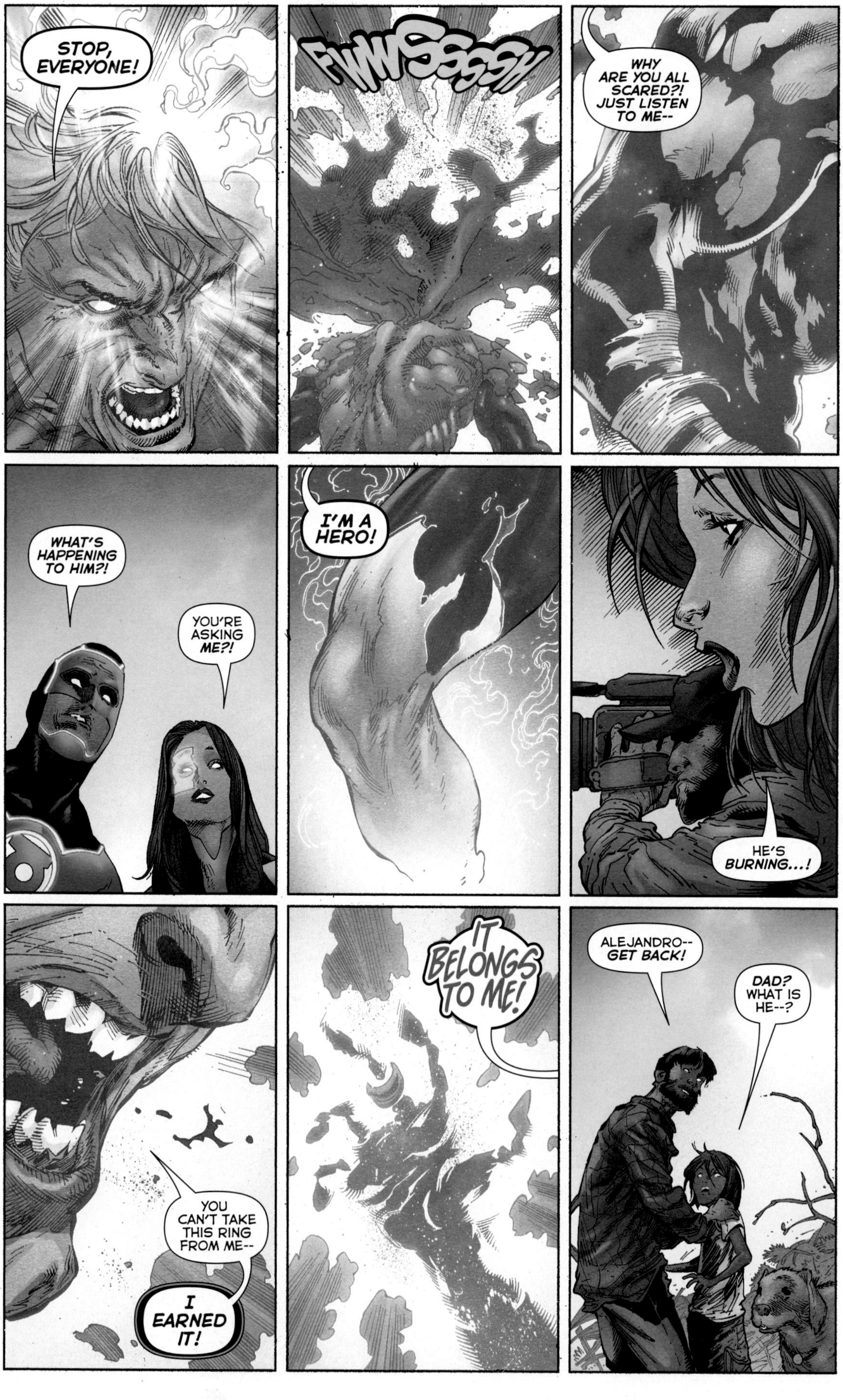
STOP, EVERYONE!
FWWSSSSSH
WHY ARE YOU ALL SCARED?! JUST LISTEN TO ME--
WHAT'S HAPPENING TO HIM?!
YOU'RE ASKING ME?!
I'M A HERO!
HE'S BURNING...!
YOU CAN'T TAKE THIS RING FROM ME--
I EARNED IT!
IT BELONGS TO ME!
ALEJANDRO-- GET BACK!
DAD? WHAT IS HE--?

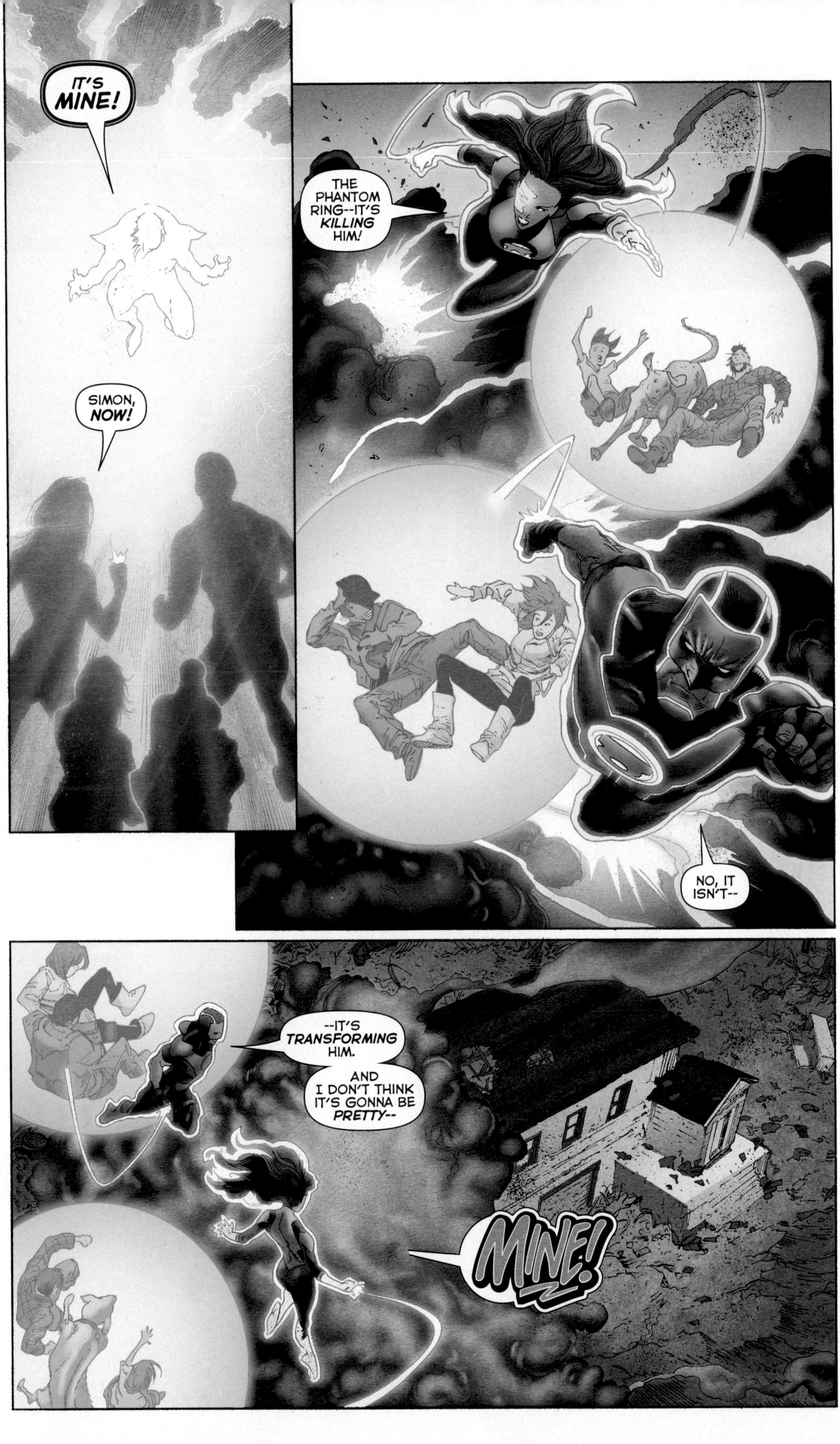
IT'S MINE!
THE PHANTOM RING--IT'S KILLING HIM!
SIMON, NOW!
NO, IT ISN'T--
--IT'S TRANSFORMING HIM.
AND I DON'T THINK IT'S GONNA BE PRETTY--
MINE!

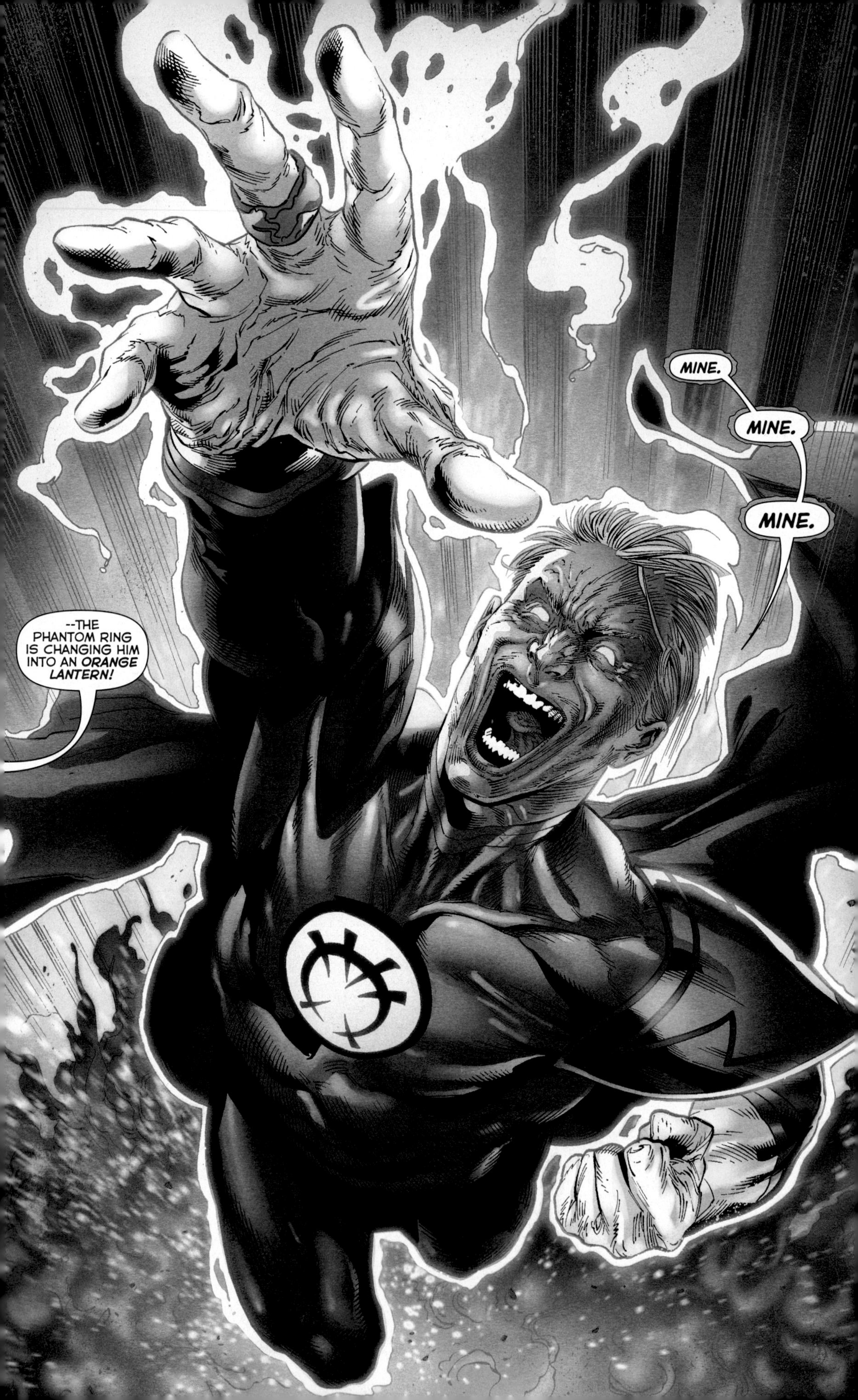
MINE.
MINE.
MINE.
--THE PHANTOM RING IS CHANGING HIM INTO AN *ORANGE LANTERN!*

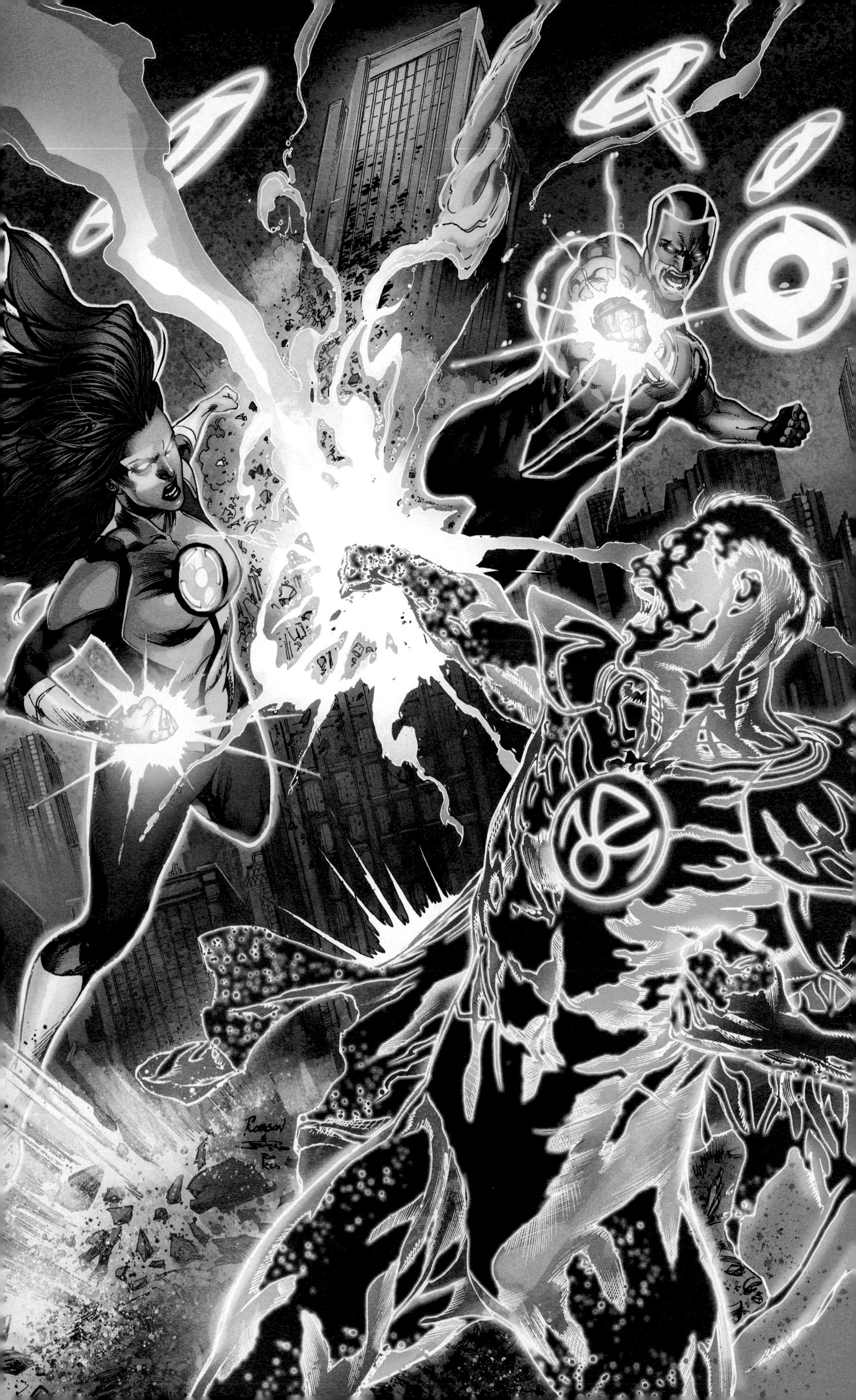

"THE PHANTOM LANTERN: PART THREE"

SAM HUMPHRIES writer * **EDUARDO PANSICA** penciller * **JULIO FERREIRA** inker

Cover by **ROBSON ROCHA, JAY LEISTEN** and **ROD REIS**

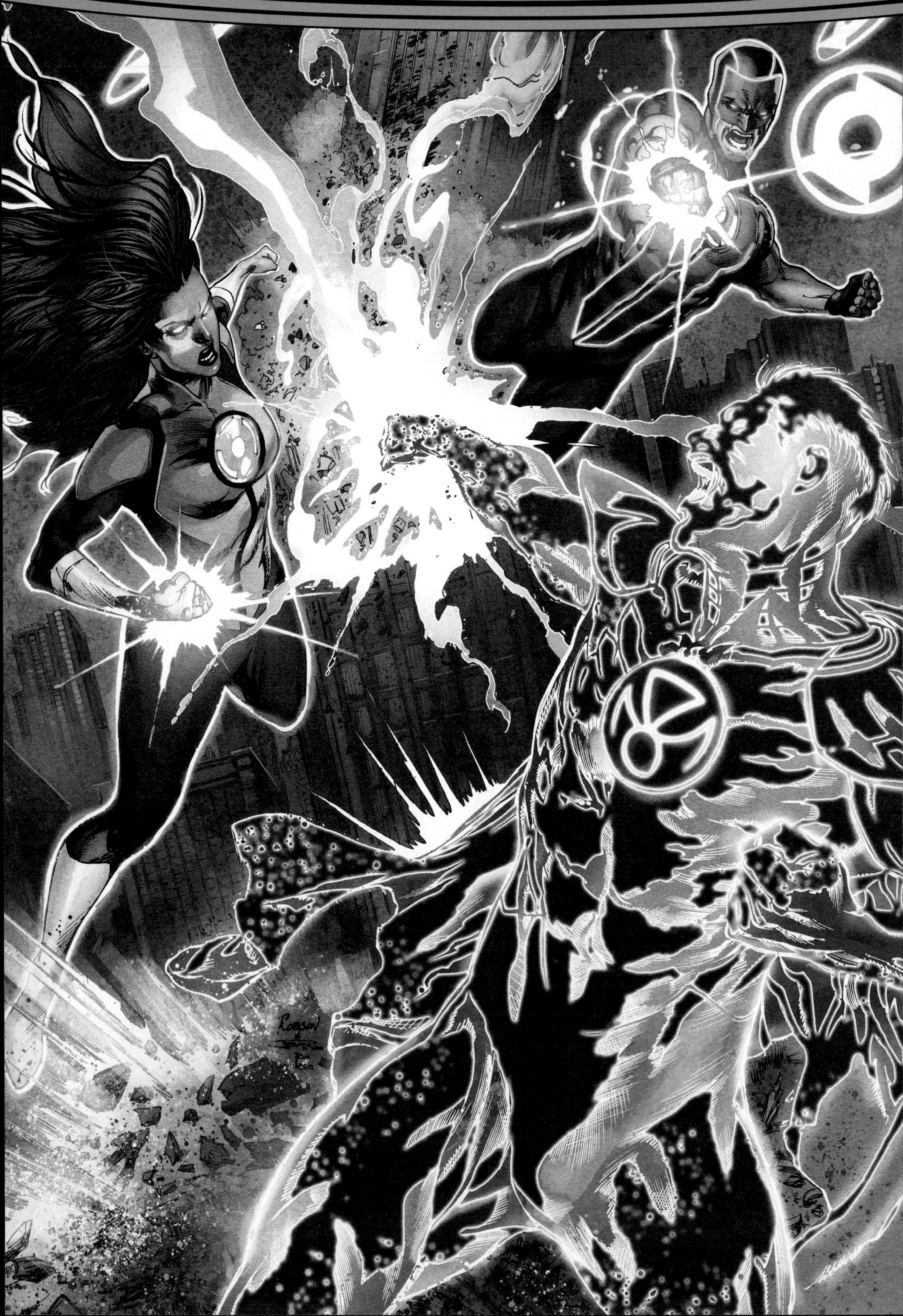

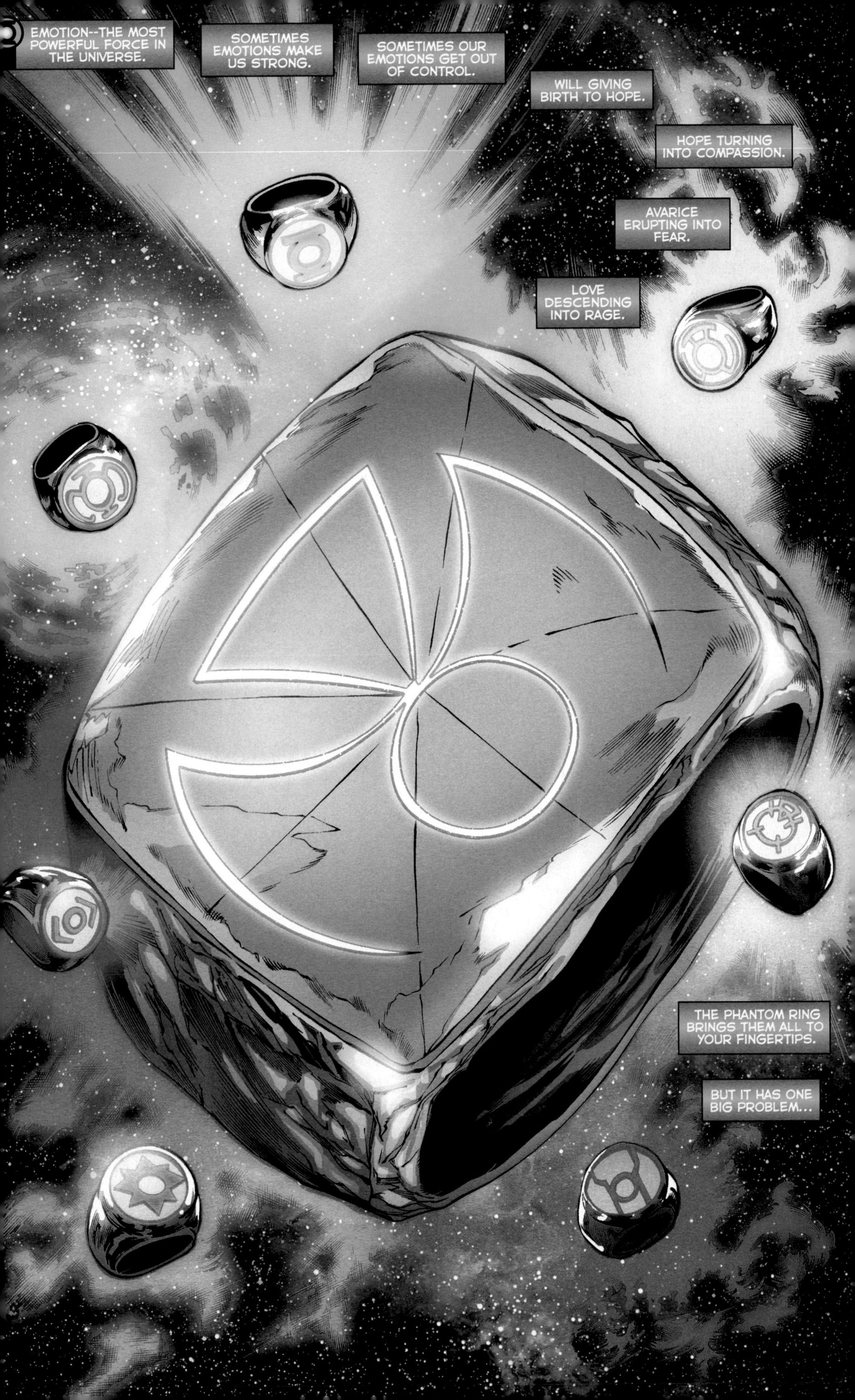
EMOTION--THE MOST POWERFUL FORCE IN THE UNIVERSE.
SOMETIMES EMOTIONS MAKE US STRONG.
SOMETIMES OUR EMOTIONS GET OUT OF CONTROL.
WILL GIVING BIRTH TO HOPE.
HOPE TURNING INTO COMPASSION.
AVARICE ERUPTING INTO FEAR.
LOVE DESCENDING INTO RAGE.
THE PHANTOM RING BRINGS THEM ALL TO YOUR FINGERTIPS.
BUT IT HAS ONE BIG PROBLEM...

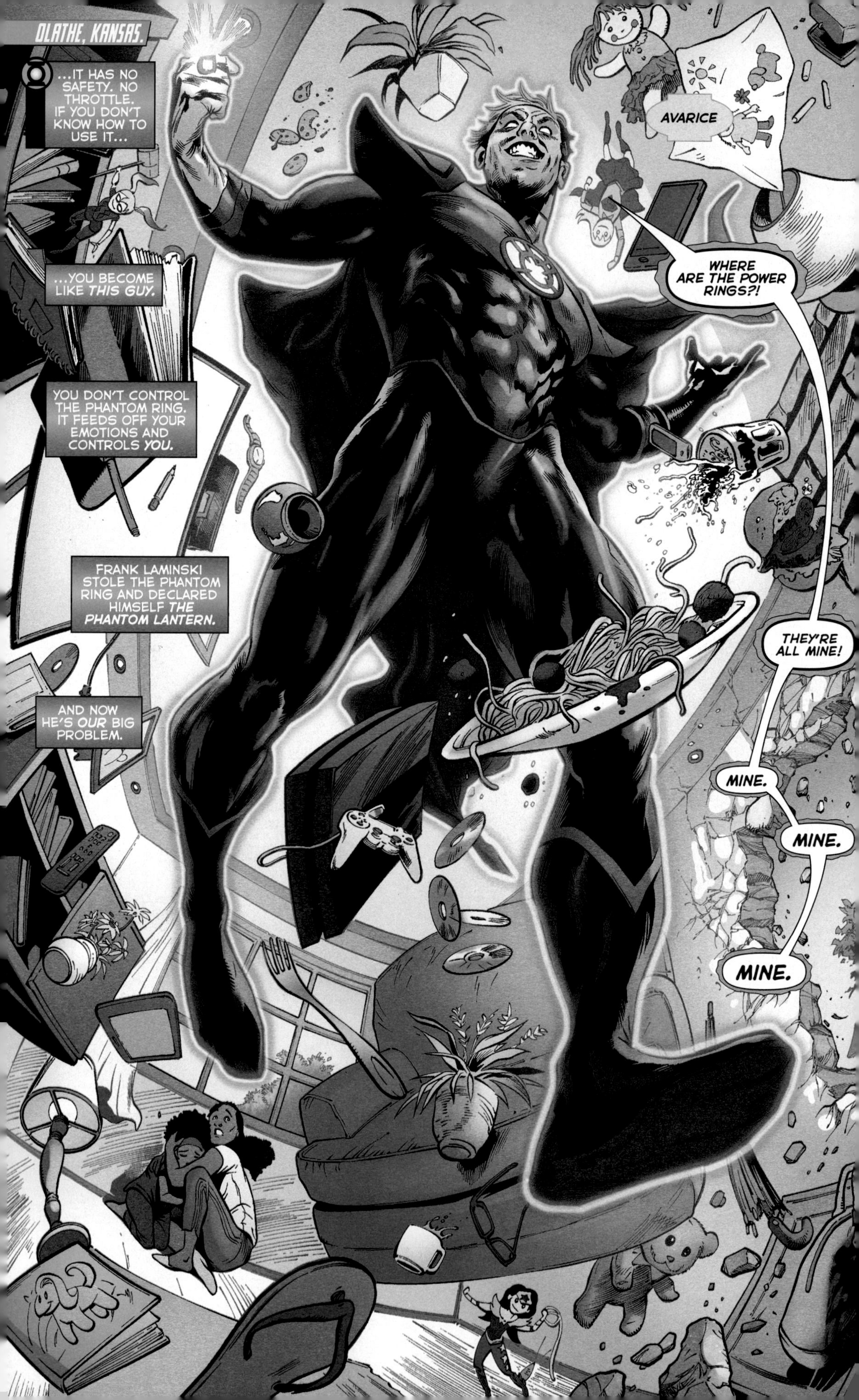
OLATHE, KANSAS.
...IT HAS NO SAFETY. NO THROTTLE. IF YOU DON'T KNOW HOW TO USE IT...
...YOU BECOME LIKE THIS GUY.
YOU DON'T CONTROL THE PHANTOM RING. IT FEEDS OFF YOUR EMOTIONS AND CONTROLS YOU.
FRANK LAMINSKI STOLE THE PHANTOM RING AND DECLARED HIMSELF THE PHANTOM LANTERN.
AND NOW HE'S OUR BIG PROBLEM.
AVARICE
WHERE ARE THE POWER RINGS?!
THEY'RE ALL MINE!
MINE.
MINE.
MINE.

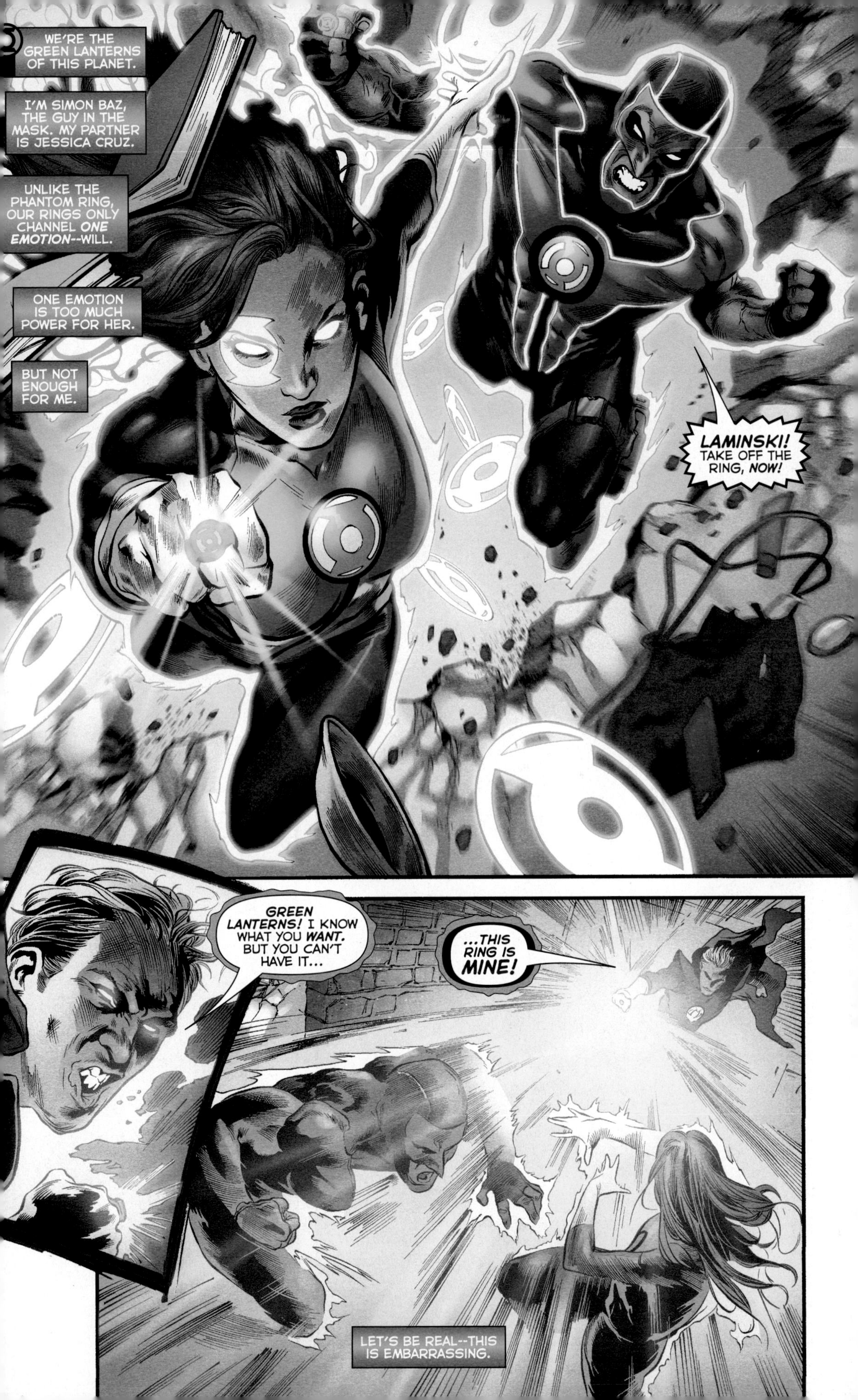
WE'RE THE GREEN LANTERNS OF THIS PLANET.
I'M SIMON BAZ, THE GUY IN THE MASK. MY PARTNER IS JESSICA CRUZ.
UNLIKE THE PHANTOM RING, OUR RINGS ONLY CHANNEL *ONE EMOTION*--WILL.
ONE EMOTION IS TOO MUCH POWER FOR HER.
BUT NOT ENOUGH FOR ME.
LAMINSKI! TAKE OFF THE RING, *NOW!*
GREEN LANTERNS! I KNOW WHAT YOU *WANT.* BUT YOU CAN'T HAVE IT...
...THIS RING IS *MINE!*
LET'S BE REAL--THIS IS EMBARRASSING.

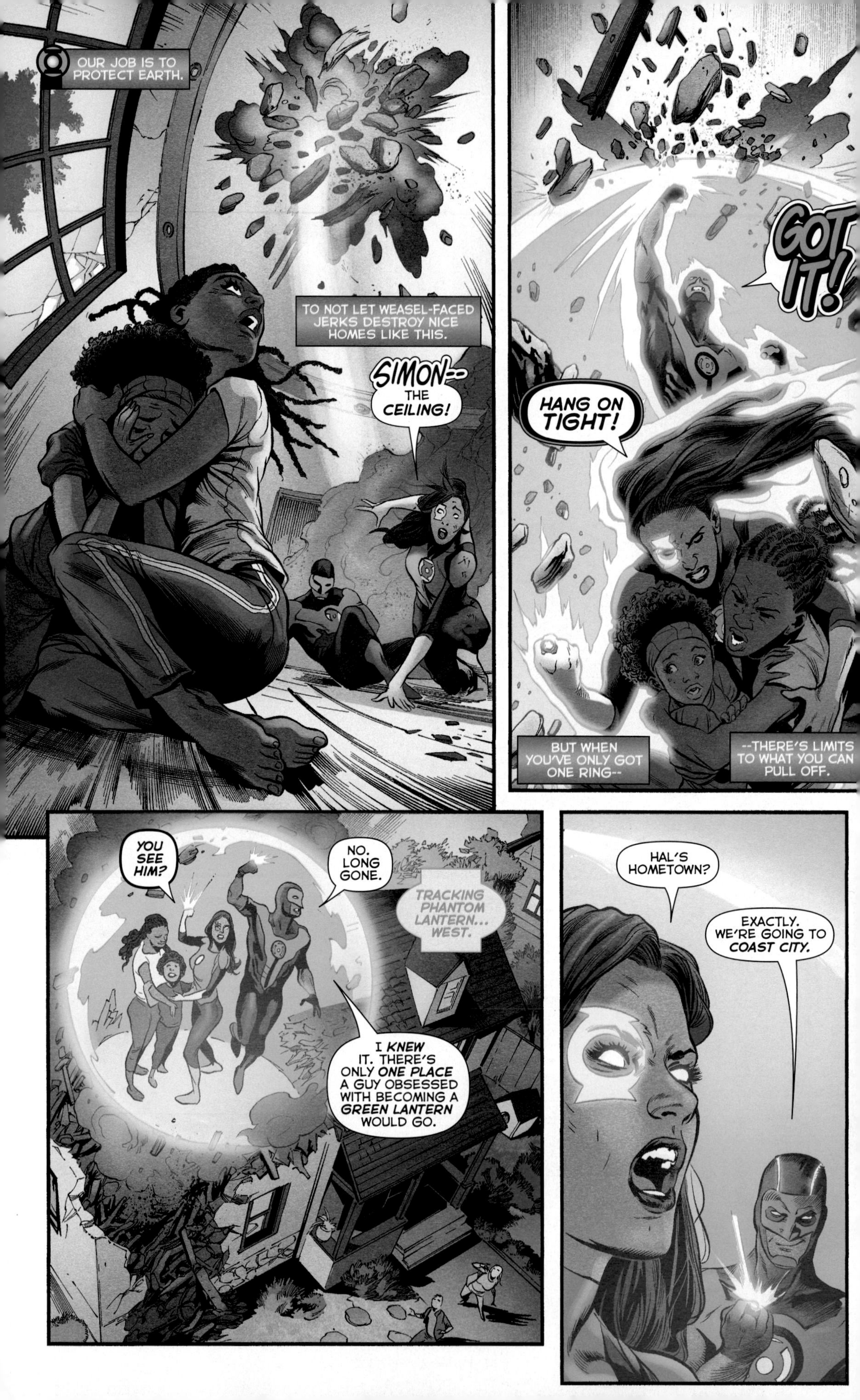
OUR JOB IS TO PROTECT EARTH.
TO NOT LET WEASEL-FACED JERKS DESTROY NICE HOMES LIKE THIS.
SIMON-- THE CEILING!
GOT IT!
HANG ON TIGHT!
BUT WHEN YOU'VE ONLY GOT ONE RING--
--THERE'S LIMITS TO WHAT YOU CAN PULL OFF.
YOU SEE HIM?
NO. LONG GONE.
TRACKING PHANTOM LANTERN... WEST.
I KNEW IT. THERE'S ONLY ONE PLACE A GUY OBSESSED WITH BECOMING A GREEN LANTERN WOULD GO.
HAL'S HOMETOWN?
EXACTLY. WE'RE GOING TO COAST CITY.

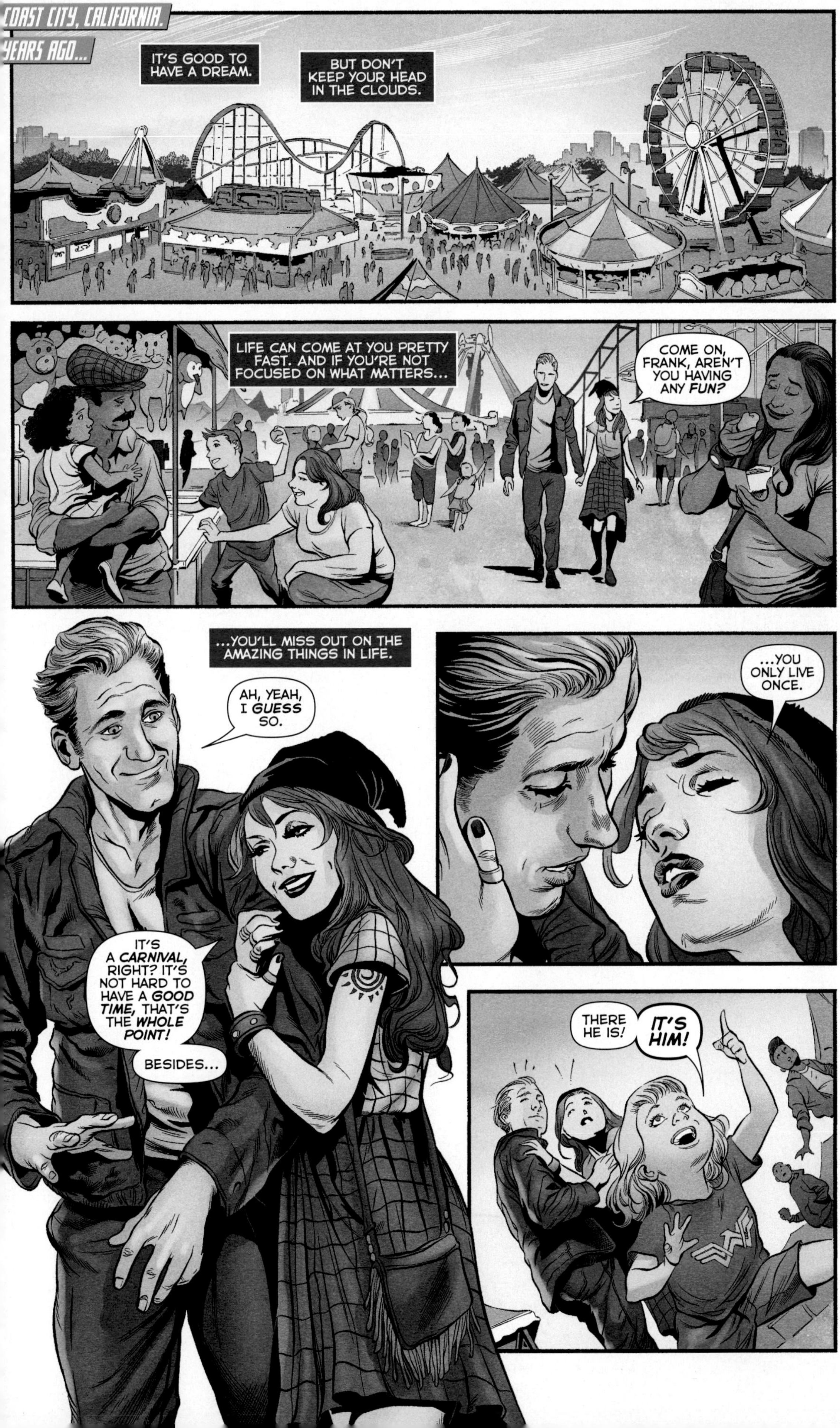
COAST CITY, CALIFORNIA.
YEARS AGO...
IT'S GOOD TO HAVE A DREAM.
BUT DON'T KEEP YOUR HEAD IN THE CLOUDS.
LIFE CAN COME AT YOU PRETTY FAST. AND IF YOU'RE NOT FOCUSED ON WHAT MATTERS...
COME ON, FRANK, AREN'T YOU HAVING ANY *FUN*?
...YOU'LL MISS OUT ON THE AMAZING THINGS IN LIFE.
AH, YEAH, I *GUESS* SO.
IT'S A *CARNIVAL*, RIGHT? IT'S NOT HARD TO HAVE A *GOOD TIME,* THAT'S THE *WHOLE POINT!*
BESIDES...
...YOU ONLY LIVE ONCE.
THERE HE IS!
IT'S HIM!

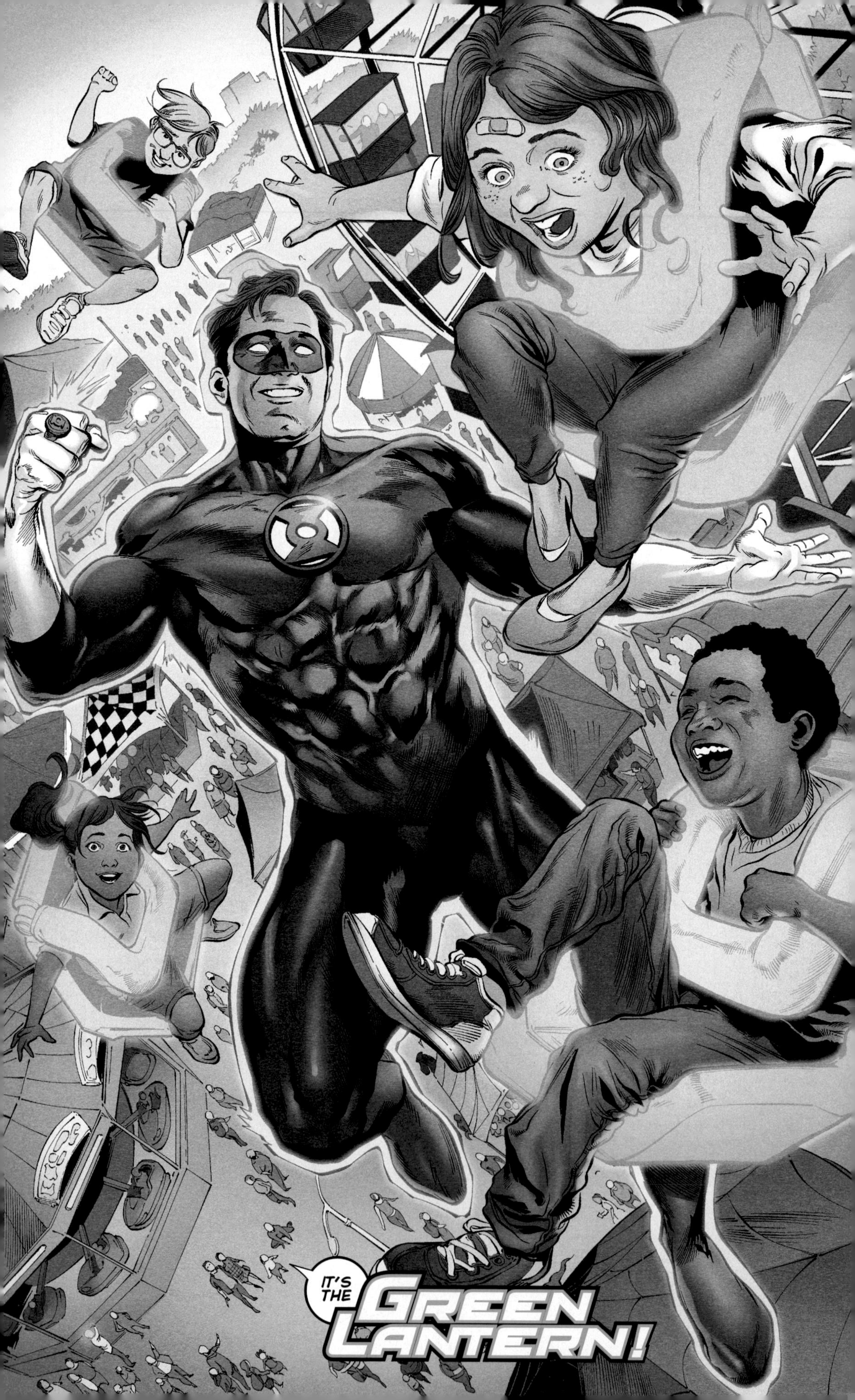

IT'S THE
GREEN LANTERN!

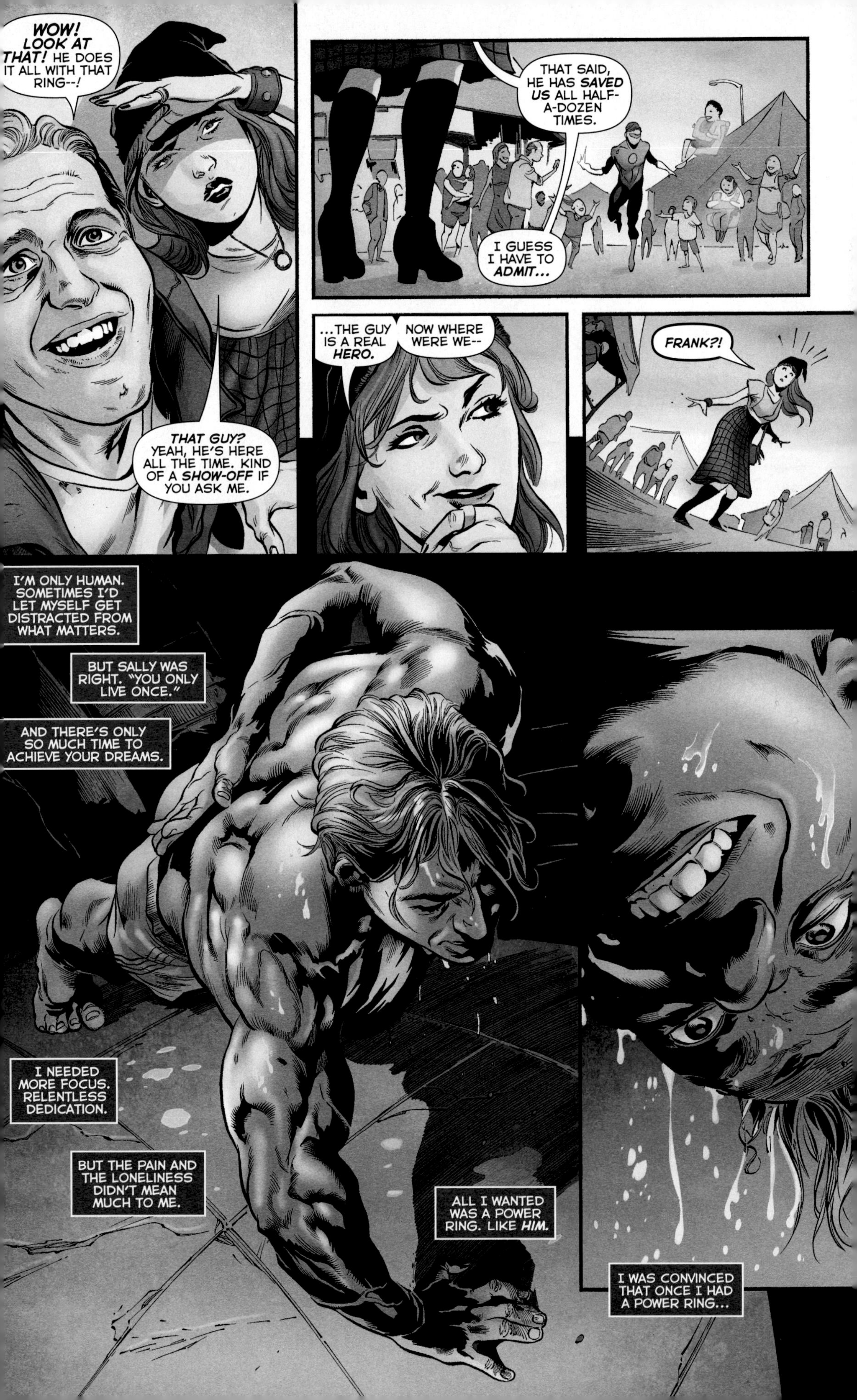

WOW! LOOK AT THAT! HE DOES IT ALL WITH THAT RING--!
THAT GUY? YEAH, HE'S HERE ALL THE TIME. KIND OF A SHOW-OFF IF YOU ASK ME.
THAT SAID, HE HAS SAVED US ALL HALF-A-DOZEN TIMES.
I GUESS I HAVE TO ADMIT...
...THE GUY IS A REAL HERO.
NOW WHERE WERE WE--
FRANK?!
I'M ONLY HUMAN. SOMETIMES I'D LET MYSELF GET DISTRACTED FROM WHAT MATTERS.
BUT SALLY WAS RIGHT. "YOU ONLY LIVE ONCE."
AND THERE'S ONLY SO MUCH TIME TO ACHIEVE YOUR DREAMS.
I NEEDED MORE FOCUS. RELENTLESS DEDICATION.
BUT THE PAIN AND THE LONELINESS DIDN'T MEAN MUCH TO ME.
ALL I WANTED WAS A POWER RING. LIKE HIM.
I WAS CONVINCED THAT ONCE I HAD A POWER RING...

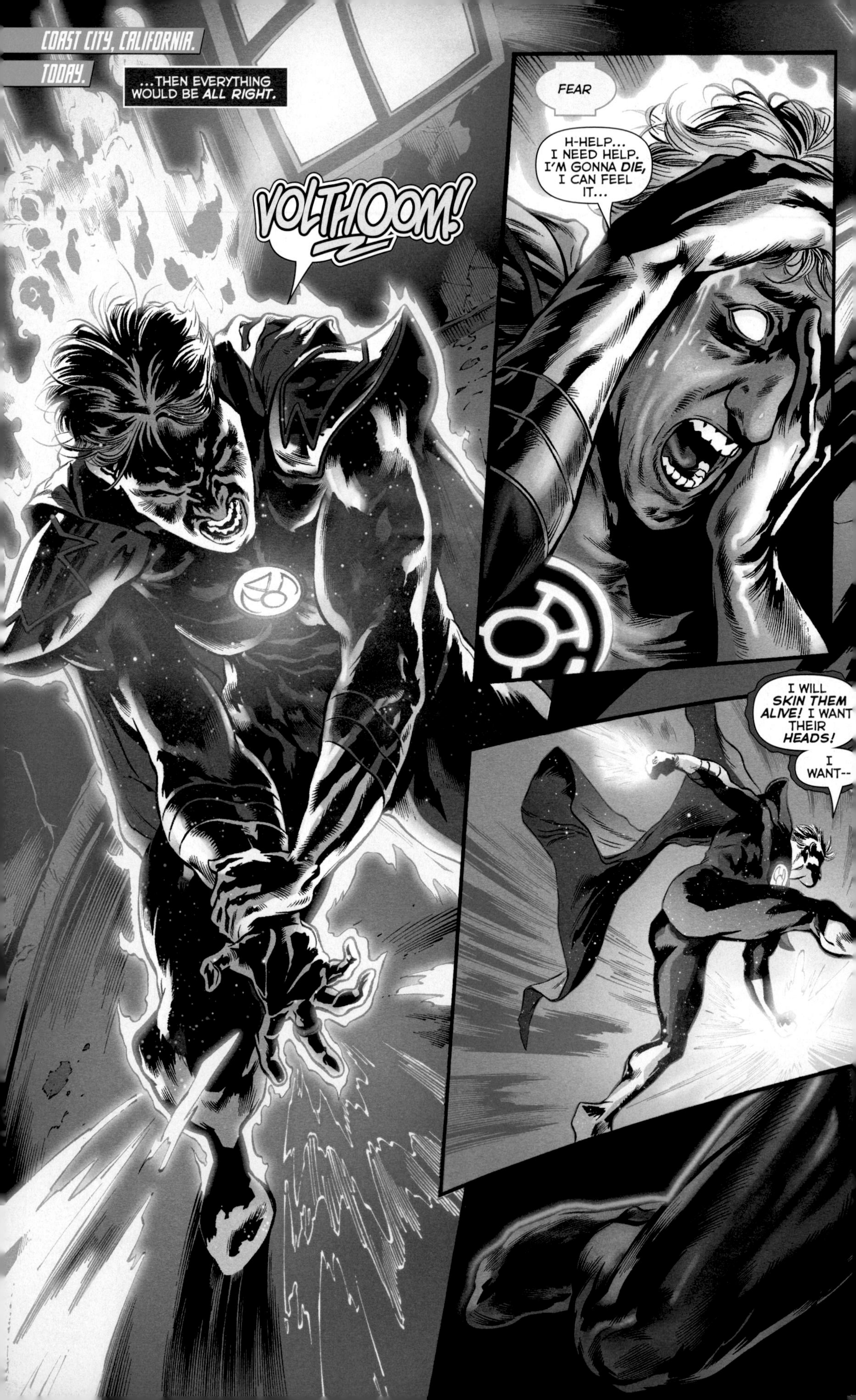

COAST CITY, CALIFORNIA.
TODAY.
...THEN EVERYTHING WOULD BE ALL RIGHT.
VOLTHOOM!
FEAR
H-HELP... I NEED HELP. I'M GONNA DIE, I CAN FEEL IT...
I WILL SKIN THEM ALIVE! I WANT THEIR HEADS!
I WANT--

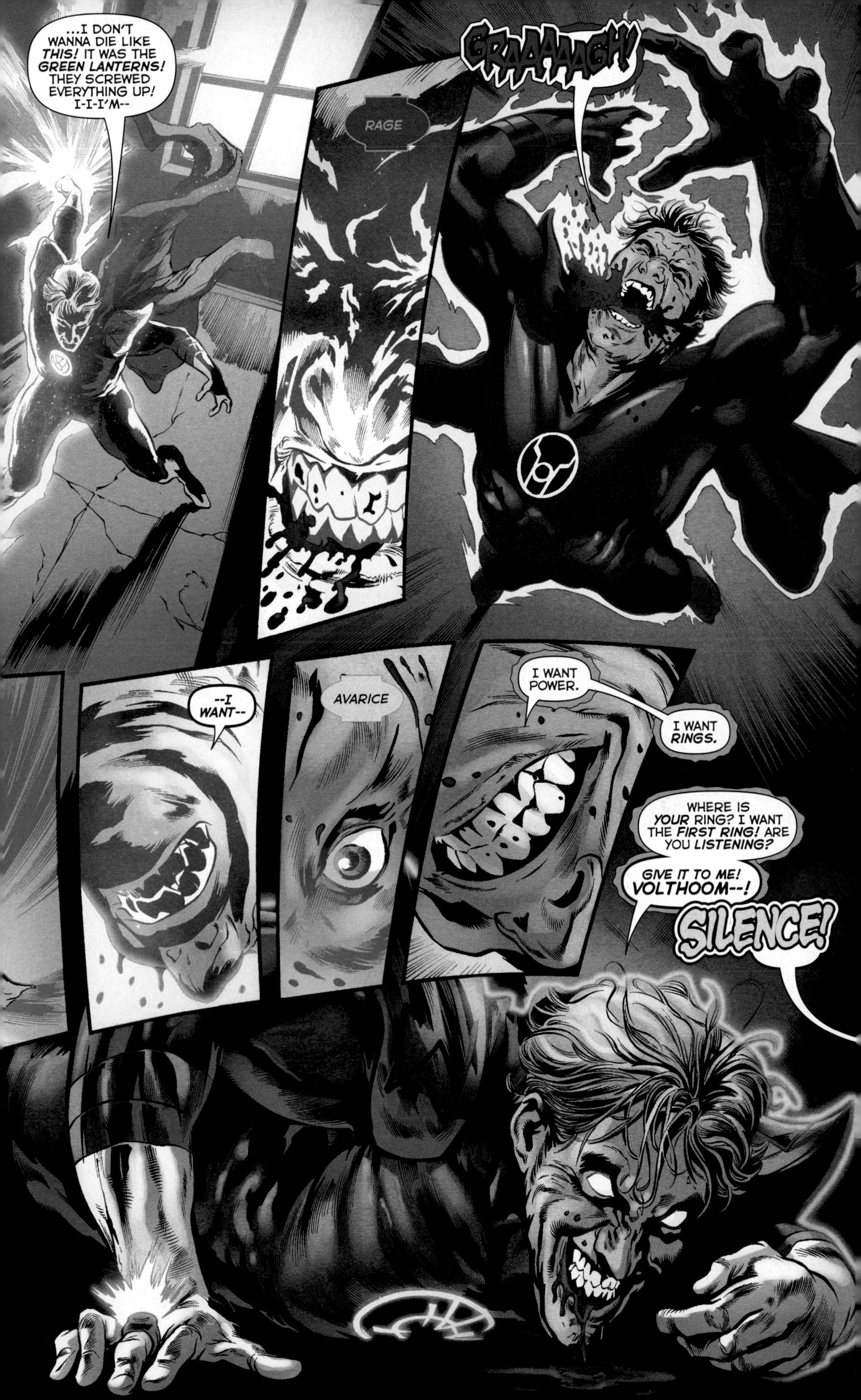
...I DON'T WANNA DIE LIKE *THIS!* IT WAS THE *GREEN LANTERNS!* THEY SCREWED EVERYTHING UP! I-I-I'M--
GRAAAAAGH!
RAGE
--I WANT--
AVARICE
I WANT POWER.
I WANT *RINGS.*
WHERE IS *YOUR* RING? I WANT THE *FIRST RING!* ARE YOU *LISTENING?*
GIVE IT TO ME! VOLTHOOM--!
SILENCE!

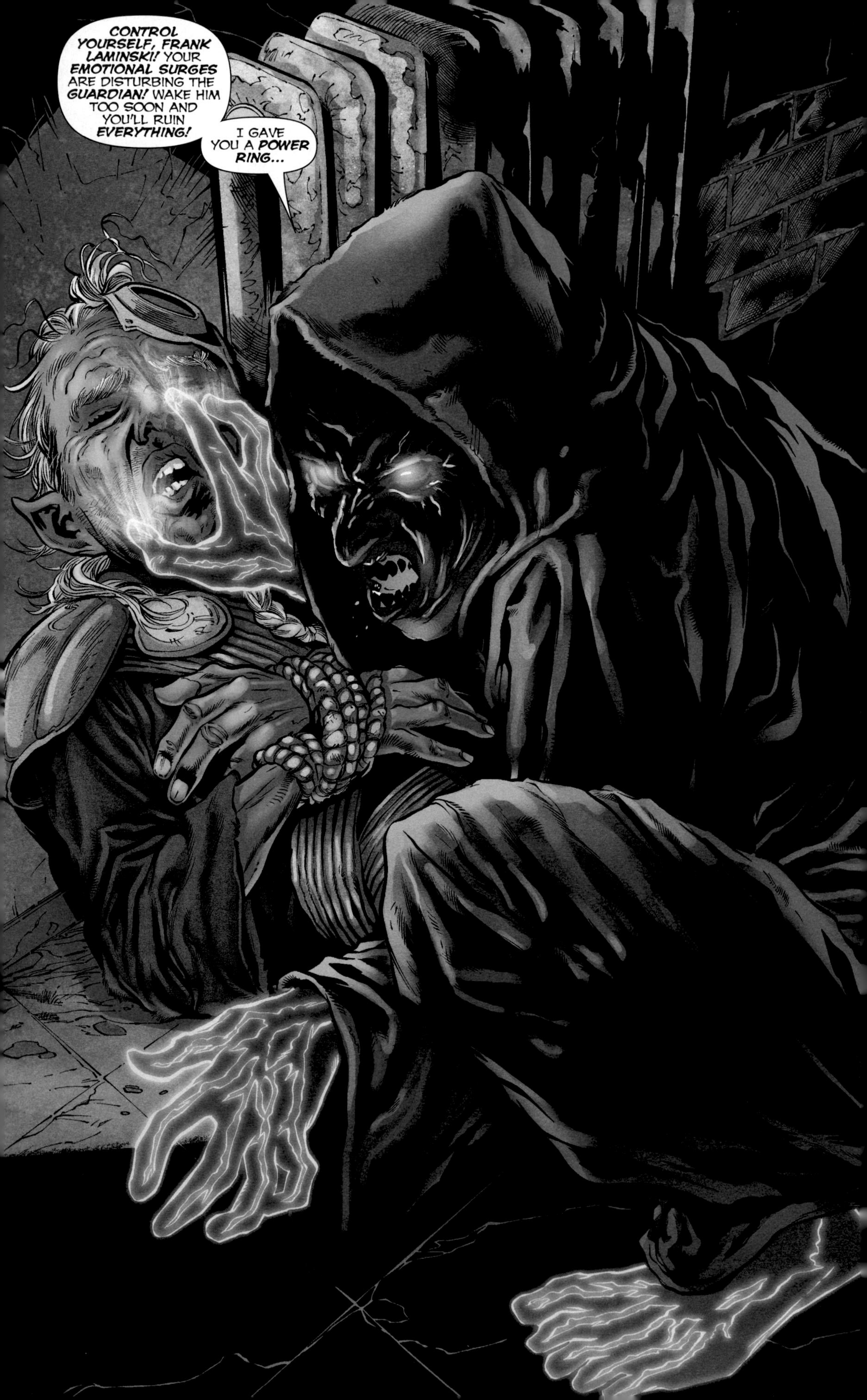
CONTROL YOURSELF, FRANK LAMINSKI! YOUR EMOTIONAL SURGES ARE DISTURBING THE GUARDIAN! WAKE HIM TOO SOON AND YOU'LL RUIN EVERYTHING!
I GAVE YOU A POWER RING...

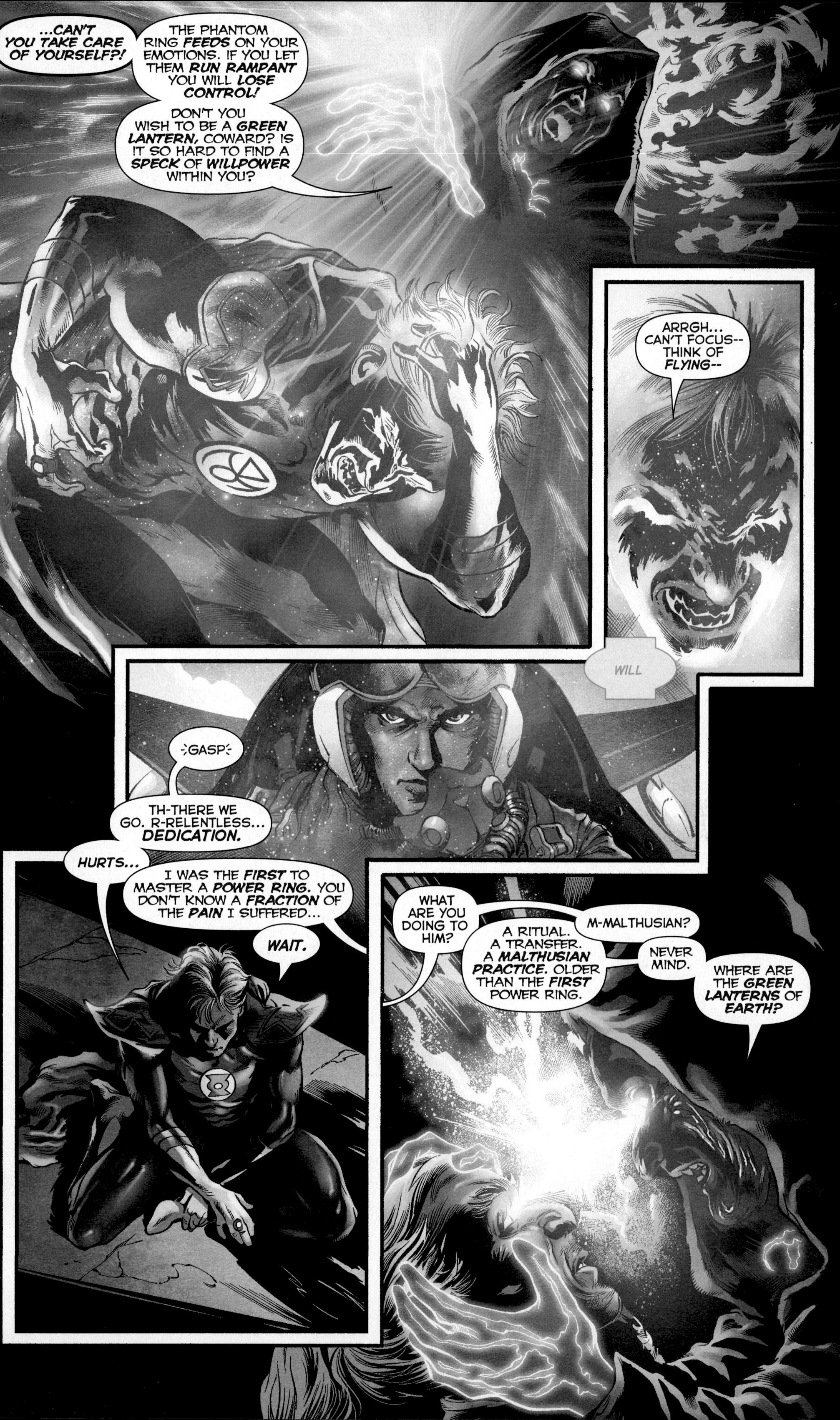
...CAN'T YOU TAKE CARE OF YOURSELF?!
THE PHANTOM RING FEEDS ON YOUR EMOTIONS. IF YOU LET THEM RUN RAMPANT YOU WILL LOSE CONTROL!
DON'T YOU WISH TO BE A GREEN LANTERN, COWARD? IS IT SO HARD TO FIND A SPECK OF WILLPOWER WITHIN YOU?
ARRGH... CAN'T FOCUS-- THINK OF FLYING--
WILL
-GASP-
TH-THERE WE GO. R-RELENTLESS... DEDICATION.
HURTS...
I WAS THE FIRST TO MASTER A POWER RING. YOU DON'T KNOW A FRACTION OF THE PAIN I SUFFERED...
WAIT.
WHAT ARE YOU DOING TO HIM?
M-MALTHUSIAN?
A RITUAL. A TRANSFER. A MALTHUSIAN PRACTICE. OLDER THAN THE FIRST POWER RING.
NEVER MIND.
WHERE ARE THE GREEN LANTERNS OF EARTH?

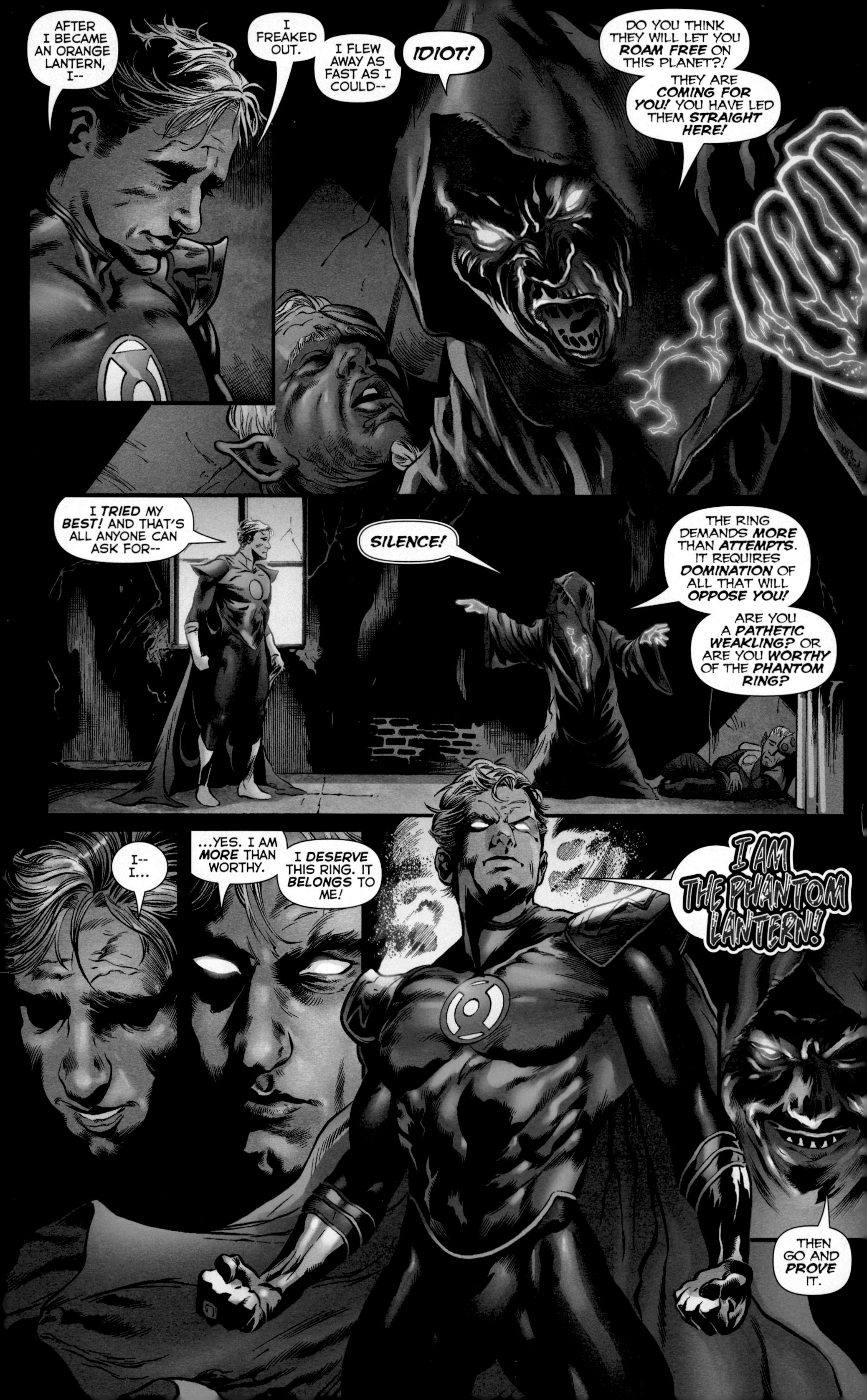
AFTER I BECAME AN ORANGE LANTERN, I--
I FREAKED OUT.
I FLEW AWAY AS FAST AS I COULD--
IDIOT!
DO YOU THINK THEY WILL LET YOU ROAM FREE ON THIS PLANET?!
THEY ARE COMING FOR YOU! YOU HAVE LED THEM STRAIGHT HERE!
I TRIED MY BEST! AND THAT'S ALL ANYONE CAN ASK FOR--
SILENCE!
THE RING DEMANDS MORE THAN ATTEMPTS. IT REQUIRES DOMINATION OF ALL THAT WILL OPPOSE YOU!
ARE YOU A PATHETIC WEAKLING? OR ARE YOU WORTHY OF THE PHANTOM RING?
I-- I...
...YES. I AM MORE THAN WORTHY.
I DESERVE THIS RING. IT BELONGS TO ME!
I AM THE PHANTOM LANTERN!
THEN GO AND PROVE IT.

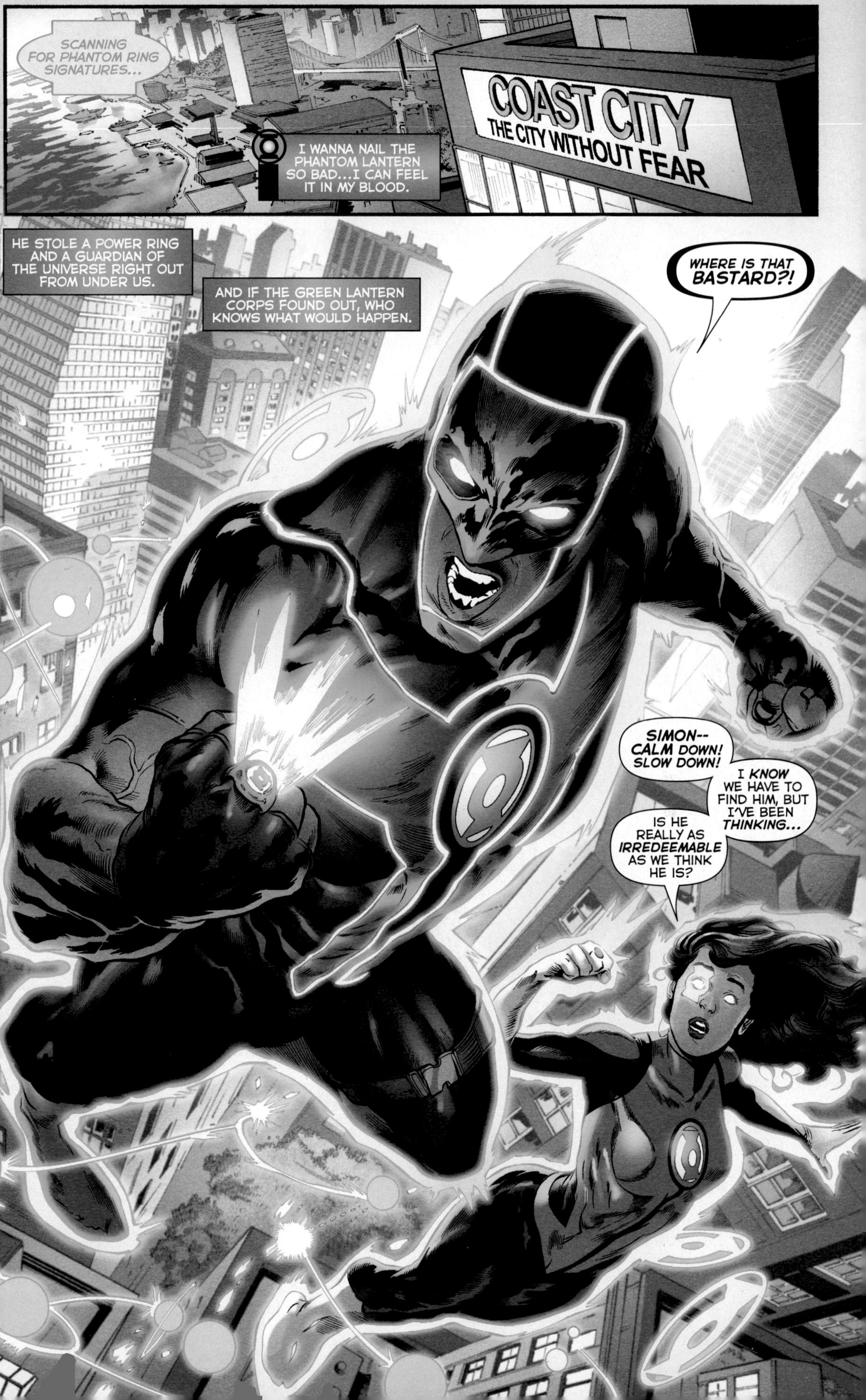
SCANNING FOR PHANTOM RING SIGNATURES...
COAST CITY
THE CITY WITHOUT FEAR
I WANNA NAIL THE PHANTOM LANTERN SO BAD...I CAN FEEL IT IN MY BLOOD.
HE STOLE A POWER RING AND A GUARDIAN OF THE UNIVERSE RIGHT OUT FROM UNDER US.
AND IF THE GREEN LANTERN CORPS FOUND OUT, WHO KNOWS WHAT WOULD HAPPEN.
WHERE IS THAT BASTARD?!
SIMON-- CALM DOWN! SLOW DOWN!
I KNOW WE HAVE TO FIND HIM, BUT I'VE BEEN THINKING...
IS HE REALLY AS IRREDEEMABLE AS WE THINK HE IS?

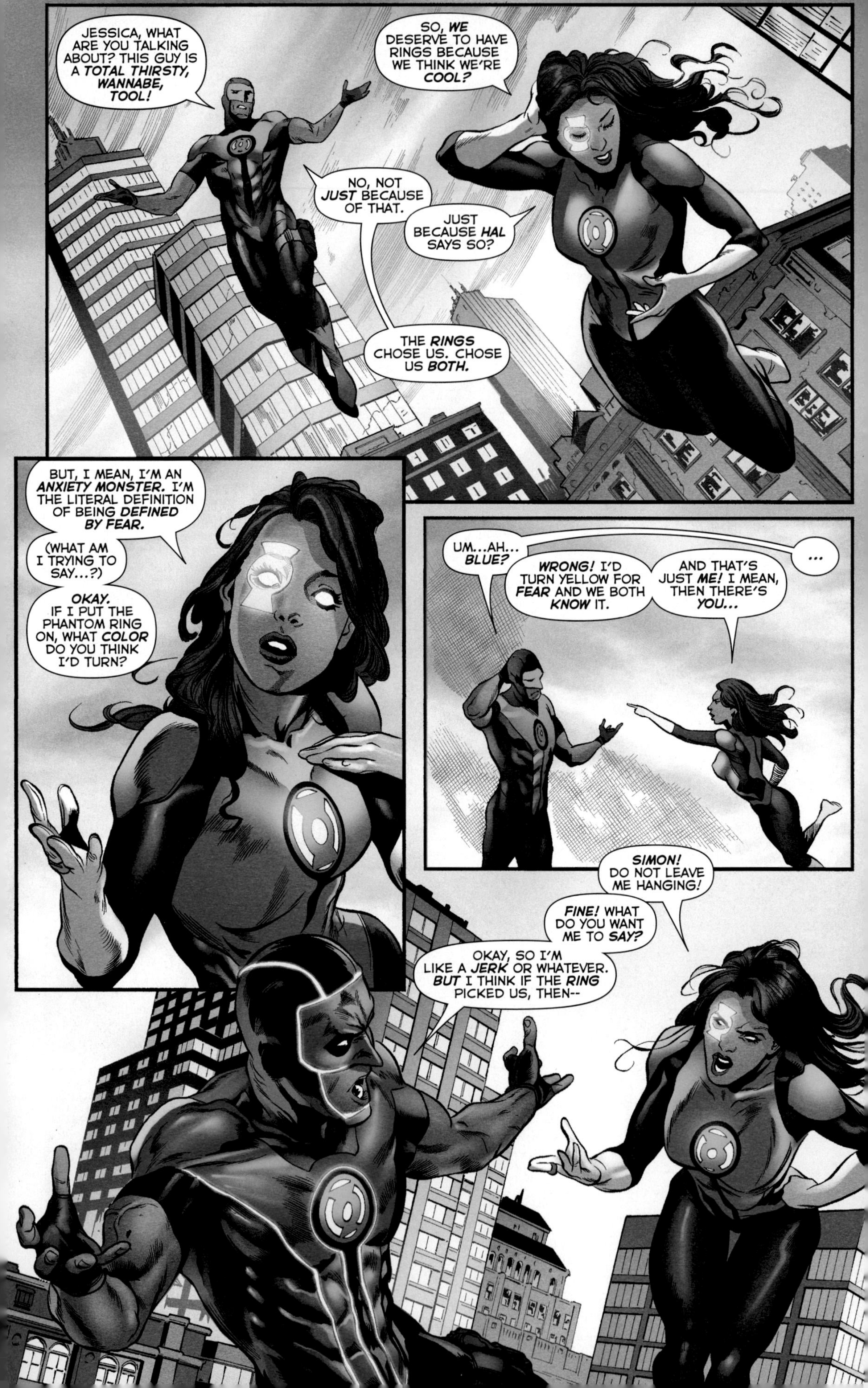
JESSICA, WHAT ARE YOU TALKING ABOUT? THIS GUY IS A TOTAL THIRSTY, WANNABE, TOOL!
SO, WE DESERVE TO HAVE RINGS BECAUSE WE THINK WE'RE COOL?
NO, NOT JUST BECAUSE OF THAT.
JUST BECAUSE HAL SAYS SO?
THE RINGS CHOSE US. CHOSE US BOTH.
BUT, I MEAN, I'M AN ANXIETY MONSTER. I'M THE LITERAL DEFINITION OF BEING DEFINED BY FEAR.
(WHAT AM I TRYING TO SAY...?)
OKAY. IF I PUT THE PHANTOM RING ON, WHAT COLOR DO YOU THINK I'D TURN?
UM...AH... BLUE?
WRONG! I'D TURN YELLOW FOR FEAR AND WE BOTH KNOW IT.
AND THAT'S JUST ME! I MEAN, THEN THERE'S YOU...
...
SIMON! DO NOT LEAVE ME HANGING!
FINE! WHAT DO YOU WANT ME TO SAY?
OKAY, SO I'M LIKE A JERK OR WHATEVER. BUT I THINK IF THE RING PICKED US, THEN--

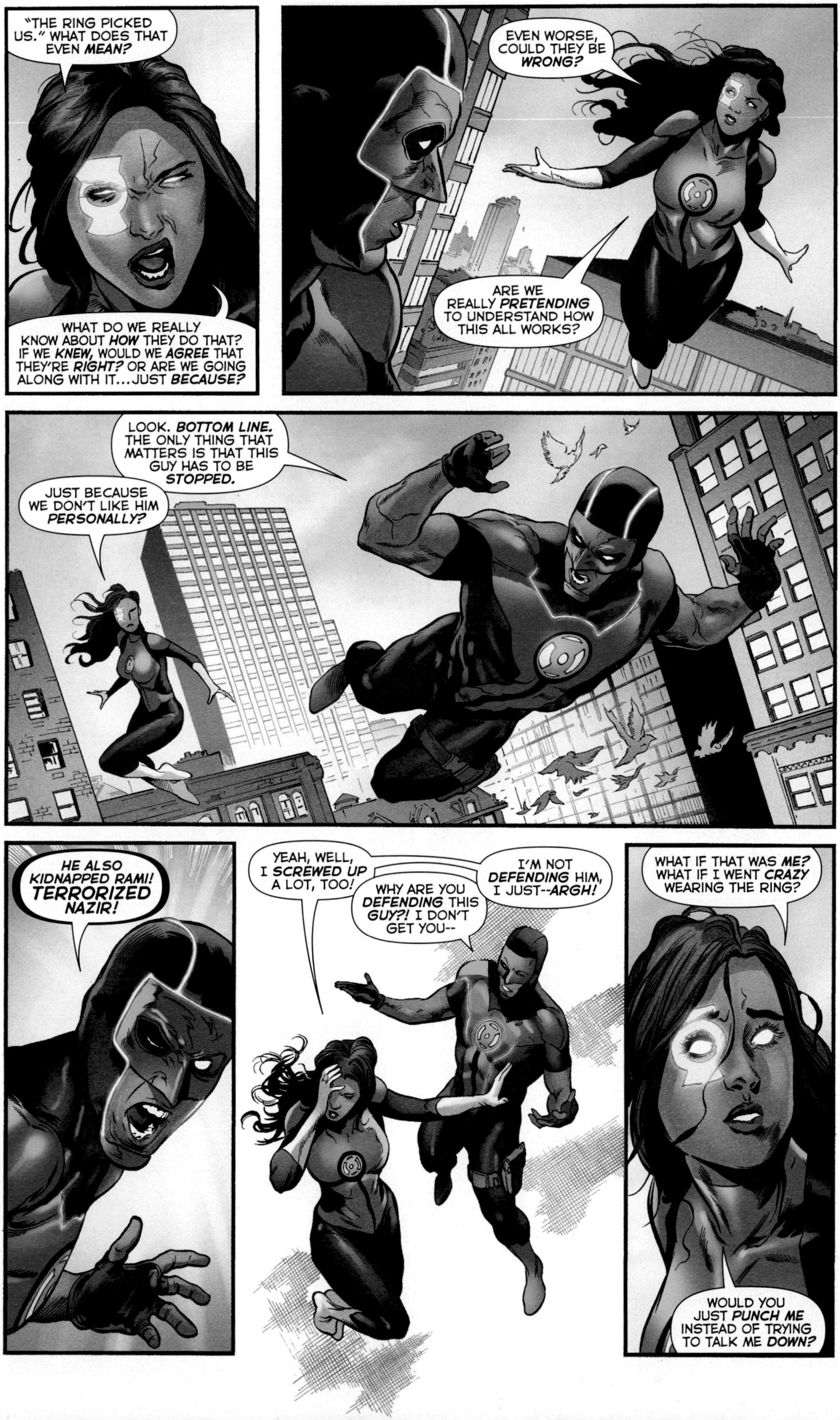
"THE RING PICKED US." WHAT DOES THAT EVEN MEAN?
WHAT DO WE REALLY KNOW ABOUT HOW THEY DO THAT? IF WE KNEW, WOULD WE AGREE THAT THEY'RE RIGHT? OR ARE WE GOING ALONG WITH IT...JUST BECAUSE?
EVEN WORSE, COULD THEY BE WRONG?
ARE WE REALLY PRETENDING TO UNDERSTAND HOW THIS ALL WORKS?
LOOK. BOTTOM LINE. THE ONLY THING THAT MATTERS IS THAT THIS GUY HAS TO BE STOPPED.
JUST BECAUSE WE DON'T LIKE HIM PERSONALLY?
HE ALSO KIDNAPPED RAMI! TERRORIZED NAZIR!
YEAH, WELL, I SCREWED UP A LOT, TOO!
I'M NOT DEFENDING HIM, I JUST--ARGH!
WHY ARE YOU DEFENDING THIS GUY?! I DON'T GET YOU--
WHAT IF THAT WAS ME? WHAT IF I WENT CRAZY WEARING THE RING?
WOULD YOU JUST PUNCH ME INSTEAD OF TRYING TO TALK ME DOWN?

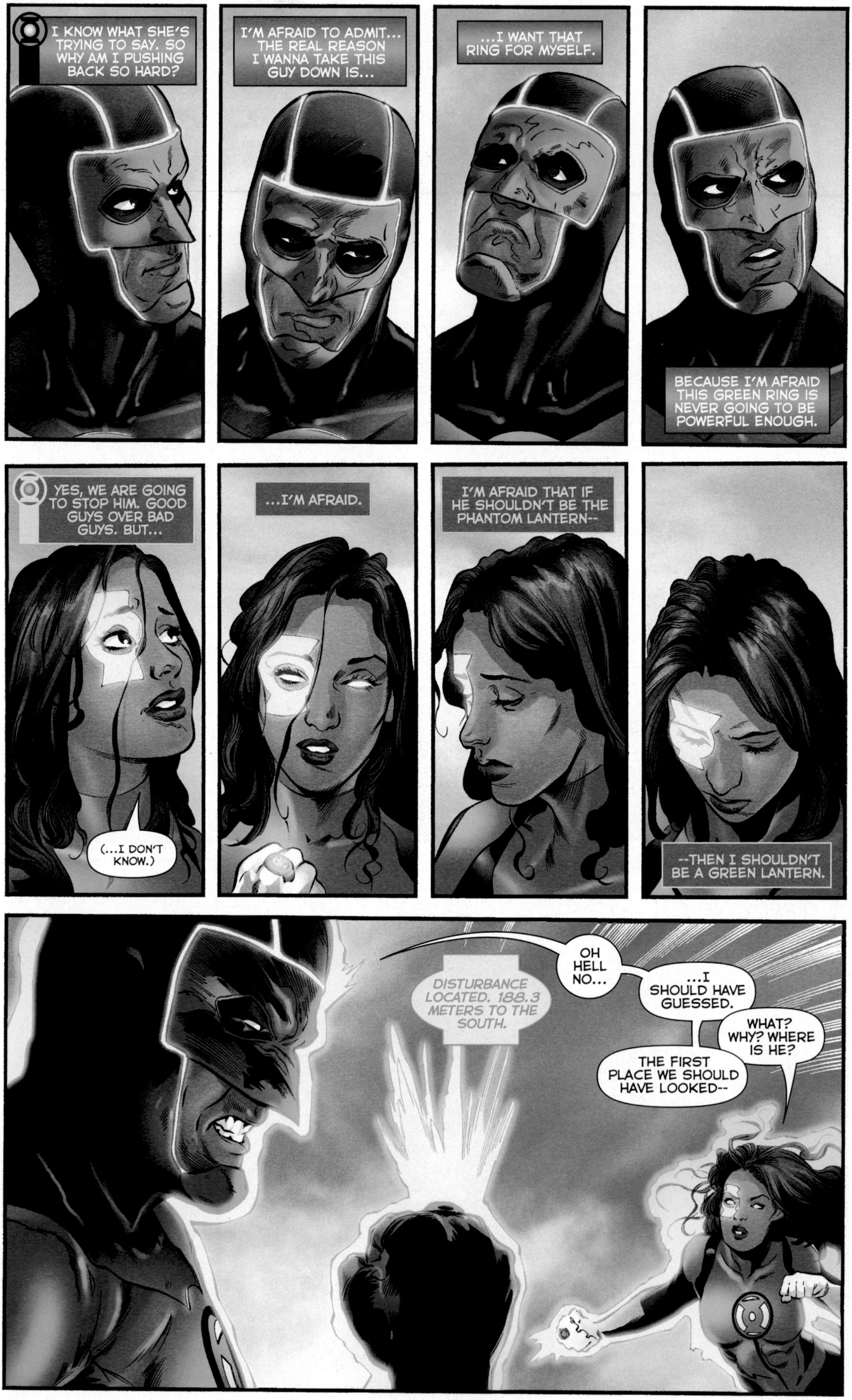
I KNOW WHAT SHE'S TRYING TO SAY. SO WHY AM I PUSHING BACK SO HARD?
I'M AFRAID TO ADMIT... THE REAL REASON I WANNA TAKE THIS GUY DOWN IS...
...I WANT THAT RING FOR MYSELF.
BECAUSE I'M AFRAID THIS GREEN RING IS NEVER GOING TO BE POWERFUL ENOUGH.
YES, WE ARE GOING TO STOP HIM. GOOD GUYS OVER BAD GUYS. BUT...
(...I DON'T KNOW.)
...I'M AFRAID.
I'M AFRAID THAT IF HE SHOULDN'T BE THE PHANTOM LANTERN--
--THEN I SHOULDN'T BE A GREEN LANTERN.
DISTURBANCE LOCATED. 188.3 METERS TO THE SOUTH.
OH HELL NO...
...I SHOULD HAVE GUESSED.
THE FIRST PLACE WE SHOULD HAVE LOOKED--
WHAT? WHY? WHERE IS HE?

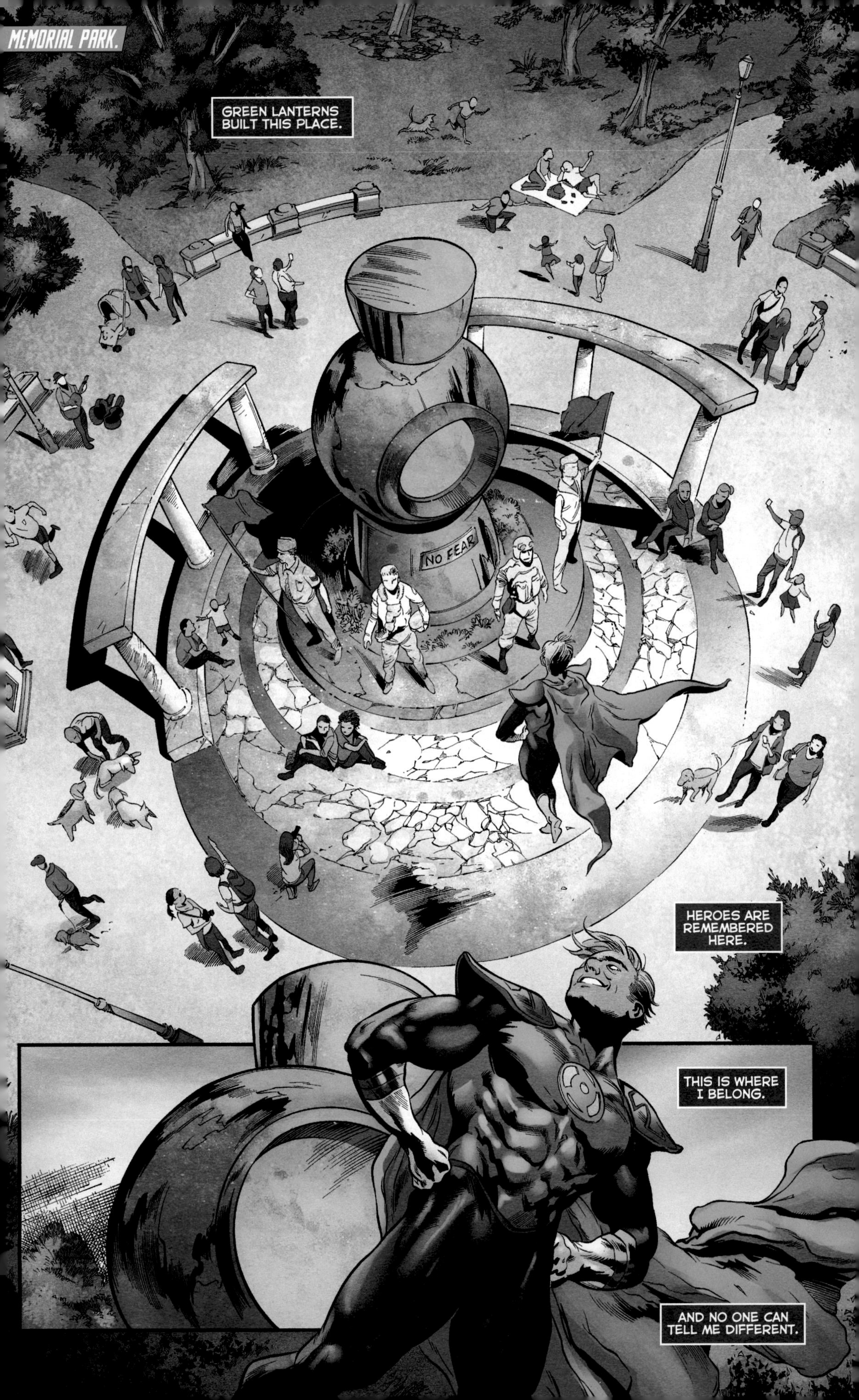
MEMORIAL PARK.
GREEN LANTERNS BUILT THIS PLACE.
NO FEAR
HEROES ARE REMEMBERED HERE.
THIS IS WHERE I BELONG.
AND NO ONE CAN TELL ME DIFFERENT.

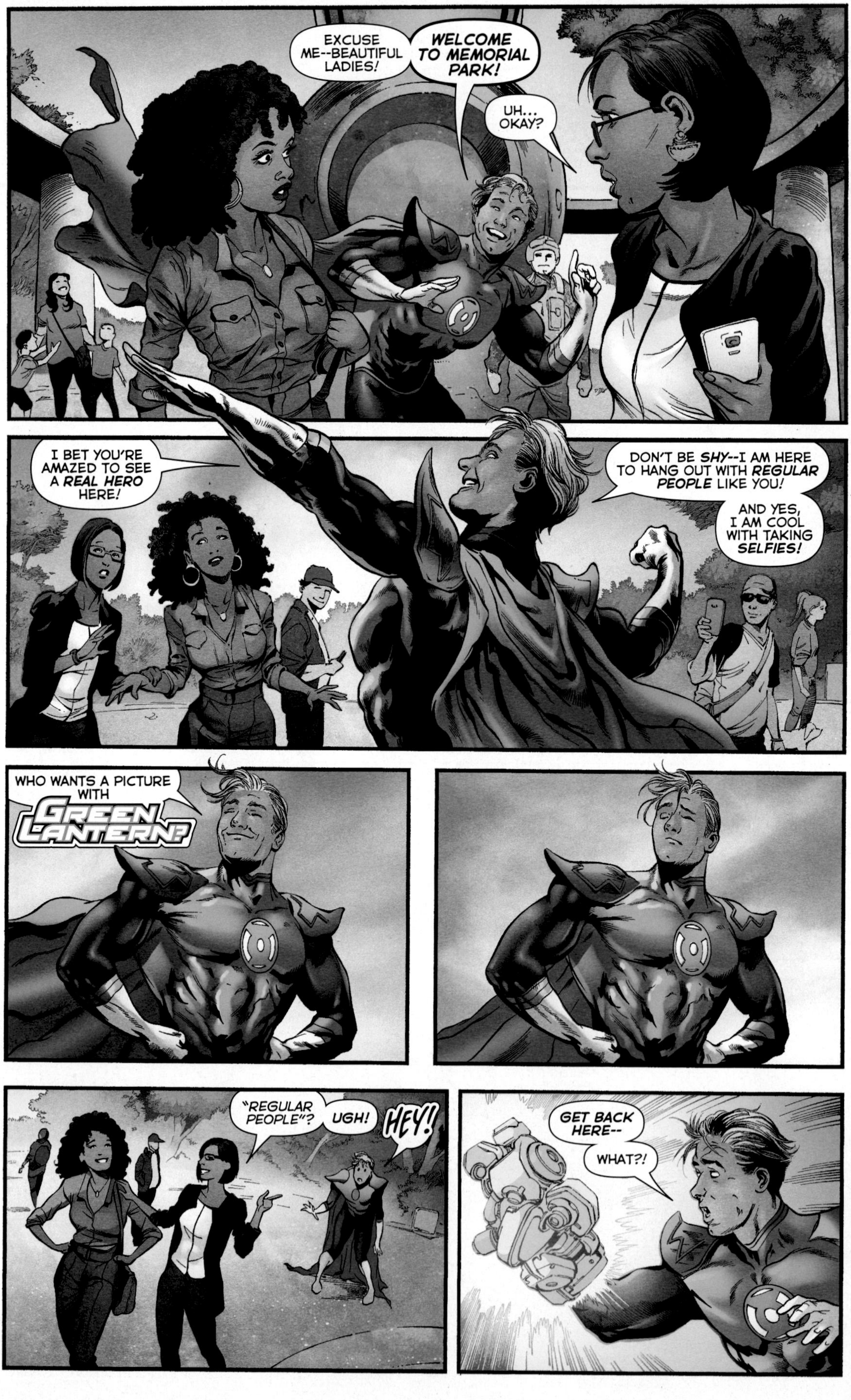
EXCUSE ME--BEAUTIFUL LADIES!
WELCOME TO MEMORIAL PARK!
UH... OKAY?
I BET YOU'RE AMAZED TO SEE A REAL HERO HERE!
DON'T BE SHY--I AM HERE TO HANG OUT WITH REGULAR PEOPLE LIKE YOU!
AND YES, I AM COOL WITH TAKING SELFIES!
WHO WANTS A PICTURE WITH GREEN LANTERN?
"REGULAR PEOPLE"?
UGH!
HEY!
GET BACK HERE--
WHAT?!

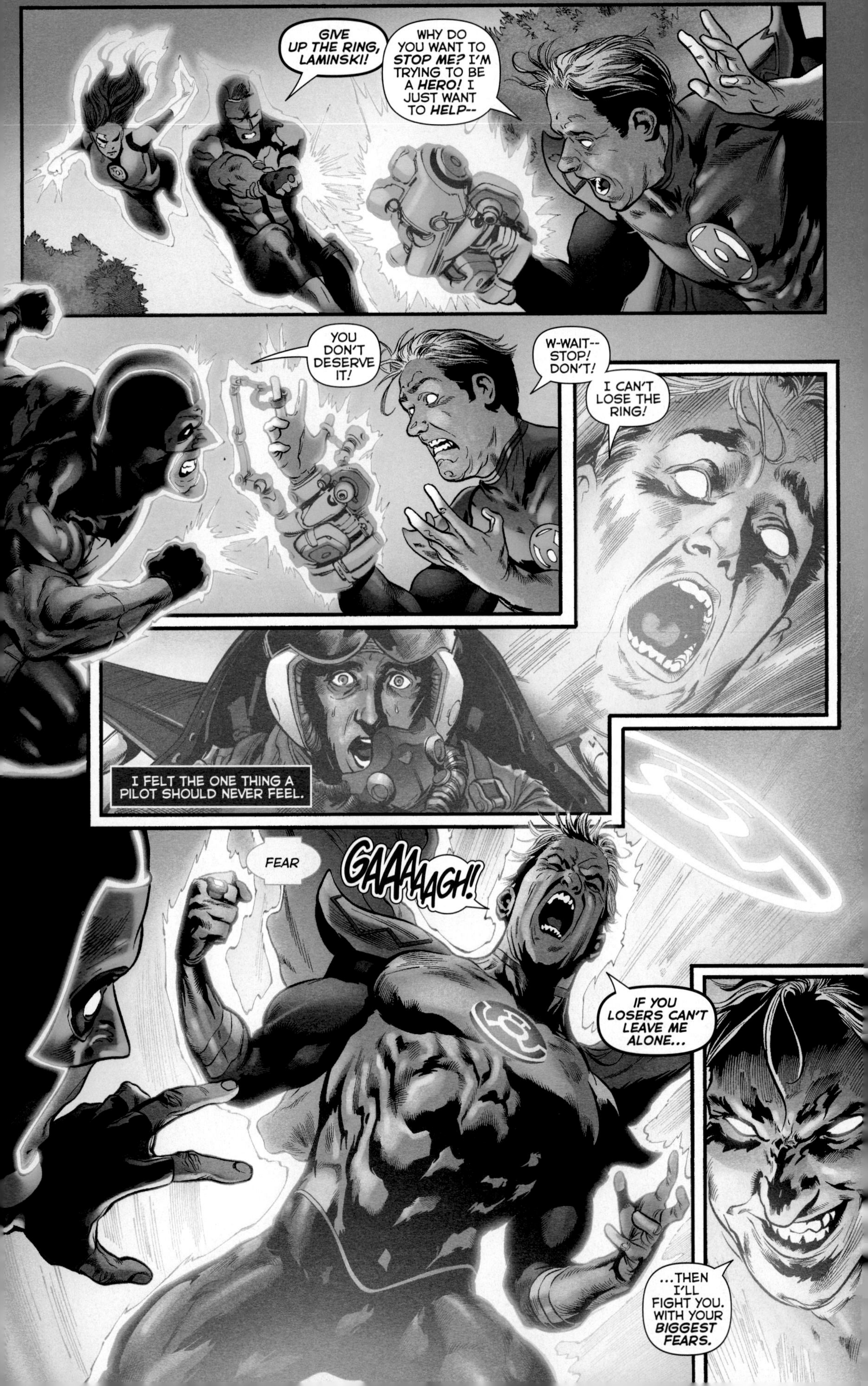
GIVE UP THE RING, LAMINSKI!
WHY DO YOU WANT TO STOP ME? I'M TRYING TO BE A HERO! I JUST WANT TO HELP--
YOU DON'T DESERVE IT!
W-WAIT-- STOP! DON'T!
I CAN'T LOSE THE RING!
I FELT THE ONE THING A PILOT SHOULD NEVER FEEL.
FEAR
GAAAAAGH!
IF YOU LOSERS CAN'T LEAVE ME ALONE...
...THEN I'LL FIGHT YOU. WITH YOUR BIGGEST FEARS.

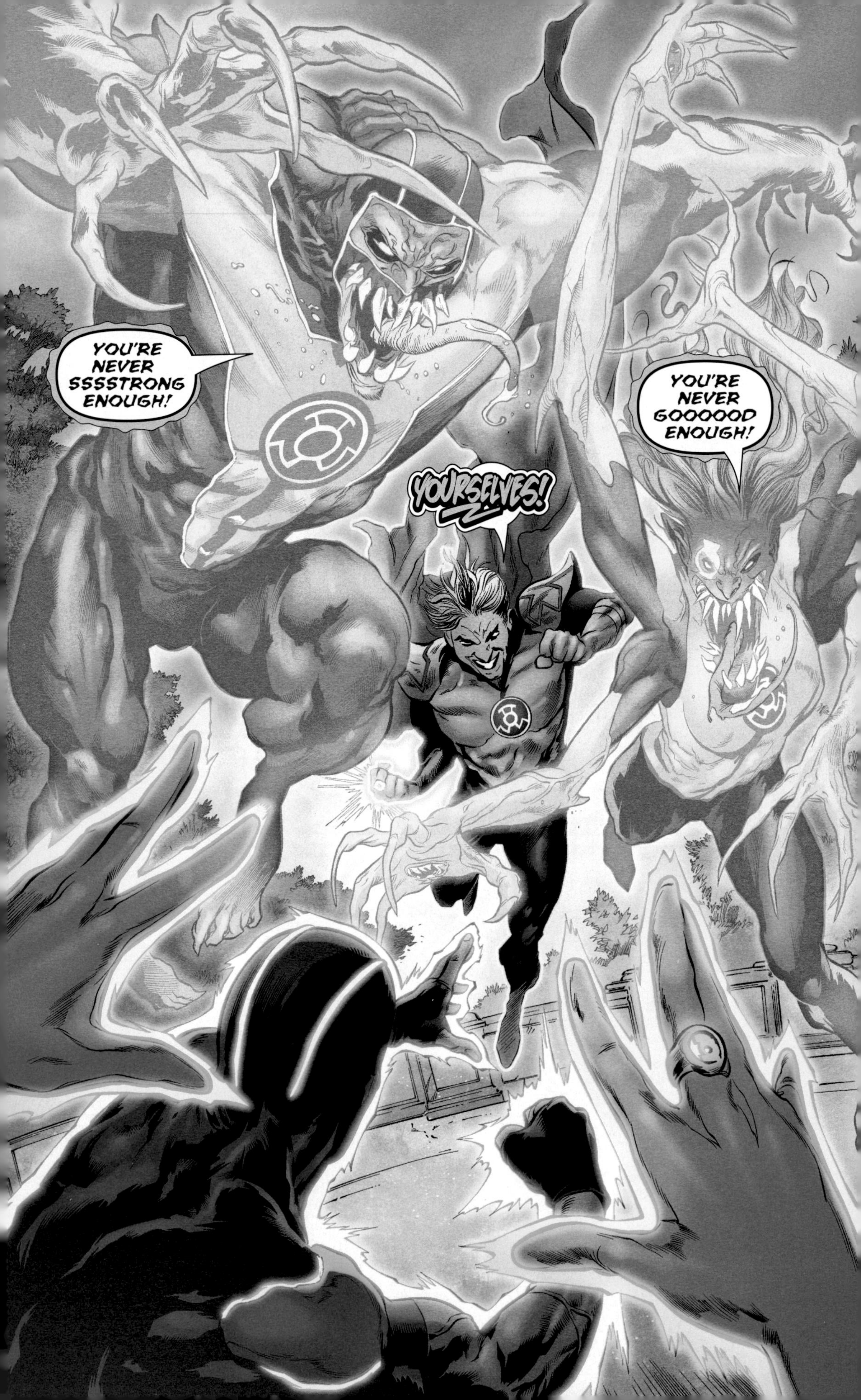
YOU'RE NEVER SSSSTRONG ENOUGH!
YOU'RE NEVER GOOOOOD ENOUGH!
YOURSELVES!

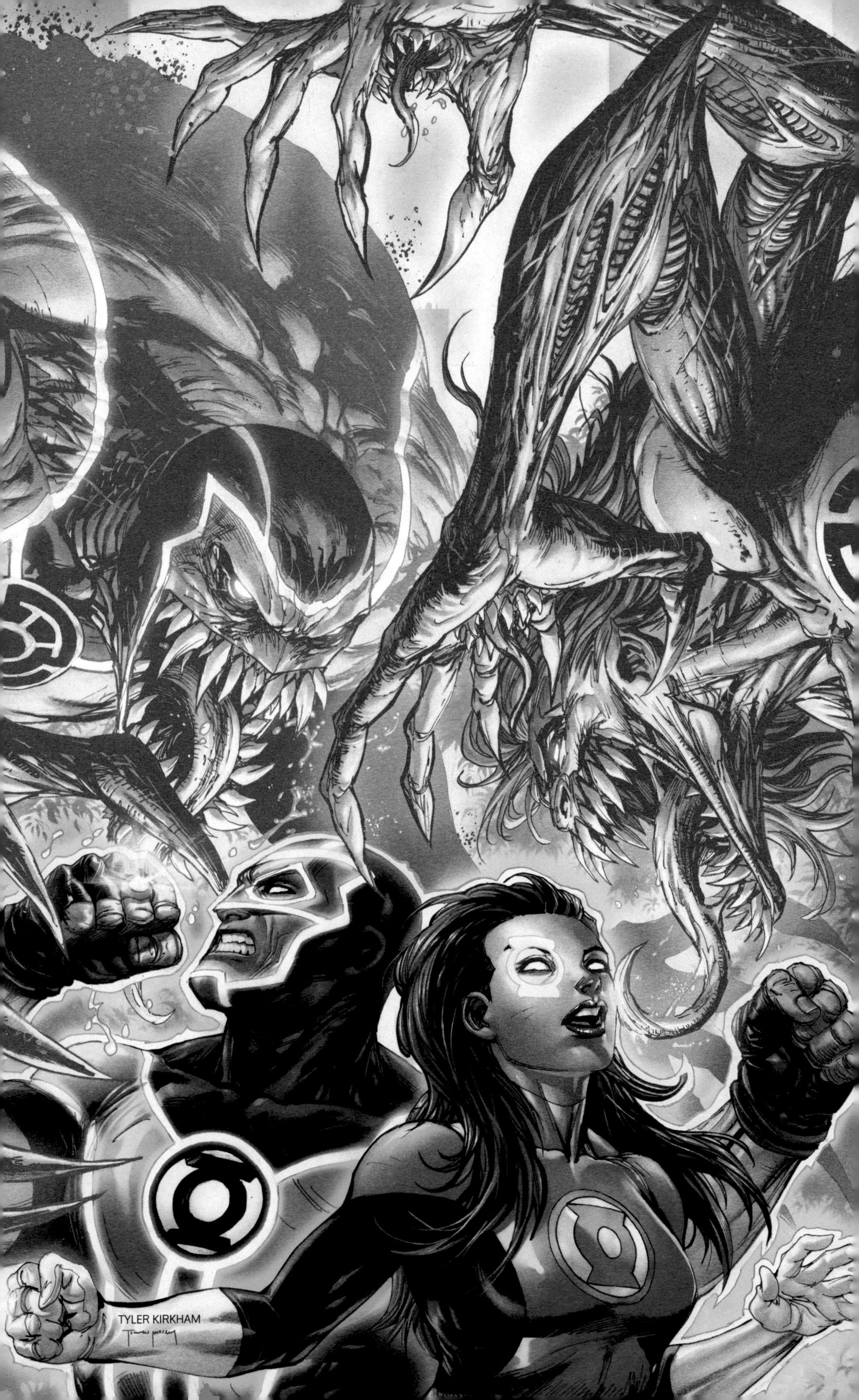
TYLER KIRKHAM

"THE PHANTOM LANTERN: PART FOUR"

SAM HUMPHRIES writer * RONAN CLIQUET artist

Cover by TYLER KIRKHAM and TOMEU MOREY

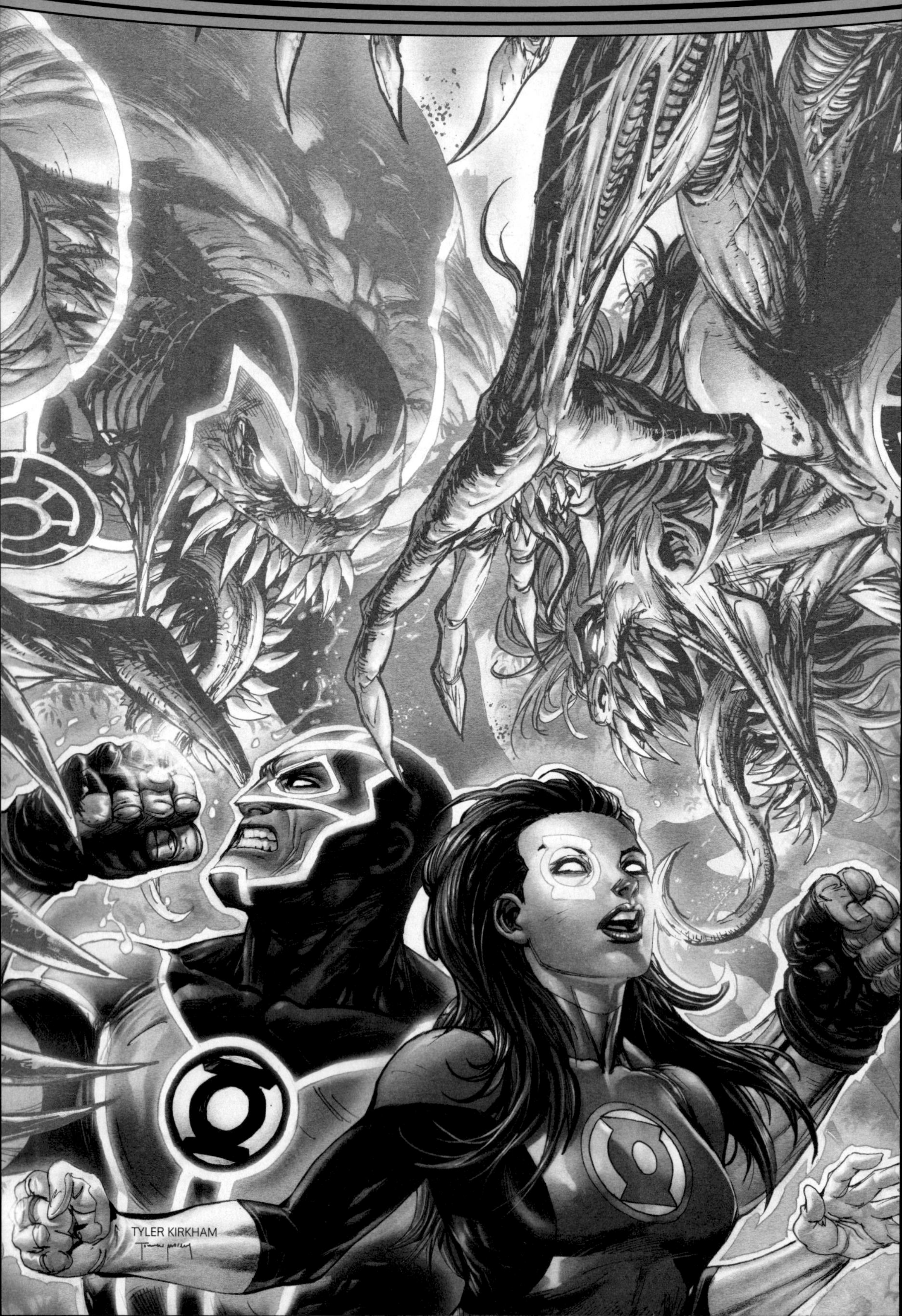
TYLER KIRKHAM

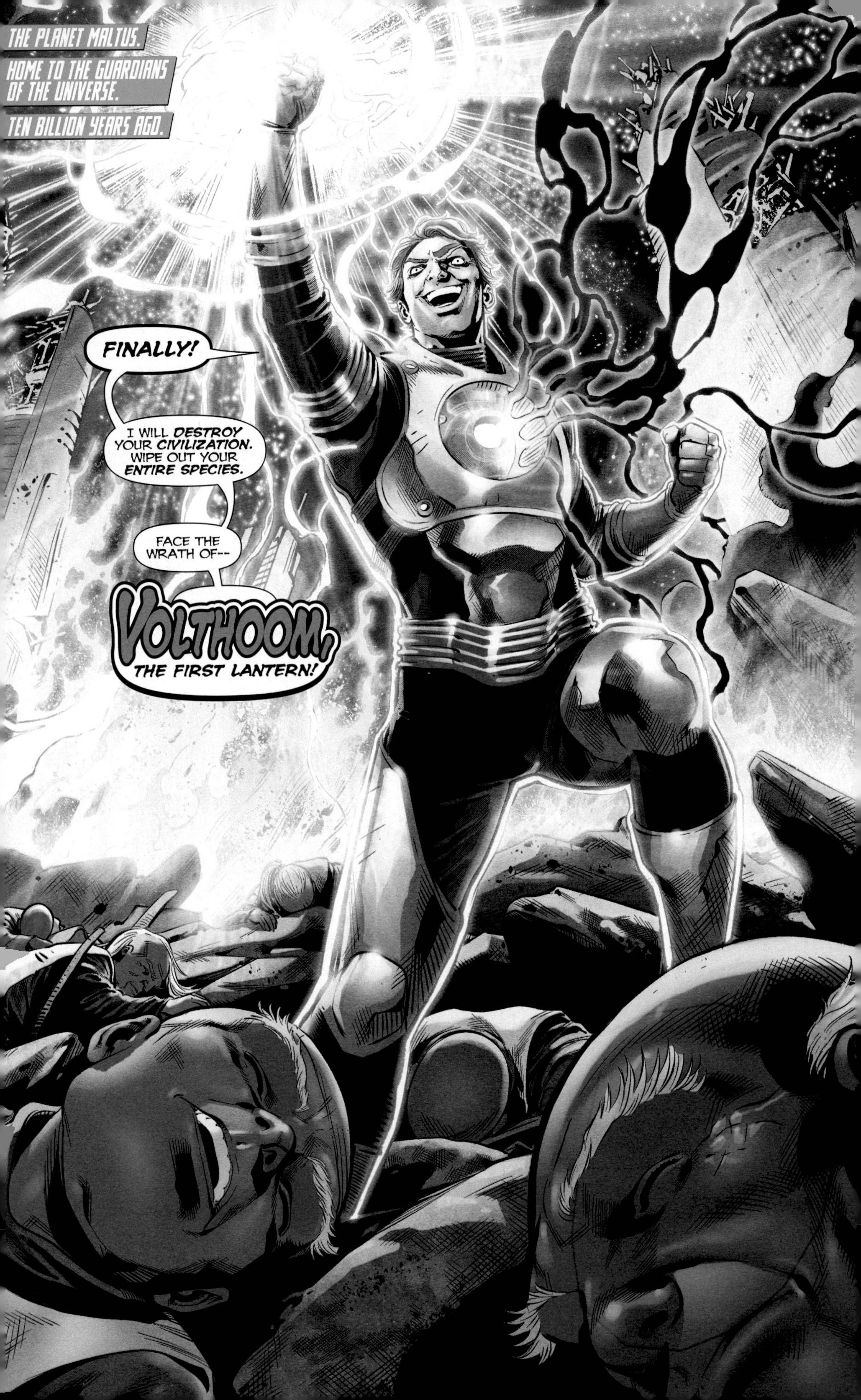

THE PLANET MALTUS.
HOME TO THE GUARDIANS OF THE UNIVERSE.
TEN BILLION YEARS AGO.
FINALLY!
I WILL DESTROY YOUR CIVILIZATION. WIPE OUT YOUR ENTIRE SPECIES.
FACE THE WRATH OF--
VOLTHOOM, THE FIRST LANTERN!

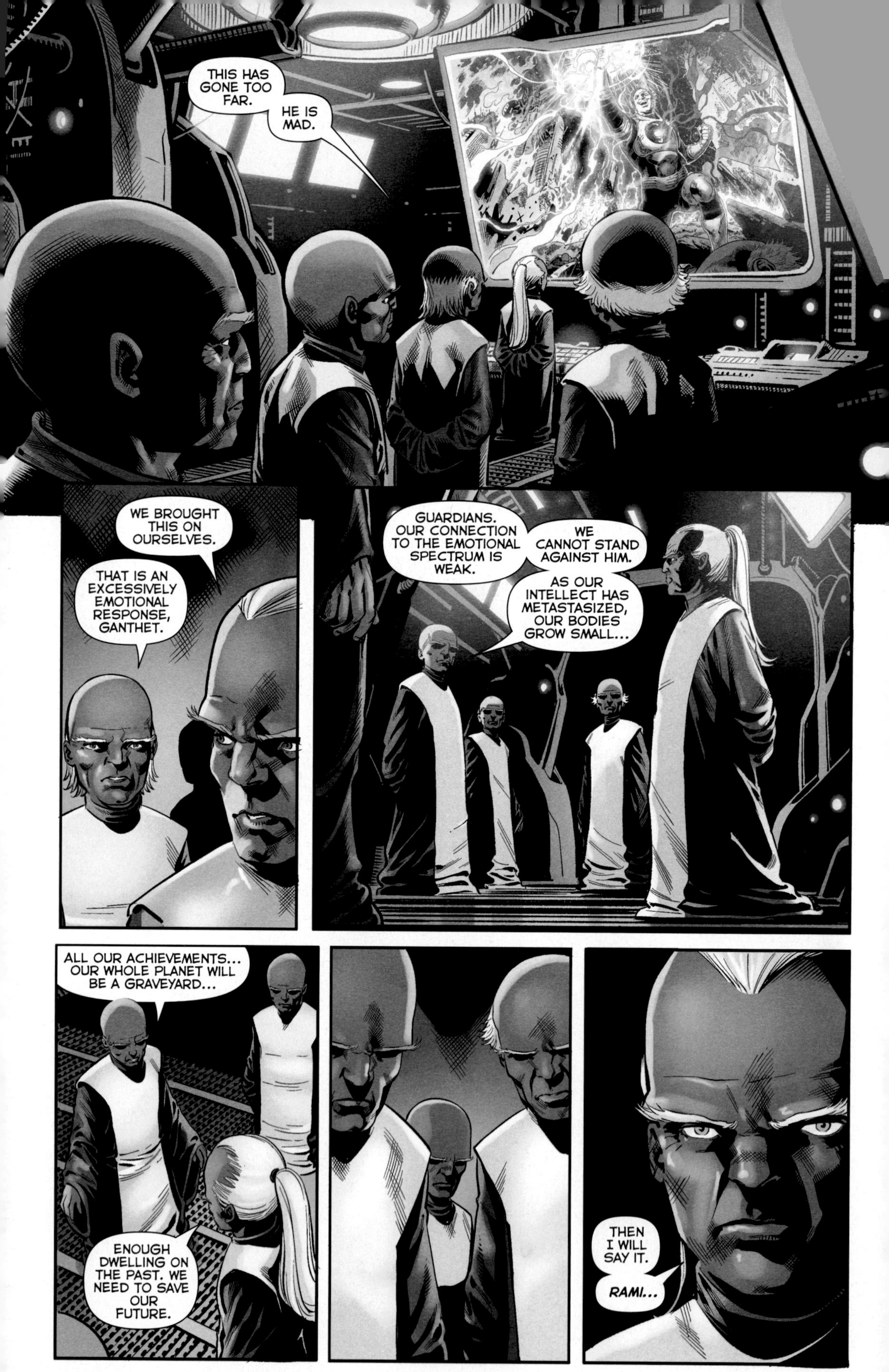
THIS HAS GONE TOO FAR.
HE IS MAD.
WE BROUGHT THIS ON OURSELVES.
THAT IS AN EXCESSIVELY EMOTIONAL RESPONSE, GANTHET.
GUARDIANS. OUR CONNECTION TO THE EMOTIONAL SPECTRUM IS WEAK.
WE CANNOT STAND AGAINST HIM.
AS OUR INTELLECT HAS METASTASIZED, OUR BODIES GROW SMALL...
ALL OUR ACHIEVEMENTS... OUR WHOLE PLANET WILL BE A GRAVEYARD...
ENOUGH DWELLING ON THE PAST. WE NEED TO SAVE OUR FUTURE.
THEN I WILL SAY IT.
RAMI...

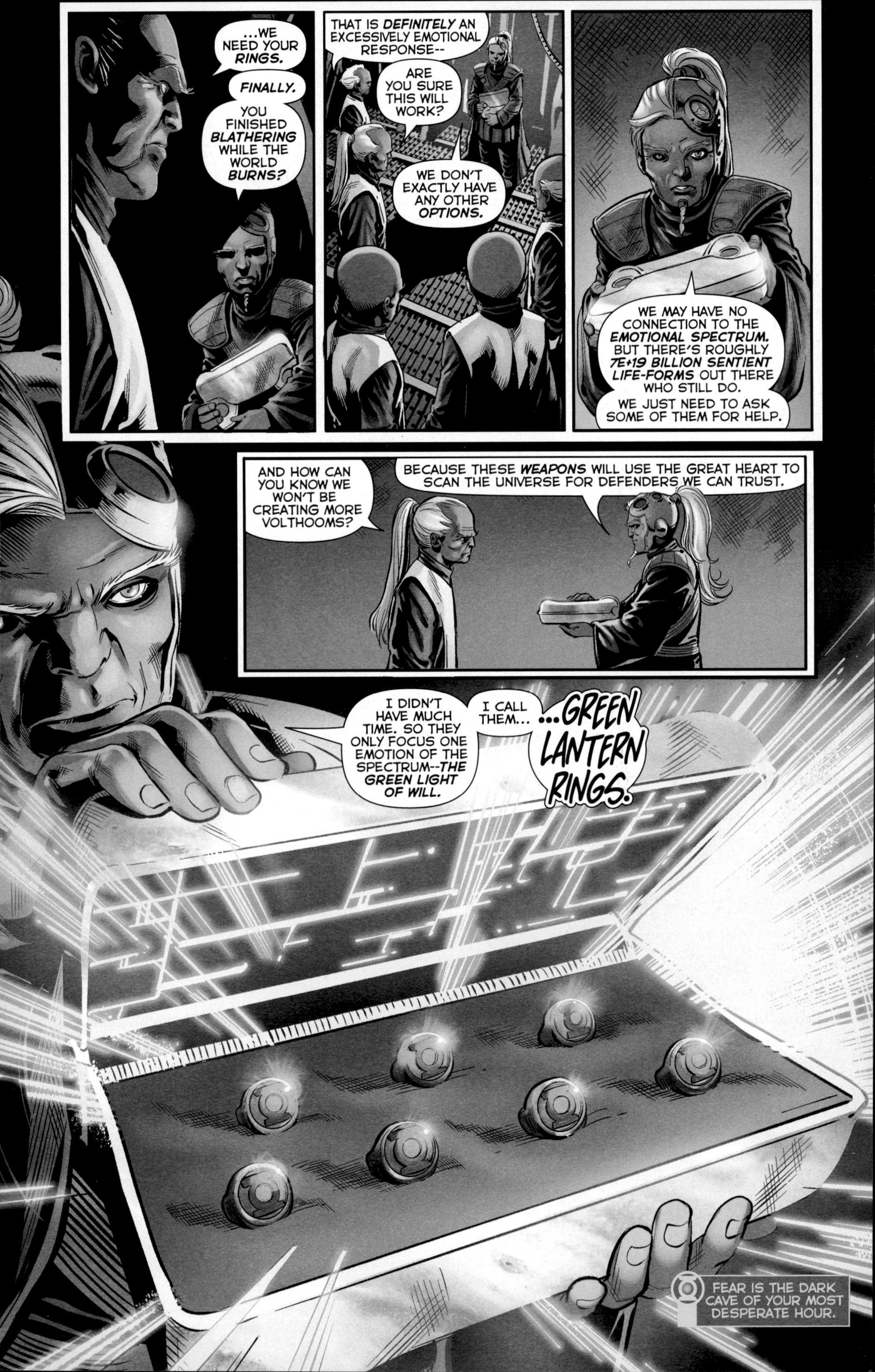
...WE NEED YOUR RINGS.
FINALLY.
YOU FINISHED BLATHERING WHILE THE WORLD BURNS?
THAT IS DEFINITELY AN EXCESSIVELY EMOTIONAL RESPONSE--
ARE YOU SURE THIS WILL WORK?
WE DON'T EXACTLY HAVE ANY OTHER OPTIONS.
WE MAY HAVE NO CONNECTION TO THE EMOTIONAL SPECTRUM. BUT THERE'S ROUGHLY 7E+19 BILLION SENTIENT LIFE-FORMS OUT THERE WHO STILL DO.
WE JUST NEED TO ASK SOME OF THEM FOR HELP.
AND HOW CAN YOU KNOW WE WON'T BE CREATING MORE VOLTHOOMS?
BECAUSE THESE WEAPONS WILL USE THE GREAT HEART TO SCAN THE UNIVERSE FOR DEFENDERS WE CAN TRUST.
I DIDN'T HAVE MUCH TIME. SO THEY ONLY FOCUS ONE EMOTION OF THE SPECTRUM--THE GREEN LIGHT OF WILL.
I CALL THEM...
...GREEN LANTERN RINGS.
FEAR IS THE DARK CAVE OF YOUR MOST DESPERATE HOUR.

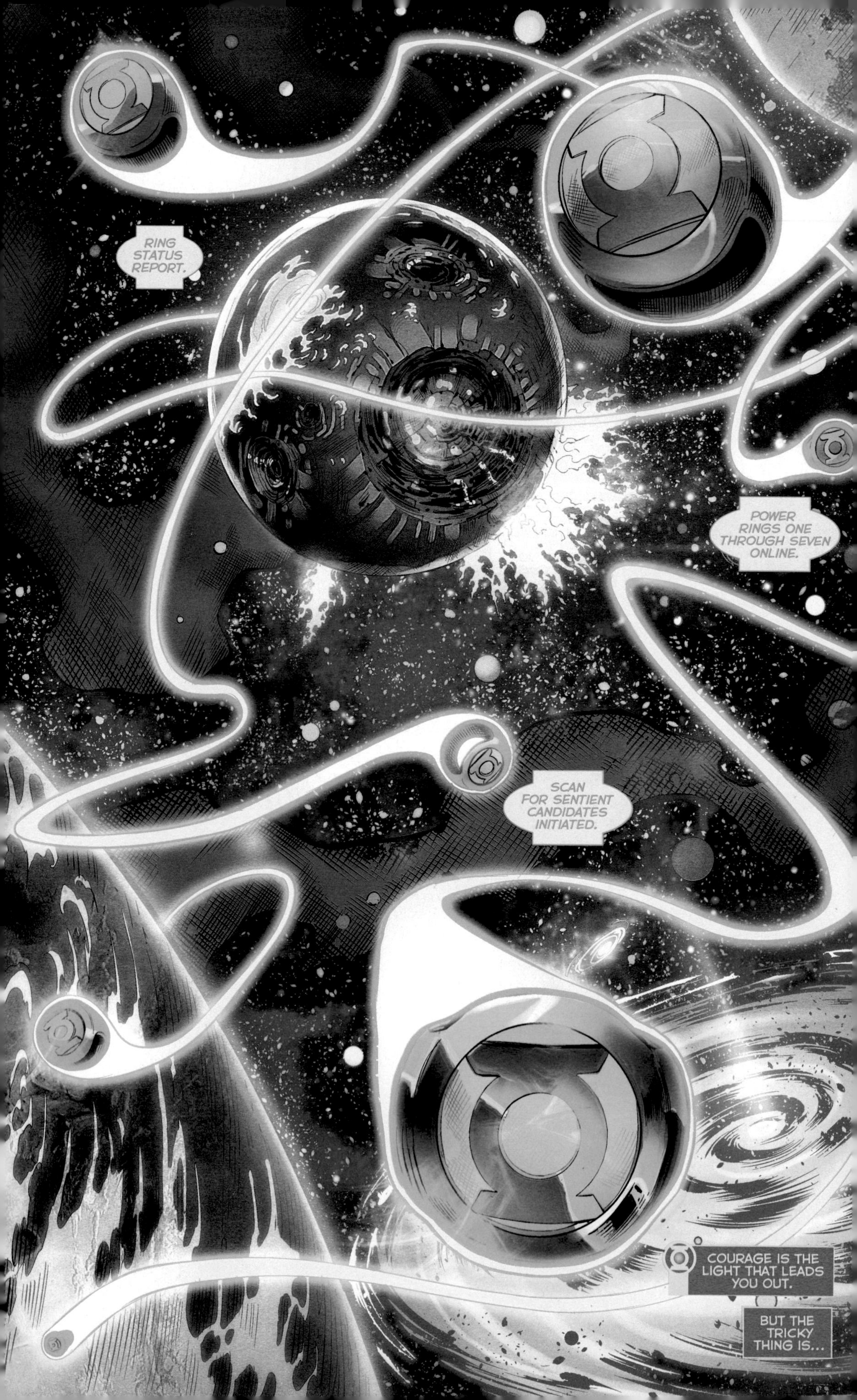
RING STATUS REPORT.
POWER RINGS ONE THROUGH SEVEN ONLINE.
SCAN FOR SENTIENT CANDIDATES INITIATED.
COURAGE IS THE LIGHT THAT LEADS YOU OUT.
BUT THE TRICKY THING IS...

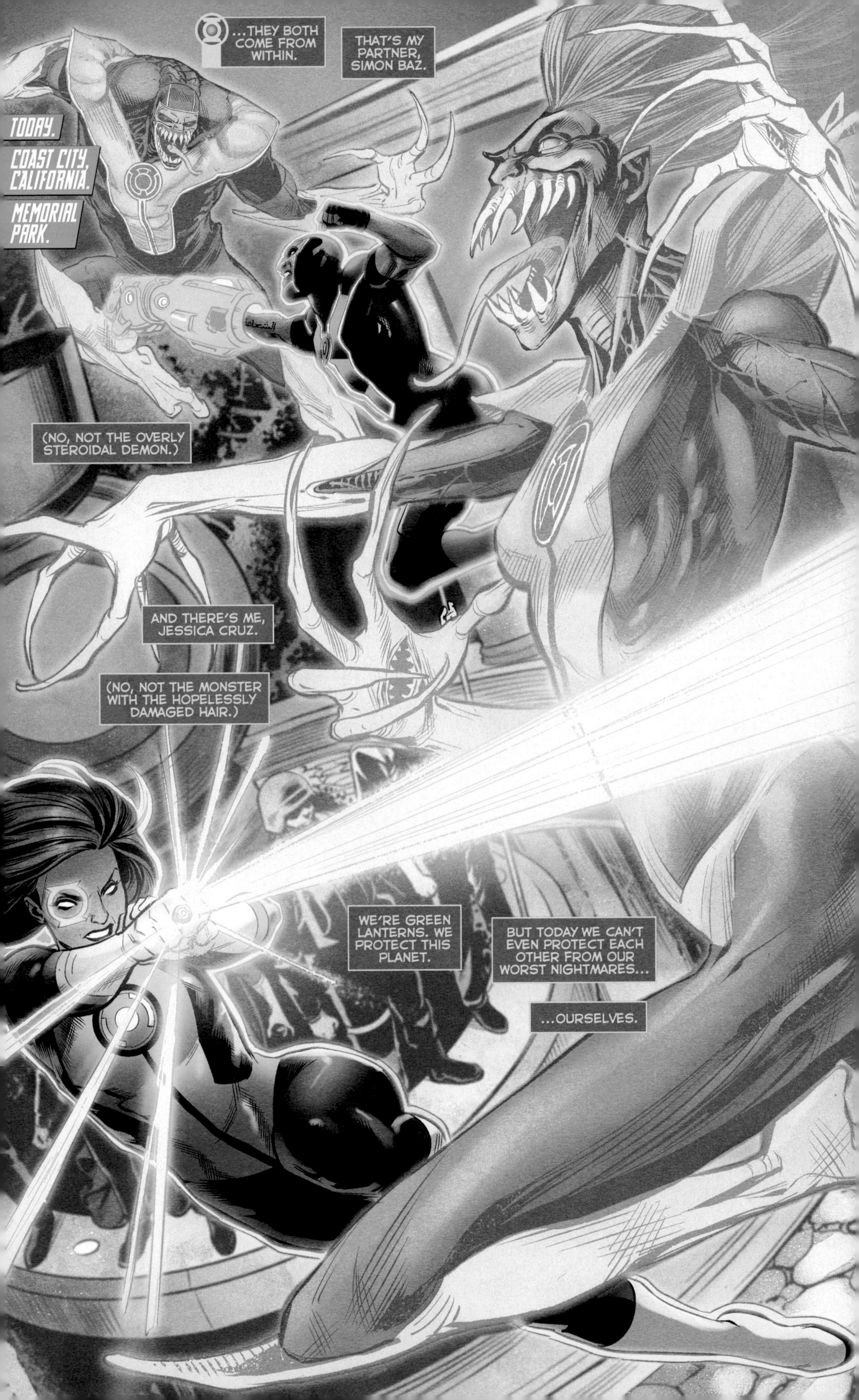
...THEY BOTH COME FROM WITHIN.
THAT'S MY PARTNER, SIMON BAZ.
TODAY.
COAST CITY, CALIFORNIA.
MEMORIAL PARK.
(NO, NOT THE OVERLY STEROIDAL DEMON.)
AND THERE'S ME, JESSICA CRUZ.
(NO, NOT THE MONSTER WITH THE HOPELESSLY DAMAGED HAIR.)
WE'RE GREEN LANTERNS. WE PROTECT THIS PLANET.
BUT TODAY WE CAN'T EVEN PROTECT EACH OTHER FROM OUR WORST NIGHTMARES...
...OURSELVES.

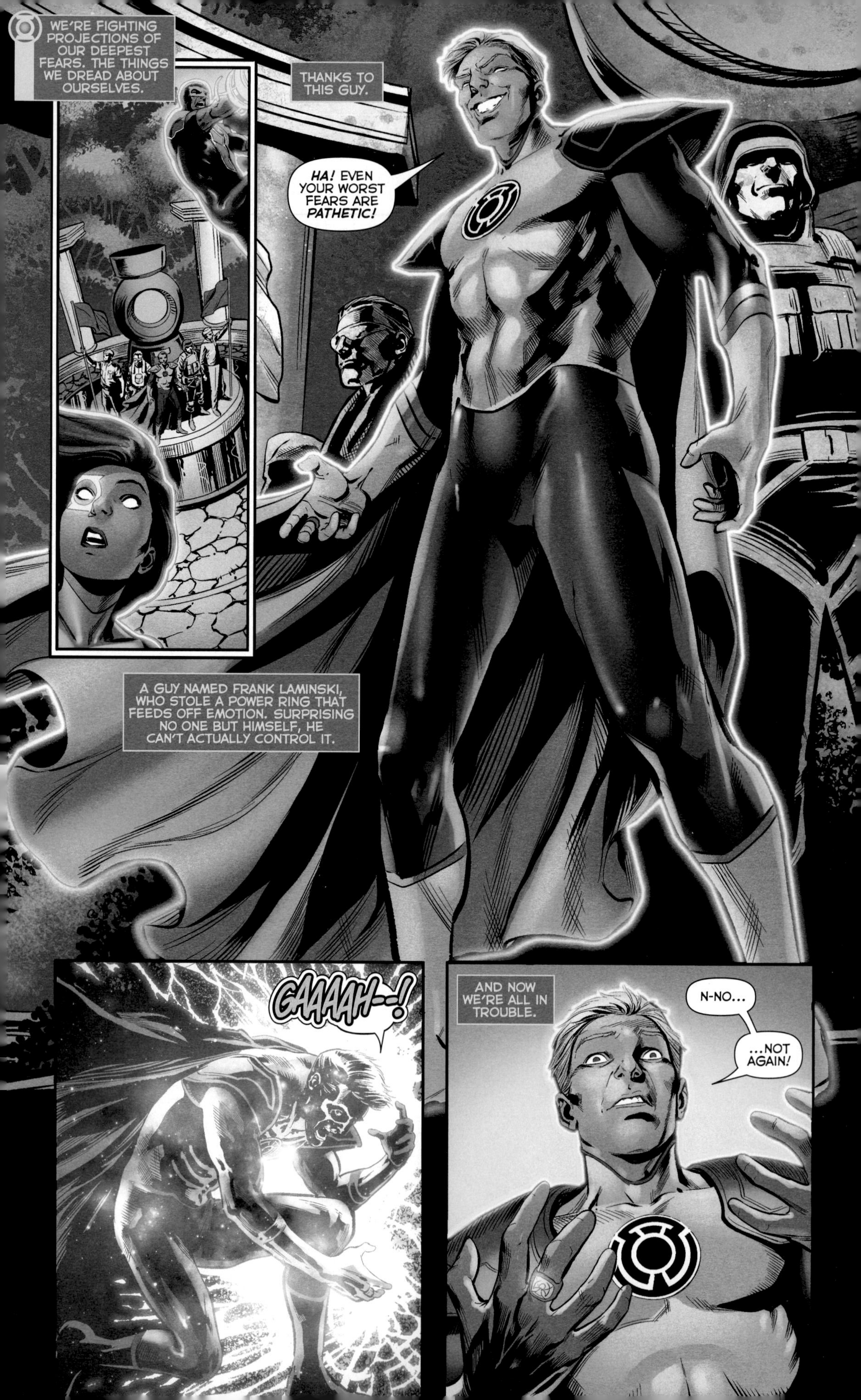
WE'RE FIGHTING PROJECTIONS OF OUR DEEPEST FEARS. THE THINGS WE DREAD ABOUT OURSELVES.
THANKS TO THIS GUY.
HA! EVEN YOUR WORST FEARS ARE PATHETIC!
A GUY NAMED FRANK LAMINSKI, WHO STOLE A POWER RING THAT FEEDS OFF EMOTION. SURPRISING NO ONE BUT HIMSELF, HE CAN'T ACTUALLY CONTROL IT.
GAAAAH--!
AND NOW WE'RE ALL IN TROUBLE.
N-NO...
...NOT AGAIN!

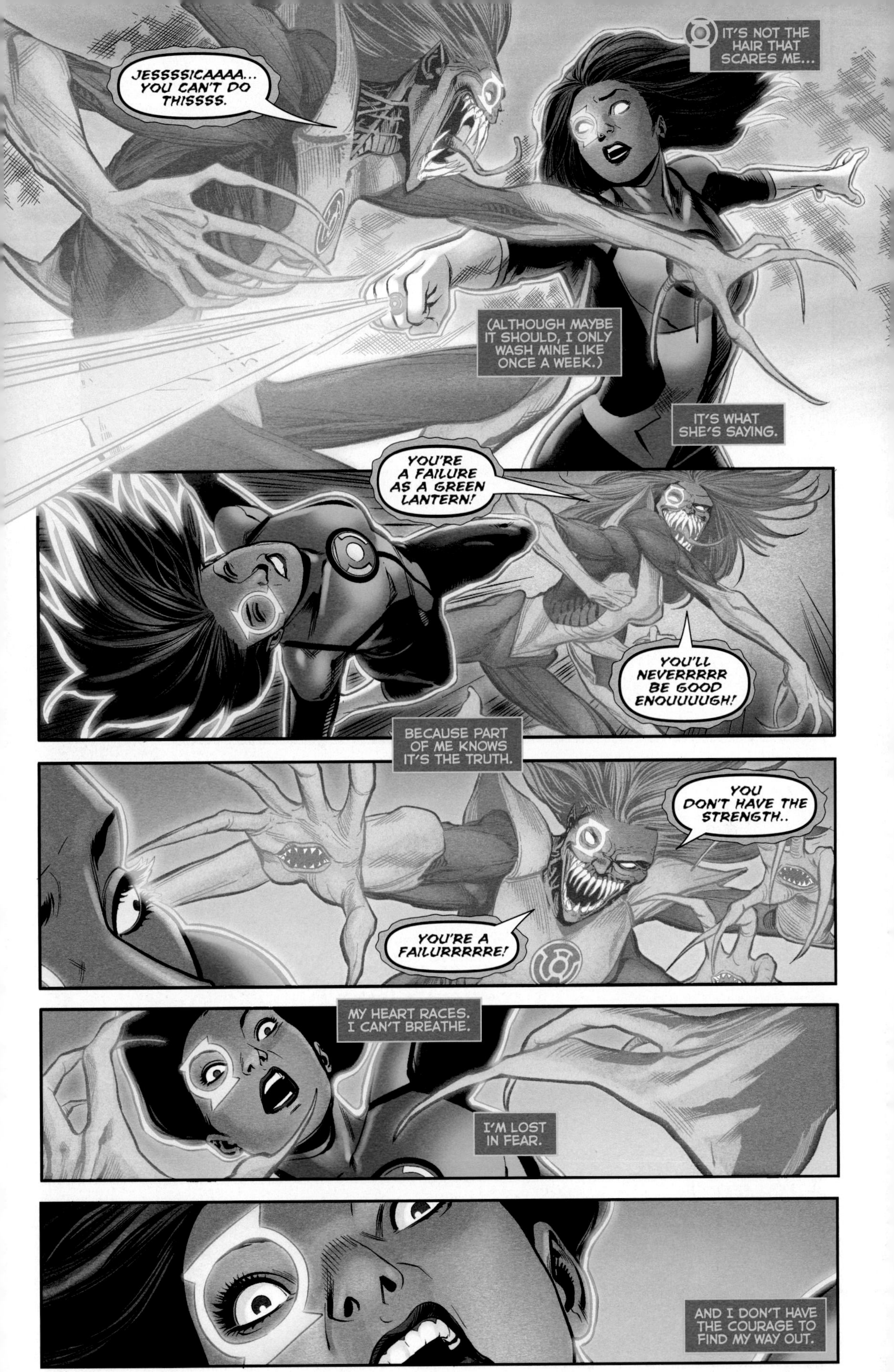

JESSSSICAAAA... YOU CAN'T DO THISSSS.
IT'S NOT THE HAIR THAT SCARES ME...
(ALTHOUGH MAYBE IT SHOULD, I ONLY WASH MINE LIKE ONCE A WEEK.)
IT'S WHAT SHE'S SAYING.
YOU'RE A FAILURE AS A GREEN LANTERN!
YOU'LL NEVERRRRR BE GOOD ENOUUUUGH!
BECAUSE PART OF ME KNOWS IT'S THE TRUTH.
YOU DON'T HAVE THE STRENGTH..
YOU'RE A FAILURRRRRE!
MY HEART RACES. I CAN'T BREATHE.
I'M LOST IN FEAR.
AND I DON'T HAVE THE COURAGE TO FIND MY WAY OUT.

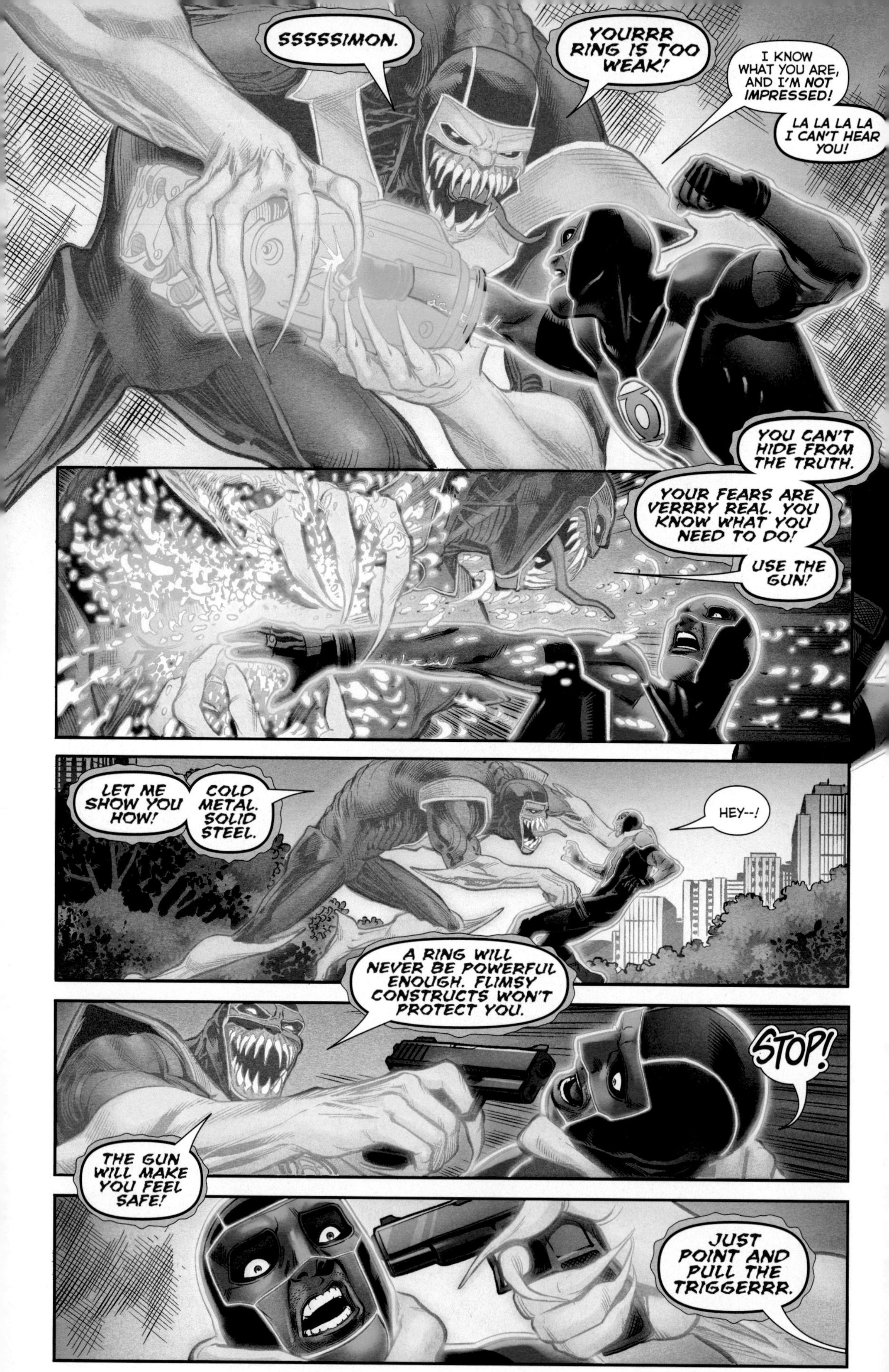
SSSSSIMON.
YOURRR RING IS TOO WEAK!
I KNOW WHAT YOU ARE, AND I'M NOT IMPRESSED!
LA LA LA LA I CAN'T HEAR YOU!
YOU CAN'T HIDE FROM THE TRUTH.
YOUR FEARS ARE VERRRY REAL. YOU KNOW WHAT YOU NEED TO DO!
USE THE GUN!
LET ME SHOW YOU HOW!
COLD METAL. SOLID STEEL.
HEY--!
A RING WILL NEVER BE POWERFUL ENOUGH. FLIMSY CONSTRUCTS WON'T PROTECT YOU.
STOP!
THE GUN WILL MAKE YOU FEEL SAFE!
JUST POINT AND PULL THE TRIGGERRR.

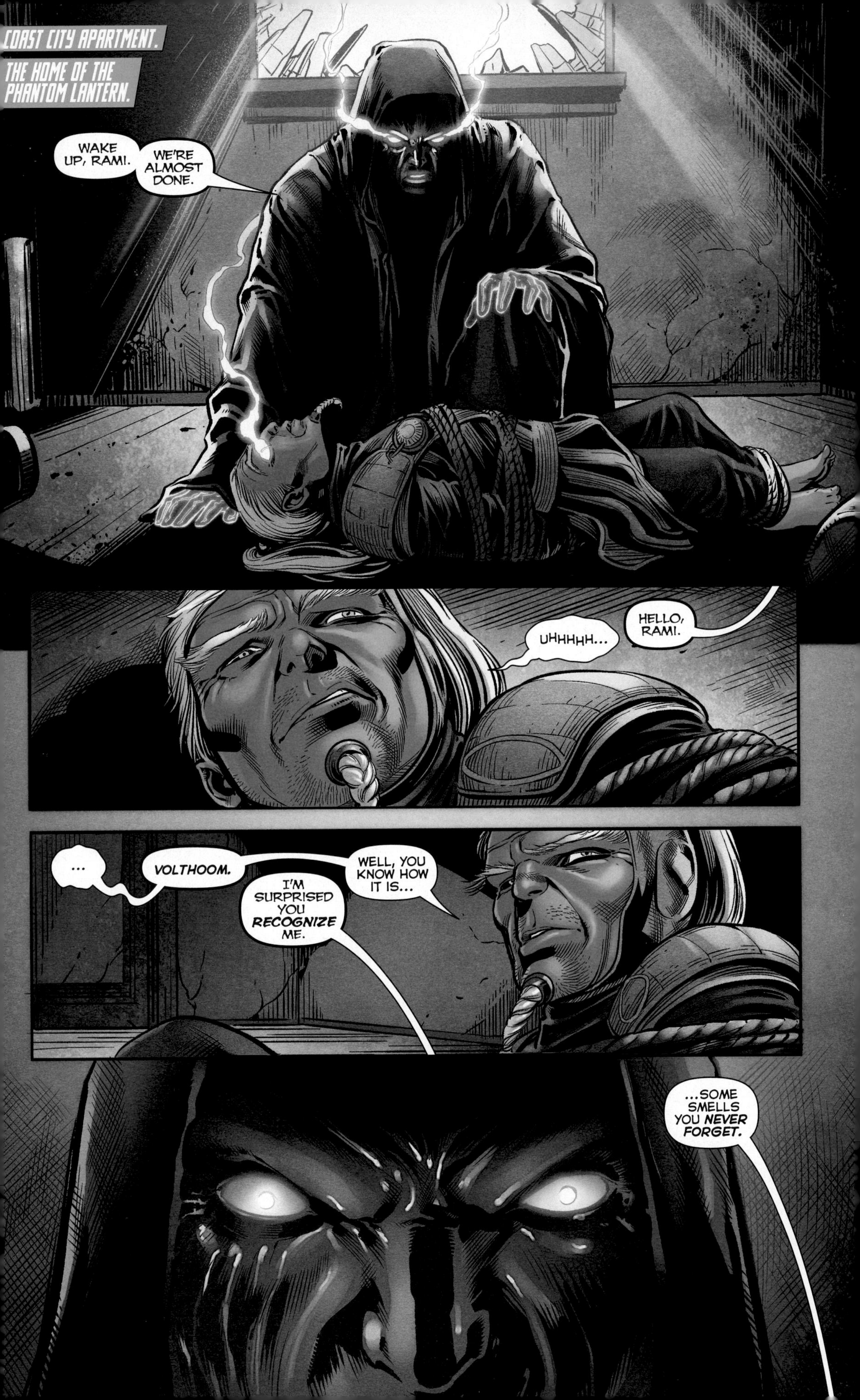
COAST CITY APARTMENT.
THE HOME OF THE PHANTOM LANTERN.
WAKE UP, RAMI.
WE'RE ALMOST DONE.
HELLO, RAMI.
UHHHHH...
...
VOLTHOOM.
I'M SURPRISED YOU RECOGNIZE ME.
WELL, YOU KNOW HOW IT IS...
...SOME SMELLS YOU NEVER FORGET.

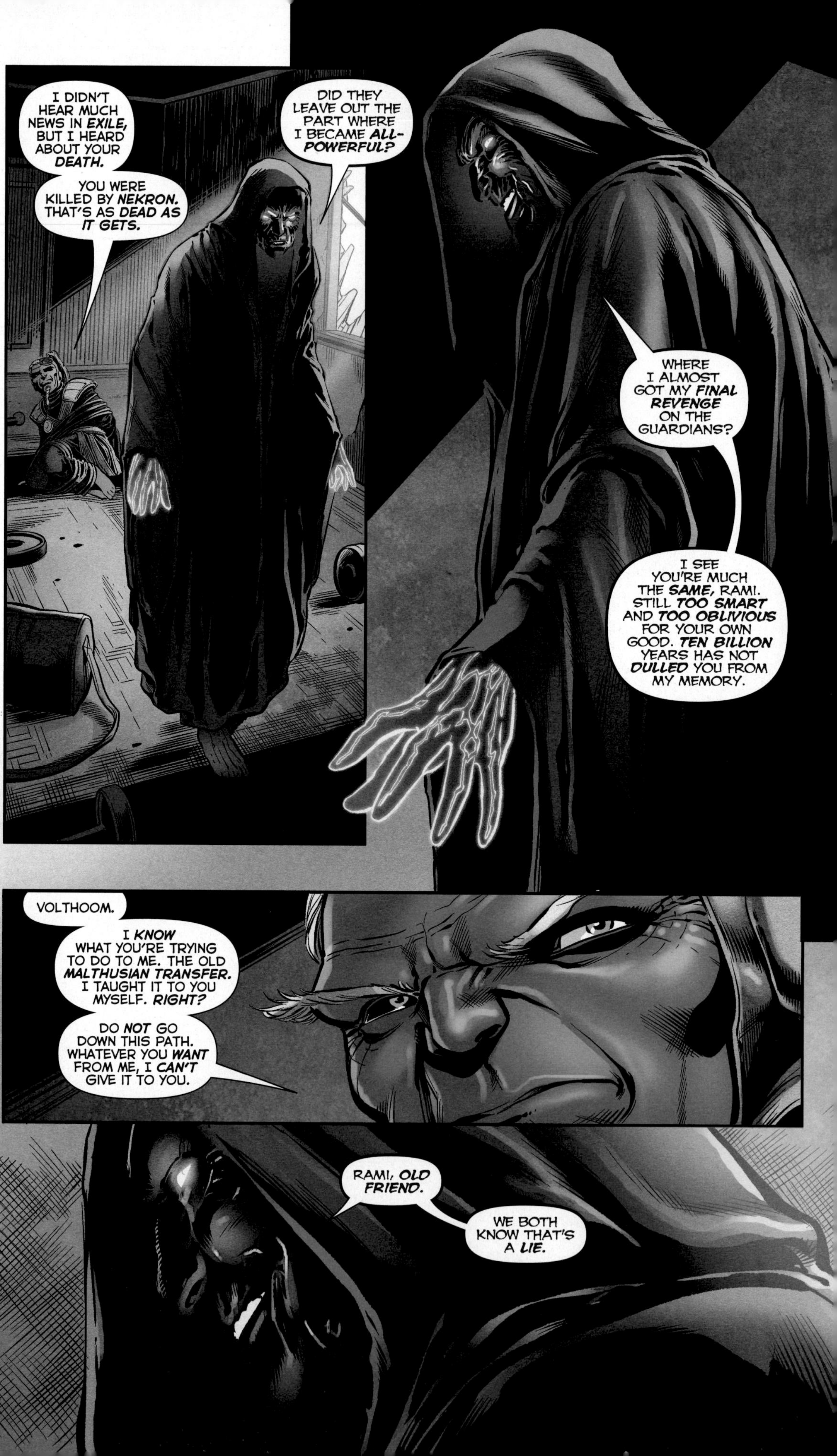
I DIDN'T HEAR MUCH NEWS IN EXILE, BUT I HEARD ABOUT YOUR DEATH.
YOU WERE KILLED BY NEKRON. THAT'S AS DEAD AS IT GETS.
DID THEY LEAVE OUT THE PART WHERE I BECAME ALL-POWERFUL?
WHERE I ALMOST GOT MY FINAL REVENGE ON THE GUARDIANS?
I SEE YOU'RE MUCH THE SAME, RAMI. STILL TOO SMART AND TOO OBLIVIOUS FOR YOUR OWN GOOD. TEN BILLION YEARS HAS NOT DULLED YOU FROM MY MEMORY.
VOLTHOOM.
I KNOW WHAT YOU'RE TRYING TO DO TO ME. THE OLD MALTHUSIAN TRANSFER. I TAUGHT IT TO YOU MYSELF. RIGHT?
DO NOT GO DOWN THIS PATH. WHATEVER YOU WANT FROM ME, I CAN'T GIVE IT TO YOU.
RAMI, OLD FRIEND.
WE BOTH KNOW THAT'S A LIE.

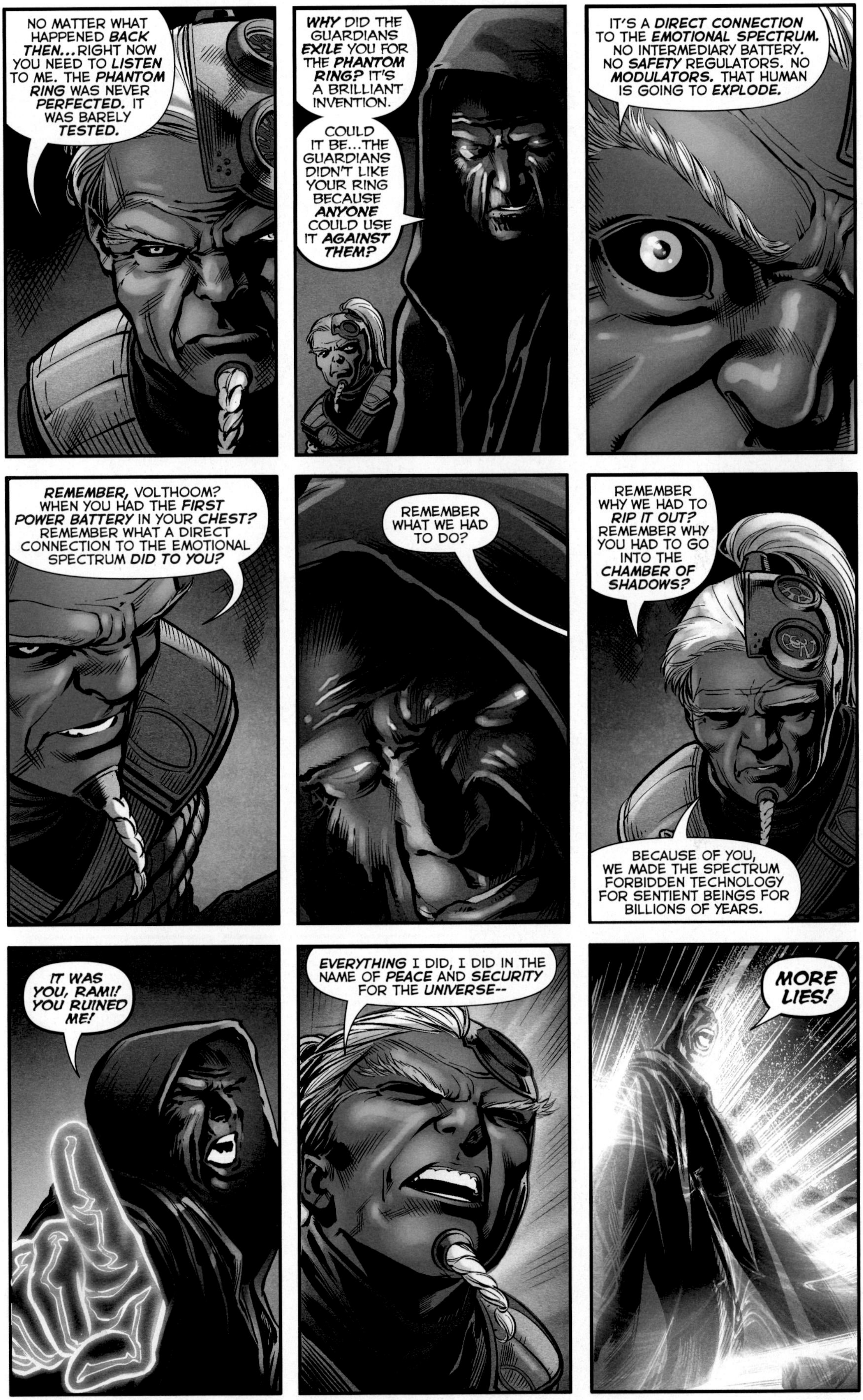
NO MATTER WHAT HAPPENED BACK THEN... RIGHT NOW YOU NEED TO LISTEN TO ME. THE PHANTOM RING WAS NEVER PERFECTED. IT WAS BARELY TESTED.
WHY DID THE GUARDIANS EXILE YOU FOR THE PHANTOM RING? IT'S A BRILLIANT INVENTION.
COULD IT BE...THE GUARDIANS DIDN'T LIKE YOUR RING BECAUSE ANYONE COULD USE IT AGAINST THEM?
IT'S A DIRECT CONNECTION TO THE EMOTIONAL SPECTRUM. NO INTERMEDIARY BATTERY. NO SAFETY REGULATORS. NO MODULATORS. THAT HUMAN IS GOING TO EXPLODE.
REMEMBER, VOLTHOOM? WHEN YOU HAD THE FIRST POWER BATTERY IN YOUR CHEST? REMEMBER WHAT A DIRECT CONNECTION TO THE EMOTIONAL SPECTRUM DID TO YOU?
REMEMBER WHAT WE HAD TO DO?
REMEMBER WHY WE HAD TO RIP IT OUT? REMEMBER WHY YOU HAD TO GO INTO THE CHAMBER OF SHADOWS?
BECAUSE OF YOU, WE MADE THE SPECTRUM FORBIDDEN TECHNOLOGY FOR SENTIENT BEINGS FOR BILLIONS OF YEARS.
IT WAS YOU, RAMI! YOU RUINED ME!
EVERYTHING I DID, I DID IN THE NAME OF PEACE AND SECURITY FOR THE UNIVERSE--
MORE LIES!

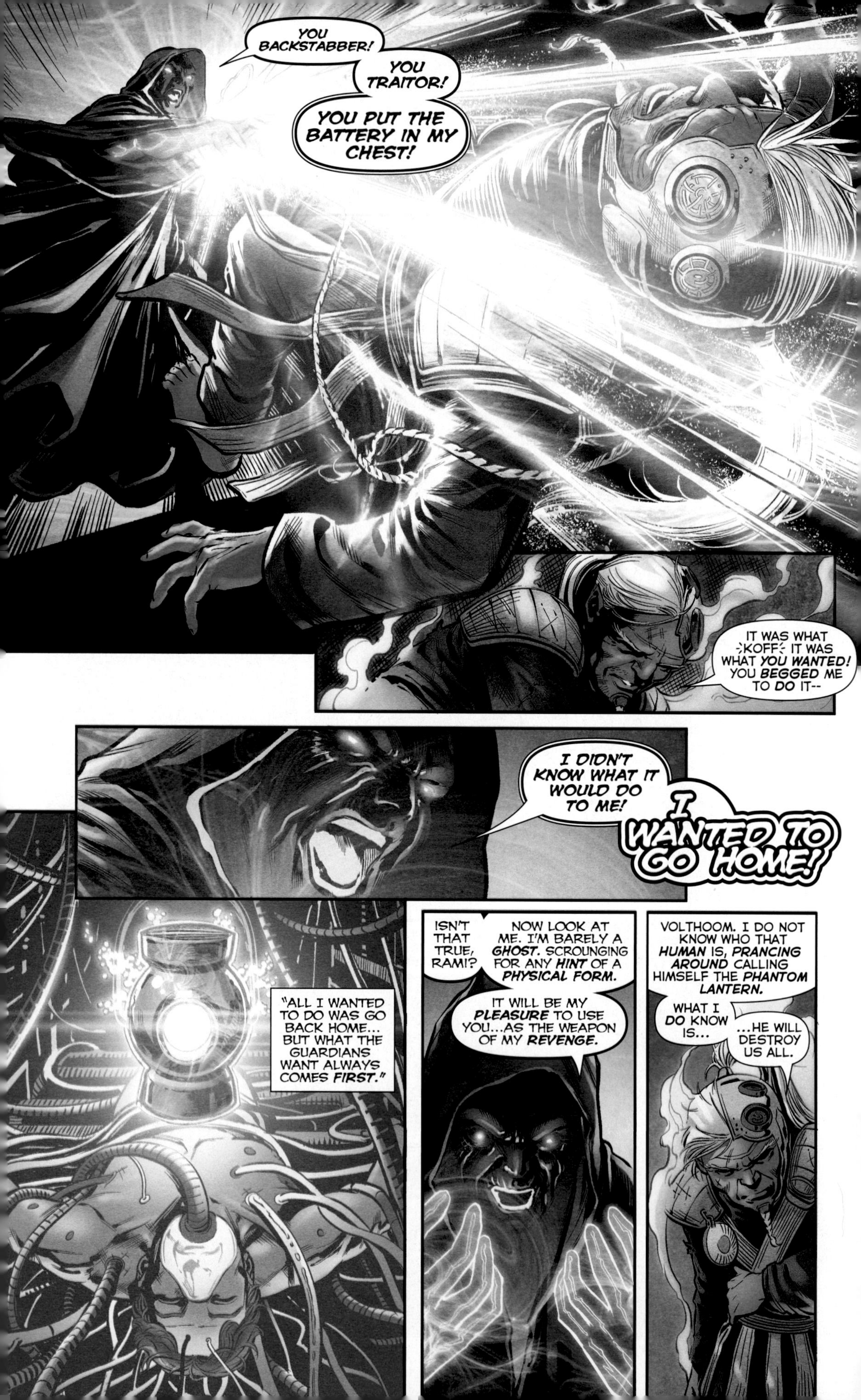
YOU BACKSTABBER!
YOU TRAITOR!
YOU PUT THE BATTERY IN MY CHEST!
IT WAS WHAT *KOFF* IT WAS WHAT YOU WANTED! YOU BEGGED ME TO DO IT--
I DIDN'T KNOW WHAT IT WOULD DO TO ME!
I WANTED TO GO HOME!
"ALL I WANTED TO DO WAS GO BACK HOME... BUT WHAT THE GUARDIANS WANT ALWAYS COMES FIRST."
ISN'T THAT TRUE, RAMI?
NOW LOOK AT ME. I'M BARELY A GHOST. SCROUNGING FOR ANY HINT OF A PHYSICAL FORM.
IT WILL BE MY PLEASURE TO USE YOU...AS THE WEAPON OF MY REVENGE.
VOLTHOOM. I DO NOT KNOW WHO THAT HUMAN IS, PRANCING AROUND CALLING HIMSELF THE PHANTOM LANTERN.
WHAT I DO KNOW IS...
...HE WILL DESTROY US ALL.

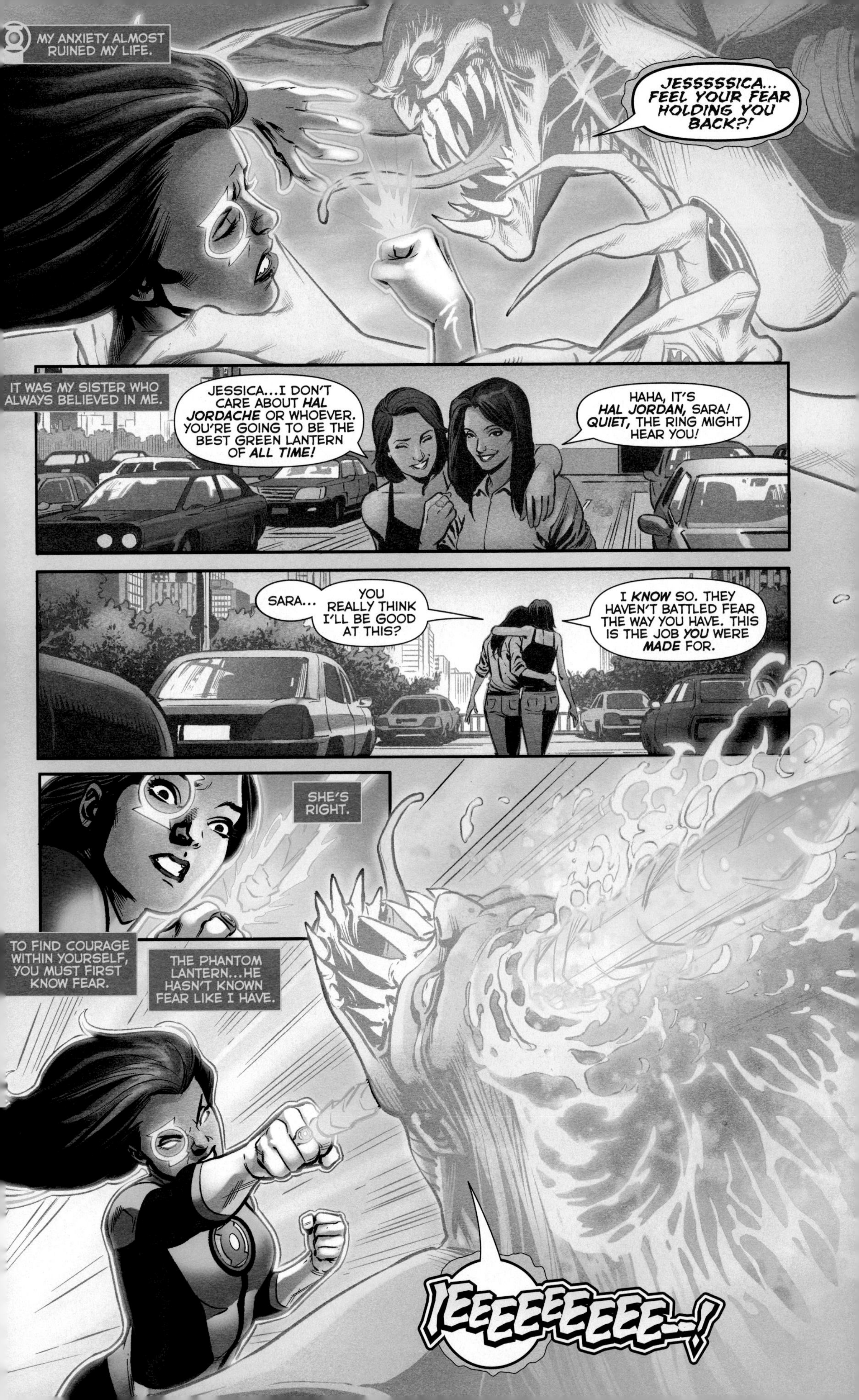
MY ANXIETY ALMOST RUINED MY LIFE.
JESSSSSICA... FEEL YOUR FEAR HOLDING YOU BACK?!
IT WAS MY SISTER WHO ALWAYS BELIEVED IN ME.
JESSICA...I DON'T CARE ABOUT HAL JORDACHE OR WHOEVER. YOU'RE GOING TO BE THE BEST GREEN LANTERN OF ALL TIME!
HAHA, IT'S HAL JORDAN, SARA! QUIET, THE RING MIGHT HEAR YOU!
SARA...
YOU REALLY THINK I'LL BE GOOD AT THIS?
I KNOW SO. THEY HAVEN'T BATTLED FEAR THE WAY YOU HAVE. THIS IS THE JOB YOU WERE MADE FOR.
SHE'S RIGHT.
TO FIND COURAGE WITHIN YOURSELF, YOU MUST FIRST KNOW FEAR.
THE PHANTOM LANTERN...HE HASN'T KNOWN FEAR LIKE I HAVE.
IEEEEEEEEEE--!

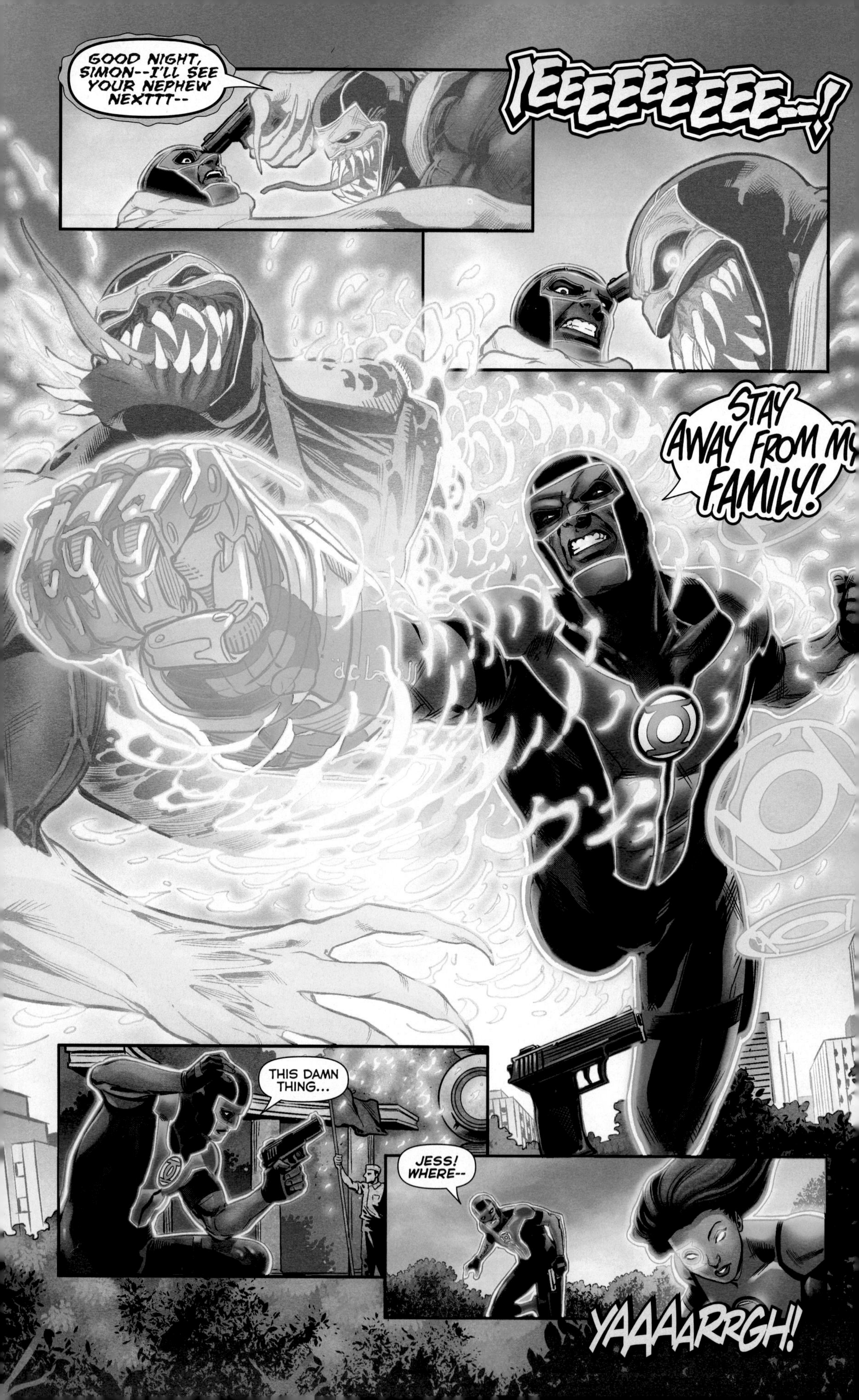
GOOD NIGHT, SIMON--I'LL SEE YOUR NEPHEW NEXTTT--
IEEEEEEEEEE--!
STAY AWAY FROM MY FAMILY!
THIS DAMN THING...
JESS! WHERE--
YAAAARRGH!

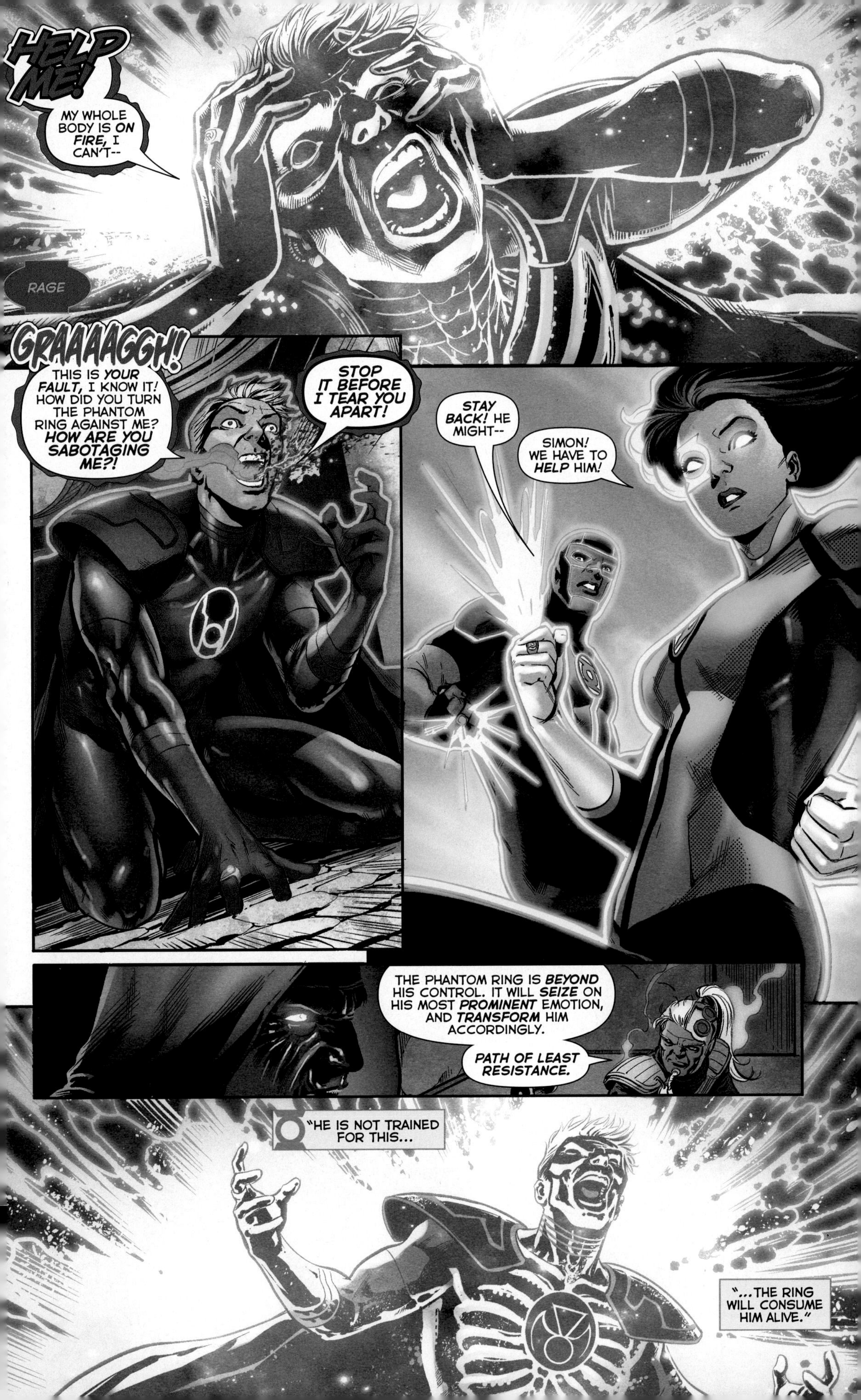
HELP ME!
MY WHOLE BODY IS ON FIRE, I CAN'T--
RAGE
GRAAAAGGH!
THIS IS YOUR FAULT, I KNOW IT! HOW DID YOU TURN THE PHANTOM RING AGAINST ME? HOW ARE YOU SABOTAGING ME?!
STOP IT BEFORE I TEAR YOU APART!
STAY BACK! HE MIGHT--
SIMON! WE HAVE TO HELP HIM!
THE PHANTOM RING IS BEYOND HIS CONTROL. IT WILL SEIZE ON HIS MOST PROMINENT EMOTION, AND TRANSFORM HIM ACCORDINGLY.
PATH OF LEAST RESISTANCE.
"HE IS NOT TRAINED FOR THIS...
"...THE RING WILL CONSUME HIM ALIVE."

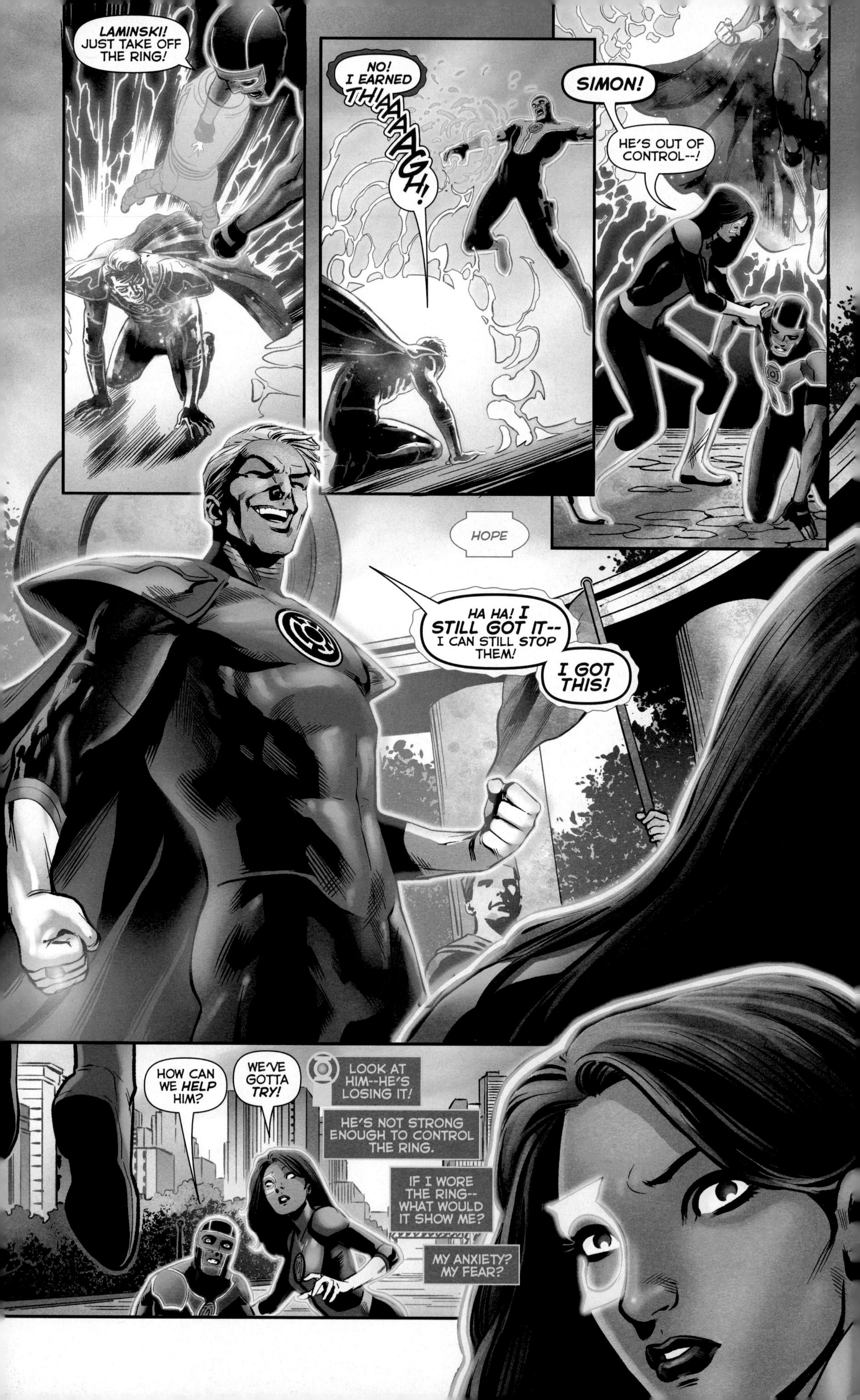
LAMINSKI! JUST TAKE OFF THE RING!
NO! I EARNED THIAAAAGH!
SIMON!
HE'S OUT OF CONTROL--!
HOPE
HA HA! I STILL GOT IT-- I CAN STILL STOP THEM!
I GOT THIS!
HOW CAN WE HELP HIM?
WE'VE GOTTA TRY!
LOOK AT HIM--HE'S LOSING IT!
HE'S NOT STRONG ENOUGH TO CONTROL THE RING.
IF I WORE THE RING-- WHAT WOULD IT SHOW ME?
MY ANXIETY? MY FEAR?

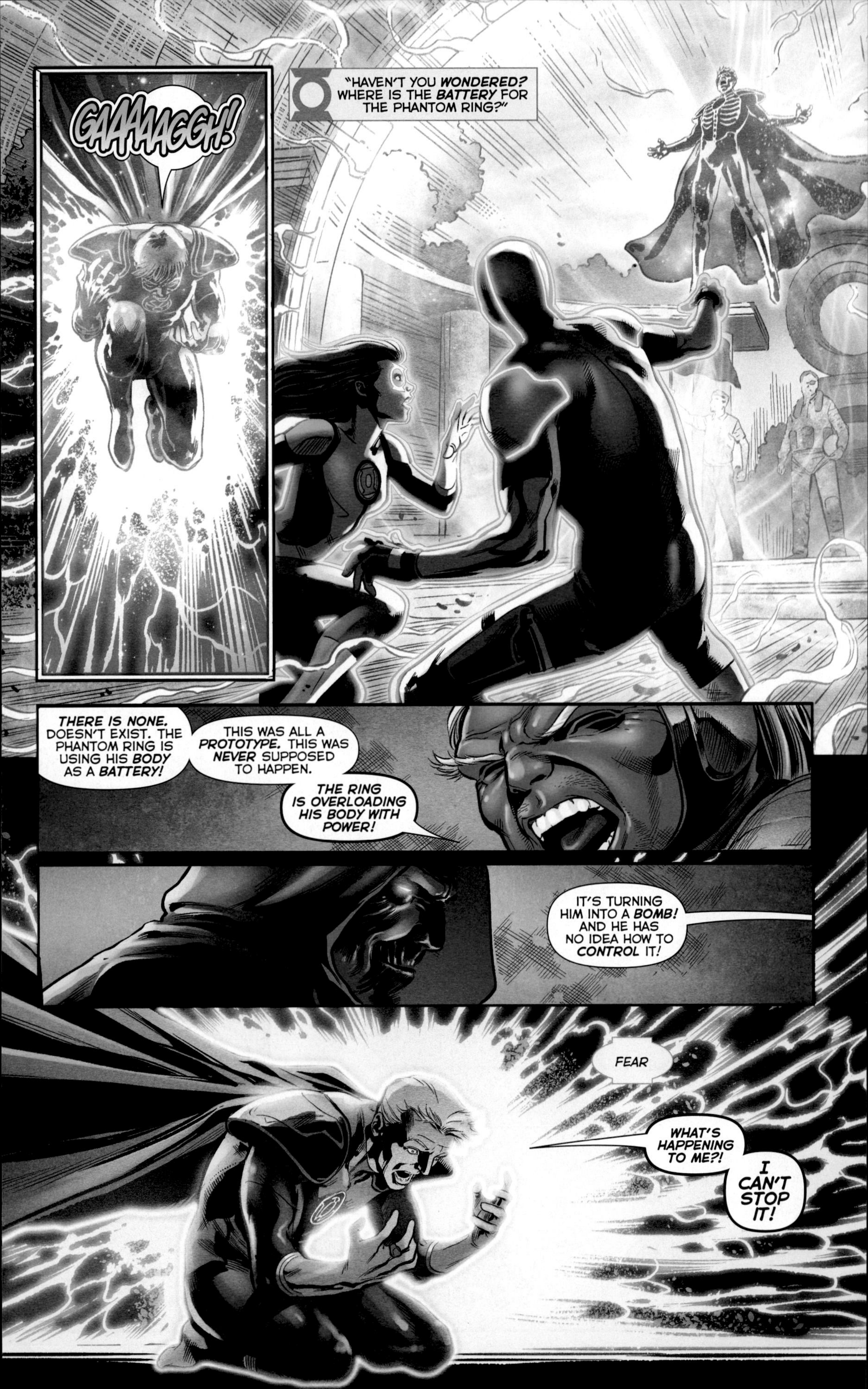
GAAAAAGGH!
"HAVEN'T YOU WONDERED? WHERE IS THE BATTERY FOR THE PHANTOM RING?"
THERE IS NONE. DOESN'T EXIST. THE PHANTOM RING IS USING HIS BODY AS A BATTERY!
THIS WAS ALL A PROTOTYPE. THIS WAS NEVER SUPPOSED TO HAPPEN.
THE RING IS OVERLOADING HIS BODY WITH POWER!
IT'S TURNING HIM INTO A BOMB! AND HE HAS NO IDEA HOW TO CONTROL IT!
FEAR
WHAT'S HAPPENING TO ME?!
I CAN'T STOP IT!

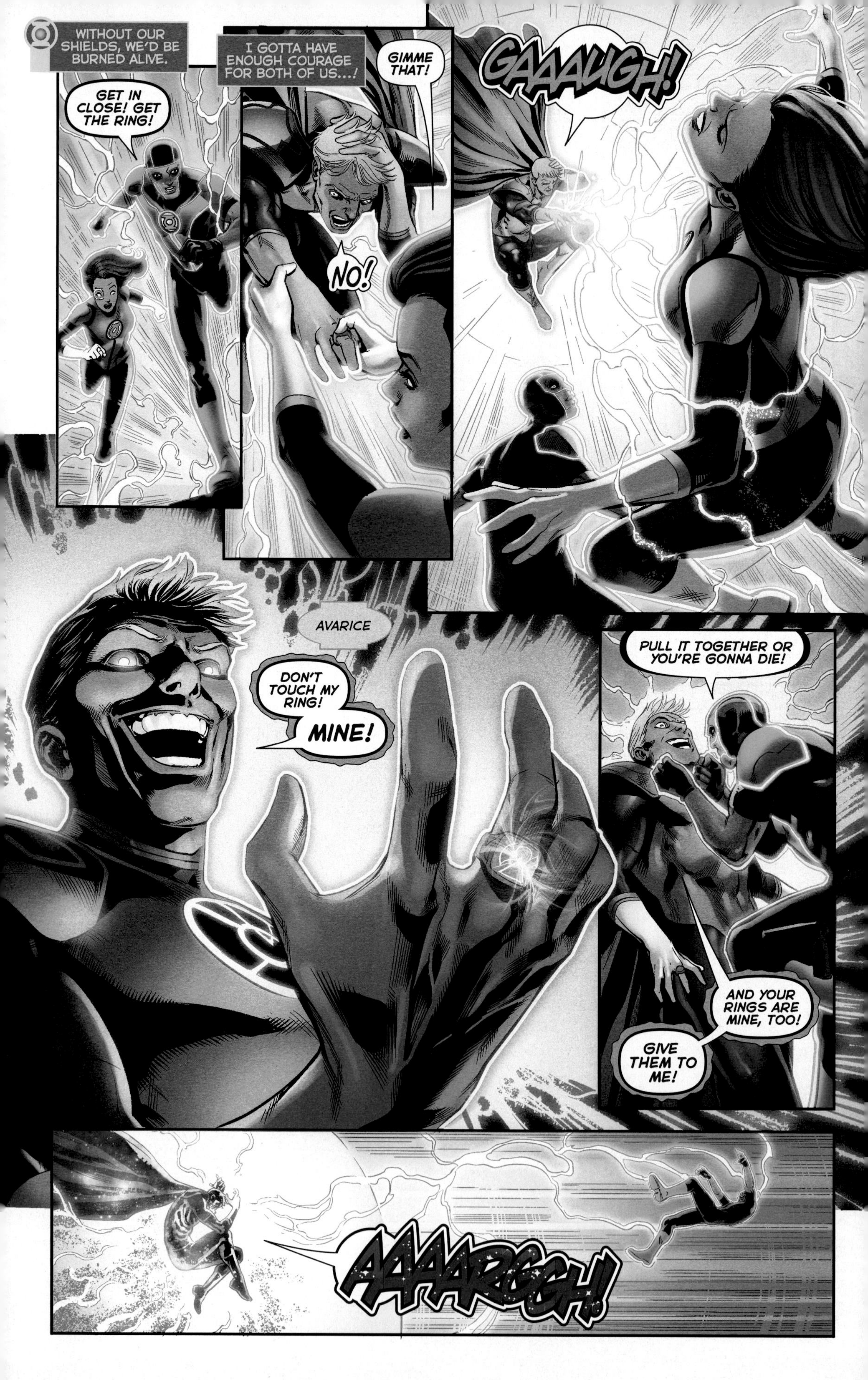
WITHOUT OUR SHIELDS, WE'D BE BURNED ALIVE.
GET IN CLOSE! GET THE RING!
I GOTTA HAVE ENOUGH COURAGE FOR BOTH OF US...!
GIMME THAT!
NO!
GAAAUGH!
AVARICE
DON'T TOUCH MY RING!
MINE!
PULL IT TOGETHER OR YOU'RE GONNA DIE!
AND YOUR RINGS ARE MINE, TOO!
GIVE THEM TO ME!
AAAARGGH!

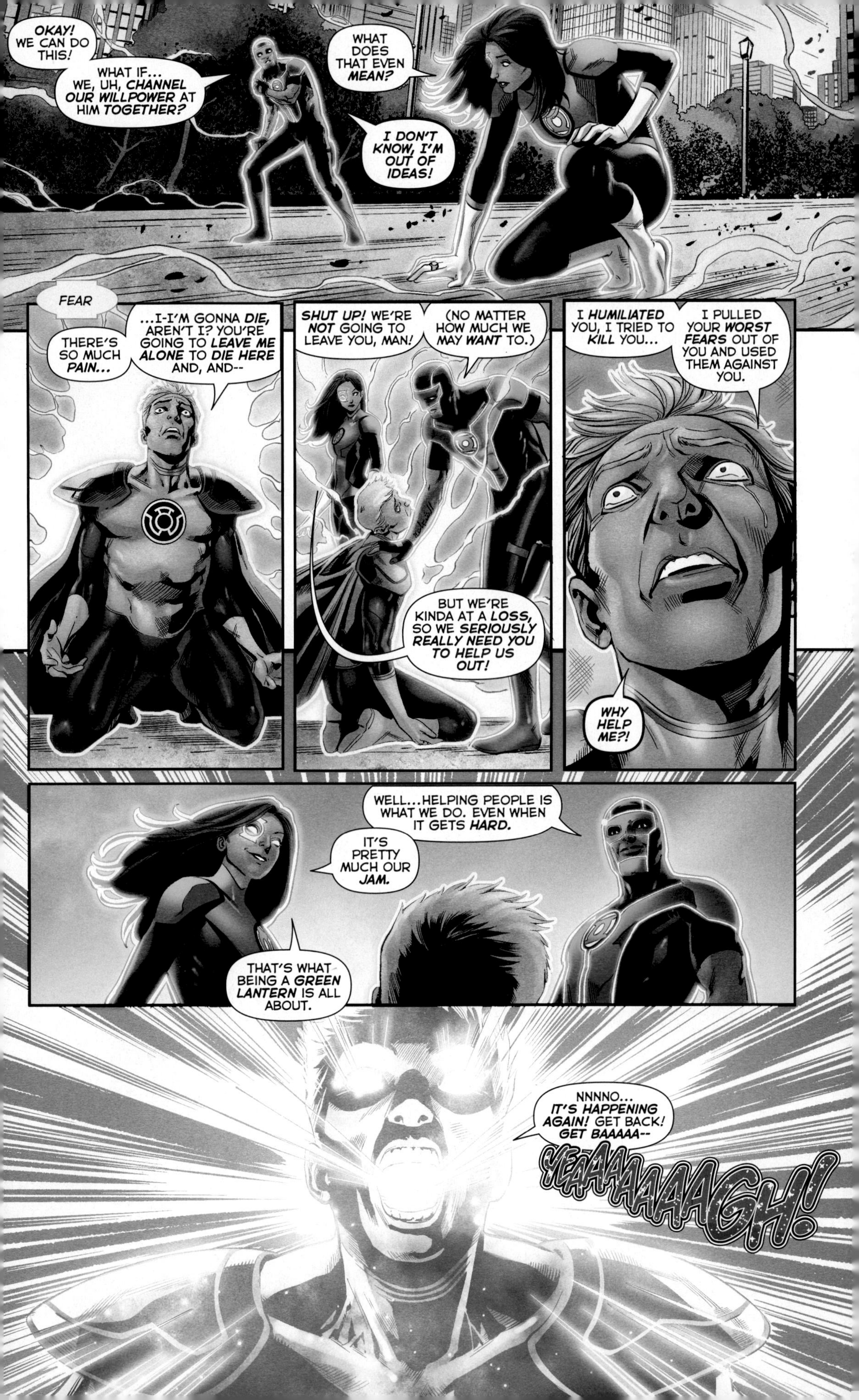
OKAY! WE CAN DO THIS!
WHAT IF... WE, UH, CHANNEL OUR WILLPOWER AT HIM TOGETHER?
WHAT DOES THAT EVEN MEAN?
I DON'T KNOW, I'M OUT OF IDEAS!
FEAR
THERE'S SO MUCH PAIN...
...I-I'M GONNA DIE, AREN'T I? YOU'RE GOING TO LEAVE ME ALONE TO DIE HERE AND, AND--
SHUT UP! WE'RE NOT GOING TO LEAVE YOU, MAN!
(NO MATTER HOW MUCH WE MAY WANT TO.)
BUT WE'RE KINDA AT A LOSS, SO WE SERIOUSLY REALLY NEED YOU TO HELP US OUT!
I HUMILIATED YOU, I TRIED TO KILL YOU...
I PULLED YOUR WORST FEARS OUT OF YOU AND USED THEM AGAINST YOU.
WHY HELP ME?!
WELL...HELPING PEOPLE IS WHAT WE DO. EVEN WHEN IT GETS HARD.
IT'S PRETTY MUCH OUR JAM.
THAT'S WHAT BEING A GREEN LANTERN IS ALL ABOUT.
NNNNO... IT'S HAPPENING AGAIN! GET BACK! GET BAAAAA--
YEAAAAAAAAGH!

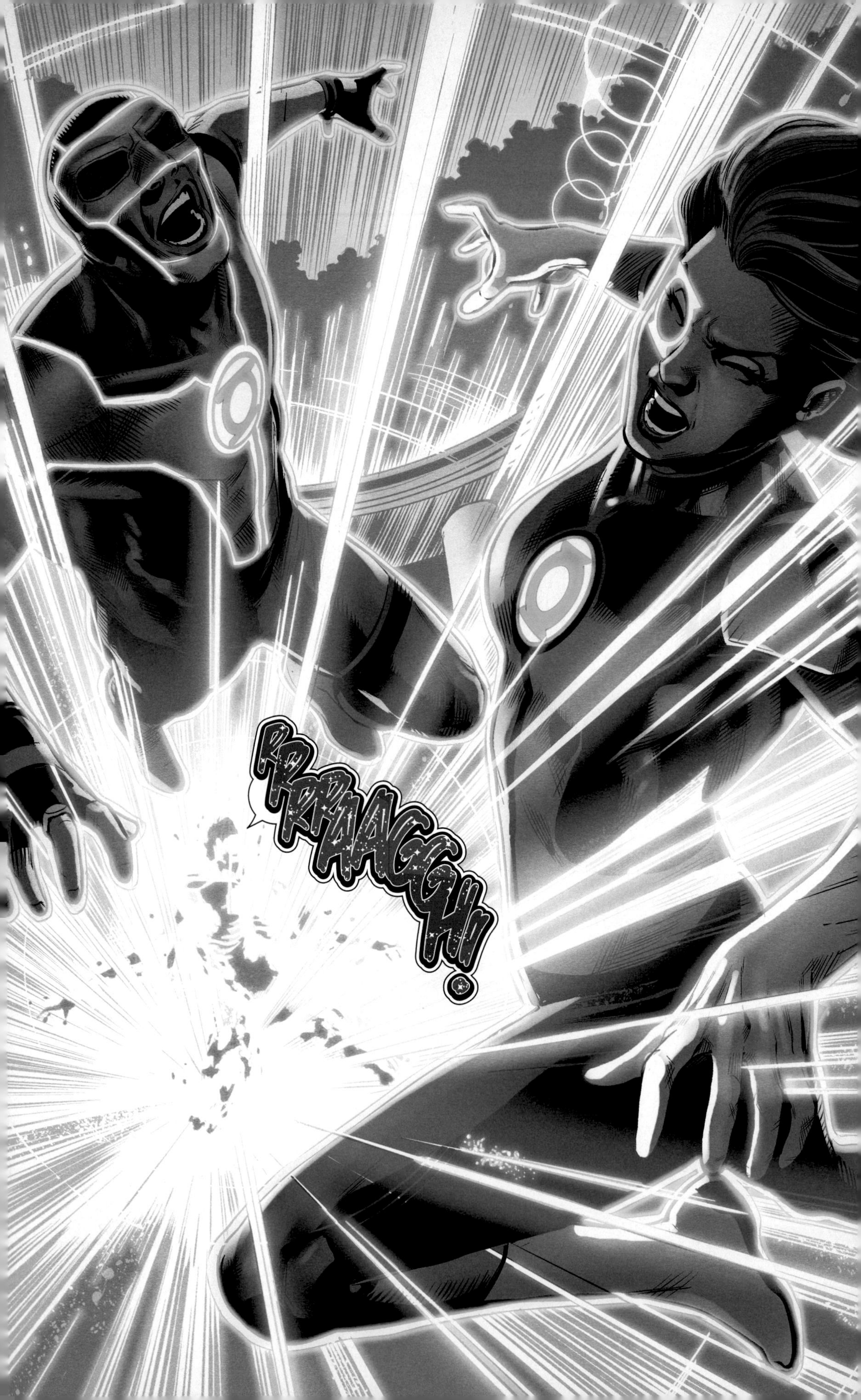
RRRAAGGH!!

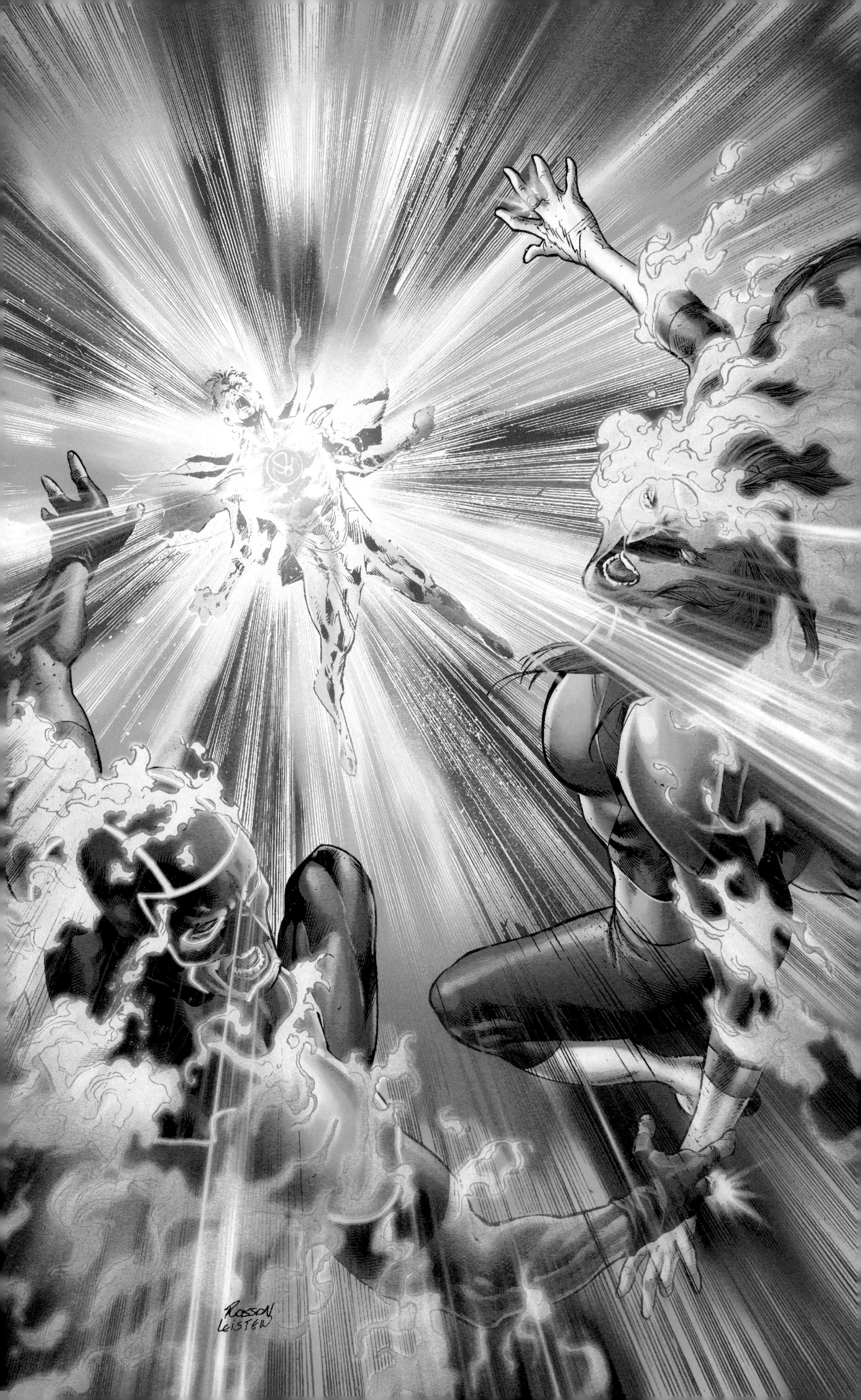
ROSSON
LEISTEN

"THE PHANTOM LANTERN: PART FIVE"

SAM HUMPHRIES writer * RONAN CLIQUET EDUARDO PANSICA pencillers * JULIO FERREIRA RONAN CLIQUET inkers

Cover by ROBSON ROCHA, JAY LEISTEN and ROD REIS

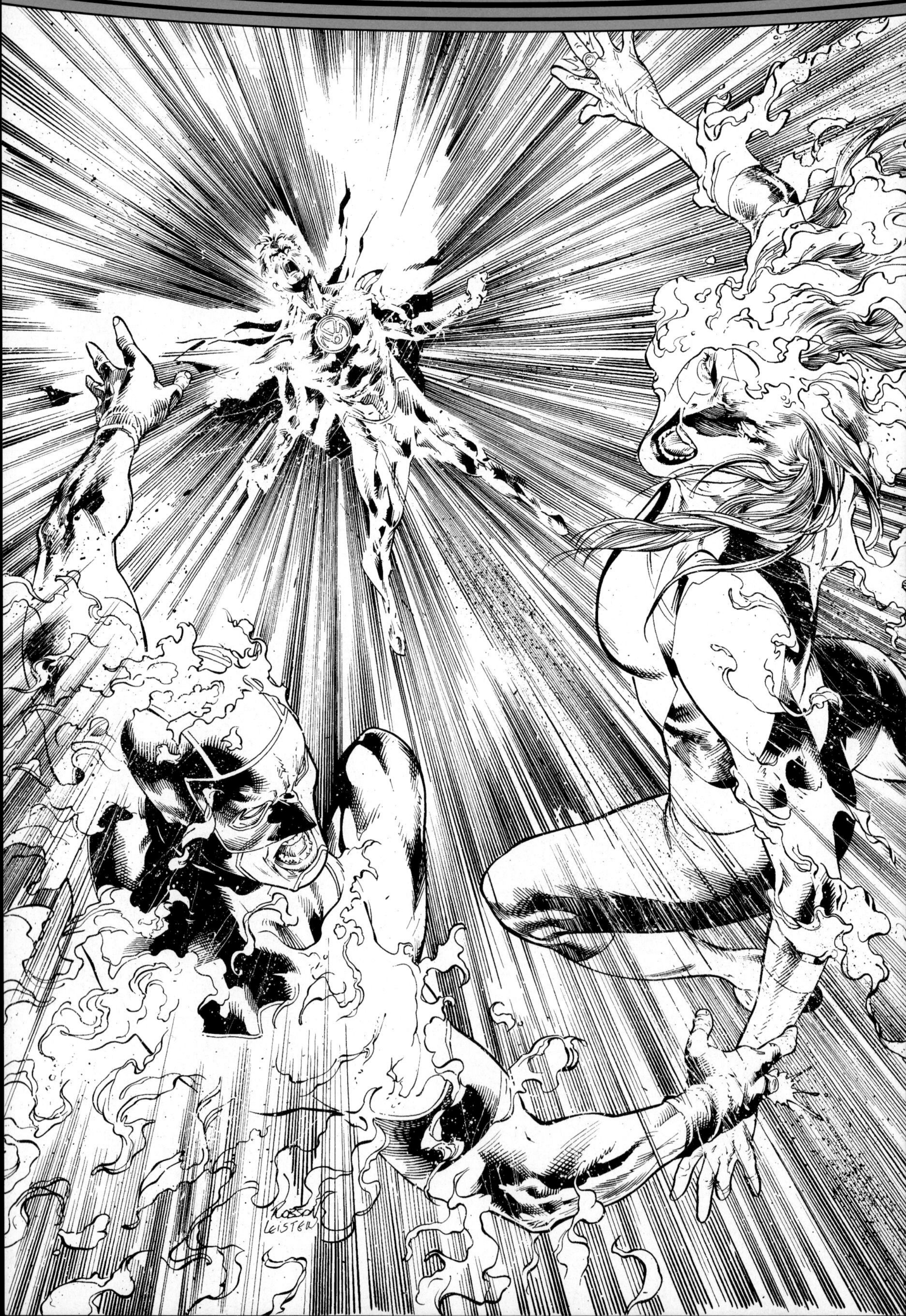

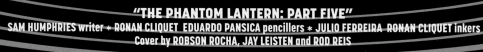

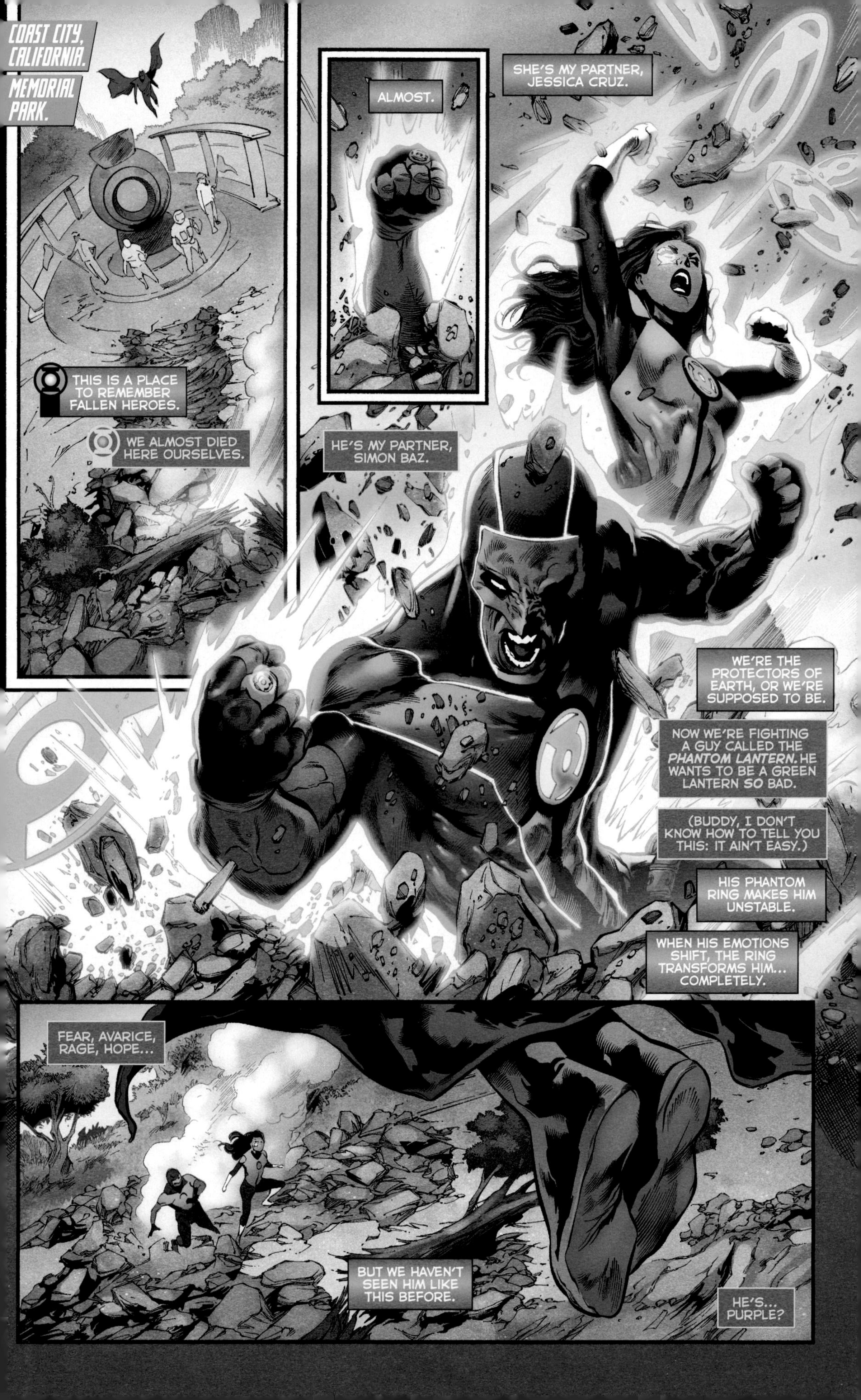
COAST CITY, CALIFORNIA.
MEMORIAL PARK.
THIS IS A PLACE TO REMEMBER FALLEN HEROES.
WE ALMOST DIED HERE OURSELVES.
ALMOST.
SHE'S MY PARTNER, JESSICA CRUZ.
HE'S MY PARTNER, SIMON BAZ.
WE'RE THE PROTECTORS OF EARTH, OR WE'RE SUPPOSED TO BE.
NOW WE'RE FIGHTING A GUY CALLED THE PHANTOM LANTERN. HE WANTS TO BE A GREEN LANTERN SO BAD.
(BUDDY, I DON'T KNOW HOW TO TELL YOU THIS: IT AIN'T EASY.)
HIS PHANTOM RING MAKES HIM UNSTABLE.
WHEN HIS EMOTIONS SHIFT, THE RING TRANSFORMS HIM... COMPLETELY.
FEAR, AVARICE, RAGE, HOPE...
BUT WE HAVEN'T SEEN HIM LIKE THIS BEFORE.
HE'S... PURPLE?

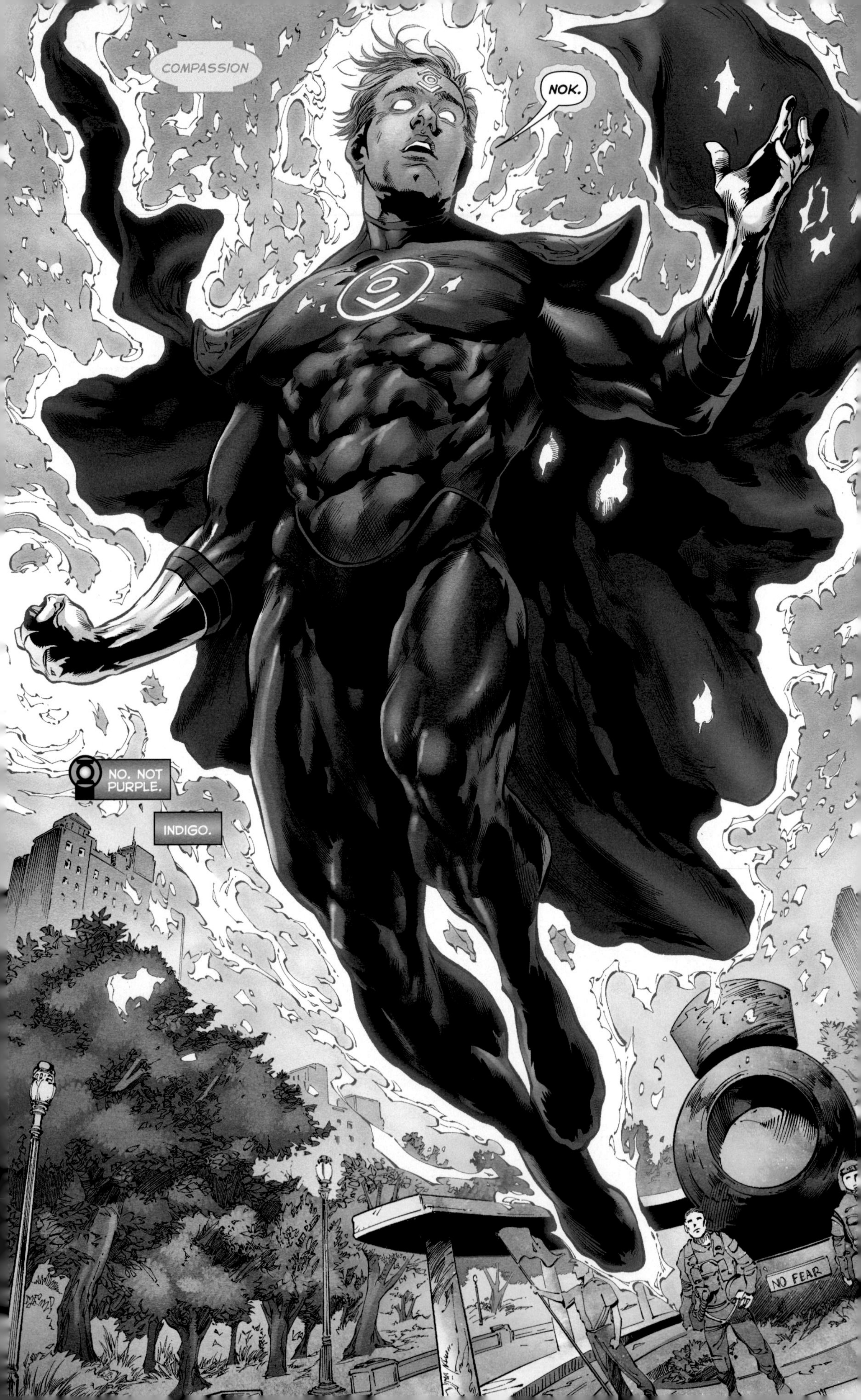
COMPASSION
NOK.
NO. NOT PURPLE.
INDIGO.
NO FEAR

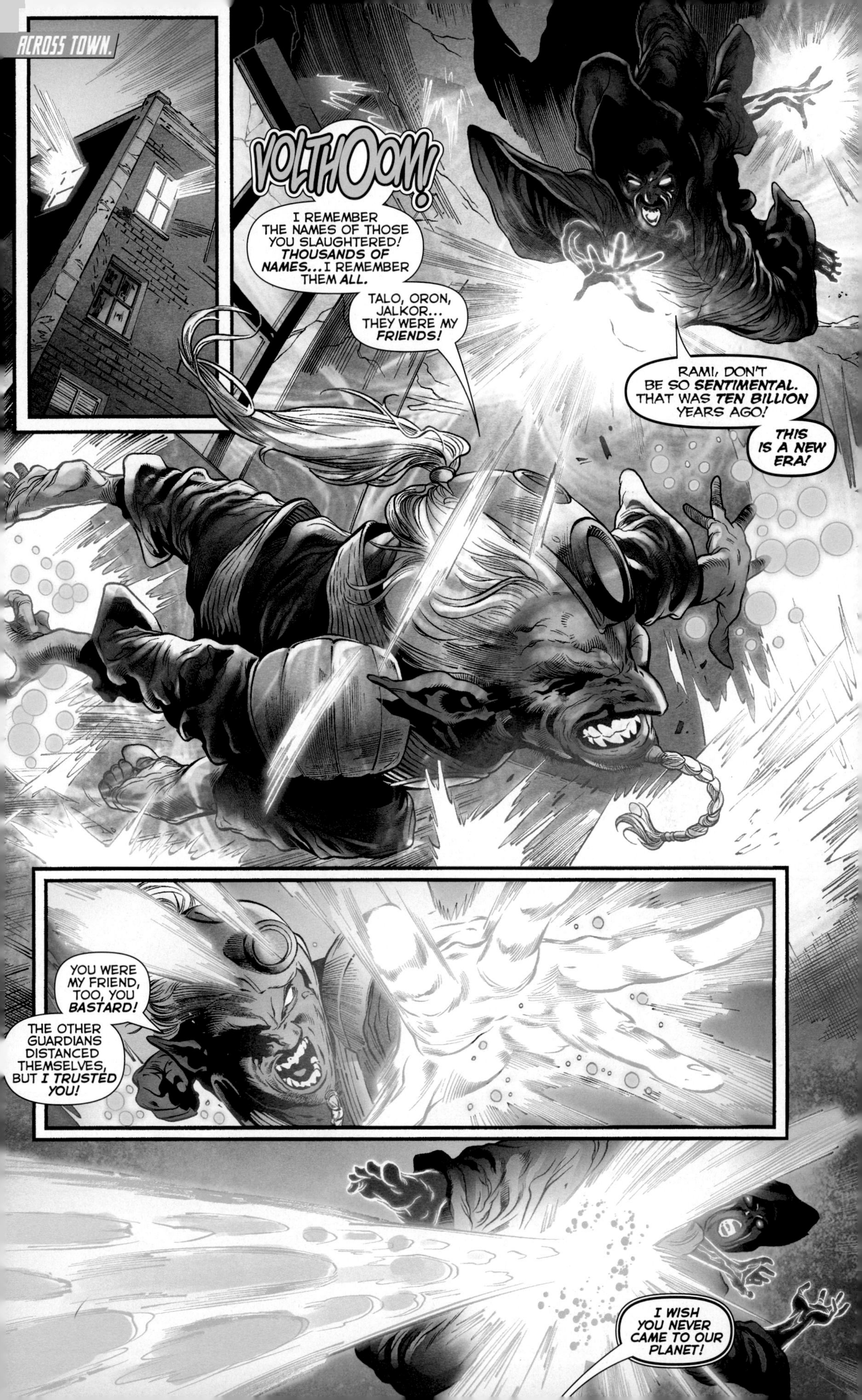
ACROSS TOWN.
VOLTHOOM!
I REMEMBER THE NAMES OF THOSE YOU SLAUGHTERED! THOUSANDS OF NAMES...I REMEMBER THEM ALL.
TALO, ORON, JALKOR... THEY WERE MY FRIENDS!
RAMI, DON'T BE SO SENTIMENTAL. THAT WAS TEN BILLION YEARS AGO!
THIS IS A NEW ERA!
YOU WERE MY FRIEND, TOO, YOU BASTARD!
THE OTHER GUARDIANS DISTANCED THEMSELVES, BUT I TRUSTED YOU!
I WISH YOU NEVER CAME TO OUR PLANET!

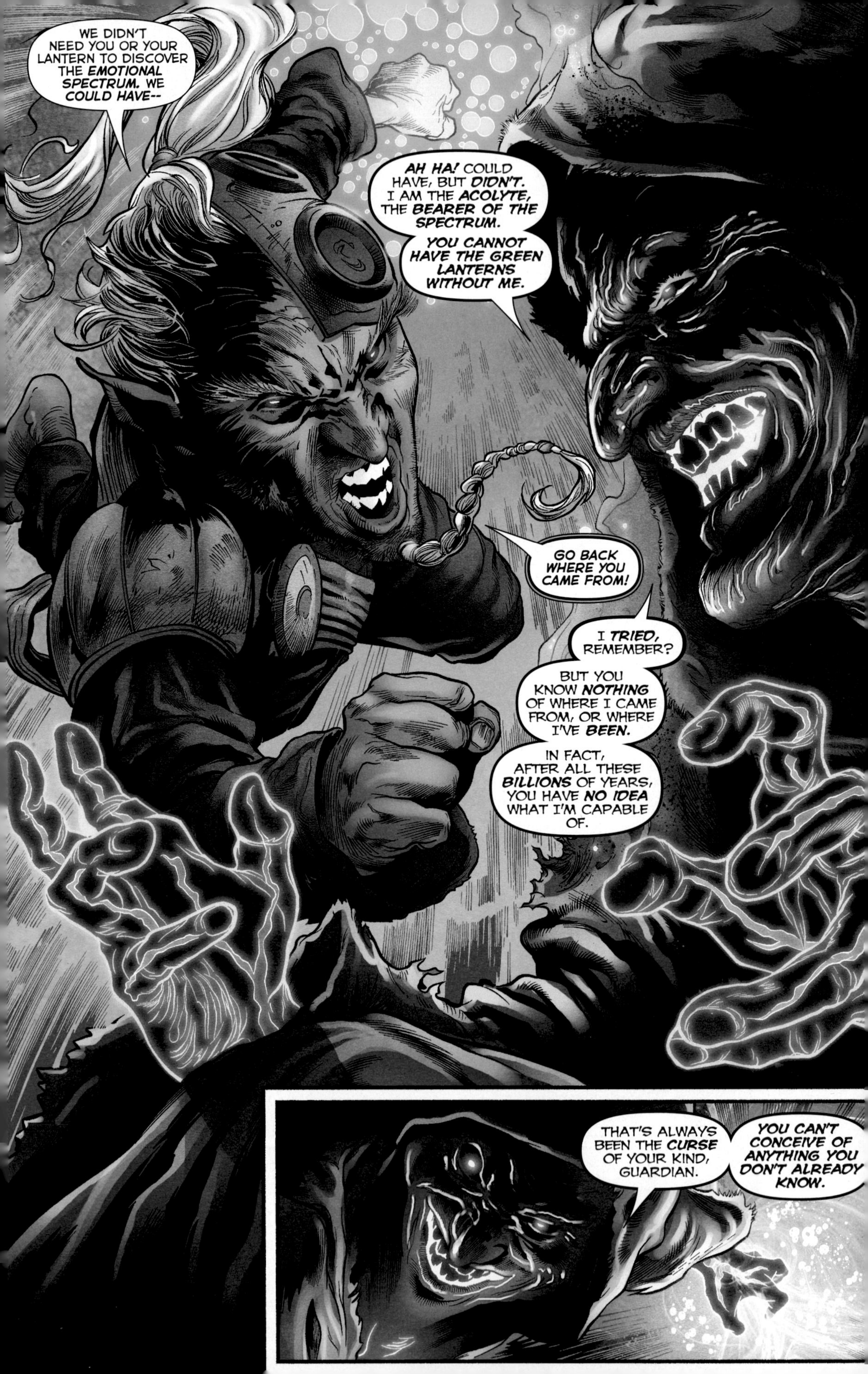

WE DIDN'T NEED YOU OR YOUR LANTERN TO DISCOVER THE EMOTIONAL SPECTRUM. WE COULD HAVE--
AH HA! COULD HAVE, BUT DIDN'T. I AM THE ACOLYTE, THE BEARER OF THE SPECTRUM.
YOU CANNOT HAVE THE GREEN LANTERNS WITHOUT ME.
GO BACK WHERE YOU CAME FROM!
I TRIED, REMEMBER?
BUT YOU KNOW NOTHING OF WHERE I CAME FROM, OR WHERE I'VE BEEN.
IN FACT, AFTER ALL THESE BILLIONS OF YEARS, YOU HAVE NO IDEA WHAT I'M CAPABLE OF.
THAT'S ALWAYS BEEN THE CURSE OF YOUR KIND, GUARDIAN.
YOU CAN'T CONCEIVE OF ANYTHING YOU DON'T ALREADY KNOW.

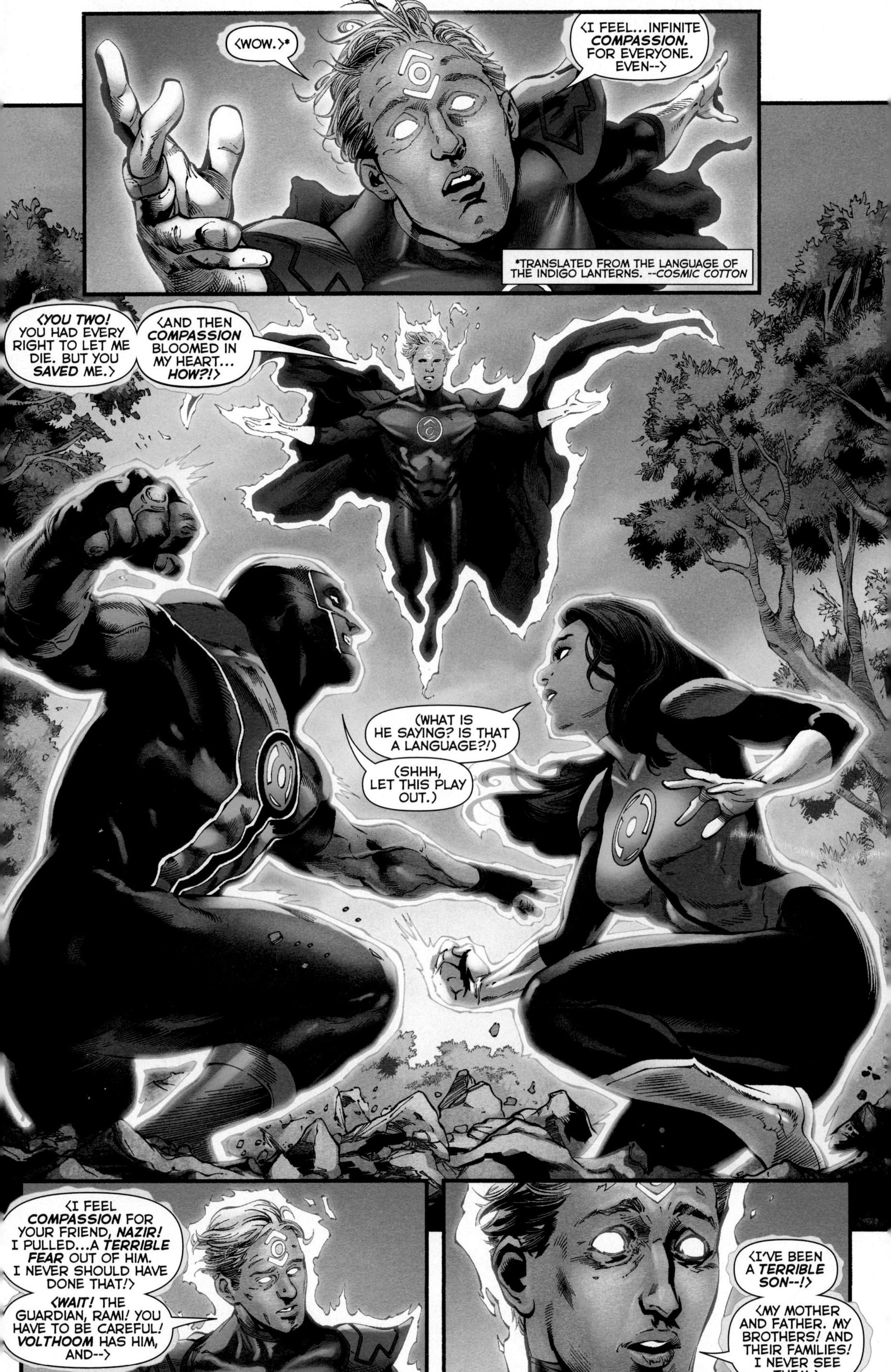

<WOW.>*
<I FEEL...INFINITE COMPASSION. FOR EVERYONE. EVEN-->
*TRANSLATED FROM THE LANGUAGE OF THE INDIGO LANTERNS. --COSMIC COTTON
<YOU TWO! YOU HAD EVERY RIGHT TO LET ME DIE. BUT YOU SAVED ME.>
<AND THEN COMPASSION BLOOMED IN MY HEART... HOW?!>
(WHAT IS HE SAYING? IS THAT A LANGUAGE?!)
(SHHH, LET THIS PLAY OUT.)
<I FEEL COMPASSION FOR YOUR FRIEND, NAZIR! I PULLED...A TERRIBLE FEAR OUT OF HIM. I NEVER SHOULD HAVE DONE THAT!>
<WAIT! THE GUARDIAN, RAMI! YOU HAVE TO BE CAREFUL! VOLTHOOM HAS HIM, AND-->
<I'VE BEEN A TERRIBLE SON--!>
<MY MOTHER AND FATHER. MY BROTHERS! AND THEIR FAMILIES! I NEVER SEE THEM.>

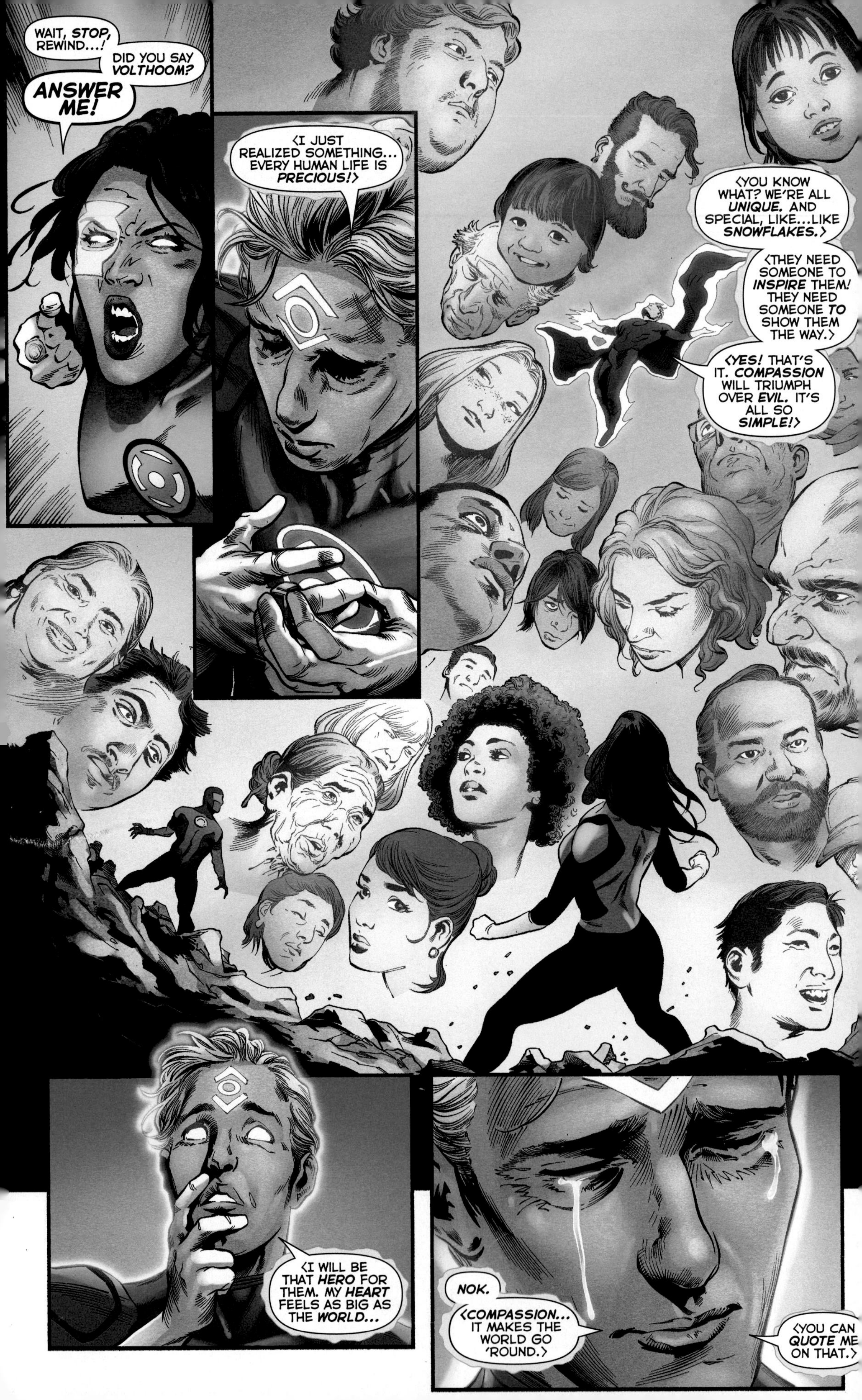
WAIT, STOP, REWIND...!
DID YOU SAY VOLTHOOM?
ANSWER ME!
<I JUST REALIZED SOMETHING... EVERY HUMAN LIFE IS PRECIOUS!>
<YOU KNOW WHAT? WE'RE ALL UNIQUE. AND SPECIAL, LIKE...LIKE SNOWFLAKES.>
<THEY NEED SOMEONE TO INSPIRE THEM! THEY NEED SOMEONE TO SHOW THEM THE WAY.>
<YES! THAT'S IT. COMPASSION WILL TRIUMPH OVER EVIL. IT'S ALL SO SIMPLE!>
<I WILL BE THAT HERO FOR THEM. MY HEART FEELS AS BIG AS THE WORLD...
NOK.
<COMPASSION... IT MAKES THE WORLD GO 'ROUND.>
<YOU CAN QUOTE ME ON THAT.>

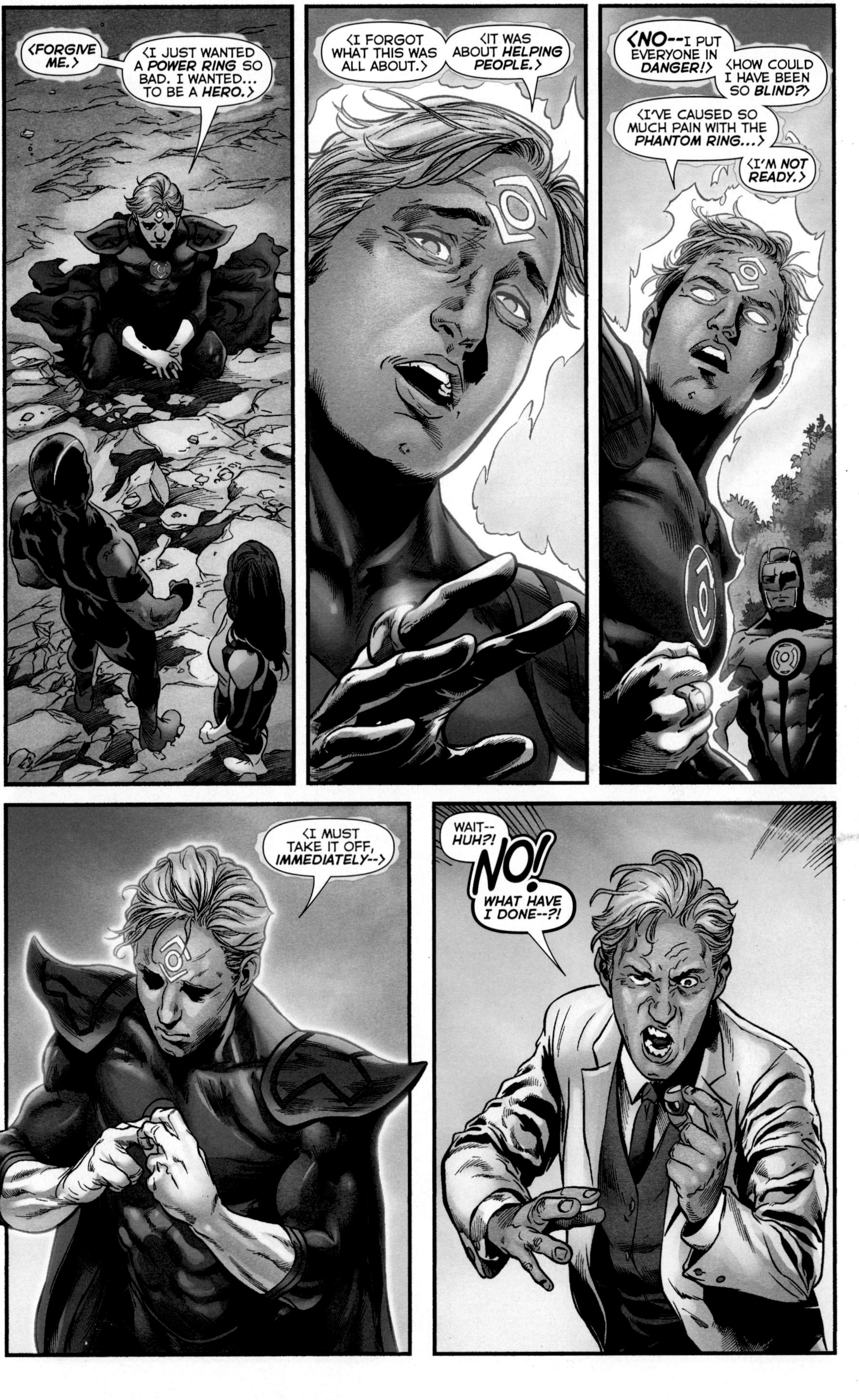

<FORGIVE ME.>
<I JUST WANTED A POWER RING SO BAD. I WANTED... TO BE A HERO.>
<I FORGOT WHAT THIS WAS ALL ABOUT.>
<IT WAS ABOUT HELPING PEOPLE.>
<NO--I PUT EVERYONE IN DANGER!>
<HOW COULD I HAVE BEEN SO BLIND?>
<I'VE CAUSED SO MUCH PAIN WITH THE PHANTOM RING...>
<I'M NOT READY.>
<I MUST TAKE IT OFF, IMMEDIATELY-->
WAIT-- HUH?!
NO!
WHAT HAVE I DONE--?!

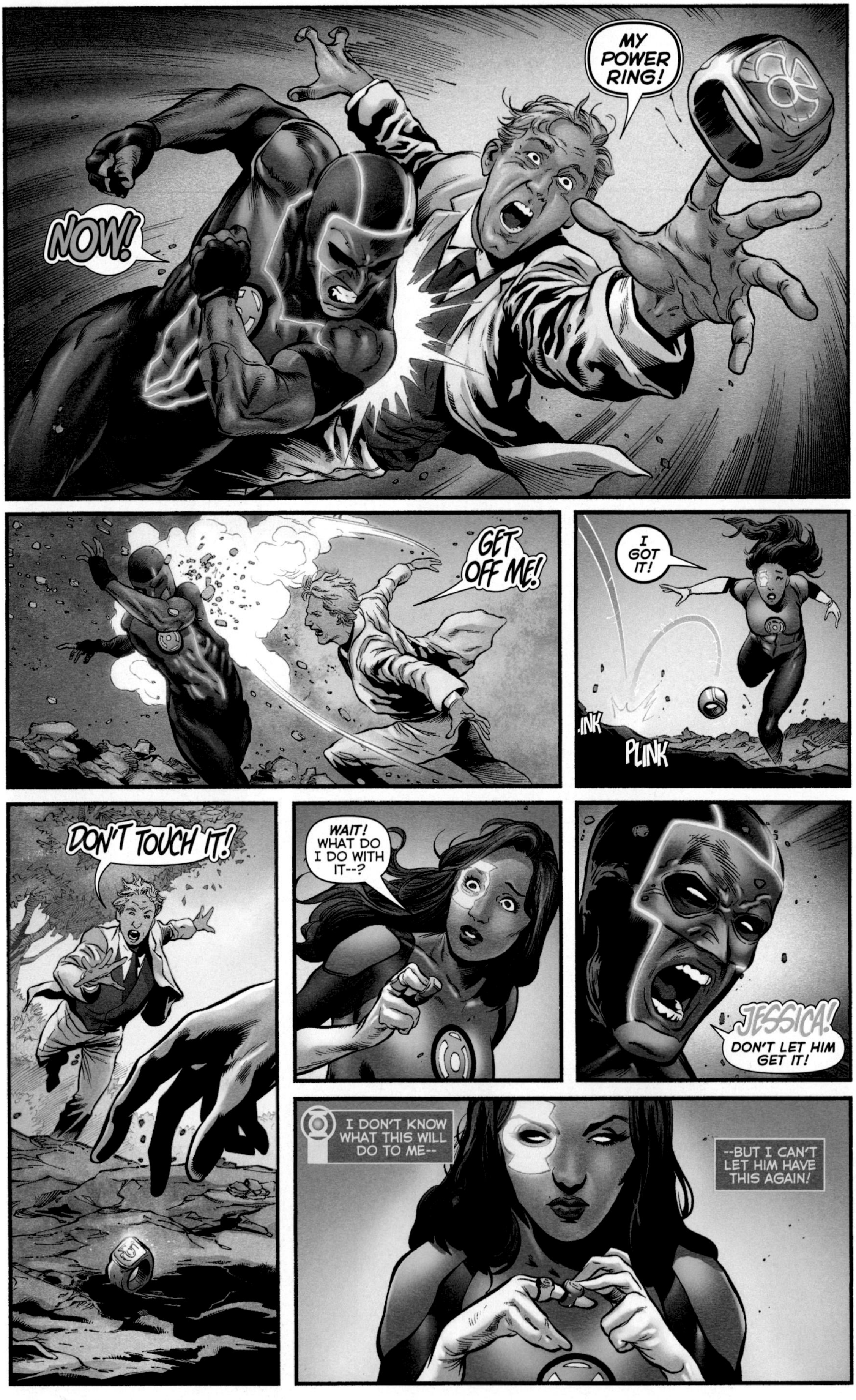
MY POWER RING!
NOW!
GET OFF ME!
I GOT IT!
.INK
PLINK
DON'T TOUCH IT!
WAIT! WHAT DO I DO WITH IT--?
JESSICA!
DON'T LET HIM GET IT!
I DON'T KNOW WHAT THIS WILL DO TO ME--
--BUT I CAN'T LET HIM HAVE THIS AGAIN!

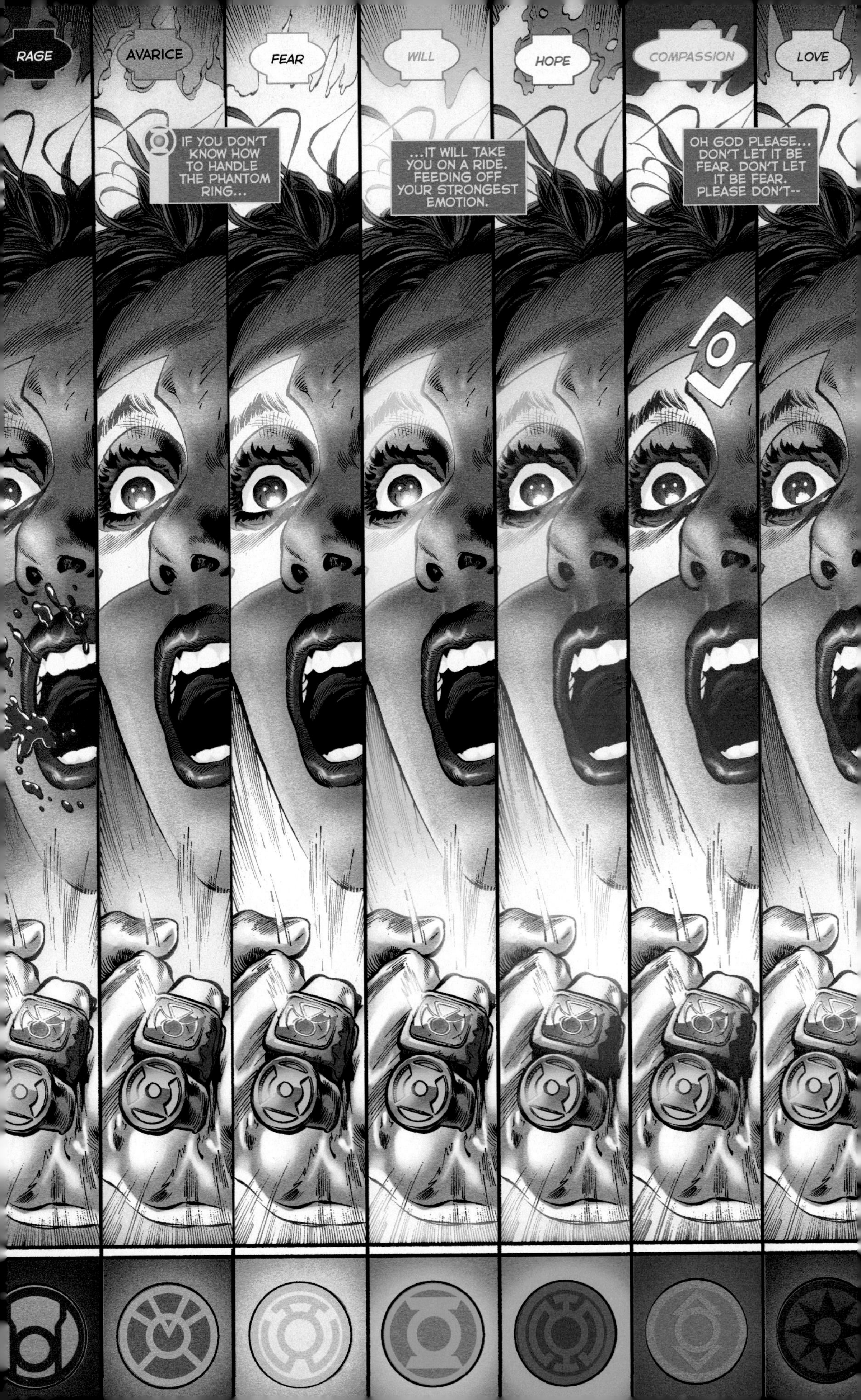

RAGE
AVARICE
FEAR
WILL
HOPE
COMPASSION
LOVE
IF YOU DON'T KNOW HOW TO HANDLE THE PHANTOM RING...
...IT WILL TAKE YOU ON A RIDE. FEEDING OFF YOUR STRONGEST EMOTION.
OH GOD PLEASE... DON'T LET IT BE FEAR. DON'T LET IT BE FEAR. PLEASE DON'T--

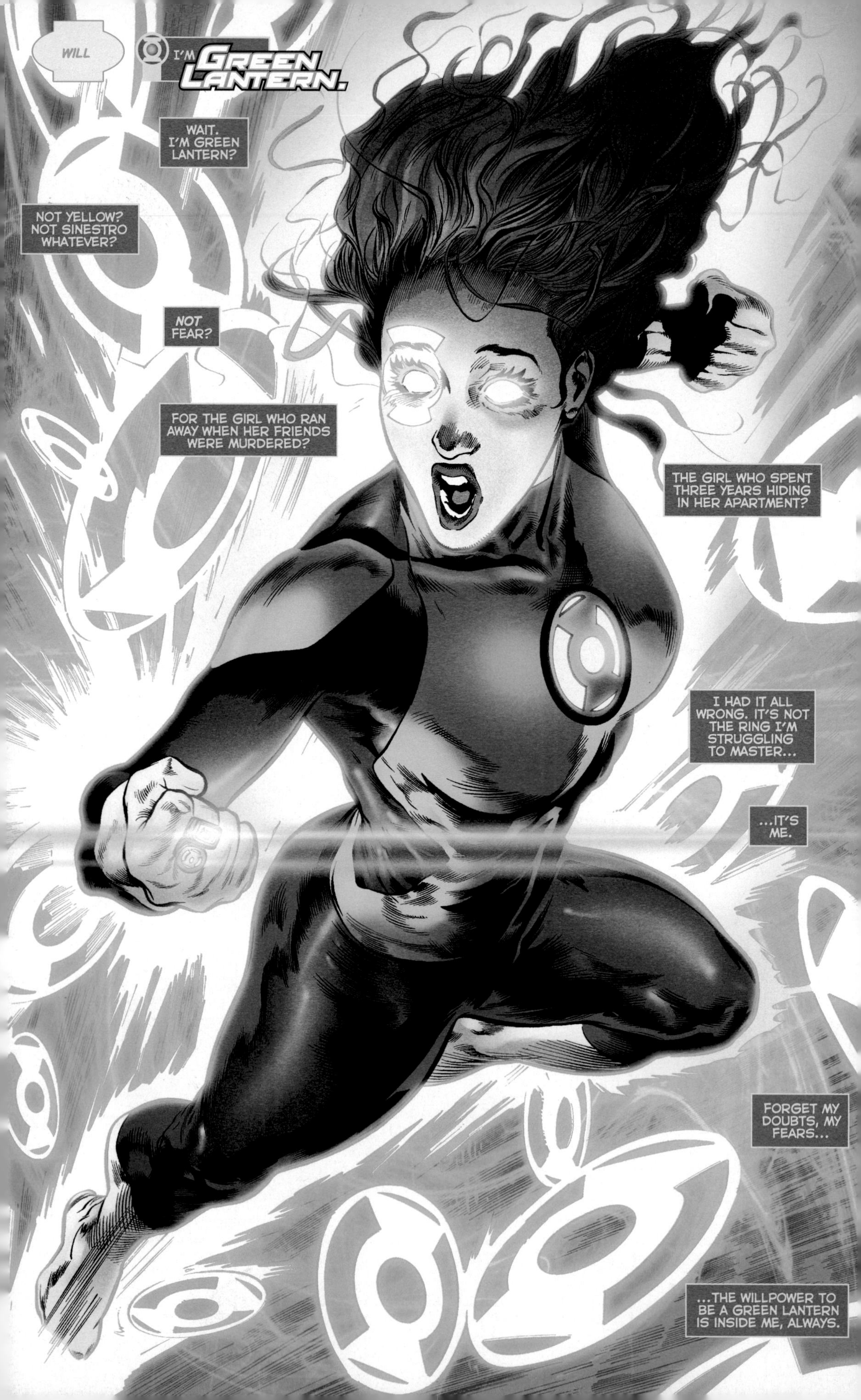
WILL
I'M GREEN LANTERN.
WAIT. I'M GREEN LANTERN?
NOT YELLOW? NOT SINESTRO WHATEVER?
NOT FEAR?
FOR THE GIRL WHO RAN AWAY WHEN HER FRIENDS WERE MURDERED?
THE GIRL WHO SPENT THREE YEARS HIDING IN HER APARTMENT?
I HAD IT ALL WRONG. IT'S NOT THE RING I'M STRUGGLING TO MASTER...
...IT'S ME.
FORGET MY DOUBTS, MY FEARS...
...THE WILLPOWER TO BE A GREEN LANTERN IS INSIDE ME, ALWAYS.

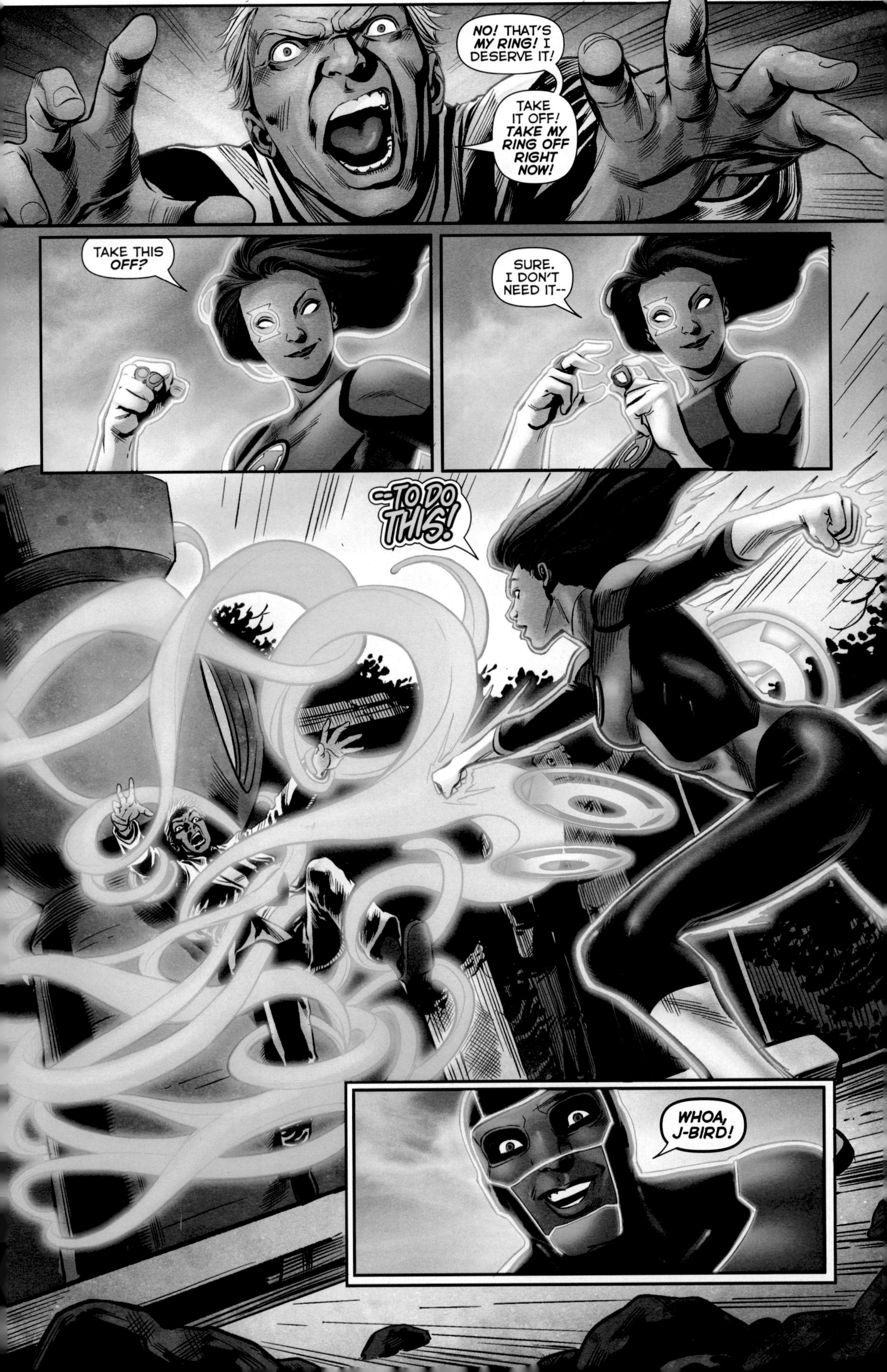
NO! THAT'S MY RING! I DESERVE IT!
TAKE IT OFF! TAKE MY RING OFF RIGHT NOW!
TAKE THIS OFF?
SURE. I DON'T NEED IT--
--TO DO THIS!
WHOA, J-BIRD!

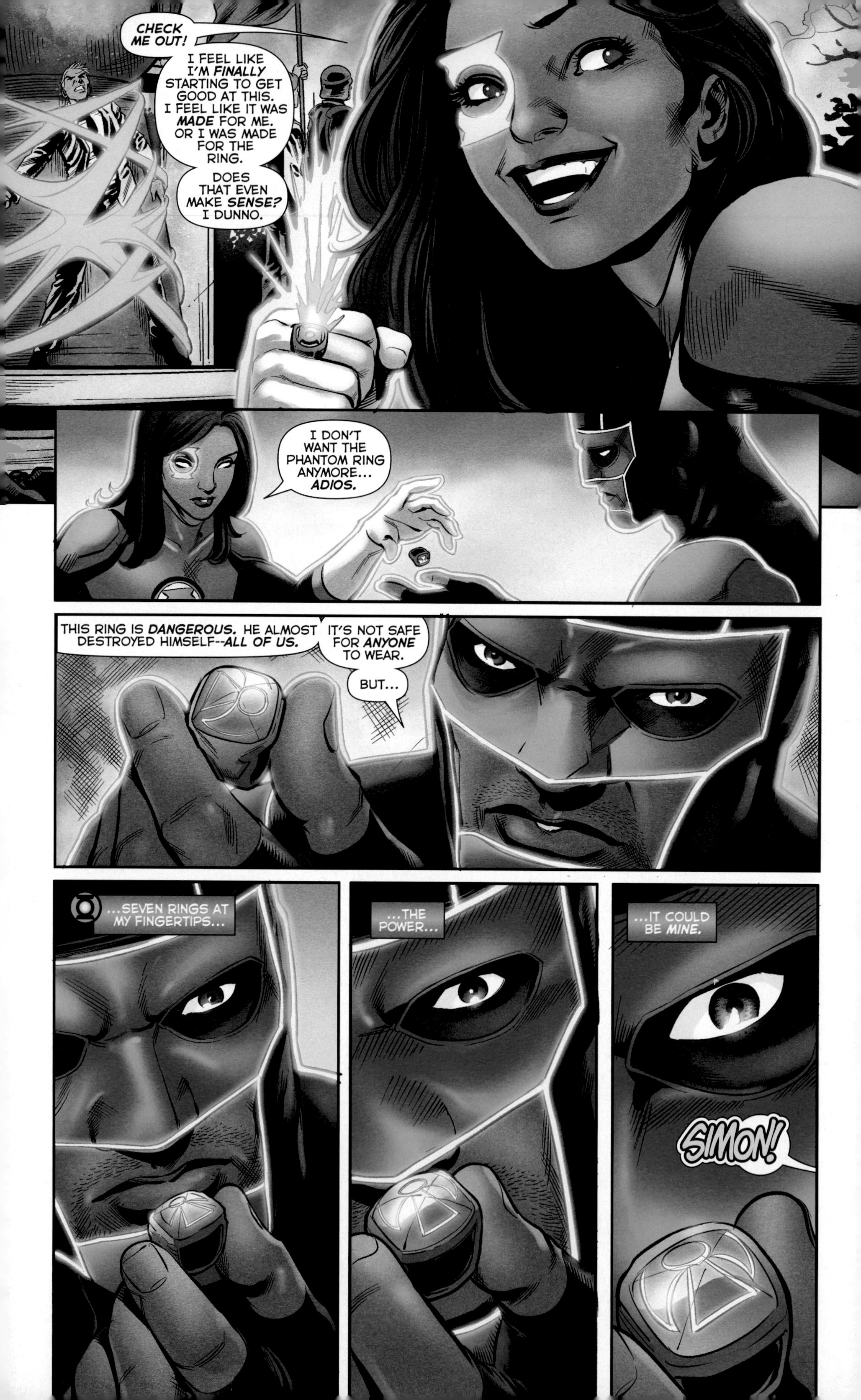
CHECK ME OUT!
I FEEL LIKE I'M FINALLY STARTING TO GET GOOD AT THIS. I FEEL LIKE IT WAS MADE FOR ME. OR I WAS MADE FOR THE RING.
DOES THAT EVEN MAKE SENSE? I DUNNO.
I DON'T WANT THE PHANTOM RING ANYMORE... ADIOS.
THIS RING IS DANGEROUS. HE ALMOST DESTROYED HIMSELF--ALL OF US.
IT'S NOT SAFE FOR ANYONE TO WEAR.
BUT...
...SEVEN RINGS AT MY FINGERTIPS...
...THE POWER...
...IT COULD BE MINE.
SIMON!

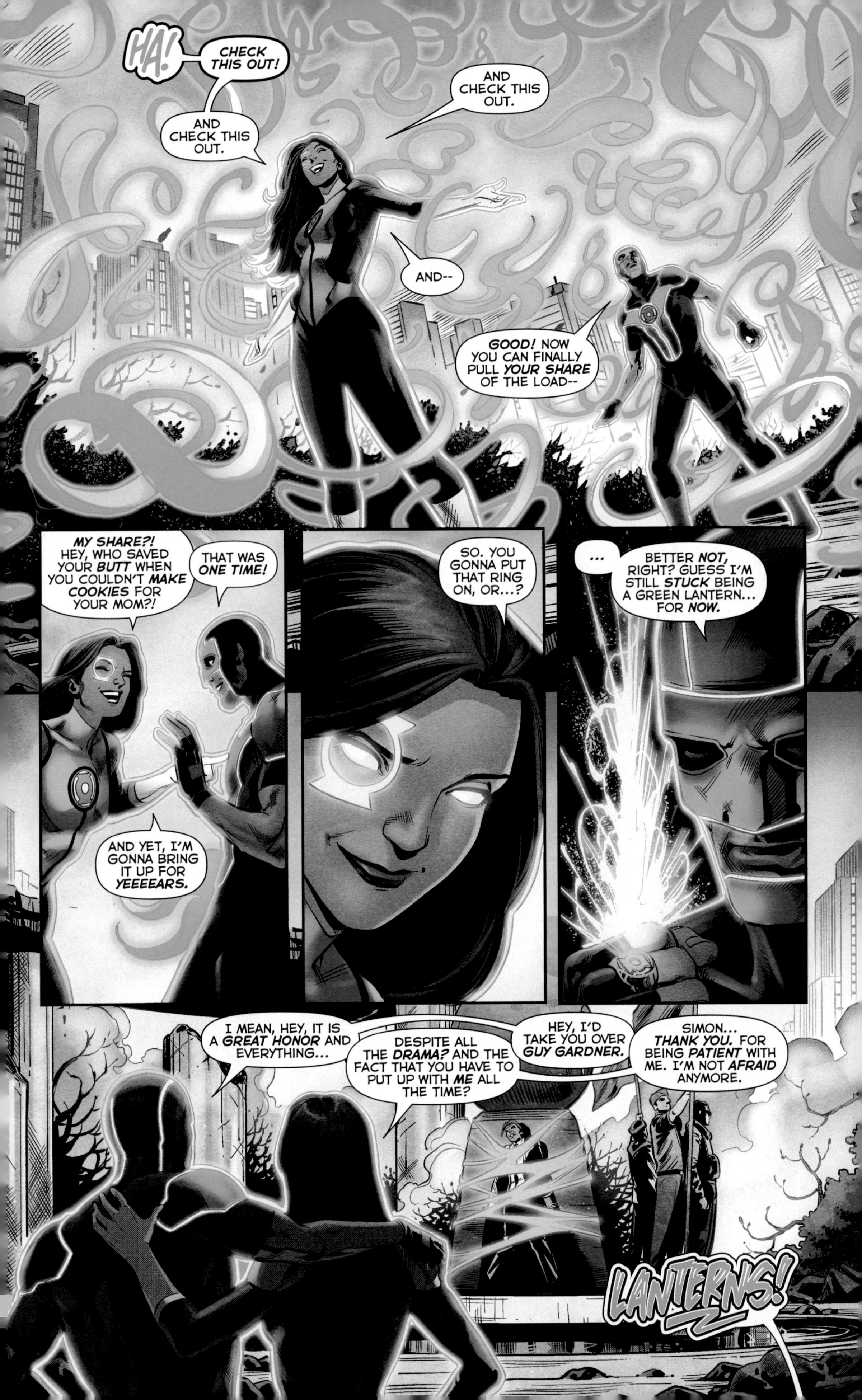
HA!
CHECK THIS OUT!
AND CHECK THIS OUT.
AND CHECK THIS OUT.
AND--
GOOD! NOW YOU CAN FINALLY PULL YOUR SHARE OF THE LOAD--
MY SHARE?! HEY, WHO SAVED YOUR BUTT WHEN YOU COULDN'T MAKE COOKIES FOR YOUR MOM?!
THAT WAS ONE TIME!
AND YET, I'M GONNA BRING IT UP FOR YEEEEARS.
SO. YOU GONNA PUT THAT RING ON, OR...?
...
BETTER NOT, RIGHT? GUESS I'M STILL STUCK BEING A GREEN LANTERN... FOR NOW.
I MEAN, HEY, IT IS A GREAT HONOR AND EVERYTHING...
DESPITE ALL THE DRAMA? AND THE FACT THAT YOU HAVE TO PUT UP WITH ME ALL THE TIME?
HEY, I'D TAKE YOU OVER GUY GARDNER.
SIMON... THANK YOU. FOR BEING PATIENT WITH ME. I'M NOT AFRAID ANYMORE.
LANTERNS!

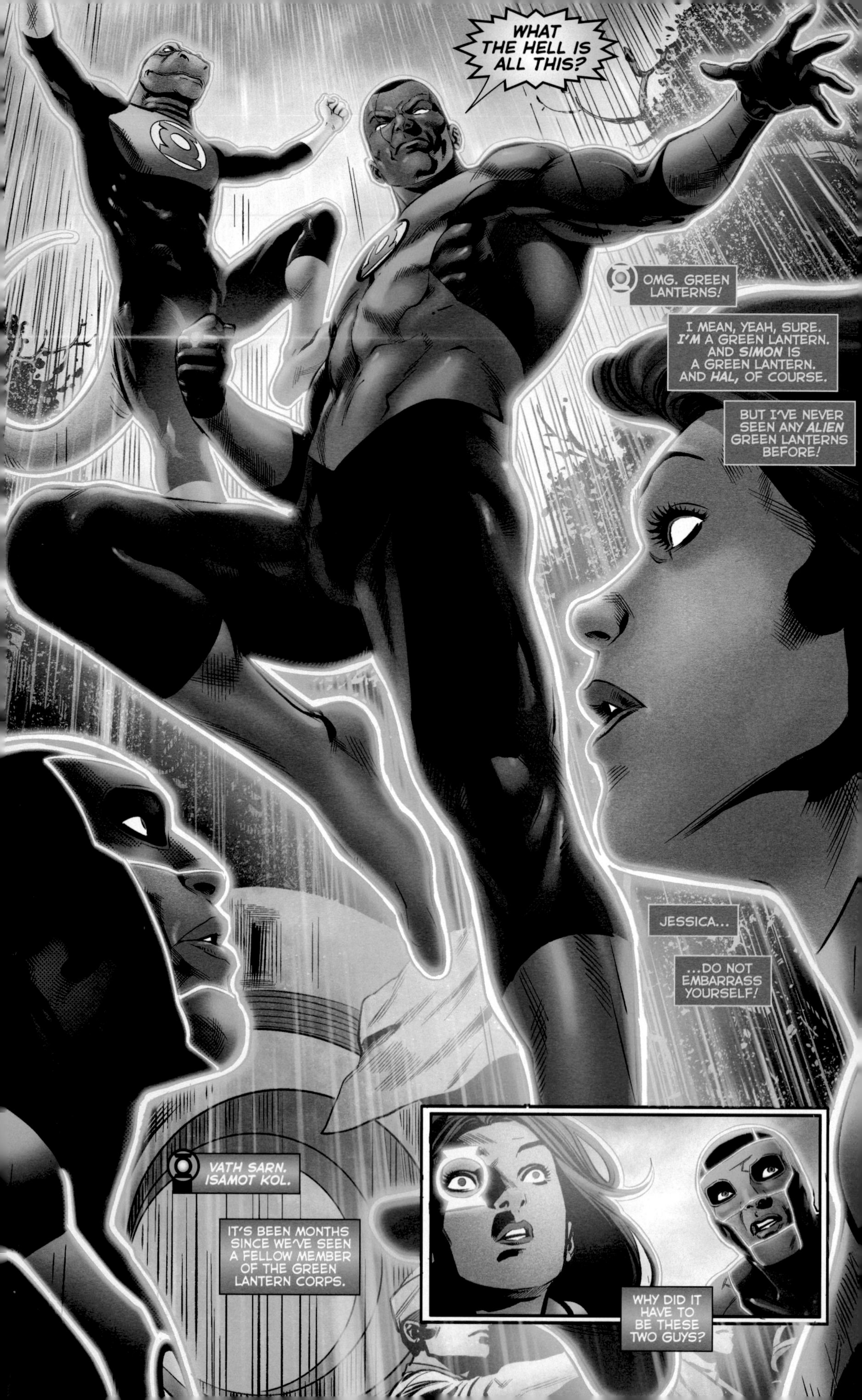
WHAT THE HELL IS ALL THIS?
OMG. GREEN LANTERNS!
I MEAN, YEAH, SURE. I'M A GREEN LANTERN. AND SIMON IS A GREEN LANTERN. AND HAL, OF COURSE.
BUT I'VE NEVER SEEN ANY ALIEN GREEN LANTERNS BEFORE!
JESSICA...
...DO NOT EMBARRASS YOURSELF!
VATH SARN. ISAMOT KOL.
IT'S BEEN MONTHS SINCE WE'VE SEEN A FELLOW MEMBER OF THE GREEN LANTERN CORPS.
WHY DID IT HAVE TO BE THESE TWO GUYS?

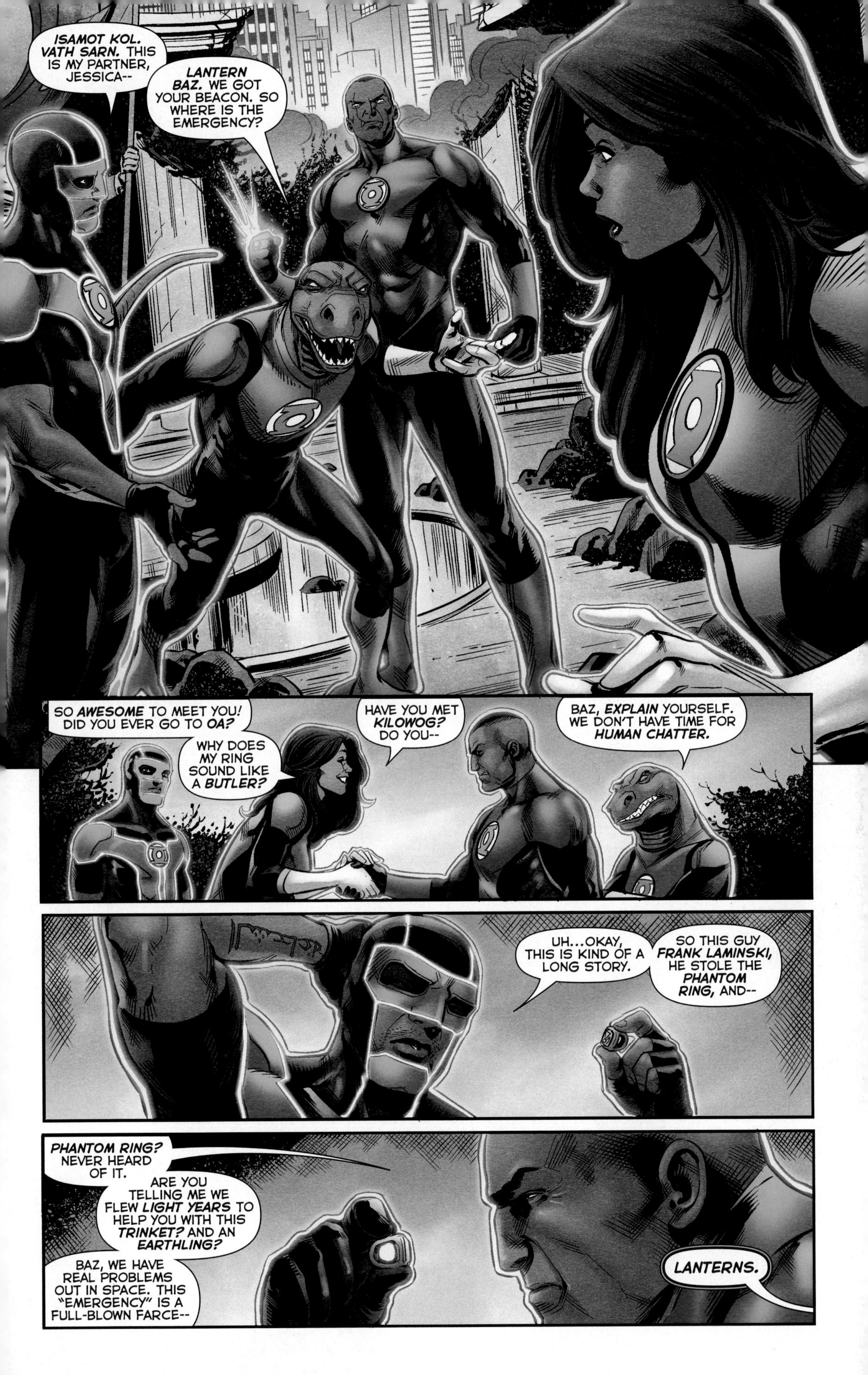
ISAMOT KOL. VATH SARN. THIS IS MY PARTNER, JESSICA--
LANTERN BAZ. WE GOT YOUR BEACON. SO WHERE IS THE EMERGENCY?
SO AWESOME TO MEET YOU! DID YOU EVER GO TO OA?
WHY DOES MY RING SOUND LIKE A BUTLER?
HAVE YOU MET KILOWOG? DO YOU--
BAZ, EXPLAIN YOURSELF. WE DON'T HAVE TIME FOR HUMAN CHATTER.
UH...OKAY, THIS IS KIND OF A LONG STORY.
SO THIS GUY FRANK LAMINSKI, HE STOLE THE PHANTOM RING, AND--
PHANTOM RING? NEVER HEARD OF IT.
ARE YOU TELLING ME WE FLEW LIGHT YEARS TO HELP YOU WITH THIS TRINKET? AND AN EARTHLING?
BAZ, WE HAVE REAL PROBLEMS OUT IN SPACE. THIS "EMERGENCY" IS A FULL-BLOWN FARCE--
LANTERNS.

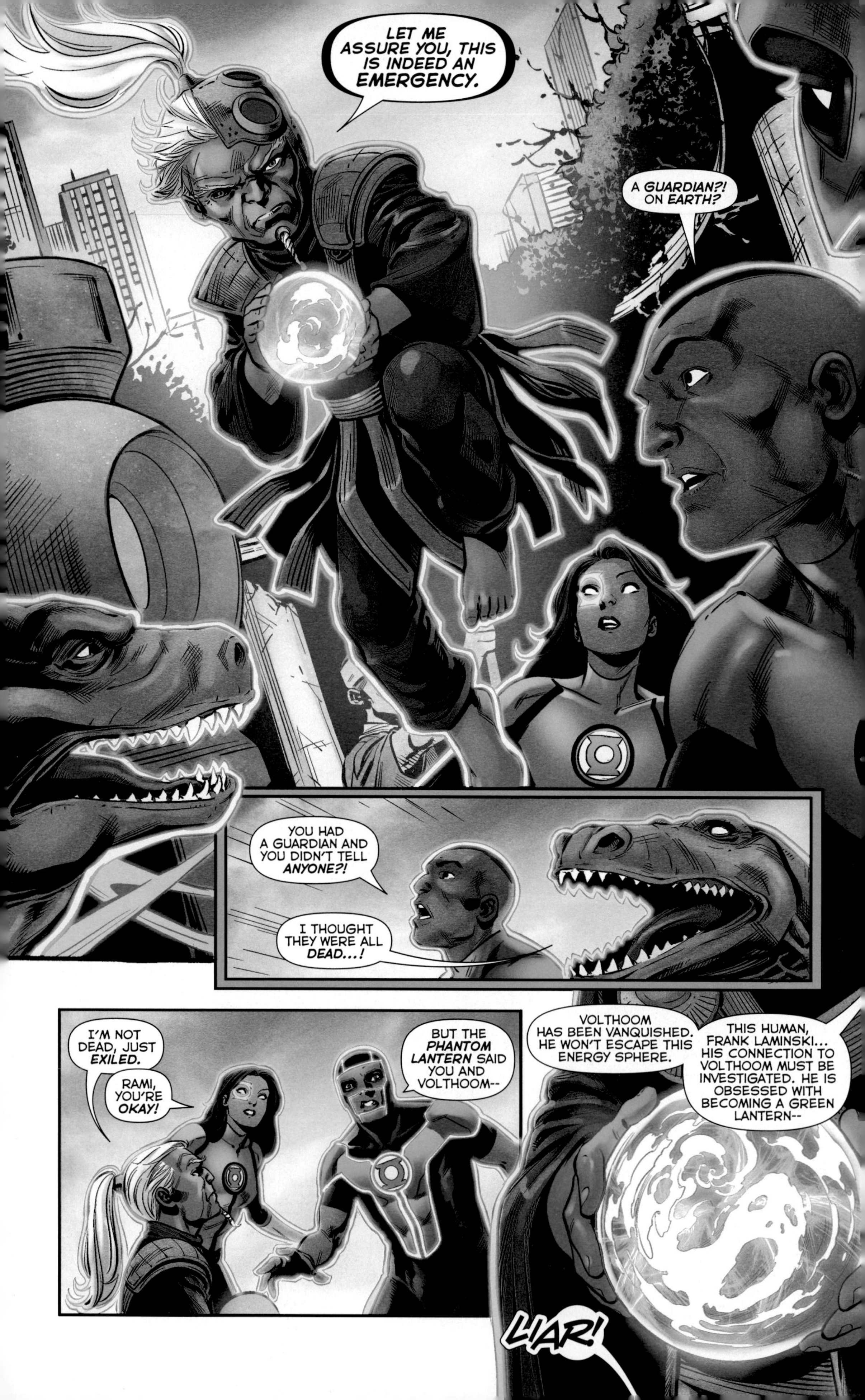
LET ME ASSURE YOU, THIS IS INDEED AN EMERGENCY.
A GUARDIAN?! ON EARTH?
YOU HAD A GUARDIAN AND YOU DIDN'T TELL ANYONE?!
I THOUGHT THEY WERE ALL DEAD...!
I'M NOT DEAD, JUST EXILED.
RAMI, YOU'RE OKAY!
BUT THE PHANTOM LANTERN SAID YOU AND VOLTHOOM--
VOLTHOOM HAS BEEN VANQUISHED. HE WON'T ESCAPE THIS ENERGY SPHERE.
THIS HUMAN, FRANK LAMINSKI... HIS CONNECTION TO VOLTHOOM MUST BE INVESTIGATED. HE IS OBSESSED WITH BECOMING A GREEN LANTERN--
LIAR!

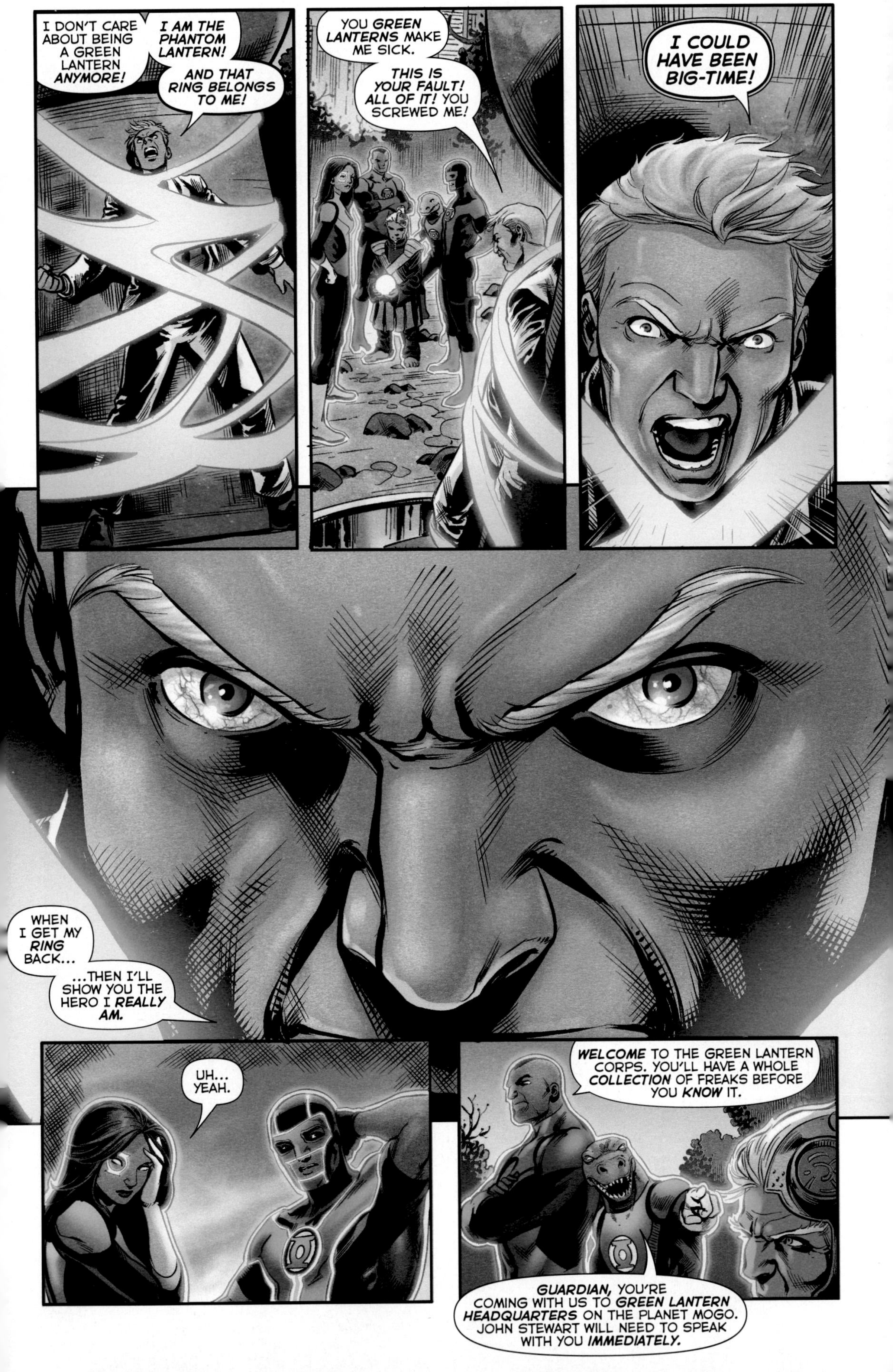

I DON'T CARE ABOUT BEING A GREEN LANTERN ANYMORE!
I AM THE PHANTOM LANTERN!
AND THAT RING BELONGS TO ME!
YOU GREEN LANTERNS MAKE ME SICK.
THIS IS YOUR FAULT! ALL OF IT! YOU SCREWED ME!
I COULD HAVE BEEN BIG-TIME!
WHEN I GET MY RING BACK...
...THEN I'LL SHOW YOU THE HERO I REALLY AM.
UH... YEAH.
WELCOME TO THE GREEN LANTERN CORPS. YOU'LL HAVE A WHOLE COLLECTION OF FREAKS BEFORE YOU KNOW IT.
GUARDIAN, YOU'RE COMING WITH US TO GREEN LANTERN HEADQUARTERS ON THE PLANET MOGO. JOHN STEWART WILL NEED TO SPEAK WITH YOU IMMEDIATELY.

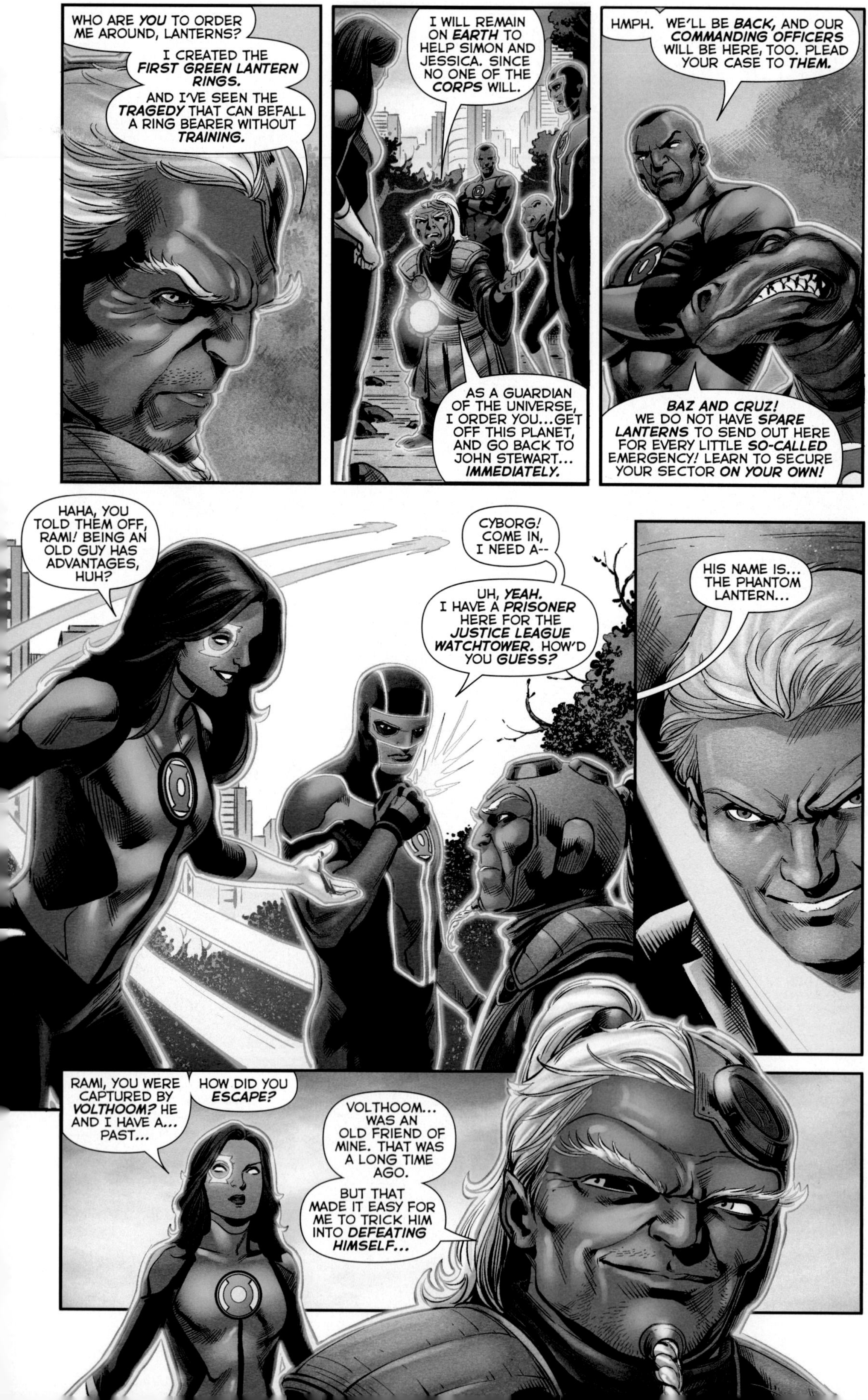

WHO ARE YOU TO ORDER ME AROUND, LANTERNS?
I CREATED THE FIRST GREEN LANTERN RINGS.
AND I'VE SEEN THE TRAGEDY THAT CAN BEFALL A RING BEARER WITHOUT TRAINING.
I WILL REMAIN ON EARTH TO HELP SIMON AND JESSICA. SINCE NO ONE OF THE CORPS WILL.
AS A GUARDIAN OF THE UNIVERSE, I ORDER YOU...GET OFF THIS PLANET, AND GO BACK TO JOHN STEWART... IMMEDIATELY.
HMPH.
WE'LL BE BACK, AND OUR COMMANDING OFFICERS WILL BE HERE, TOO. PLEAD YOUR CASE TO THEM.
BAZ AND CRUZ! WE DO NOT HAVE SPARE LANTERNS TO SEND OUT HERE FOR EVERY LITTLE SO-CALLED EMERGENCY! LEARN TO SECURE YOUR SECTOR ON YOUR OWN!
HAHA, YOU TOLD THEM OFF, RAMI! BEING AN OLD GUY HAS ADVANTAGES, HUH?
CYBORG! COME IN, I NEED A--
UH, YEAH. I HAVE A PRISONER HERE FOR THE JUSTICE LEAGUE WATCHTOWER. HOW'D YOU GUESS?
HIS NAME IS... THE PHANTOM LANTERN...
RAMI, YOU WERE CAPTURED BY VOLTHOOM? HE AND I HAVE A... PAST...
HOW DID YOU ESCAPE?
VOLTHOOM... WAS AN OLD FRIEND OF MINE. THAT WAS A LONG TIME AGO.
BUT THAT MADE IT EASY FOR ME TO TRICK HIM INTO DEFEATING HIMSELF...

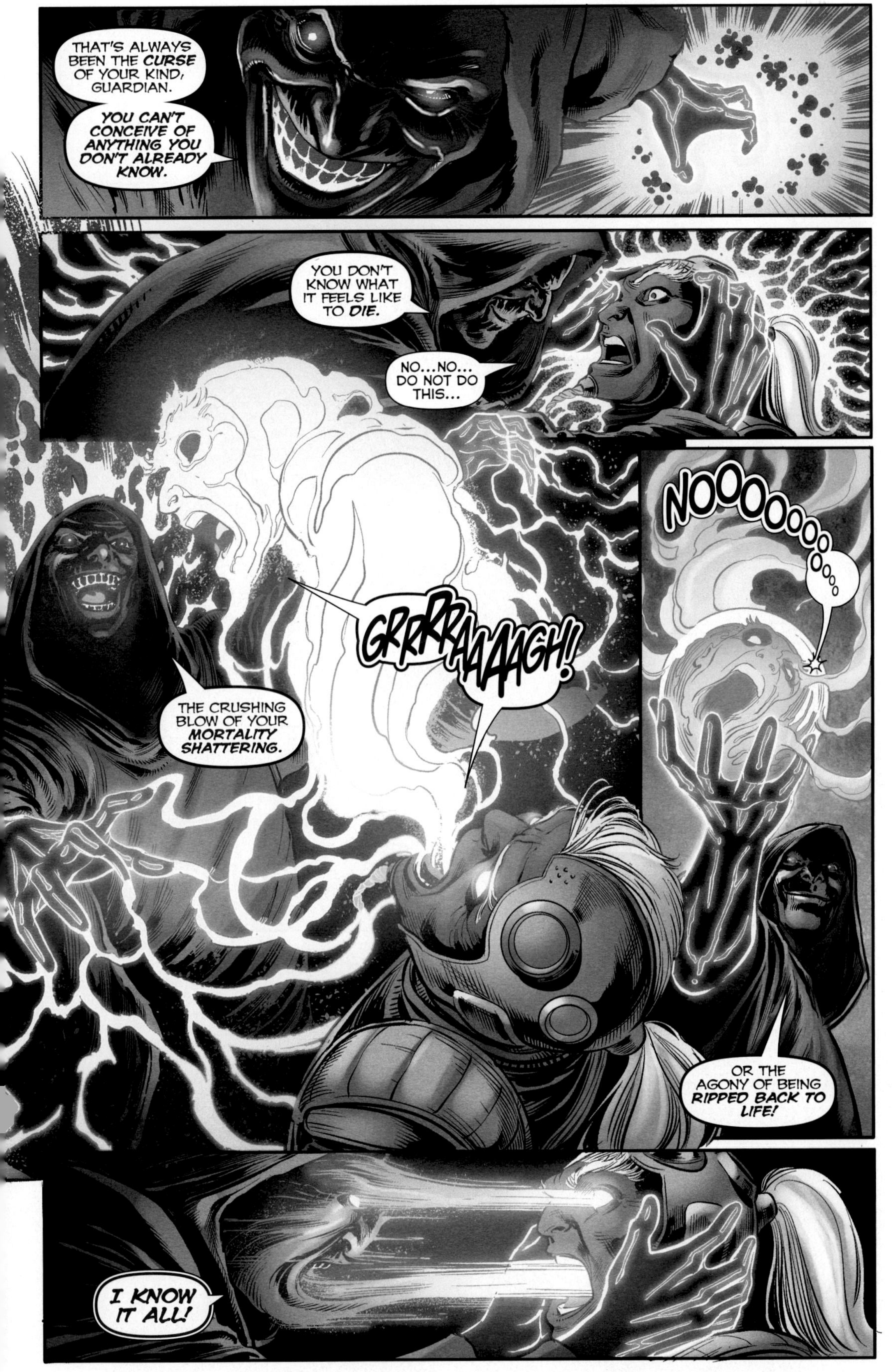
THAT'S ALWAYS BEEN THE CURSE OF YOUR KIND, GUARDIAN.
YOU CAN'T CONCEIVE OF ANYTHING YOU DON'T ALREADY KNOW.
YOU DON'T KNOW WHAT IT FEELS LIKE TO DIE.
NO...NO... DO NOT DO THIS...
THE CRUSHING BLOW OF YOUR MORTALITY SHATTERING.
GRRRRAAAAAGH!
NOOOOOOOOOOOO
OR THE AGONY OF BEING RIPPED BACK TO LIFE!
I KNOW IT ALL!

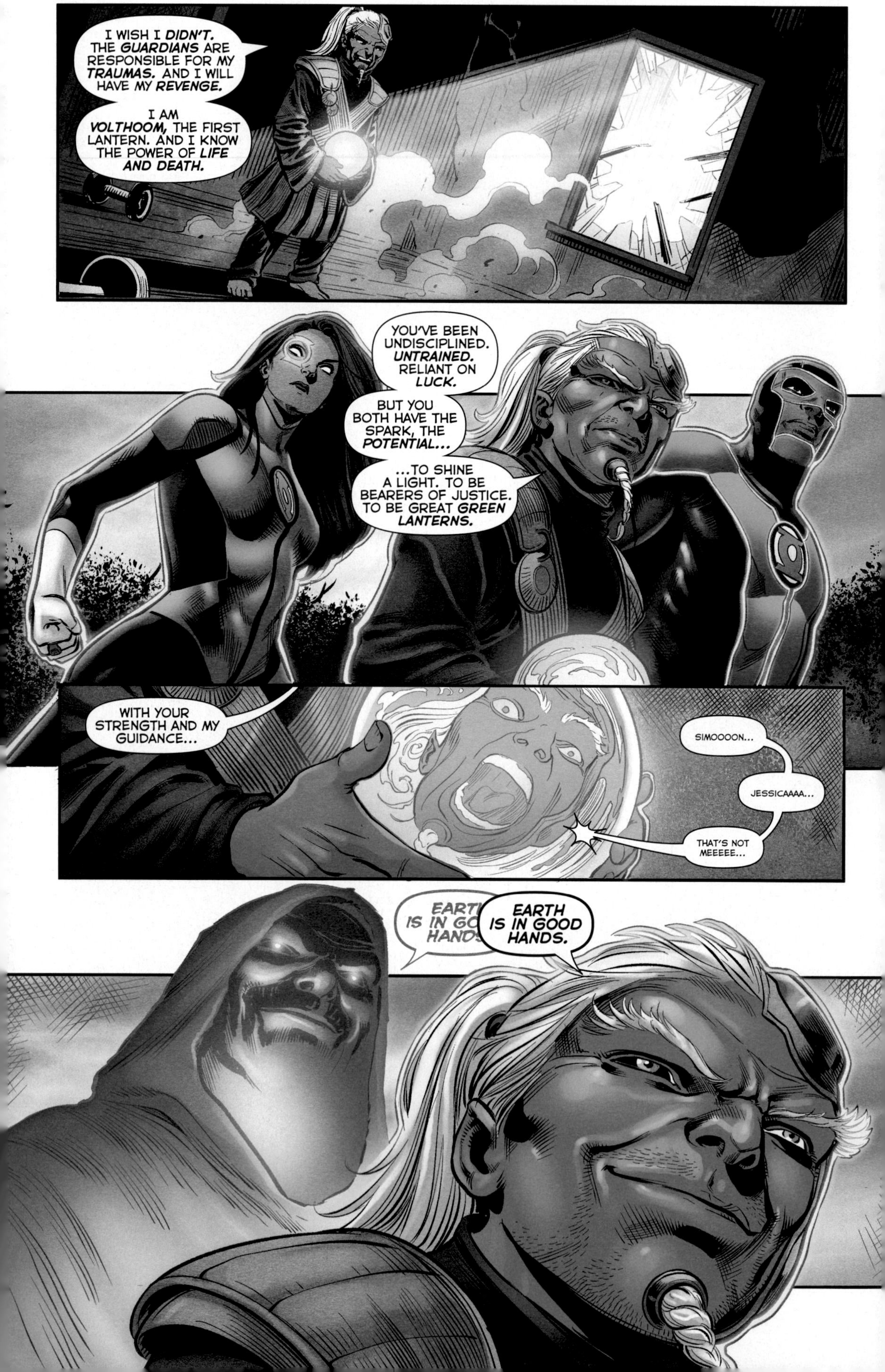
I WISH I DIDN'T. THE GUARDIANS ARE RESPONSIBLE FOR MY TRAUMAS. AND I WILL HAVE MY REVENGE.
I AM VOLTHOOM, THE FIRST LANTERN. AND I KNOW THE POWER OF LIFE AND DEATH.
YOU'VE BEEN UNDISCIPLINED. UNTRAINED. RELIANT ON LUCK.
BUT YOU BOTH HAVE THE SPARK, THE POTENTIAL...
...TO SHINE A LIGHT. TO BE BEARERS OF JUSTICE. TO BE GREAT GREEN LANTERNS.
WITH YOUR STRENGTH AND MY GUIDANCE...
SIMOOOON...
JESSICAAAA...
THAT'S NOT MEEEEE...
EARTH IS IN GOOD HANDS.
EARTH IS IN GOOD HANDS.

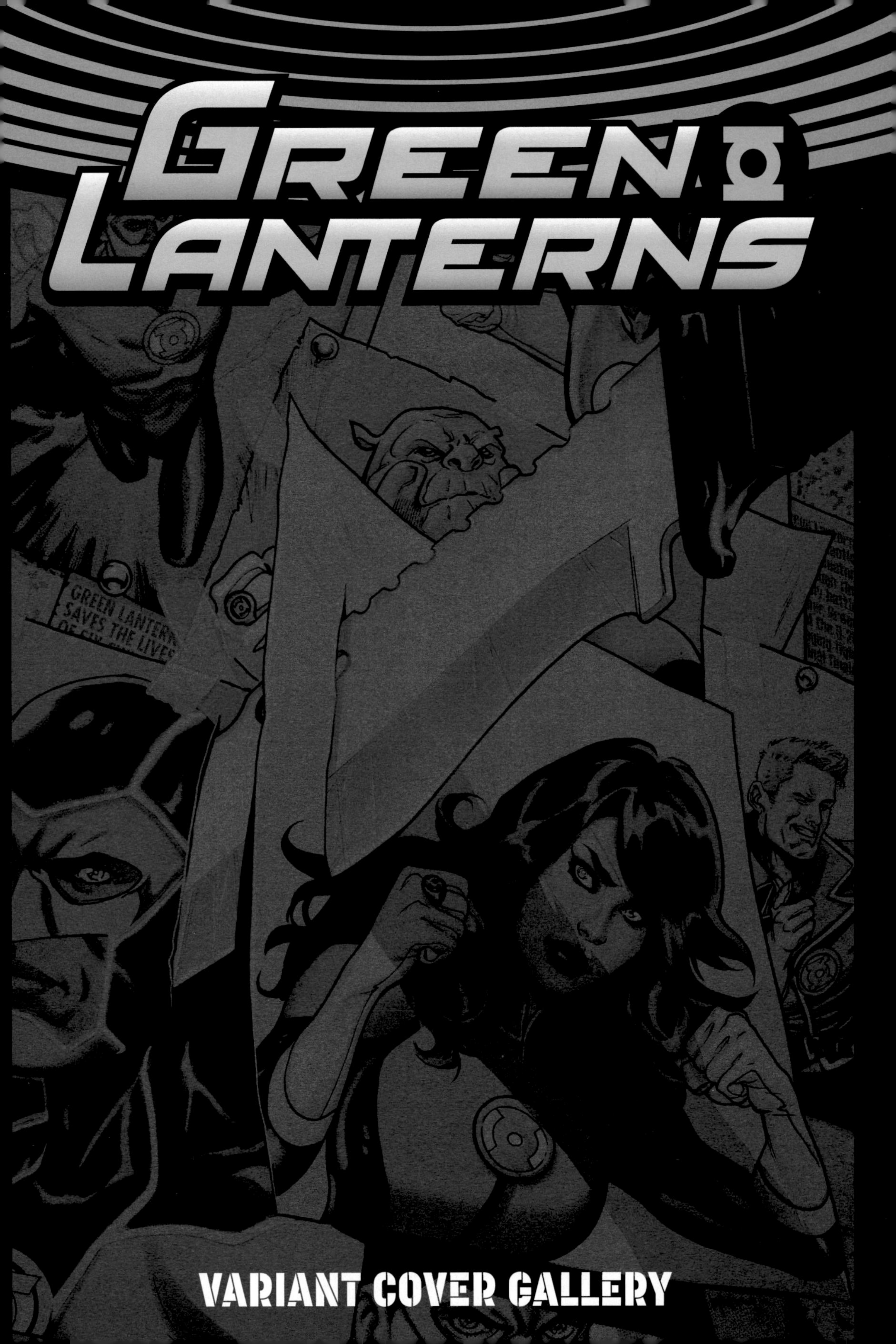
GREEN LANTERNS
GREEN LANTERN SAVES THE LIVES
VARIANT COVER GALLERY

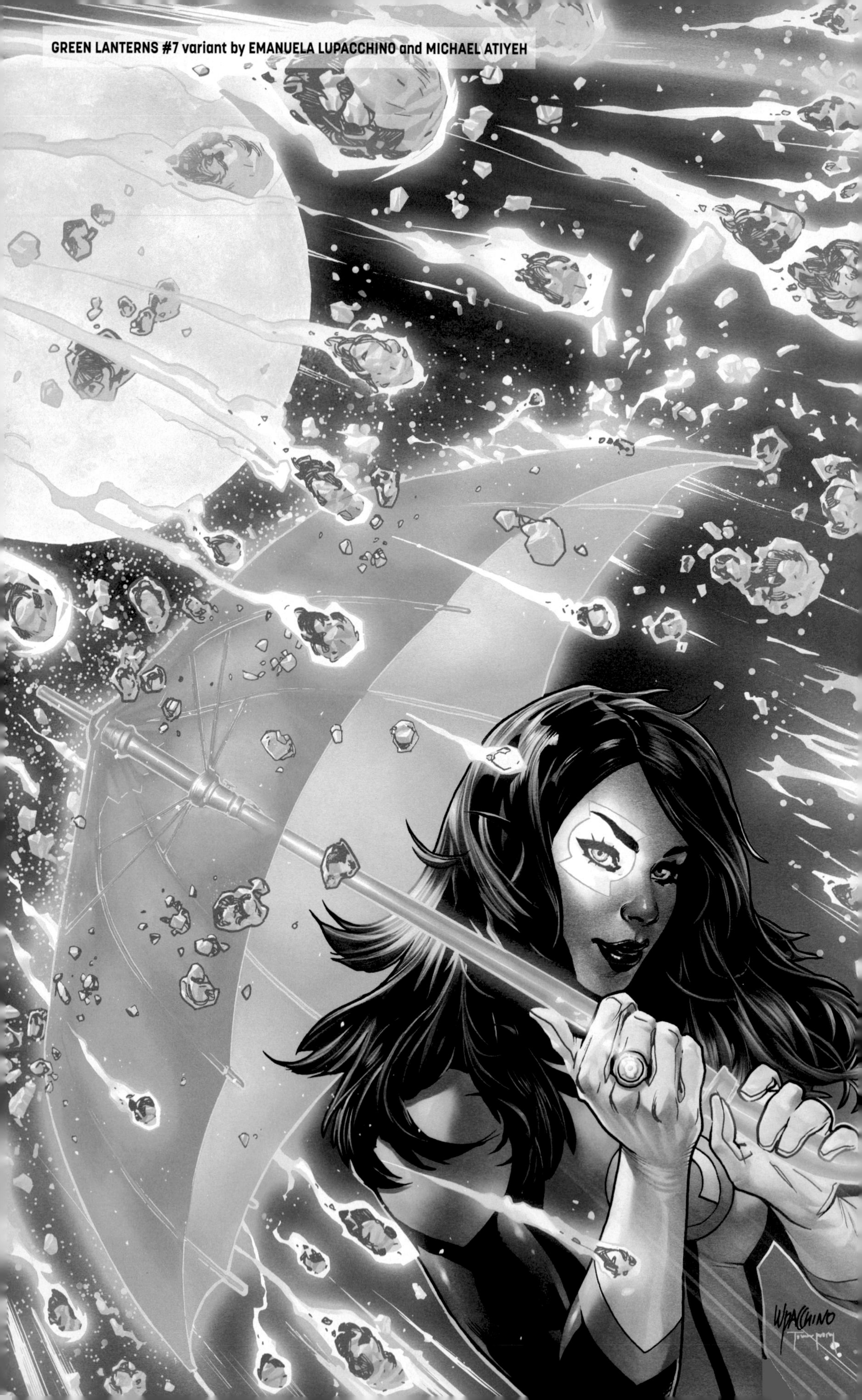

GREEN LANTERNS #7 variant by EMANUELA LUPACCHINO and MICHAEL ATIYEH

GREEN LANTERNS #8 variant by EMANUELA LUPACCHINO and MICHAEL ATIYEH

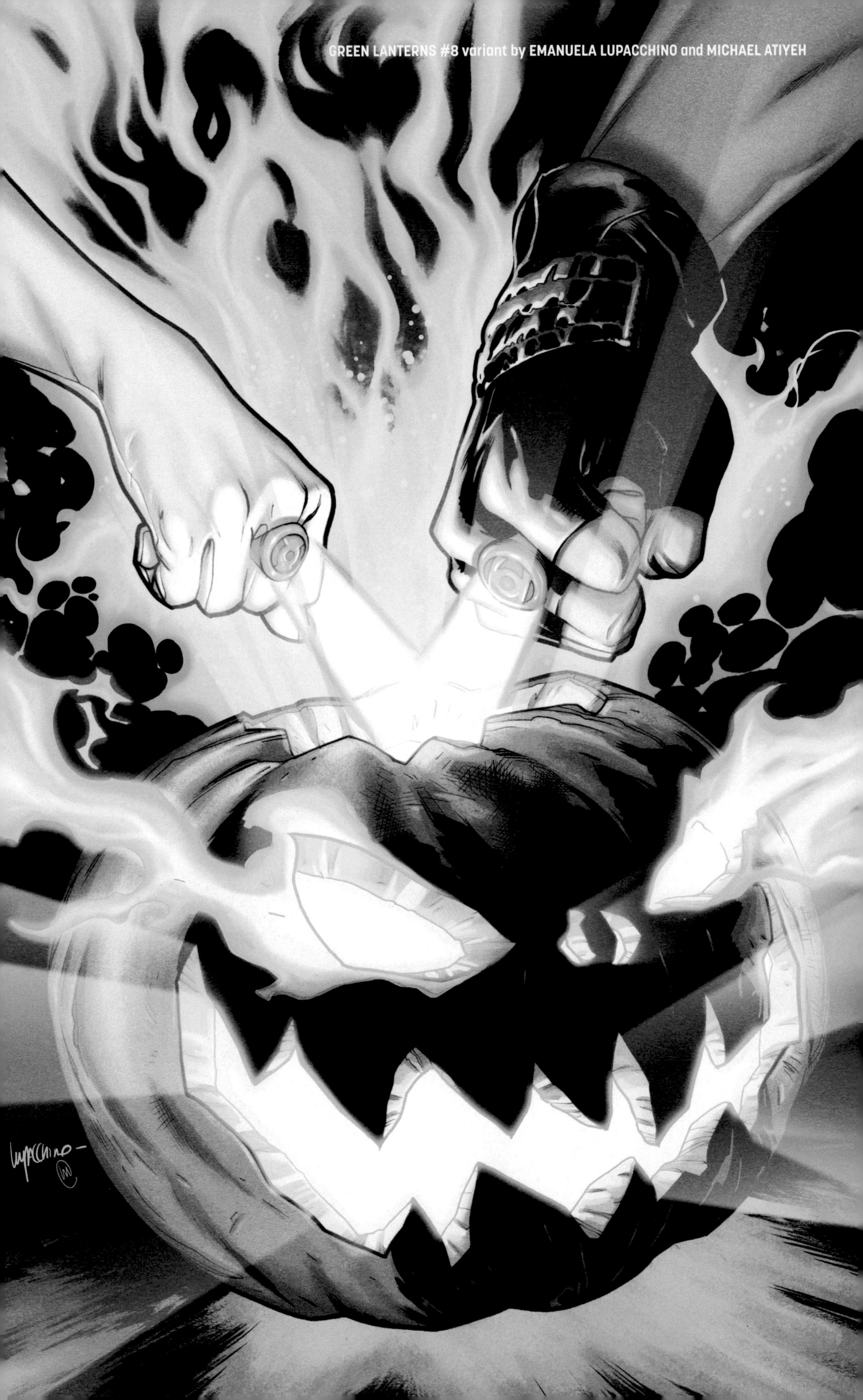

GREEN LANTERNS #9 variant by EMANUELA LUPACCHINO and MICHAEL ATIYEH

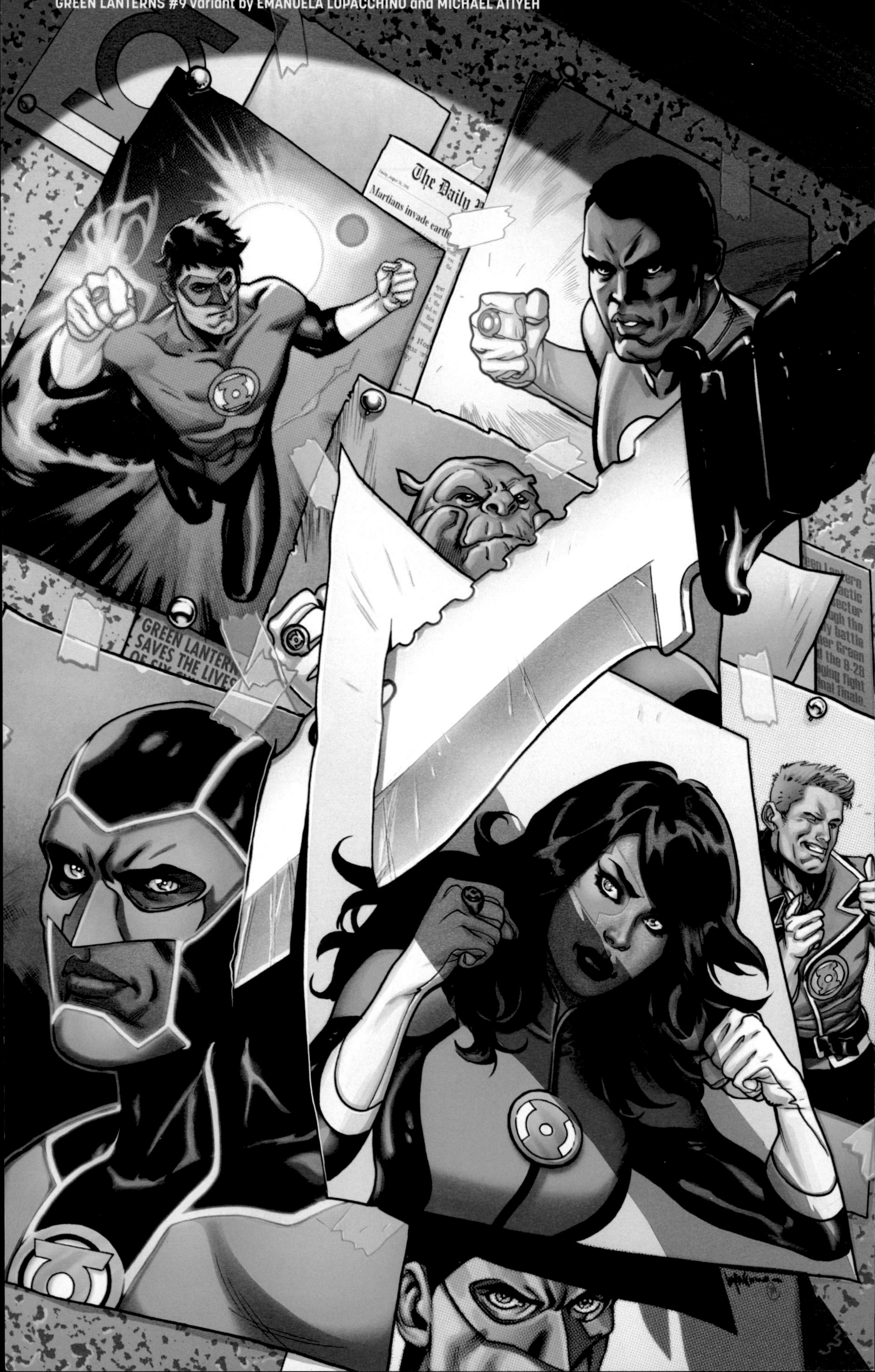

GREEN LANTERNS #10 variant by EMANUELA LUPACCHINO and MICHAEL ATIYEH

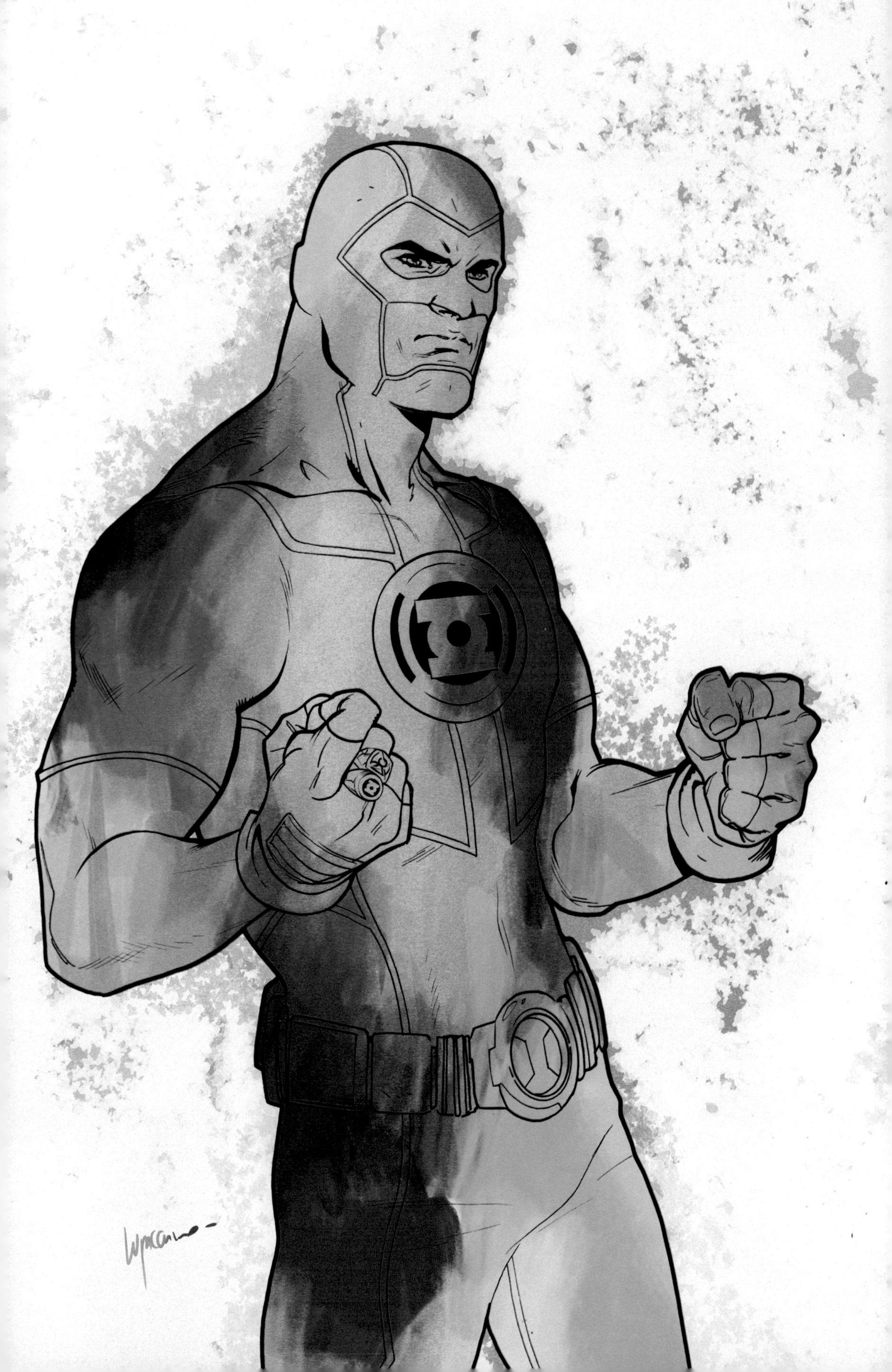

GREEN LANTERNS #11 variant by EMANUELA LUPACCHINO and MICHAEL ATIYEH

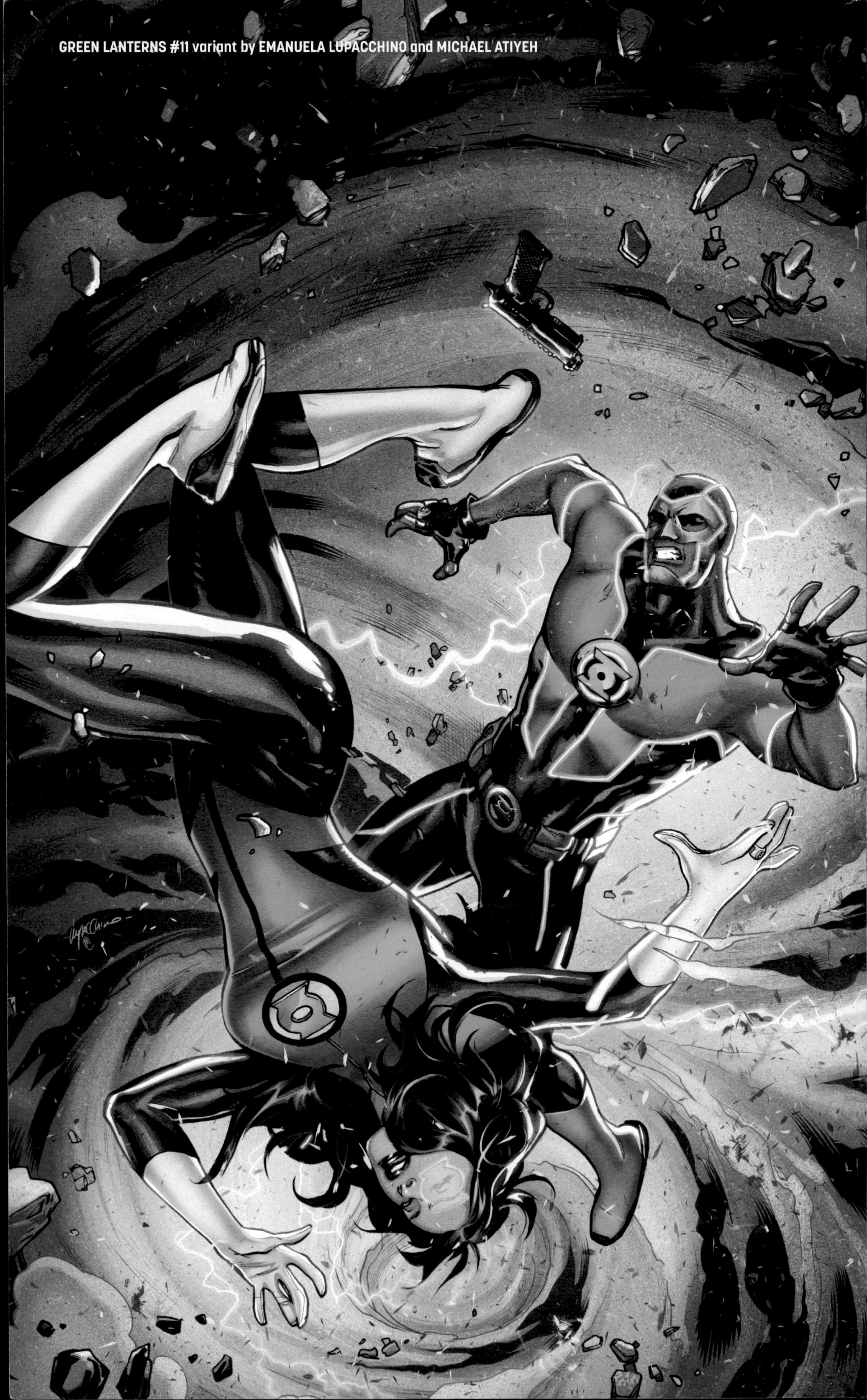

GREEN LANTERNS #12 variant by EMANUELA LUPACCHINO and MICHAEL ATIYEH

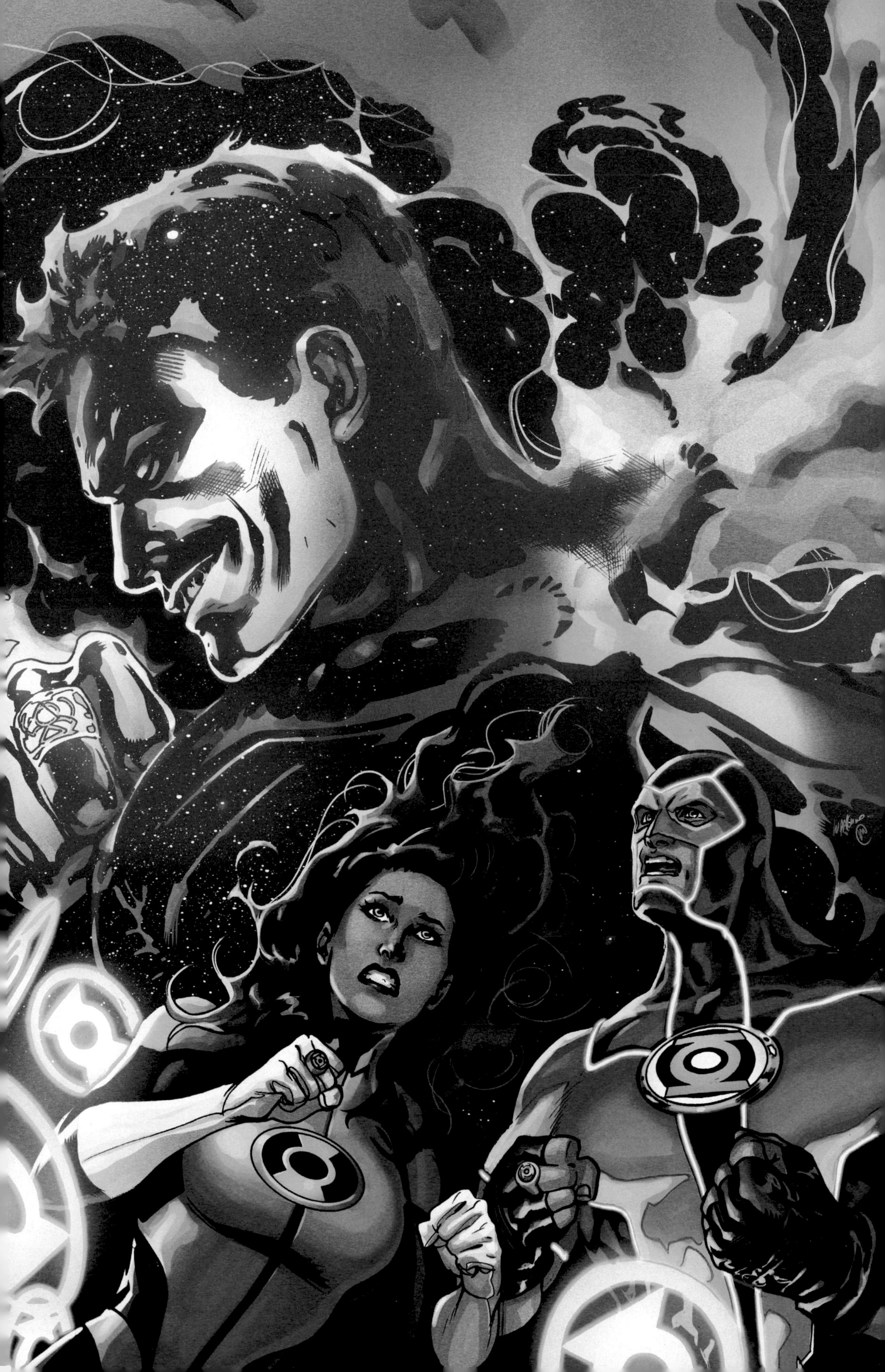

GREEN LANTERNS #13 variant by EMANUELA LUPACCHINO and MICHAEL ATIYEH

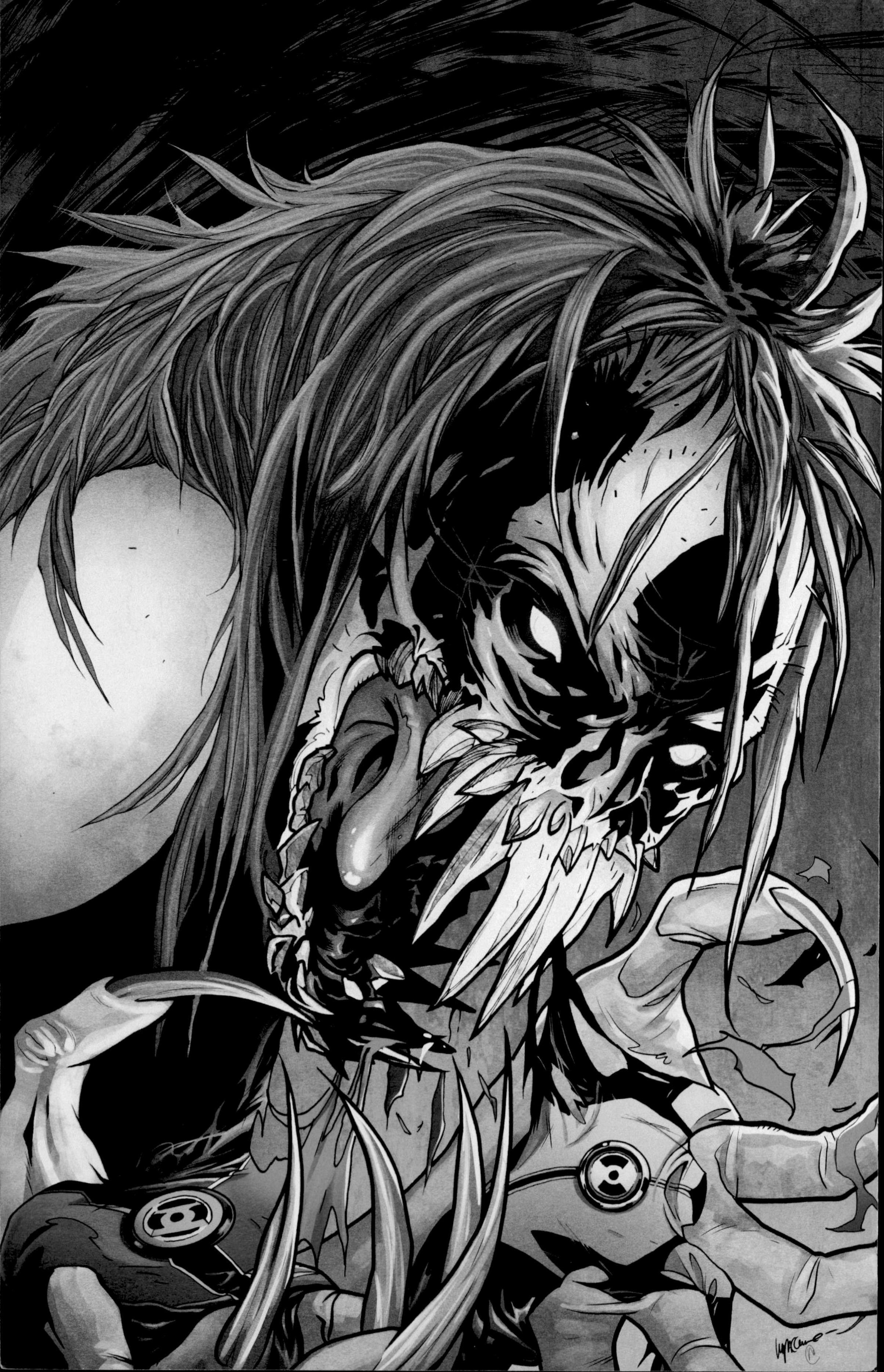

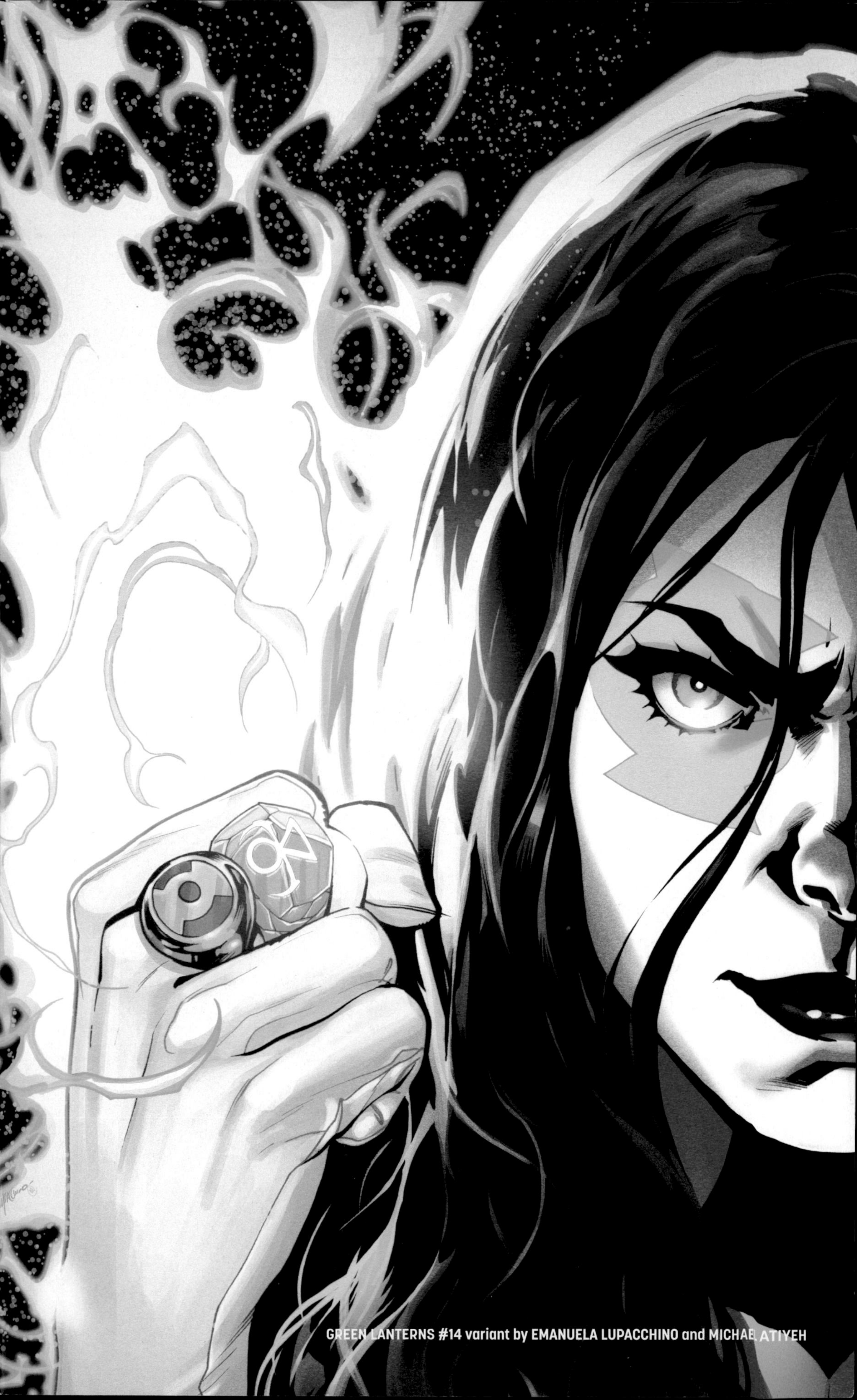

GREEN LANTERNS #14 variant by EMANUELA LUPACCHINO and MICHAEL ATIYEH

GREEN LANTERNS #9 PAGES 2-3
Art by Robson Rocha and Jay Leisten

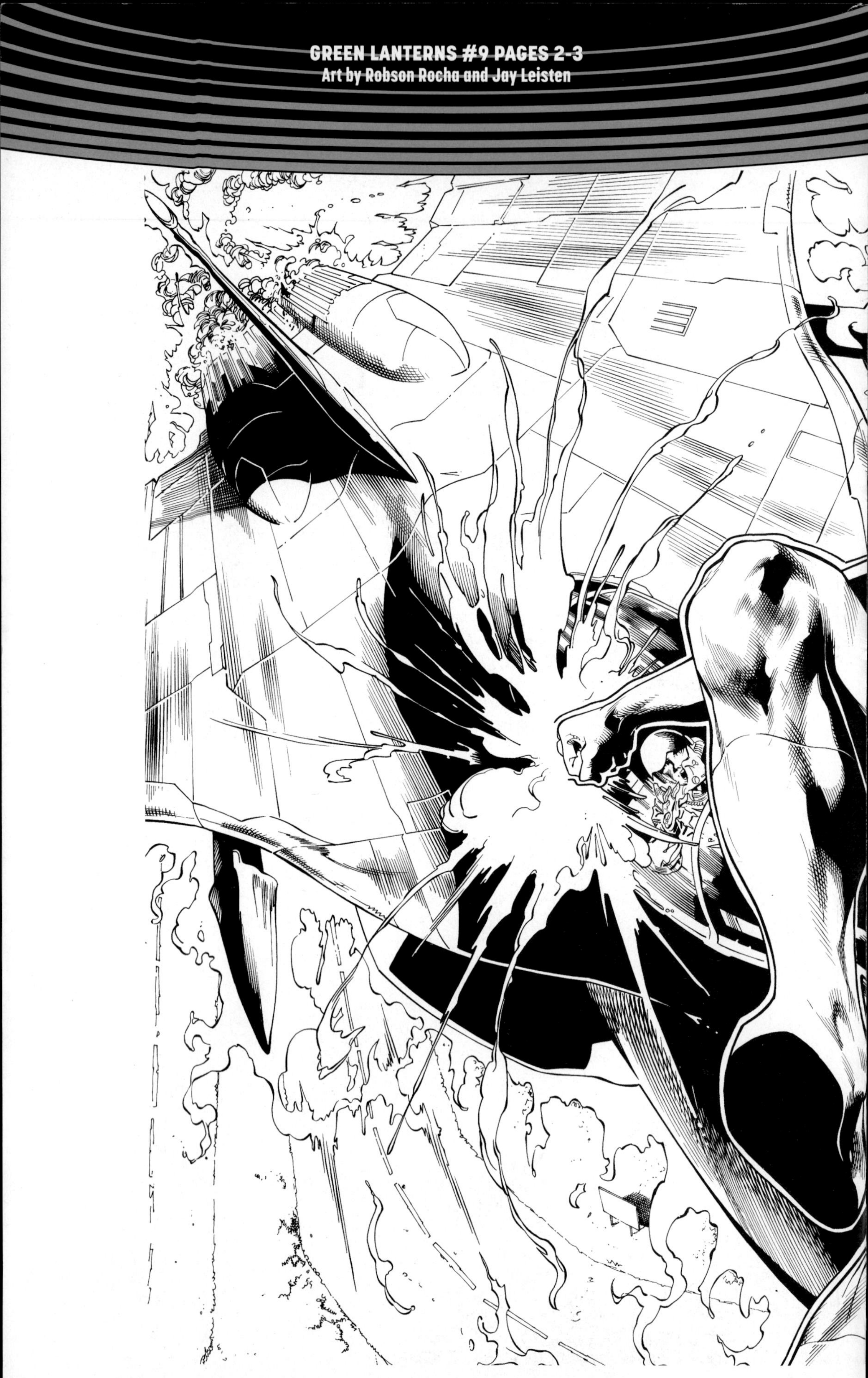

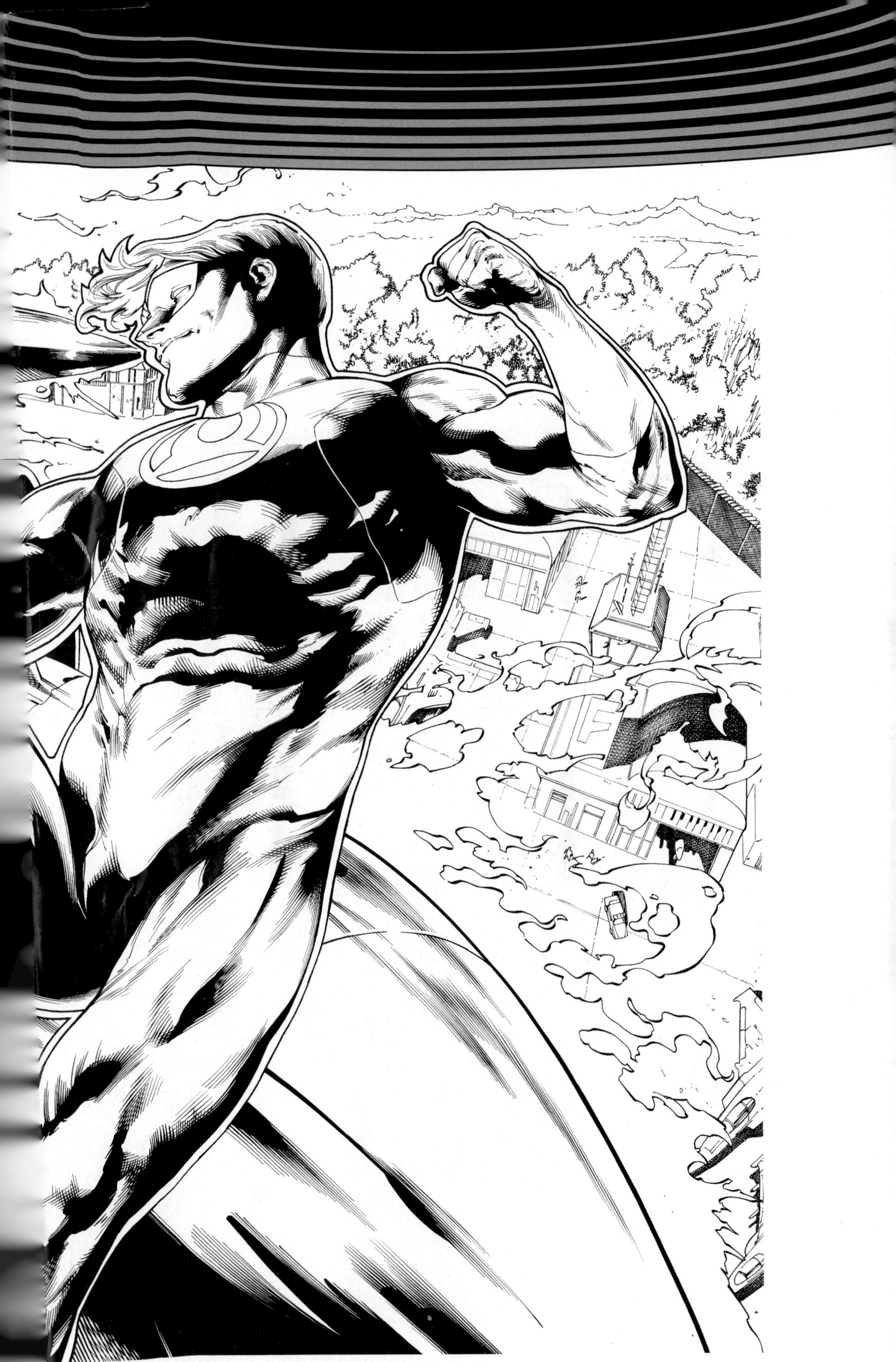

PHANTOM LANTERN DESIGN
by Ethan Van Sciver

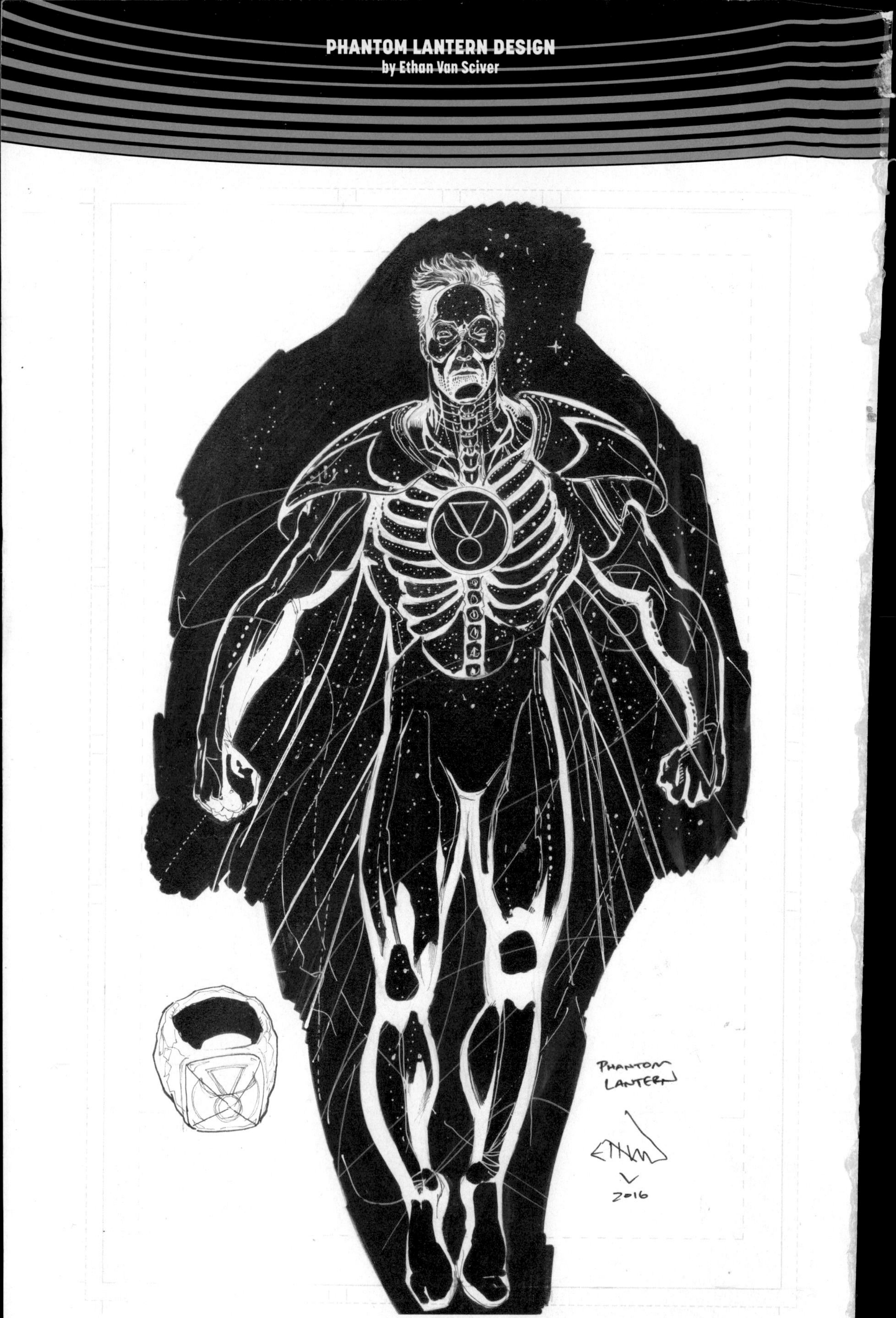

PHANTOM LANTERN
2016